PREFACE

PERSONAL BUSINESS MANAGEMENT is a one-semester course designed for high school students. The major purpose of this textbook is to provide students with the tools necessary to meet a variety of future needs—making career decisions, managing money, providing economic security, managing credit, and keeping up to date with technology. Personal business management is a relevant topic for all students in order that they may better understand and adapt to the financial world into which they will enter. From personal planning decisions to credit conditions, the informed citizen is better able to be a productive part of, draw maximum benefits from, and be well adjusted to the social, economic, and technological changes that are inevitable. The study of personal business management is an examination of societal and self-expectations, needs and wants, controls and restraints. It explores the opportunities and possibilities, the barriers and roadblocks that citizens will encounter when planning personal and financial decisions for the present and future. Personal business management is an examination of the decisions made daily and the results of careful planning, study, and analysis, with emphasis on decision-making skills and awareness of the consequences of personal and societal choices on self, the economy, and the world.

All 18 chapters in PERSONAL BUSINESS MANAGEMENT are practical as well as informational; students are given opportunities to experience the topics presented. Learning objectives given at the beginning of each chapter are fulfilled through study of the chapter narrative and completion of end-of-chapter activities. A vocabulary exercise, items for discussion, applications, and case problems and activities provide practical experiences.

Part One, "Career Decisions," includes four chapters on employment: "Choosing Your Career," "Planning Your Career," "Adapting to Your Job," and "Keeping Your Job." Part Two, "Money Management," includes four chapters on managing your finances: "Employee Pay and Benefits," "Budgets and Financial Records," "Banking," and "Federal Income Tax." Part Three, "Economic Security," includes three chapters: "Saving for the Future," "Investment Choices," and "Insurance." Part Four, "Credit Management," consists of five chapters including "Credit in America," "Buying on Credit," "Cost of Credit," "Personal Decision Making," and "Personal Economic Decisions." Part Five, "Electronic Information," includes two chapters: "Information Technology" and "Coping with Technology and Change." The Appendix includes the annual percentage rate formula and the Rule of 78 with several practice problems. A glossary of terms used throughout the text is also provided.

The STUDENT ACTIVITY GUIDE FOR PERSONAL BUSINESS MANAGEMENT provides students with additional reinforcement exercises. Each STUDENT ACTIVITY GUIDE chapter contains sections on vocabulary, review questions (true/false and multiple choice), and applied activities. Through the numerous practical applications offered in the text and supplemental materials, students gain a thorough understanding of personal business management. In the PERSONAL BUSINESS MANAGEMENT course, students conduct an intensive examination of career choice decisions, money management principles and practices, financial security and planning for the future, managing credit responsibilities, and an introduction to the world of technology in business.

Joan S. Ryan

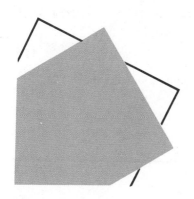

CONTENTS

PART ONE
CAREER DECISIONS

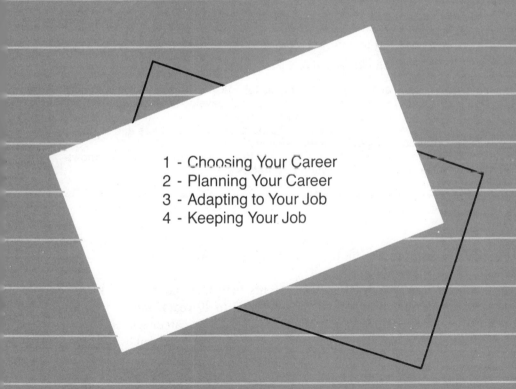

1

Choosing Your Career

PREPARING FOR CAREERS OF THE 1990s AND BEYOND

Your grandparents or even parents may have gone to work for one employer, remained at the same job for 25 to 40 years, and then comfortably retired. But chances are that your beginning career will change drastically every five years. Because of new technology, you will either be retrained or change jobs. *Technology* is a general term for advances resulting from improvements in technical processes that increase productivity of machines and eliminate manual operations or operations done by older machines.

Major Occupational Groups

In the early 1900s, farmers constituted more than one third of the total work force; now, farmers make up less than 3 percent. Today, the

ILLUSTRATION 1–1
Professional workers have information jobs.

Three percent of the population is in agriculture.

occupation with the largest number of employees is clerk (according to John Naisbitt, author of *Megatrends*). There are more people working at universities today than in agriculture.

The second largest career group is in the professions, where knowledge is the key job skill. Professional workers are said to have information jobs, where the creation, processing, storage, and retrieval of information *is* the job. From an industrial society, we have moved into an information society.

Many historians agree that the industrial age ended with Sputnik—when worldwide communications became the standard, and the accumulation of information rose abruptly with satellite communications. Before telecommunications, it took hours, and even days, for news of world events to reach audiences around the globe. Today, the reach is instantaneous. When we turn on the television for the evening news, the telecast is worldwide, up-to-the-minute coverage.

Service careers will flourish through the 1990s.

Service workers will be a large part of the job market in the 1990s and beyond. But service jobs will also be intertwined with the creation, processing, storage, and retrieval of information. Service workers will be using the most sophisticated information storage and retrieval devices in history!

Many historians, economists, and futurists foresaw this extraordinary transfiguration in occupations. Labels have included Space Age, Electronic Era, Global Village, Technological Revolution, Post-Industrial Society, Information Age, and Technetronic Age. All recognize the significance of technology and the rapidly increasing storehouse of knowledge.

Job Titles and Descriptions

Most careers of the 1990s appear to be the same as they were 10 or 20 years ago. However, these careers are considerably different when you compare job descriptions, job qualifications, and employment opportunities. Careful research into job titles and descriptions of your potential career choices will prepare you for making that very important decision. Several U.S. government publications provide detailed descriptions of many job titles. Three of these publications are available in most public libraries—the *Dictionary of Occupational Titles* (DOT), the *Occupational Outlook Handbook*, and the *Monthly Labor Review*.

Many government publications help you make career choices.

The *Dictionary of Occupational Titles* classifies jobs by nine-digit categories according to functions and duties. Listed within major job categories are the numerous specific jobs that are available in the United States. Figure 1–1 is an excerpt from the DOT which lists several specific jobs under the general category of "Cashiers and Tellers." To use the *Dictionary of Occupational Titles*, you first consult the index to locate the reference number for Cashiers and Tellers. Jobs may be further divided into functions and duties, with a brief description given of the job duties and responsibilities.

The *Occupational Outlook Handbook* is a yearly publication of the U.S. Department of Labor. It provides in-depth job descriptions and includes additional information about job opportunities nationwide. As you can see in Figure 1–2, the *Handbook* makes reference to the DOT numbers for jobs that are being described. The *Handbook* descriptions include topics such as nature of the work, working conditions, employment, training and qualifications, job outlook, earnings, related occupations, and sources of additional information.

The Monthly Labor Review is a monthly magazine.

Additional statistics and graphic information are available on a monthly basis in the *Monthly Labor Review*. Articles in this publication are written by business people, teachers, researchers, and government statisticians. These articles provide current information about specific occupation clusters across the nation. The *Monthly Labor Review* is found in most libraries and is published by the U. S. Department of Labor.

FIGURE 1–1
DOT Job
Descriptions

Source: U.S.
Employment
Service,
*Dictionary of
Occupational
Titles*
(Washington:
U.S.
Government
Printing Office,
1983), p. 166.

211 CASHIERS AND TELLERS

This group includes occupations concerned with receiving and disbursing money and recording transactions. Most occupations involve use of adding machines, cash registers, and change makers. It includes occupations concerned with receiving and disbursing money in banks and financial institutions.

211.132-010 TELLER, HEAD (finan. inst.)

Supervises and coordinates activities of workers engaged in receiving and paying out money and keeping records of transactions in banks and similar financial institutions: Assigns duties and work schedules to workers to insure efficient functioning of department. Trains employees in customer service and banking procedures. Approves checks for payment. Adjusts customer complaints. Examines TELLERS (finan. inst.) reports of daily tranactions for accuracy. Consolidates and balances reports, using adding machine. Insures supply of money for bank's needs based on legal requirements and business demand. May be designated according to transactions involved as TELLER, COLLECTION AND EXCHANGE, HEAD (finan. inst.); TELLER, FOREIGN EXCHANGE, HEAD (finan. inst.); TELLER, NOTE, HEAD (finan. inst.); TELLER, PAYING AND RECEIVING, HEAD (finan. inst.); TELLER, SAVINGS, HEAD (finan. inst.). Performs other duties as described under SUPERVISOR (clerical).

211.137-010 SUPERVISOR, CASHIERS (hotel & rest.; ret. tr.)

Supervises and coordinates activities of workers engaged in receiving cash or credit-card payment for merchandise or services and keeping records of funds received in retail establishments or places of public accommodation: Performs cashiering and other clerical duties to relieve subordinates during peak work periods. Searches records to assist subordinates in locating and reconciling posting errors on customers' invoices, such as hotel bills or sales tickets, or compares cash register totals with receipts in register to verify accuracy of transactions. Withdraws monies from bank and keeps custody of operating funds, or retains next day's operating funds from daily receipts. Allocates operating funds to cashiering stations. Totals and summarizes funds received, endorses checks, and prepares bank deposit slip. Performs duties as described under SUPERVISOR (clerical).

211.137-014 SUPERVISOR, FOOD CHECKERS AND CASHIERS (hotel & rest.)

Plans, supervises, and coordinates activities of FOOD-AND-BEVERAGE CHECKERS (hotel & rest.) and CASHIERS (clerical) II at multiple stations in large food-service establishment: Establishes food-checking and cashiering stations to support activities, such as dining rooms, bars, clubs, banquets, and social functions. Hires and trains workers. Observes food-checking, billing, and cashiering activities; counts cash; and reconciles charge sales and cash receipts with total sales to verify accuracy of transactions. Compiles reports, such as cash receipts, guest-bill charges, and sales for accounting and management purposes, or supervises clerical workers preparing reports.

211.137-018 SUPERVISOR, MONEY-ROOM (amuse. & rec.)

Supervises and coordinates activities of money-room workers engaged in keeping account of money wagered on each race at racetrack: Keeps continuous balance sheet of cash transactions and verifies with cash on hand. Requisitions additional cash as needed. Determines workers needed each day and assigns their duties. Performs duties as described under SUPERVISOR (clerical).

Computer Operating Personnel

(D.O.T. 203.382-018, .582-022, -026, -030, -070; 206.387-030; 208.685-030; and 213.132-010 and -014, .362-010, .382-010, and .685-010)

Nature of the Work

All computer systems require specialized workers to enter data and instructions, operate the computer, and retrieve the results. The data to be processed and the instructions for the computer are called "input;" the results are called "output." Information is entered into a computer system by data entry personnel in a variety of ways.

Working Conditions

Because electronic computers must be operated at carefully controlled temperatures, computer operating personnel work in well-ventilated rooms; air-conditioning counteracts the heat generated by machine operations.

Some computer and peripheral equipment operators work evening or night shifts because many organizations use their computers 24 hours a day.

Employment

Computer operating personnel held 580,000 jobs in 1982: Computer operators 211,000, peripheral equipment operators 49,000, and data entry operators 320,000.

Although computer and peripheral equipment operators and data entry operators are employed in almost every industry, most work in manufacturing firms, banks, insurance firms, colleges and universities, wholesale and retail trade establishments, and firms that provide data processing services for a fee.

Training, Other Qualifications, and Advancement

In some firms, other clerical workers such as tabulating and bookkeeping machine operators may be transferred to jobs as data entry, peripheral equipment, or computer operators. Most often, however, employers recruit workers who already have some of the necessary skills to operate the equipment.

Employers in private industry usually require a high school education, and many prefer to hire computer operators who have some community or junior college training, especially in data processing.

Job Outlook

Changes in data processing technology will have differing effects on computer operating occupations. Employment of computer and peripheral equipment operators, for example, is expected to rise much faster than the average for all occupations through the mid-1990s.

Related Occupations

Other occupations in which workers organize data and process information on electronic equipment include secretaries and typists, printing typesetters and compositors, transcribing machine operators, and file clerks.

Earnings

In 1982, median weekly earnings of full-time computer operating personnel were $285 for computer and peripheral equipment operators and $240 for data entry operators. The middle 50 percent earned between $220 and $380 and between $205 and $300, respectively. The lowest 10 percent of computer and peripheral equipment operators earned $180 or less a week, and the top 10 percent earned more than $485.

Sources of Additional Information

People who want further information about work opportunities in computer operations should contact firms that use computers such as banks, manufacturing and insurance firms, colleges and universities, and data processing service organizations. The local office of the State employment services is another source of information about employment and training opportunities.

FIGURE 1–2 Portions of an *Occupational Outlook Handbook* Job Description

Source: Adapted from U.S. Department of Labor, *Occupational Outlook Handbook* (Washington: U.S. Government Printing Office, 1984-85), pp. 205, 206.

JOB ANALYSIS

While considering the type of work for which you will be best suited, you may find it useful to do a *job analysis* such as the one shown in Figure 1-3. The job analysis shows the positive and negative attributes of a given career choice. After careful analysis, you may find that a certain career will not meet most of your career objectives. If this happens, continue with your analyses of other careers that interest you. Since you will probably spend a number of years in your first career choice, selecting the right career for you is important.

Do a complete job analysis for all possible choices.

Positive Features of Employment

When considering the *salary*, which is the amount of your monthly or annual pay, you need also to consider the potential salary after a month, six months, or a year. Some companies offer frequent evaluations, merit

FIGURE 1–3
Job Analysis Form

JOB ANALYSIS

Job title: *Junior Accountant*

Positive features:

Beginning salary: *$22-25,000*

Benefits: *Health insurance;*
profit-sharing; bonus;
unlimited sick leave; vacation 2
weeks/year; professional leaves

Promotion opportunities:
Senior accountant after 2 years;
need CPA license after 3 years
to become self-employed

Other considerations:
A good way to prepare for having
my own business in a few years

Negative features:

Employee costs: *4-year degree*
and continuing education classes;
must be able to travel two days
a month (out of town); must
wear business suits daily

Work characteristics:
Work with numbers; at desk
most of time; little contact with
public; tiring; precise

Other considerations:
Round-trip travel expenses to
work; work-related travel

---

raises, and more liberal pay schedules. ***Benefits*** include sick pay, vacation time, profit-sharing plans, health-insurance provisions, and other company-provided supplements to your income, as discussed in Chapter 5. ***Promotion opportunities***, the chance to advance, accept more responsibilities, and eventually work your way up the corporate ladder (receiving recognition for your achievements with higher paying and more challenging jobs), should be very important to you. For example, a junior accountant will want to work for a company in which advancement to senior accountant and partner is possible. Other considerations might be travel arrangements (how far and how difficult it is to get to the work site), company stability in the community, work hours and flexibility, and company personnel policies.

Benefits are an important consideration.

Negative Features of Employment

On the negative features side of the job analysis, you should first consider ***employee costs*** and include such things as uniforms and their cleaning, special clothing requirements, and other expenses to be paid by the employee that are not reimbursed by the employer. Although many such expenses may be tax deductible, they nevertheless could be very costly to the employee, and they could make the job less attractive. For example, if you choose to become a real estate agent and work independently (rather than as an employee of an agency), you will pay your own advertising costs, automobile expenses, membership dues to a multiple-listing service, license fees, and many other expenses normally paid by an agency (employer).

Consider carefully what your costs will be.

Work characteristics should also be of particular concern, since you will do this work for eight or more hours a day. Consider such things as routine or boring activities; indoor or outdoor work; working with people or alone; pressure that goes with the job; time between breaks; supervisory relationships (who will be your boss); number of employees with whom you will work; and company rules and policies. Other considerations might be your transportation arrangements and costs; how you feel about the company, its employees, or your supervisor; your attitude toward the particular job description or responsibilities; or how this job fits into your overall career and life goals.

Working conditions are important.

If you wish to gain insight into how workers in actual career choices feel about their jobs, the *Vocational Biographies*, published by Vocational Biographies, Sauk Centre, Minnesota, will help you. These biographies are a series of short descriptions of persons in many different occupations. These persons relate their personal likes and dislikes about their jobs. They also give more details about their jobs than you may be able to find elsewhere. In each series there are seven volumes. Within each volume there are as many as 27 biographies.

Do career research at the library.

You can continue your in-depth career research by searching the subject headings in your library's card catalog and magazine indexes, such as the *Business Periodicals Index*, and the *Readers' Guide to Periodical Literature*. Most career information sources can be found in the reference section of the library.

COPING WITH CHANGE

With increasing numbers of advanced technologies, one thing should be fairly clear to most American workers: Change is certain. Psychologists agree that there are three things you can do about change—you can accept it, you can reject it, or you can ignore it. If you accept change, then you can get in, be a part of it, and help it to happen. If you reject change, you will get run over by it because there is no stopping progress

Technology is highly valued in our society.

and technological advancements. They are commodities that are highly valued in our country and in the world. If you ignore change, you will be left behind and wondering what happened. By either rejecting or ignoring change, you will be very frustrated, unemployed, or both.

As mentioned just now, one of the best ways for you to cope with change is to become a part of it. Being aware of what is new and "state of the art" can be done in a number of ways.

Read Widely

There are a variety of magazines that follow business and international technologies, from general technologies to specific industries. If you work with computers, one of the many computer magazines will keep you

Keep informed of new technological advances.

informed of new technological advancements entering the marketplace almost daily. In addition, you need to read newspapers and magazines that keep you informed of what is going on in the United States and in the world. In this way, you will be aware of and better prepared to meet the challenges of change that are inevitable.

Be a Lifetime Learner

Both at work and in your personal life, be interested in what is going on. Ask questions; talk to people; follow news and special events; participate in community activities and events, both social and leisure; care about what is going on in your local area, in your state, in your country, and in the world. This will make you a more interesting person to talk to, to work with, and to be around. And it is essential to your successful career development and enhancement. Actively participating in your right to vote is one way of showing that you are involved and that you care about what is going on in your country.

Take Classes

Take classes to keep yourself up-to-date.

Sometimes technological advancements are too complex to learn by yourself, so you should actively seek new knowledge by taking classes to learn new life skills. According to John Naisbitt (*Megatrends*), people are choosing to go to college in greater numbers in the 1980s than 30 years ago (many people after age 30 for the first time). More college education is now being geared to retraining for displaced workers than to preparation for first-time opening-entry positions.

Outdated jobs are being replaced by new technology, methods, and machines. It is often necessary for workers to retrain and prepare for different types of work in relatively short periods of time. Twenty-three million Americans—10 million more than 15 years ago—are involved in continuing-education programs, and more than two thirds of them are taking job-related courses.

Be eager and willing to accept change.

Technical courses are often available through corporations for the retraining of their own employees. Those who volunteer and are eager to learn and make progress will be putting themselves in position for advancement. Other training is available through technical schools, vocational centers, job placement services, business colleges, and community colleges. For many careers, it will be necessary for applicants to have a bachelor's degree before being hired. Most higher paying jobs will be for those with bachelor's or advanced degrees—people who work smarter, not harder. Statistics show that Americans place a high value on education. From 1960 to 1980, the number of students earning bachelor's degrees more than doubled. More doctoral degrees were conferred by Yale between 1970 and 1981 than in the previous 109 years. *Advanced degrees* are obtained through specialized, intensive postbaccalaureate programs which prepare the recipients for higher level work responsibilities with more challenge and higher pay. Advanced degrees may be an MBA (Master of Business Administration); a PhD (doctorate in education or a specialized field); or a degree in special areas as medicine, law, veterinary medicine, engineering, aerospace technology, and so on. Advanced degrees usually require three to five years' formal education beyond a bachelor's degree.

You may need higher degrees for your career choice.

Complete a Self-Assessment

As you go through life, your needs and values often change. It is important to look inward to define what it is that is important to you and to make plans for the future. You need to be thinking continually about what you like doing, what you do well, and what skills and knowledge you want to develop further. For those who choose some form of college or technical training, **college placement centers** offer advice and counseling to help you determine a career direction. You may be asked to participate in an autobiographical approach, in which you write or tape-record your life story. Then, counselors help you analyze this data and determine where it is you would really like to go with your life. Vocational testing is also available through these college placement centers. You might want to compare your interests with those of successful people in various professions. A values clarification test will help you determine what is of significance to you, personally and professionally.

Private counselors are listed in the Yellow Pages, and some may specialize in career counseling. Fees may range from $25 to $75 an hour. Your own independent research will lead you through sources already listed in this chapter, as well as to *The American Almanac of Jobs and Salaries*. This book evaluates job potentials in many career fields and gives a full range of salaries for levels and positions. You can do industry research and look into major job categories (service, professional, and so on, as listed in Chapter 2). Specific company research will help you to learn which companies can provide you with the best career opportunities. You might want to check your library to find sources such as *Standard & Poor's Register of Corporations, Directors and Executives, United States and Canada* or *The 100 Best Companies to Work for in America* to learn about major American companies and why they are successful. You can learn about their history, their structure, and their future plans. And finally, you can do field research where you talk to people working in careers that interest you. These interviews will allow you to see strengths and weaknesses in some careers that you might not have anticipated. All this information is important to you in determining what you need and want, and then matching it to a career that will meet those needs.

Seek professional help early in career planning.

Industry and company research will give you insight into jobs.

Your career must meet your needs and wants.

THE DEVELOPMENT OF OCCUPATIONS

Alvin Toffler wrote two bestsellers which describe the development of occupations throughout history: *Future Shock* and *The Third Wave*. According to Toffler, we are now in the Third Wave.

Humankind began without organization, or plans, or control. The First Wave is labeled "agriculture." It is an era with simple tools, machinery, and limited capital. People spread to villages and settlements, and they cultivated land to make a way of life. The world economy was based on barter and self-dependence. Nations fortified themselves against other nations that attempted to take over and rule them. But very little progress was made in occupations—son followed father who followed grandfather. The rich were rich by inheritance and were the ones who were entitled to education and culture. Life was based on fishing, hunting, or herding. Agriculture was crude, and small, inefficient tools and methods were used to produce food for sale and for the grower's own use. Weapons were not accurate or dependable; farm equipment was powered by animals or human beings; most jobs consisted of family operations or hard manual labor. And so it went until late in the seventeenth century.

Occupations began with isolation and lack of dependence on others.

The First Wave had not exhausted itself (and indeed still exists in some undeveloped nations of Africa) when the Second Wave, called the Industrial Revolution, hit Europe. This new giant—industrialization—swept rapidly across nations and continents. It brought factories and wages, machinery, tools and equipment, the first automobile and airplane, the first steam-powered train and boat, typing machines and communications, and a whole new era of employment. The United States caught on quickly and began its own factories and tools of production, declaring independence in 1776 with many resources, natural and manufactured, to its advantage.

Industrialization destroyed isolationism.

Coming from nowhere a little over 200 years ago, the United States rose to become an industrial giant. We built steel mills, auto plants, textile factories, railroads, and food-processing plants. While the Second Wave has already reached its peak in most industrially developed nations, it has still not completely run its course. But even as its momentum continues, a new wave has begun.

We are now in the Third Wave.

The Third Wave was ushered in about 1955—the middle of a decade which saw more white-collar workers than blue-collar workers for the first time in history. With the launching of space satellites, a new communication era began. And with it, the "information age" in which the computer, commercial jet travel, and many other high-impact innovations arrived. The Third Wave is characterized by rapid and profound changes. In a short time, amazing technologies and advancements are proven obsolete. Therefore, change is an essential ingredient in the formula for success in this technological era.

Modern high-technology nations are reeling from the collision between the Third Wave and the nearly obsolete economies and institutes

Future shock is the
realization of truth.

of the Second Wave. This is what is described as "future shock"—the realization that things have changed beyond the point of return. While having lost much of its industrial advantage (in the Second Wave) to Japan and other nations which have lower costs of production, the United States has gained a lead in and a control of the information age. This is because the United States was able to make the rapid changes necessary in the Third Wave.

Career planning is as never before. It is not a permanent and final decision at its beginning, but subject to change within relatively short periods of time. To understand how our careers will be affected, let us examine some of the major changes that are sweeping the country and the world.

Long-Term Planning

Long-range planning is
a necessity today.

Businesses are forced to be concerned about what will happen in the long run, rather than just being concerned about showing a profit for this quarter. Otherwise, they will be totally unprepared as new technologies appear on the horizon which require massive changes and improvements. Individuals also must look to long-term planning to protect themselves from the effects of a rapidly changing technology—they must be in the midst of the change and help it to happen. Career plans must span several decades and must be as broad, diversified, and open to opportunities and challenges of the future as possible.

A World Economy

We are interdependent
internationally.

The United States is
the leader in the tech-
nological information
era.

The idea that we can isolate ourselves from the rest of the world and be in peace and security is a myth. We are now in the midst of a world interdependence structure; as a nation, we must seek ways to survive and grow internationally. As individuals, we need to understand and be aware of the changes and progress that are worldwide—for example, the growing significance of Third World countries. *Third World* countries include undeveloped and underdeveloped nations. The 20 fastest growing economies of the 1970s and 1980s were all in Third World nations. Included are the oil exporting countries of Saudi Arabia and Iran, plus South Korea, Singapore, Dominican Republic, Taiwan, Mexico, and Brazil. The economic powers of the Third World are growing with purpose and design— they are taking over the industrial production tasks. And they have the potential work force to do it. Should we try to go back and recapture the Industrial Revolution? Most experts agree that the answer is "No."

Instead, we need to adapt to it and move forward in the area in which we are the leader—the new information age.

Networking

Businesses and individuals are involved in a new system—which is really just a new way of getting the job done. From formal structures, we are moving toward networks. *Networks* are communication lines established for people to talk to each other and share information. Networking is making calls, sharing lunch, and creating opportunities to give ideas, information, and resources, and to receive information from someone who has information you need. To find a career, you will need to pursue networking (setting up your own system of contacts and information sources). Through networking, you are able to get inside information without being an "insider."

Networking is your key to opportunities.

Adapting to the world of work in the 1990s and beyond will necessitate successful networking structures. You can begin now with a master list of people you know through your parents, friends in business, and personal friends and associates. By communicating within your network, you will learn about what is going on, how to prepare yourself, where the openings are to be found, and when you will be ready to pursue them.

VOCABULARY

Directions: Can you find the definition for each of the following terms used in Chapter 1?

technology	work characteristics
job analysis	advanced degrees
salary	college placement centers
benefits	private counselors
promotion opportunities	Third World
employee costs	networks (networking)

1. A procedure to list the positive and negative attributes of a given career choice.

2. A source for help in career counseling which will cost you from $25 to $75 an hour.

3. A source of career counseling available at colleges or technical training institutes.

4. Advances resulting from improvements in technical processes.

5. Communication lines established for people to talk to each other and share information.

6. The amount of monthly or annual pay.

7. The daily activities at work, such as indoor or outdoor work, or working with people or alone.

8. Expenses paid by employees and not reimbursed by employers.

9. Chances for recognition of your abilities and accomplishments.

10. Sick pay, vacation time, profit sharing, and other company-provided supplements to income.

11. Specialized, intensive postbaccalaureate programs.

12. Underdeveloped and undeveloped nations of the world.

ITEMS FOR DISCUSSION

1. What is the number one occupation (numerically) today?

2. What is the second largest career group today?

3. List some of the names given in this chapter and others that you may have heard that describe today's electronic era.

4. List three publications of the U.S. government that will assist you with career choices.

5. Describe the types of information that would be listed on a job analysis.

6. List some employee costs which you might expect to pay in your first occupation choice.

7. What are the three things you can do about change?

8. List four ways you can keep up on what is new and keep yourself prepared for tomorrow's career choices.

9. How much education do you need to earn an advanced degree?

10. What is the label given to Toffler's First Wave?

11. What is the label given to Toffler's Second Wave?

12. When is the Third Wave (information age) said to have begun?

13. List some Third World countries that have made great economic gains.

APPLICATIONS

1. Can you describe some new technology that has been introduced in the past few months?

2. Can you describe some technological advance made just a year or two ago that is now obsolete?

3. What do workers in the information age do?

4. How has telecommunications changed our perspective and position in the world?

5. What are some positive features of employment?

6. What are some negative features of employment?

7. Describe ways you plan to keep in touch with what is going on in the world technologically.

8. What types of independent research can you do to determine the type of work you want and the company you want to work for?

9. List and briefly describe the three waves identified by Toffler.

10. What is meant by "future shock"?

11. How has the United States been able to keep up with the Third Wave?

12. Why is long-term planning necessary for individuals as well as for businesses?

CASE PROBLEMS AND ACTIVITIES

1. Look up three career choices in the *Dictionary of Occupational Titles*. Summarize your findings into one paragraph about each choice. Look up the same three occupations in the *Occupational Outlook Handbook* and add a paragraph about each.

2. From a current issue of *Monthly Labor Review*, summarize an article about an industry or employment trend.

3. Complete a job analysis, using the form in Figure 1-3 as a guide, for three different occupations. To get this information, consult one of the sources listed in this chapter, or interview someone working in each occupation field. List your source(s) of information on the job analysis form.

4. Explain to a friend why it is necessary to be aware of what is new and what is happening technologically in the world. Give suggestions as to what she or he can do to keep up with changes.

5. Pick a large company or corporation you think you would like to work for in the future. Research to learn more about the company. (Suggestions: *Standard & Poor's, The 100 Best Companies to Work for in America.* Summarize your findings into a one- or two-paragraph article.)

6. Develop a networking plan—a list of all possible communication sources you may have and add to it each time you make a contact. List some contacts you plan to set up, people you would like to meet, places you would like to visit.

2
Planning Your Career

CHAPTER OBJECTIVES

After studying this chapter and completing the activities, you will be able to:

1. Identify and describe good job search techniques.
2. Complete self-analysis and goal activity steps in career planning.
3. List sources of job opportunity information and formulate a personal plan of action to get the job you want.

WHY PEOPLE WORK

Most of you will work at sometime during your life. After completing high school and other forms of additional training or education, many of you will work for twenty-five to forty years. Today it is common to see two-income families, teenagers with part-time jobs, and family members with more than one job.

Two-income families are common.

People work to meet their needs, wants, and goals. They work to provide themselves with everything from food, clothing, and shelter to vacations, education, and luxuries. If working does not make it possible for a person to meet personal goals, that person is likely to become frustrated or unhappy in her or his job.

People also work to gain a sense of *identity*—of who and what they are. Because a person's work is most often life's central activity, it often becomes a way of life, or a person's main identity in life. For example, as a student, your main activities center around school. Your identity is that

Work is a central life activity.

**ILLUSTRATION
2–1**
Apply for a job
that will meet
your needs,
wants, and
goals.

of student. When you are asked what you do, you describe activities, classes, grades in school, and events related to your education. When you are out of school, your main identity will be based on your career. When adults are introduced, the first question asked is usually "What do you do for a living?" When one person answers, "I'm a financial economist," and another says, "I'm a sports announcer," two entirely different images come to mind.

FACTORS AFFECTING CAREER CHOICE

Because your career will have an impact on nearly every part of your life, the choice of a career is a very important decision. Many factors affect your career decision; some of these are values and life-style, aptitudes and interests, and personal qualities and traits.

Values and Life-Style

Values are the things in life that are important to you. While you are living at home, your values will probably reflect your parents' values. During your years in high school, you begin to form values of your own—keeping many of your parents' values and rejecting others. For example, you may retain your parents' value that it is proper to wear a tie while

During high school you form your own values.

attending a religious service. But you may reject a value that modern music is worthless.

Life-style may be defined as the way people choose to live their lives, based on the values they have chosen or rejected. Your life-style is displayed to others by the clothes you wear and by the things you buy, rent or use, do, enjoy, and feel. A career is considered an important value in most peoples' lives because it dictates life-style. With careful planning, a career can be rewarding and satisfying and also provide the money needed to support the life-style you desire.

A career can make possible a desired life-style.

Aptitudes and Interests

An *aptitude* is a natural physical or mental ability that permits you to do certain tasks well. Examples of aptitudes include *finger dexterity*, the ability to use your fingers to move small objects quickly and accurately; and *manual dexterity*, the ability to move your hands skillfully. Certain types of work require certain types of aptitudes. Aptitude tests are valuable tools in career planning because they help you to become aware of your strengths and weaknesses. Aptitude tests can be taken through counseling or career guidance departments of most high schools. You may want to test your physical and mental abilities before you begin making career plans.

Aptitude tests are valuable tools.

In addition to your aptitudes, you should also think about your interests—the things you like to do and the reasons why you enjoy doing them. By examining the types of things you enjoy, you can better choose a career that has activities that are similar and will be satisfying and enjoyable. For example, a person who enjoys being with large groups of people and helping others will likely prefer a job working with others rather than one working alone. Consider the options listed in Figure 2–1.

Choose a career that offers things you like to do.

FIGURE 2–1
Types of Work Activities

Which of these work activities appeal to you?	
indoor work	outdoor work
physically active work	physically inactive work
various tasks	same tasks
manual work	thinking work
working with machines	working with others
working alone	leading and directing
following directions	creating and designing
helping others	presenting or speaking
self-motivated work	analyzing and recording

Personal Qualities and Traits

Your *personality* is made up of the many personal qualities and traits that make you unique. Personal qualities include such things as your appearance, intelligence, creativity, sense of humor, and general attitude. Many times a certain position requires an individual with a particular set of personal qualities and traits. For example, a person who represents a company to the public or to potential customers needs a different set of personal qualities and traits than does a machine operator. Examining your personal qualities and traits can help you to choose a career that's right for you. How many of the traits listed in Figure 2–2 apply to you?

Your personality is a job qualification.

FIGURE 2–2
Personality Traits

1. Has a good attitude toward own work and toward others' work.
2. Shows courtesy and respect toward others.
3. Is dependable and will do what is promised.
4. Has a desire to succeed and do a good job.
5. Has enthusiasm for the job and for life.
6. Is clean and has a healthy appearance.
7. Is friendly and helpful.
8. Has a good sense of humor and cares about others.

CAREER PLANNING

Planning for your future career is an important task. Consider the total time spent in life's central activity of working. Eight hours a day, five days a week, 50 weeks a year totals 2,000 hours each year. If you work the average career span of 43 years (from age 22 to age 65), you will have spent 86,000 hours on the job. In addition, you will have spent time in traveling to and from work, in getting ready for work, in overtime (paid and unpaid), and in other work-related activities performed away from the workplace. Because your work will likely take so much of your time, you will want to choose and plan for your career carefully.

The average worker spends 86,000 hours on the job.

Steps in Career Planning

Effective career planning involves careful investigation and analysis—a long process that may take years to complete. Career planning involves self-assessment, research, and a plan of action.

Self-Assessment. Using resources available to you (at schools, employment offices, testing services, etc.), you can explore personal factors that relate to your career choice. You should:

1. Determine your wants and needs.

What is your desired life-style?

2. Determine your values and desired life-style.
3. Assess your aptitudes and interests and how they match job descriptions and activities.
4. Analyze your personal qualities and traits—those you have and those you need to improve.

Research. Based on a good self-assessment, you can determine which careers interest you most and which suit you best. You should:

1. Seek information in books, pamphlets, articles, and other resources available from libraries, counseling centers, and employment offices.
2. Compare some of your interests, abilities, and personal qualities with job descriptions and requirements. Most careers can fit into one of the nine classifications shown in Figure 2-3. Can you choose one or more of these areas that you might want to pursue in which you would be able to meet the requirements? Can you decide which cluster the job of your choice would fit into?
3. Interview people in the fields of work you find interesting.
4. Observe occupations, spend time learning about jobs and companies, and seek part-time work to get direct exposure and experience.

Plan of Action. After you have done some job research, you will need

Set a plan to meet your goals.

to develop a plan of action that will eventually bring you to your career goals.

1. Use good job search techniques: get organized, make a plan, follow through, and don't give up.
2. Develop necessary skills by taking courses and getting exposure to the area in which you want to pursue a career.
3. Seek a part-time or volunteer job to gain experience.

Don't get locked into a job.

4. Evaluate what you have done. If at any point you think you are following the wrong career path, change your mind before you stay too long in an occupation.

Choosing and planning for a career in the method just described may seem confusing and complicated. Most people do follow this method, however, either consciously or unconsciously. Those who do not give career choice and planning the proper thought often spend years in a job not really suited for them before they finally discover their error. Others discover their mistake, but are unable to correct it.

The Importance of Goals

A *goal* is an end toward which efforts are directed. People need to have goals to have a sense of direction and purpose in life. There are three types of goals: short-term goals, intermediate goals, and long-term goals.

JOB CLASSIFICATION	DESCRIPTION OF ACTIVITIES	TRAINING NEEDED	WORKING HOURS	BEGINNING SALARY	EXAMPLES
Clerical/Secretarial	Work in office setting. Involves contact with people and machines. Must type, have telephone skills, etc.	High school diploma plus special training in typing, shorthand, accounting, etc.	40 hours/week during normal business hours	$800+/month	Secretary, typist, word processor operator
Professional	Involves use of highly specialized knowledge. Often stressful. High-level responsibility implied.	4+ years of college. May require special training and/or apprenticeship.	40 hours/week during normal business hours plus overtime	$15,000/year to unlimited	Physician, lawyer, teacher, accountant
Skilled Labor	Emphasis on use of highly specialized skill. Special clothing required. Involves use of tools, machines, etc.	High school diploma plus special training, apprenticeship, licensing, or bonding.	40 hours/week plus overtime	Minimum wage to set salary. $1,000-1,200/month	Builder, mechanic, construction worker
Sales and Marketing	Emphasis on persuading others to buy products and services. Salesperson represents company, self.	High school diploma plus special training. License usually required.	Varied. Often seasonal.	Commission. Often self-employed.	Real estate agent, insurance agent, retail salesperson
Service	Involves labor that does not produce a material good. May or may not involve personal contact.	None to specialized 2-year degree program	Varied. Split shift, as needed	Minimum wage to $1,000/month	Custodian, barber, chef, police officer
Management	Emphasis on supervision of operations, decision making, and direction giving.	College degree plus in-service training.	40 hours or more/week.	$2,000/month or salary plus percentage of profits	Store manager, bank officer, supervisor
Semiskilled and Unskilled Labor	Involves assembly line and other manual work. Physical fitness and good health needed.	In-service training or vocational diploma.	40 hours/week plus overtime	Minimum wage. $10-$15/hour when advanced.	Assembly worker, farm laborer
Entertainment and Recreation	Emphasis on entertaining people. Special quality or talent needed.	None required. Dancing, singing, and music lessons helpful.	Varied. Often under contract.	$0 to unlimited.	Singer, dancer, athlete
Military Service	Emphasis on defense of the country. Discipline and training stressed. Ability to follow orders needed. Must fulfill minimum service requirement.	High school diploma usually required.	Daily during set number of years' commitment.	$7,000/year and up, depending on rank.	Armed Forces service people

FIGURE 2–3 Job Clusters

A *short-term goal* is one that is set to happen in the next few days or weeks. You will work consistently and with certainty to achieve it because you will have to account for the results in a very short time. A short-term goal could be preparing to pass a math test next week—you know you must plan your studying to be ready for the test or suffer the consequences.

Short-term goals take care of daily living.

Intermediate goals are those you wish to accomplish in the next few months or years. Some examples are graduation from high school, a trip you would like to take, or your plans for the coming summer.

Long-term goals include college, career, marriage, and family planning goals. All are activities or plans that will materialize in five to ten years or longer.

If they are to be meaningful, goals should be defined and worked on every day. If goals are to give direction to your life, they must be carefully considered, clearly defined, and actively sought after in an organized manner. Many people find a checklist a handy way to keep on target. For example, your goals, which you would look at and work on daily, might be listed as in Figure 2–4.

Work on your goals every day.

A checklist keeps you current on your goals.

You might want to make up your own checklist form and include your own short-term, intermediate, and long-term goals. Remember: if you don't know where you're going, you'll probably end up somewhere else.

Making the Right Choices

How do you know what kind of job you will be best suited for? How can you possibly decide now, while in high school, what you will want to do for the rest of your life? You may not be able to decide. Yet, unfair as it may seem, the fact is that what you do now can greatly affect what you will do in the future.

What you learn to do, you gain *experience* doing—knowledge, skills, and practice from direct participation in a certain area. Furthermore, the more experience you gain, the more qualified you become, and the more you learn. The more experience and expertise you gain in one area, the more desirable you become as an employee in that area. Thus, you can, in effect, "set yourself up" for a career in a certain area, make yourself worth more to an employer, and increase your earnings by continuing in that area. Then you must design your life-style around that work and salary.

Experience makes you a valuable employee.

Unfortunately, the longer you work at one type of job, the greater the chance of becoming *locked into* that job—of feeling that you cannot change to another type of work because you cannot afford to take the cut in pay that may accompany starting over. This is true even of part-time

FIGURE 2–4
Checklist Plan

CHECKLIST
Week of _____

                                                                    Accomplished

Short-term goals (today/this week)
1. Buy birthday gift for Mom.   _____
2. Get haircut (Saturday).   _____
3. See counselor about chemistry class.   _____

Intermediate goals (next month/year)
1. Get a C or better on Chemistry test (test in
    2 weeks).   _____
2. Prepare for SAT test (test in October).   _____
3. Finish term report (due November 9).   _____
4. Complete college admission forms (by
    January 15).   _____

Long-term goals (future)   Things to do now
1. Graduate from college.   —Extra work in
                                                                      science
                                                                    —Bring up GPA
                                                                      to 3.5
2. Begin full-time job.   —Update place-
                                                                      ment folder
3. Buy a car.   —Get part-time
                                                                      job (save $50
                                                                      a month)

work. If you take a job as a clerk, for instance, rather than take a job that pays less but would prepare you for your preferred career, you are in the process of locking into the clerk job. Taking a temporary position to earn a living while you are preparing for your chosen career is a common practice. However, to achieve your career goals, you must continue to pursue jobs in your field.

Through a careful self-assessment, thorough research, a good plan of action, and well-defined goals, you will be able to choose the career that is right for you. These steps are essential for obtaining employment in the job that you want and in the career field that you want.

SOURCES OF JOB OPPORTUNITY INFORMATION

There are several sources of job opportunity information available: word of mouth and personal contacts; school counseling and placement services; periodicals, books, and other publications; public and private employment agencies; and newspaper, telephone book, and private job listings.

Word of Mouth and Personal Contacts

Most job openings are filled by word of mouth.

Many job openings are filled before they are ever advertised. They are filled from within the company, or by people outside the company who have been privately informed of the opening by a friend or other contact within the company. Each of you has a certain amount of exposure to *contacts*. Relatives, friends, people you have worked for, and others may be able to provide you with inside information on job openings. Therefore, the more people you know, the better your chances of hearing about a job opening before it is made public and of getting the job because you had a contact.

If you are seeking a job in an area in which you have no contacts, it may be necessary for you to make contacts within that work area before you will be able to find an opening. If, for example, you want to work in a bank, you will find it to your advantage to get to know people who work in banks and to make yourself known to the personnel manager and other key employees.

School Counseling and Placement Services

Many schools have programs to assist students in preparing for careers, in making career choices, and in securing part-time and full-time work. One such program is the *cooperative work experience program*. In this program, students receive high school credits for on-the-job experiences that directly relate to classroom studies in a chosen career area. Students placed in work situations are given grades on their work and are paid minimum wages for their efforts. Employers receive tax credits for the wages the students receive during training.

Employers get tax credits for some wages paid.

School counselors and teachers are also good sources of job opportunity information. They often know about specific job openings and are asked by employers to recommend students for job openings. If you are interested in an office job, you should talk to counselors and business teachers as you complete business courses.

College and universities (and some high schools) offer *placement services*. Placement services help students find employment; they are usually offered free of charge. These services include keeping a placement folder on each student that contains school records employers most often ask for. Records kept include: attendance, academic, and discipline. Job openings are posted at the school, and qualified students are given information so that they can apply. When employers ask for information about a student, they are given copies of information kept in a student's placement folder. If your school offers a placement service, perhaps through the counseling center, you should examine your folder and have teachers and other adults write recommendations to put in your folder. You should also see that all school records are in the folder. Be sure to check at your school to see what other types of assistance are available to you.

Employers ask about attendance.

Periodicals, Books, and Other Publications

Your library has much information about jobs.

Your local public library and your school library are good resource centers where you can find information about jobs. You can find facts about which jobs will be available in the future and about which jobs may not be around very long. You can read job descriptions, opportunities for employment, benefits, and requirements.

One good job sourcebook is the *Occupational Outlook Handbook*, published yearly by the U.S. Department of Labor. This book contains current information about most jobs throughout the country. At the library you will also find many government and industry publications that present information about job trends, kinds of jobs, employment possibilities, skills needed, and education requirements. Your librarian can assist you in finding and using such publications.

In addition, many current periodicals contain timely information about selected occupations. You might want to look at magazines such as *Time, Newsweek, U.S. News & World Report, Fortune,* and *Business Week.* The library's *Guide to Current Periodicals* will assist you in locating information by topic, article title, or author.

Public and Private Employment Agencies

Employment agency fees vary greatly.

All major cities have private and public employment agencies whose business is to help you find jobs for which you are prepared and help employers locate the best applicants for job openings. Private employment agencies may or may not charge a fee for their services. Such fees vary within a community; so you should compare prices before you sign with an agency. Some of these employment agencies charge a fee to the employer, others charge the person seeking work a fee when a job is found, and still others divide the fee between the employer and the person hired. The state employment office does not charge a fee because it is a government agency.

At the state employment office, you can also obtain information about government jobs training assistance programs, YES (Youth Employment

Services), Youth Corps, Civil Service (state and federal), and apprenticeship boards, as well as other government employment programs that exist from time to time. You may qualify for one or more of these types of work programs.

Newspaper, Telephone Book, and Private Job Listings

Job openings are often advertised.

The *help wanted ads* in the classified section of your local newspaper consist of job openings in your area. Brief descriptions of the positions are given, often with salary ranges specified. By keeping close watch on these ads, you can tell when a new job enters the market and be quick to respond. Both employers and employment agencies advertise job openings to attract qualified applicants. You may be asked to send a letter of application and a résumé to an employer before you will be granted an interview. In the next chapter you will learn how to prepare a letter of application and a résumé.

The *Yellow Pages* of the telephone book is an alphabetic, subject listing of businesses advertising their services. If you are looking for a job in a certain field, determine the subject heading under which that type of work might be classified. Under that heading, you will find a list of companies to help you begin your job search. You may want to send letters of application and résumés to all those listed, asking to be considered for the next opening.

Many companies, government offices, and schools place job opening announcements on bulletin boards, circulate them within the company, and post them in other special locations. Checking in these places may give you inside information to apply for a position at the right time. Often the first persons to apply for a job opening have an advantage over those who apply at the last minute.

JOB SEARCH TECHNIQUES

Finding and getting the right job does not happen by accident. It takes hard work, careful planning, and often a great deal of time. Nevertheless, it is important that you put in sufficient time and effort to ensure that you get a job you enjoy and can stay with. Dissatisfaction leads to frequent job changing, which may damage your employment chances in the future. Your *work history*, a record of the jobs you have held and how long you stayed with each employer, will be important to future employers. If your record shows that you changed jobs six times in six months, you will appear immature and unstable to future employers. Thus, your

Your work history should show stability.

work history, in this example, will hurt your chances of getting a job you might want very much.

Job search techniques that will help you to find and get the right job are discussed in the following paragraphs.

Get Organized

Gather all the information you can about a job.

After you have decided what kind of job you want, the first step is to get organized. Gather together all the information you will need about the type of work you want to do. Get a list of prospective companies for which you would like to work. Gather your sources of information and research job descriptions, skills and aptitudes needed, and other job requirements. Make lists of personal contacts, places to go, and people to see. Type a current résumé and letter of application. Ask previous employers, teachers, or others to write letters of recommendation for you. Update your placement folder at school. You may want to prepare a checklist of things to do and check them off as they are completed.

Make a Plan

A good plan lists all your goals in a time frame.

A plan is important to the success of your job search because it keeps you organized, shows what you have done, and indicates what you need to do in the immediate future. A good plan lists all your goals and shows a time frame for getting them done. As each step or goal is accomplished, it should be checked off. A plan you might want to follow is shown in Figure 2–5.

Follow Through

The most important, yet difficult, step is this one. After you have contacted a potential employer by letter or by filling out an application for a job opening, after you have met a personnel manager, or had an interview, it is important that you follow through. This means checking back from time to time to say you are still interested in the job. Be neatly dressed and well groomed at all times so that you will represent yourself well. Call back in a day or two to check on the job and remain courteous and optimistic.

Don't Give Up

Before you get a good job, you will probably not get several other jobs for which you applied. When your first and second efforts appear to be fruitless, remain calm and courteous, and keep checking back for open-

FIGURE 2–5
Plan to Get a
Job

Job Leads: __ State employment office
            __ Help wanted ads (newspaper)
            __ School placement office
            __ Marketing teacher

Contacts: __ Uncle Henry (knows manager of local Penney's)

Time Line—Week 1
    Day 1: __ Type résumé and letter of application.
            __ Check help wanted ads.
            __ Make list of local stores from Yellow Pages.

    Day 2: __ Send two application letters.
            __ Get two personal references.
            __ Call Uncle Henry to set a date for lunch.

    Note: Any planned activities that are not completed this
            week should be brought forward to next week's plan.

Check with your con-
tacts frequently.

ings. Try all your job leads. Be prepared at all times, so that if you are called to come in for an interview on short notice—even the same day—you can do so. Continually check the want ads for new openings. Call back when you have established a contact, and check with your contacts frequently. Although a good job search may take several weeks or months, it will pay off. With careful planning and research, you can find the job that will meet your needs, wants, and goals.

VOCABULARY

Directions: Can you find the definition for each of the following terms used in Chapter 2?

identity   goal
values   contact
life-style   placement service
aptitude   work history
personality

1. The things in your life that are important to you.

2. A natural physical or mental ability.

3. Personal qualities and traits that make you unique.

4. Person you know in a business to give you inside information about a job.

5. The record of jobs you have held.

6. A description of who and what you are.

7. The way you choose to live your life, based on your values.

8. An end toward which efforts are directed.

9. A service that sends out school records and other information used to help students secure employment.

ITEMS FOR DISCUSSION

1. Why do people work?

2. What is your identity at this time in your life? (You may have more than one.)

3. Define *values*. List three of your parents' values and three of your own.

4. Why is choice of a career considered to be an important decision?

5. What is manual dexterity? Why might it be important to you to know if you have manual dexterity?

6. What is meant by *personal traits*? List three.

7. What are the three major steps in good career planning?

8. Why do people need to set goals in life?

9. What are (*a*) short-term, (*b*) intermediate, and (*c*) long-term goals?

10. What is meant by the term *locked in*?

11. How can you establish personal contacts within a business where you don't know anyone?

12. What are placement services? What types of placement services are available at your school?

13. Who publishes the *Occupational Outlook Handbook*? What does it contain?

14. Why should you check around with different private employment agencies before signing up with one of them?

15. Describe the Yellow Pages of your telephone book. What does it contain? How is the information listed?

APPLICATIONS

1. From Figure 2–1, list the activities that appeal to you. Can you think of several occupations that offer these types of activities?

2. Make a list of personality traits that would be important in three different types of work (for example, secretary, accountant, mechanic). Your best source of information is someone in these types of work. Ask what personality traits are more successful.

3. Describe your desired life-style in ten years. Include the things you want to have and what you want to be. Consider such factors as marriage, family, housing, job title, etc. Will the job you want to work at support the life-style you desire?

4. Research three different types of careers, using the resources available to you. (Suggestions: *Occupational Outlook Handbook*, current periodicals.) List for each occupation: job description, job requirements (including education), working hours, salary range, and other information.

5. Using Figure 2–4 as an example, prepare a checklist that contains short-term, intermediate, and long-term goals. At the end of the week, check to see what you have accomplished.

6. Cut these types of want ads from the classified section of your local newspaper: three ads by private employers; three ads by private employment agencies, one ad for someone to make a cash investment, one ad for someone in a sales position (to work on commission rather than for a salary), and one ad that gives the beginning salary in a dollar amount.

7. Using your telephone book, list ten private employment agencies, their addresses, and their phone numbers. Also list the address and phone number of the state employment office. Call one of the private agencies and ask a counselor the amount of the fee for a job that will pay approximately $1,000 a month, and ask who would pay the fee.

8. Write a paragraph describing your work history. It can be current or what you would like it to be in ten years.

9. List and describe the four steps in an effective job search.

10. Using Figure 2–5 as an example, prepare a plan to get yourself a job using a one-week timetable. List your job leads, your contacts (or potential ones), and a daily plan to accomplish several things each day.

11. Define the phrase *follow through*.

CASE PROBLEMS AND ACTIVITIES

1. Give five or more activities (see Figure 2–1) that would be a part of the work involved in each of the following occupations: carpenter, forest ranger, teacher, social worker.

2. Using the *Occupational Outlook Handbook* and the following format, prepare a career report for one occupation you are interested in.

CAREER REPORT

Name of career: _____

Year of handbook: _____ Info. located on pp.: _____

1. What is the nature of the work? _____

_____

_____

2. Describe the average working conditions. _____

_____

3. List possible places of employment. _____

_____

4. What training is needed for this type of work? _____

_____

5. What is the employment outlook for this career across the country? _____

_____

6. What salary can you expect to earn as a beginning worker in this career? __

_____

7. What personality traits are needed for success in this career? _____

_____

_____

8. Where can you find additional information about this career? _____

_____

_____

---

3. John Wilson has decided that his long-term goal in life is to become an astronaut. He is now a sophomore in high school and hasn't done any planning. John's grades are average; he is active, outgoing, and bright. What can John do now, in the next few years, and beyond to prepare himself for a career as an astronaut?

4. Using Figure 2-3 as a guide, classify each of the following job titles into one of the nine job classifications. You may have to do some research to determine types of activities performed, skills and education required, working hours, and beginning pay.

   a. log scaler
   b. court reporter
   c. sheet-metal worker
   d. technical writer
   e. building custodian
   f. underwriter
   g. mechanical engineer
   h. sonar operator
   i. cosmetologist
   j. physical therapist
   k. computer programmer
   l. radio announcer
   m. singer
   n. infantry officer
   o. administrative assistant
   p. F.B.I. special agent
   q. tailor

5. Linda Garcia wants to be an accountant when she completes high school. She is taking accounting courses and is working part-time at the ice cream store. What should Linda be doing to prevent herself from becoming locked into her job at the ice cream store?

6. Henry Weinberger would like to work as a merchandising manager for a large department store. He has all the qualifications, education, and skills necessary; but he doesn't know anyone in any large stores, and most openings are filled before he even knows they existed. What can Henry do to find out about job openings in the large department stores?

7. Louise Pitts is a sophomore in high school. She plans to use the placement service of her high school to help get a part-time job in her senior year. What should Louise do between now and her senior year to be sure her placement folder is ready when she is ready to find a job?

8. Jack Adams has worked part-time after school for the past two years. He worked for two weeks as a cook, but rarely got to work on time and was fired. He worked for two months as a busboy but quit because he didn't get enough tips. Jack also worked for three weeks as a janitor but was laid off. Finally, he worked for four months as a plumber's assistant but quit because the work hurt his back. What is Jack's record of job changes called? What does it say to potential employers? Would you hire Jack?

3
Adapting to Your Job

CHAPTER OBJECTIVES:

After studying this chapter and completing the activities, you will be able to:

1. List and describe the types of listening.
2. Describe the types of speeches and tools to use in preparing for them.
3. Define types of absentees and list the causes of employee absenteeism; describe the costs and effects of absenteeism.
4. List the five levels of need as described by Maslow and discuss the results of job satisfaction.

GOOD WORK HABITS

Each worker in a company represents that company to others. When you walk into a restaurant, the person who greets you or serves you *is* that restaurant to you. When you go into a grocery store, the checker *is* the grocery store to you. When you go into a department store, the sales clerk *is* the company to you. If the first impression is good, the service is courteous, and the employee seems to care about your needs, you feel good about that company and want to continue doing business with it. But, if you are treated poorly, you are likely not to do business there again.

> When you work for a company, you *are* the company.

Authors Peters and Waterman, in *In Search of Excellence*, set out to learn the qualities of top-performing companies in the United States. They cite the reasons for business success, and one of the observations that occurred again and again was related to good employee performance. Employees of the best-run companies did these simple, but rememberable, things:

1. Remembered customers' names.
2. Made an "unusual effort" to help.
3. Demonstrated knowledge, enthusiasm, and interest in their customers and their customers' needs.
4. Displayed a genuine concern for quality and good service.
5. Seemed really to care about people.
6. Took pride in themselves and in their work and seemed happy to do
   what they were being paid to do.

Peters and Waterman developed eight basic principles which describe
the reasons why the best-run American companies stay on top. Three of
these recommendations involve people and motivation through productivity. They conclude that employees who recognize that their best efforts
are essential will perform better because they know they will share in the
rewards of the company's success.

Good effort is rewarded by companies.

Go the Extra Mile

Employers generally expect a full day's work for a full day's pay. If
you give a full day's work, you are indeed entitled to a full day's pay. But
how can you expect to receive more than a full day's pay for giving only
what is required of you? You must go beyond your basic job requirements

and do more in order to expect more. Your employer is under an obligation when you perform extra work—an obligation to recognize your achievements and reward you accordingly. Performing extra work is entirely voluntary. Because most people do not voluntarily give more without extra pay, you will stand out because you will be in the minority. Going the extra mile begins with a positive attitude: doing what is required of you and more. It means taking special care of details; thinking ahead and displaying initiative; listening carefully to what is being asked of you; and being attentive to the needs of others.

You will be recognized for going the extra mile.

Learn to Communicate by Listening

Eighty percent of all job activities include communication in one form or another. The most commonly used communication is listening, followed by speaking. Figure 3-1 illustrates the amount of time spent in communication during the work day.

Listening carefully is an excellent work habit that will bring you much reward. There are several rules to follow to become a good listener:

Being a good listener takes practice.

1. Look at the speaker and maintain eye contact. This shows interest in what the speaker is saying.
2. Ask questions. This gets you actively involved in the conversation. You may need to save your questions until the end of the presentation, however, so write them down.

FIGURE 3–1
Communication on the Job

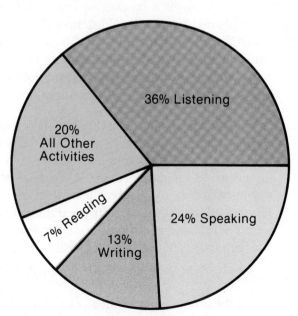

3. Avoid interrupting or changing the subject.
4. Control your emotions. Listen to what the speaker says, then evaluate it with an open mind.

Hearing is not the same thing as listening. *Hearing* is the physiological sensory process by which auditory sensations are received by ears and transmitted to the brain. It is little more than a natural process by which sound registers in the brain; it requires little or no thinking and very little effort. *Listening* is the active process that requires mental concentration and effort. You may need to use different types of listening at different times. Three types of effective listening are: sympathetic, critical, and creative.

There are three basic types of listening.

Sympathetic Listening. *Sympathetic listening* is when you follow these rules: Keep your eyes and attention on the speaker; do not interrupt the speaker or interject your opinions; ask questions which lead the speaker to make further explanations and analysis; do not make body gestures or expressions which indicate approval, disapproval, or opinion. A good sympathetic listener allows the speaker to "talk it out." In many cases, the speaker can work through the problem simply by discovery. Your own opinions should not be given unless asked for.

Critical Listening. *Critical Listening* is when a person is able to discern between facts and fiction or useless trivia. When you are receiving information about a product or service you are considering purchasing, you will need to use critical listening. For example, claims that a product is the "best buy," "top quality," "one of a kind," "really beautiful," or "a sure winner," do not tell you anything about the product. But when you hear descriptors such as "100 percent cotton," "one-year guarantee," or "wash and wear," you are receiving information that you can use.

Listen critically to sales talk.

Creative Listening. This type of listening is often used in problem solving. Each person puts forth ideas; parts that are useful in order to develop a final plan of action are taken from each idea. Brainstorming is often used in the development of *creative listening*—all ideas are written down, regardless of quality. Then, after every possible piece of information is gathered, the best parts are put together to make a workable plan. Creative listening is difficult to do because it is a group process. It takes concentration, cooperation, and skill to be able to listen creatively.

Creative listening is difficult.

Learn to Communicate by Speaking

At the place of employment, the average worker spends 24 percent of his or her time speaking. It is important that verbal communication be easily understood. You may face several different types of speaking assignments.

Purposes for Speeches. There are three basic purposes for giving speeches: to inform, to entertain, or to persuade. The information presented takes different styles, depending on which kind of speech you are preparing.

An informational speech is the easiest to prepare.

1. To inform. In this type of presentation, you are attempting to convey information to your audience. The information should be given in a manner that is easily understood. You can follow an approach in which you give a number of facts and then reach your conclusions. Or you can use an approach in which you give the conclusions first, followed by the reasons.
2. To entertain. This type of speech is humorous from beginning to end. The purpose is to get the members of your audience to relax and enjoy themselves. You want them to laugh and applaud. Subtle humor is usually better than jokes.
3. To persuade. This is the most difficult type of speech because you are trying to convince your audience to take some action or to believe something. To be convincing you must use solid information that is based on facts and statistics. You must appear to be sincere, honest, and to believe in what you are saying.

Speaking Tools. To give your speech added dimension and style, use speaking tools. Do not let the tools overshadow your message; make sure they are sending the same message or reinforcing yours; and rehearse with the tools. Speaking tools include *audiovisual aids* (overhead transparencies, slides, display boards, flip charts, chalk boards, maps and graphs, real objects, models, and handouts); *equipment* (overhead projectors, screens, recorders/players, or sound systems); the *setting* (lighting, room layout, seating, speaker's stand, and microphone). All these tools are important when preparing an effective oral presentation.

Use speaking tools to enhance your speech.

Stage Fright. Stage fright is a natural reaction. Most people experience some form of stage fright every time they speak publicly. Even experienced speakers are found to be nervous or tense before speaking. To control stage fright, there are several things you can do: build confidence, be well prepared, and practice speaking.

Everyone experiences stage fright.

1. Build confidence. To gain confidence, begin with relatively unthreatening speaking situations. Take speech classes and observe other speakers carefully. Dress appropriately to gain the respect of your audience so that you will be confident of your appearance. Learn from your mistakes.

2. Be well prepared. When organizing and writing your speech, first outline what you want to say. Time yourself several times. Prepare an additional "comfort zone" of several minutes worth of material in case time goes faster than you thought. Make sure you have enough material to cover and that the material is appropriate and well developed. Know your audience and their needs, and gear your speech to target their expectations.

Always overprepare for a speech.

3. Practice speaking. Using the telephone is a good place to begin. Expand to small groups. Begin with shorter speeches and build to longer speeches. Volunteer in class to answer questions and participate in group assignments. Practice speaking slowly and carefully when expressing your thoughts and opinions.

WORK RULES

Unwritten rules are generally understood.

Most businesses have written and unwritten work rules that are generally understood by all employees. Unwritten rules are often those that require only common understanding; many are not even verbally communicated. A dress code is one example of this. Before you interview for a job, find out how workers who are already at the job are dressed. Workers simply show up for work in appropriate clothes, and the employer rarely has to say anything. An employer has a right to expect that workers will know from common sense many work rules that will apply to their jobs and all other jobs. Courtesy and teamwork are expected. Loyalty, a positive attitude, good grooming, punctuality, and appropriate dress are other unwritten and unspoken rules.

Written rules are for the benefit of all workers.

Written work rules are many times posted in employee work areas to remind employees of strict policies that must be followed. These rules are generally written for the benefit and protection of all workers. When everyone adheres to the rules, the work flows smoothly and everyone shares in the responsibilities. When an individual breaks a rule or rules, the results are employee dissatisfaction and hard feelings among workers. Figure 3-2 is an example of work rules that might be posted in an employee lunch room.

Breaking work rules is not tolerated.

Because the rules shown in Figure 3-2 are basic discipline rules, workers who break them are subject to immediate discipline. Employers will not generally tolerate workers who are late for work (except in rare emergencies) or who leave work early. To permit one employee to break the rules will cause problems with other employees who will expect to be treated in a similar manner. It is important for a new employee to follow all the rules to the letter—and beyond, to establish an air of conformity. A new worker should arrive early, leave on time, and never stay overtime on

FIGURE 3–2
Work Rules

Employees Are Required to Obey These Work Rules:

1. Begin work promptly at 8 a.m. Leave at 5 p.m.

2. No food, drink or smoking is allowed at your work station.

3. Smoking is permitted in Lounge B during break and lunch time only.

4. All employees are allowed two 15-minute breaks, at 10 a.m. and 3 p.m.

5. To call in sick, call by 7 a.m. each day of your absence.

6. Vacations are taken by seniority; no more than three employees in the same department may be vacationing at the same time.

a break or sneak food into the work area. While these infractions are not acceptable in regular workers, they are even more intolerable in new workers because they are new.

WORK ATTITUDES AND ABSENTEEISM

Most human resource experts and managers agree that absenteeism is a special kind of problem. How to deal with the problem depends on the reasons for absence. Professor P.J. Taylor (London University) observed that of all absences:

Most absences are due to illness or injury.

60 percent are due to serious or chronic illnesses, injuries, or family emergencies;

20 percent are due to acute, short-term illnesses (such as the flu), work-related accidents, or personal problems;

10 percent are due to a minor illness such as a cold, and employees who report to work according to their attitudes about their jobs;

10 percent are due to a feigned illness so that the employee can enjoy a day off.

The absentees making up the bottom 20 percent are the most concern to businesses. Industrial psychologists call this disease "voluntary absence syndrome" and warn workers that these patterns can lead to serious emotional unbalance and disturbance in their lives. Statistics will prove that younger workers are more likely to feel this way and develop poor lifelong work habits than older workers.

Some authorities on employee absenteeism contend that the person who is chronically absent from work (without good medical reason) is

Chronically absent
employees are mentally
ill.
mentally ill. They believe that this type of person cannot deal with the reality of work, and that she or he must literally "escape from reality" by regularly staying away from work. But what the employees do not realize is the long-term effects on themselves, on their employers, and on other employees.

Types of Absentees

Absentees usually fall into groups with similar characteristics. Most absentees fit into these six categories:

Chronic Absentees. These are the people who seem to have little capacity for pressure (on the job or off) and who are prime candidates for counseling. In order to counsel with them, however, they first need to be aware that their absence is a problem and is causing other problems.

Vacationing Absentees. These are people who work only long enough to pay their bills and put a few dollars in their pocket to head down the road. These employees can be very capable on the job, but they will not accept responsibility for work, jobs, or consistency in life. Vacationers make a conscious choice to be absent from work as much as work rules will allow, and they rarely will allow or benefit from counseling.

Directionless absentees
are often young.
Directionless Absentees. This group of workers is common among young people. They have not decided what they want to do with their lives. They have not set goals—personal, professional, or career. Until they can decide what they want to do with their lives, they are likely to be poor workers and take advantage of opportunities to be absent from work.

Aggressive Absentees. Persons who willfully stay away from work, wanting their absence to cause a problem or inconvenience, are called aggressive absentees and are probably emotionally disturbed. This kind of behavior requires professional counseling to correct.

Moonlighters. People who hold more than one job are often either too tired to come to work or may be faced with conflicting work schedules. Very often, the moonlighter is forced to make a choice between jobs.

Occasional Absentees. People who seem to have a few more absences, on the average, than the rest of the employees are probably prime candidates for some counseling before their behavior becomes one of the more serious forms previously listed. Their absences are legitimate, and illnesses are real. But while their problems are usually temporarily insurmountable, these absentees need a mixture of sympathy, understanding, and good advice.

Causes of Chronic Absenteeism

Some employees can be helped through counseling.

Using the same percentages as earlier presented in this section, the top 60 percent of absentees are able to be "helped." Employees who can answer yes to any of these questions are categorized as employees who need and will respond to help.

1. Is getting to work a problem (real or imagined)?
2. Are off-the-job pressures so strong and overwhelming (such as family and marital pressures) that they weaken the employee's resolve to get to work?
3. Is the employee too eager to please others or too easily misled by others?
4. Does the work appear to be boring, disagreeable, unattractive, or somehow not living up to employee expectations?
5. Are working relationships unpleasant?
6. Are there serious problems that need immediate attention (child care, emergencies, serious illness, court appearance, and so on)?
7. Has lateness or absenteeism become a habit that is hard to break?

Some employees can only help themselves.

Other employees face more serious problems to themselves and to their employers. Employees who can answer yes to any of the following questions are categorized as employees who will probably not respond to help. In other words, overcoming these symptoms involves action and resolve on the part of the employee.

1. Does work or the pay that is associated with the work hold no strong attraction for the employee? Does the employee show general disinterest in life, work, pay, or any other rewards?
2. Do off-the-job pressures and needs have a greater appeal than work and a greater payoff in the view of the employee?
3. Is the employee intentionally absent in order to disrupt or cause problems to the employer or to other employees?

Alcoholism and Drug Abuse. The National Council for Alcoholism reports that the alcoholic is absent two to four times more often than the non-alcoholic and that on-the-job accidents are two to four times more frequent for the alcoholic than for the non-alcoholic. Absenteeism rates vary with the ages of the workers; generally, workers under 30 make up a high proportion of chronic absentees. Their causes for absenteeism are more likely to be low morale and lack of discipline than illnesses. Drug abuse is more difficult to detect by employers, but overall effects and outcomes are similar to those of alcoholics. Work efficiency is impaired, other workers are affected, and general work attitudes are inhibited when workers suffering from drug addiction attempt to perform as usual without any professional help. When drug abuse is not detected, admitted by the worker, or consciously worked on in a rehabilitation plan, it can eventually lead to the dismissal of the worker. In either event, the use or sale of alcohol or drugs on the work site is usually cause for immediate dismissal.

Repetitive Work. The highest rate of absenteeism (other than for illness) is among workers with fairly repetitive work that is considered "routine" and nonintellectual. When workers perceive their own jobs as unproductive or unimportant, they are more likely to have high absenteeism rates.

New Employees. Newly hired employees are also often among the chronic absentees. It is to an employer's benefit to request from an applicant's previous employers the applicant's records of total days absent and total number of times absent. It is beneficial to a person being interviewed to provide a *letter of reference* which specifically states the person's attendance record, as well as other qualifications for the job. A former employer writing a letter of reference will probably include this kind of specific information in the letter: attendance; total days absent in the time worked in that company; dependability; responsibility; and punctuality. Letters of reference from a teacher, minister, or friend in business will also discuss your personal qualities that are appropriate to your new job.

Costs of Absenteeism

High rates of absenteeism cost companies thousands of dollars annually. The U.S. Department of Labor has developed a formula to help businesses compute a rate of absenteeism which they can use to find their total costs.

For example, assume that a small business has an average of 25 total workers during a month's payroll period (includes part-time and full-time workers). During the average month, there are 22 workdays. If that employer had total absences among all employees of 15 full days, the absenteeism rate would be about 2.73 percent. Most experts in the labor field agree that an absenteeism rate of 2.0 is low, while a rate of 5.0 is high. For instance, a survey of 931 firms revealed an average absenteeism rate of 3.73 percent; the highest average of 4.41 percent was in manufacturing, and the lowest rate of 2.79 percent was in banking.

High absenteeism rates are expensive for companies.

Once the absenteeism rate is known, the cost to the company can be computed by figuring the average wages earned by workers. In the previous example, an absenteeism rate of 2.73 percent would cost the company about $17,000 each year in lost time due to absenteeism, assuming the average wage earned was $6.00 per hour.

Effects of Absenteeism

There are many penalties for absenteeism.

The absentee is not the only one who is affected by absenteeism; but typically, he or she is the one most seriously affected. Typically, the results range from penalties, fines (such as payroll deductions), warnings, temporary layoffs, poor recommendations, lack of respect (by employer and fellow workers), and eventually, to termination of employment.

Habits are difficult to break.

Penalties and fines are often demoralizing, create job dissatisfaction and sometimes worsen the problem. However, when such action is not taken, businesses are in effect stamping their approval (or lack of disapproval) on the absences, thereby encouraging other employees to feel free to be absent often. This type of atmosphere tends to be very demoralizing to other workers who eventually resent the absentee who originally started the trend that is now difficult to stop. The working employees resent having to do another employee's work when no corrective action is taken by the employer. The overall effects of absenteeism are certain: demoralization, lack of respect, disciplinary action, tightening of company policy, poor working conditions, and poor employment references.

FIVE LEVELS OF NEED

All human beings have some needs that are basic to survival and other needs that are beyond mere physical existence. A person's work attitudes and job satisfaction are affected by the fulfillment of his or her needs. Maslow's hierarchy divides human needs into five distinct categories, as shown in Figure 3-3.

Pay needs to be sufficient to make you feel comfortable.

Employment can be the basis for meeting all five levels of need. Levels 1 and 2 are said to be things which are essential to physical survival: pay adequate to provide food, clothing, housing, and sufficient job security to feel safe and comfortable. When pay is insufficient to provide these needs, or when your job security is so shaky that you cannot relax and be comfortable about your employment, then absence of these factors is said to be a *dissatisfier*. In other words, your work productivity will be reduced because your incentive and desire to work are diminished.

Levels 3, 4 and 5 are said to be *motivators* because accomplishments and recognition in these areas will lead to greater productivity and work

FIGURE 3–3
Maslow's
Hierarchy of
Needs

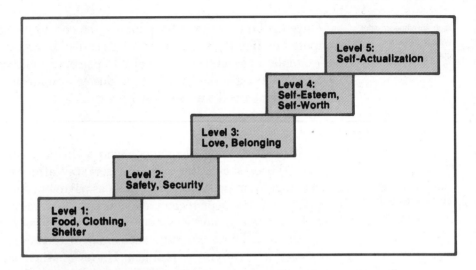

satisfaction. ***Productivity*** is a measure of the output of a production unit during a specific period of time. A measure of quality is often incorporated into the meaning of productivity.

Most businesses consider it the responsibility of management (such as the supervisor or office manager) to provide opportunities for employees to meet their needs. Every worker is motivated because every person needs fulfillment beyond her or his physical requirements.

Love means group
acceptance.

Level 3 is described by Maslow as the need to belong to the group: to be accepted, to have friendship, and to be valued as a member of the team. Love in this category is not the romantic type of love we need in marriage and personal relationships. It is the kind of love represented by kindness and caring in work relationships when we feel that we belong and have a meaningful role in the workplace. It is important to note that one level of need does not have to be completely satisfied or fulfilled before we can go on to meet needs in the next level or levels.

Self-esteem is an
important part of
productivity.

Level 4 is ***self-esteem*** and self-worth, and it refers to our inner feelings about ourselves and our accomplishments. When work is challenging and rewarding, we feel good about what we accomplish and about ourselves, and we want to do more. When workers do not feel good about themselves and their accomplishments, it is easy for them to become negative about others and their accomplishments. This brings further negative reactions and achieves little in increased work effort or productivity.

Level 5 is ***self-actualization***, the level at which workers are able to meet their needs of accomplishment and satisfaction; they are able to do the work they choose, as they choose, and receive appropriate rewards for a job well done. This is the ideal state for every worker: a job that meets not only the first four levels but is totally satisfying in terms of meeting personal goals and values. To aid workers in meeting this level, many managers seek to learn what type of work is truly satisfying and desired by their employees for self-fulfillment and self-actualization. Then they give this kind of work to their workers gradually until employees are able to handle the work well and realize their full potential.

Employers need to match employee needs and abilities.

RESULTS OF JOB SATISFACTION

The employer is not the only winner when workers are able to meet most of their needs. The worker is able to feel better about himself or herself; stress levels are reduced; efforts are rewarded by greater pay, advancement opportunities, and praise; work is a pleasant and enjoyable thing to do since it meets physical and emotional needs of workers. Employers benefit because of increased productivity, which leads to greater profits, company growth, and income potential. When things are going well at work, both employers and employees feel better about what is going on at work and in their personal lives.

Both employers and employees benefit from job satisfaction.

Increased Productivity

When employees work better, they are said to be more productive. Time is used wisely; less time is wasted. More work is produced in less time, and better work is produced in the same or less time. Increased productivity leads to higher profits for the employer, and subsequent rewards for the employees—both tangible (a raise, bonus, or promotion) and intangible (praise, commendation, and self-worth feelings).

Self-Esteem and Self-Actualization

To be the best you can be; to win the praise of employer and employees; to strive for and accept new challenges—these are valid bases for career development and satisfaction. As these goals are met and satisfied, they bring personal pride and enjoyment that are satisfying beyond the paycheck. Since you will probably have to work most of your adult life anyway, why not strive to accomplish the most and the best of your ability?

Meeting your goals brings great satisfaction.

Rewards and Opportunities

Employers often seek to motivate employees using praise and pay as reinforcements for desirable results. Your rewards will vary: oral or written commendations from employers; admiration and respect of other workers; pay raises for exemplary work (often called *merit pay*); increased opportunities for challenging work (new job assignments with increased responsibilities); opportunities for advancement to higher paying positions with more prestige and status; and respect from others inside and outside your employment for your accomplishments and quality of work. You could become known as "one of the best in the field" and gain recognition in your local area, community, state, or even nation. This makes you valuable not only to your own employer, but it also makes you more employable in future years should you desire to move to another job or another area. Increased opportunities within your field are created by excellence in work accomplishments and should be a part of your long-term career plans.

It is important to be respected for your work.

VOCABULARY

Directions: Can you find the definition for each of the following terms used in Chapter 3?

hearing	written work rules
listening	letter of reference
sympathetic listening	dissatisfier
critical listening	motivators
creative listening	productivity
audiovisual aids	self-esteem
equipment	self-actualization
setting	merit pay

1. Pay raises for exemplary work.

2. An active process (skill) that requires mental concentration and effort.

3. Transparencies, slides, or other visual materials.

4. Diminishes your desire to work.

5. Lead to greater work satisfaction.

6. A type of listening in which you decide between fact and fiction.

7. An accounting of a past employee's work record and personal traits.

8. Feelings of self-worth about ourselves and our accomplishments.

9. Overhead projectors, screens, and other systems for projecting images and sounds.

10. A measure of the output of a production unit.

11. The type of listening in which you listen but offer no advice.

12. A type of listening in which all ideas are considered and the most workable parts are saved.

13. A level at which workers meet their needs of accomplishment and satisfaction.

14. The physiological sensory process of receiving auditory sensations.

15. Lighting, room layout, speaker's stand, and other considerations of speaking.

16. Policies posted in employee work areas for the benefit of all.

ITEMS FOR DISCUSSION

1. List some examples of good employee performance as cited by Peters and Waterman in *In Search of Excellence*.

2. What is meant by "going the extra mile"?

3. In percentages, how much time on the job is spent on these activities:

    (a) listening

    (b) speaking

    (c) writing

    (d) reading

    (e) other activities

4. Define the following terms:

    (a) sympathetic listening

    (b) critical listening

    (c) creative listening

5. List three purposes of speeches.

6. List the three main categories of speaking tools.

7. List three things you can do about stage fright.

8. What percent of all absences is due to serious or chronic illness?

9. What is "voluntary absence syndrome"?

10. List six types of absentees.

11. Give three reasons or causes of chronic absenteeism.

12. What are some effects of absenteeism on the absentee? on other workers?

13. List in order Maslow's five levels of need.

14. What are three major results of job satisfaction?

APPLICATIONS

1. Listening is a skill. What are some things you can do to improve your listening skill?

2. How is hearing different from listening? Are there times when you hear but aren't listening? Give examples.

3. Under what circumstances would you use sympathetic listening? critical listening? creative listening?

4. Which type of listening (sympathetic, critical, or creative) did you last use? Describe the situation.

5. What type of speech or presentation did you hear recently (inform, entertain, or persuade)? Describe it.

6. Have you ever experienced stage fright? What did you do to help make it easier?

7. What are some examples of unwritten rules that you observe in your school? What are some examples of written rules that you observe in your school?

8. Why is it important for a new employee to observe all unwritten and written work rules?

9. What is meant by a "chronic absentee"? Why is this person said to be mentally ill?

10. What are some symptoms of chronic absenteeism which are said to be of the nature that cannot be helped by the employer?

11. How do alcoholism and drug abuse affect a worker's performance on the job?

CASE PROBLEMS AND ACTIVITIES

1. The following formula is distributed by the U.S. Department of Labor for computing a rate of absenteeism. Can you compute the rate of absenteeism based on these facts:
    Average number of workers: 45
    Number of workdays in period: 22
    Worker days lost during period: 26

$$\text{RATE OF ABSENTEEISM (\%)} = \frac{\text{WORKER DAYS LOST DURING PERIOD}}{\text{AVERAGE NUMBER OF WORKERS} \times \text{NUMBER OF WORKDAYS IN PERIOD}} \times 100$$

2. Interview a person working full time and ask how each of the following levels is met through his or her employment: Level 1 (food, clothing, and shelter); Level 2 (safety and security); Level 3 (love and belonging); Level 4 (self-esteem and self-worth); and Level 5 (self-actualization).

3. How many times were you absent from school (or from a part-time job) this year? What were the reasons for each absence?

4. Write a letter of reference. Assume that it is a letter from your previous employer and covers areas such as attendance, punctuality, work attitude, qualifications, dependability, and so on. Write the type of letter you would like to present to your next prospective employer.

5. Make a list of unwritten rules that you observe in your home or in your classroom. Compare your list to a friend's list to see the similarities and differences.

6. Visit a company and ask for a copy of its written rules, such as those shown in Figure 3-2, or interview a manager and ask about written rules (some companies may not want to share written information). In groups, compare work rules from different types of companies. What types of penalties are imposed for breaking some of these rules?

Keeping Your Job

CHAPTER OBJECTIVES

After studying this chapter and completing the activities, you will be able to:

1. Understand and complete appropriate work forms, such as W-4, social security application, and work permit application.
2. Understand and recall employee responsibilities at work and employer responsibilities to employees.
3. List and define provisions of basic employment laws enacted for protection and security of workers.

WORK FORMS

When you begin your first paying job, you will need to be aware of a number of forms. Most of these forms ask for information that employers are required by law to keep. Some of these forms can be obtained prior to beginning work (social security card and work permit, if you are under 16), while others are completed by you when you begin working (W-4) and by the employer after you have worked during the year (W-2). You should be familiar with these forms because you may need to make corrections or changes from time to time.

Form W-4, Employee's Withholding Allowance Certificate

When you report to work, you will be asked to fill out a *Form W-4, Employee's Withholding Allowance Certificate*. Form W-4 is for income tax withholding purposes and remains in effect until you make a change. On this form you declare the total number of **allowances**, persons who are dependent on your income for support. The more allowances you can claim, the less tax you will have withheld. You may automatically claim yourself. Other allowances can be for spouse, children, or if your itemized deductions allow less money to be withheld from your paycheck. You may also claim **exempt status** and not have any federal tax withheld from your paycheck, if you qualify, by writing *exempt* as shown in Figure 4–1. You may claim to be exempt from federal tax withholding if you will not earn enough money to owe any federal tax. The amount of maximum earnings necessary to qualify varies annually. Exemption may be claimed if last year you owed no federal tax and had a right to receive a full refund and if this year you do not expect to owe any federal tax and expect a full refund.

Claim exempt status if you qualify.

Social Security Forms

Because all workers in the United States must pay a social security tax from wages earned, all persons must obtain a *social security number*. Your social security number is your permanent work identification number. While you are working, your employers withhold social security taxes from your pay and contribute matching amounts. All your work life, the amounts you earn and the amounts contributed for social security are credited by the Social Security Administration to your account under your assigned number. When you become eligible, benefits are paid to you monthly based upon how much you have paid into your account.

Withholdings are credited to your account.

FIGURE 4–1
Form W-4, Employee's Withholding Allowance Certificate

Social security isn't just for retirement. If a parent covered by social security dies or becomes disabled, minor children may be eligible for payments. Persons who become severely disabled (unable to work for a year or more) are paid benefits until they return to work. If disability coverage is needed for more than two years, payments are continued under Medicare.

Disability benefits are available.

Figure 4–2 is an application for a social security number card. This application must be filled out completely and sent to the Social Security

FIGURE 4–2
Application for a Social Security Number Card

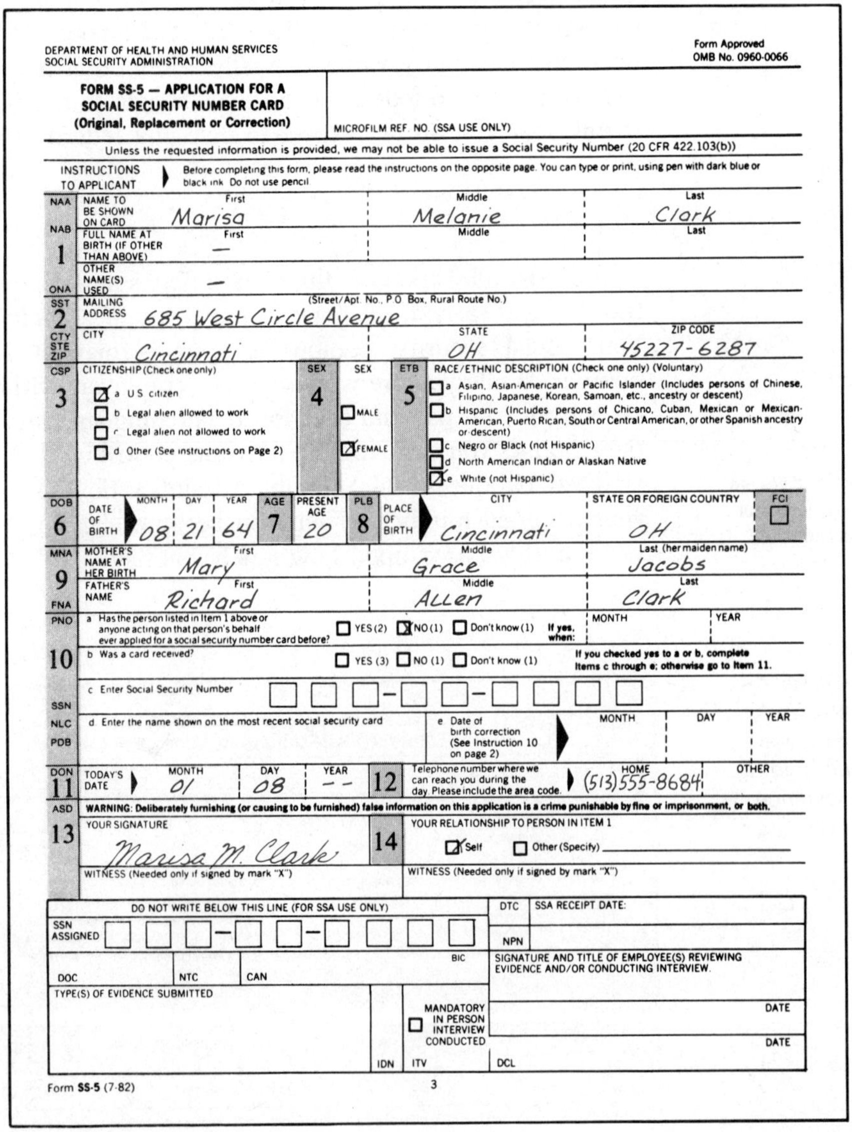

DEPARTMENT OF HEALTH AND HUMAN SERVICES
SOCIAL SECURITY ADMINISTRATION

Form Approved
OMB No. 0960-0066

FORM SS-5 — APPLICATION FOR A SOCIAL SECURITY NUMBER CARD (Original, Replacement or Correction)

MICROFILM REF. NO. (SSA USE ONLY)

Unless the requested information is provided, we may not be able to issue a Social Security Number (20 CFR 422.103(b))

INSTRUCTIONS TO APPLICANT: Before completing this form, please read the instructions on the opposite page. You can type or print, using pen with dark blue or black ink. Do not use pencil.

NAA 1	NAME TO BE SHOWN ON CARD	First: Marisa	Middle: Melanie	Last: Clark
NAB	FULL NAME AT BIRTH (IF OTHER THAN ABOVE)	First: —	Middle	Last
ONA	OTHER NAME(S) USED	—		
SST 2	MAILING ADDRESS (Street/Apt. No., P.O. Box, Rural Route No.)	685 West Circle Avenue		
CTY STE ZIP	CITY	Cincinnati	STATE: OH	ZIP CODE: 45227-6287

CSP 3 CITIZENSHIP (Check one only): [x] a U.S. citizen; [ ] b Legal alien allowed to work; [ ] c Legal alien not allowed to work; [ ] d Other (See instructions on Page 2)

SEX 4: [ ] MALE; [x] FEMALE

ETB 5 RACE/ETHNIC DESCRIPTION (Check one only) (Voluntary): [ ] a Asian, Asian-American or Pacific Islander (Includes persons of Chinese, Filipino, Japanese, Korean, Samoan, etc., ancestry or descent); [ ] b Hispanic (Includes persons of Chicano, Cuban, Mexican or Mexican-American, Puerto Rican, South or Central American, or other Spanish ancestry or descent); [ ] c Negro or Black (not Hispanic); [ ] d North American Indian or Alaskan Native; [x] e White (not Hispanic)

DOB 6 DATE OF BIRTH: MONTH 08 DAY 21 YEAR 64 — AGE 7 PRESENT AGE 20 — PLB 8 PLACE OF BIRTH: CITY Cincinnati, STATE OR FOREIGN COUNTRY OH — FCI [ ]

MNA 9 MOTHER'S NAME AT HER BIRTH: First Mary, Middle Grace, Last (her maiden name) Jacobs
FNA FATHER'S NAME: First Richard, Middle Allen, Last Clark

PNO 10 a Has the person listed in Item 1 above or anyone acting on that person's behalf ever applied for a social security number card before? [ ] YES (2) [x] NO (1) [ ] Don't know (1) If yes, when: MONTH YEAR
b Was a card received? [ ] YES (3) [ ] NO (1) [ ] Don't know (1) If you checked yes to a or b, complete items c through e; otherwise go to item 11.
SSN c Enter Social Security Number □□□-□□-□□□□
NLC PDB d Enter the name shown on the most recent social security card — e Date of birth correction (See Instruction 10 on page 2) MONTH DAY YEAR

DON 11 TODAY'S DATE: MONTH 01 DAY 08 YEAR — — 12 Telephone number where we can reach you during the day. Please include the area code. HOME (513) 555-8684 OTHER

ASD **WARNING: Deliberately furnishing (or causing to be furnished) false information on this application is a crime punishable by fine or imprisonment, or both.**

13 YOUR SIGNATURE: Marisa M. Clark — 14 YOUR RELATIONSHIP TO PERSON IN ITEM 1: [x] Self [ ] Other (Specify) ______
WITNESS (Needed only if signed by mark "X") — WITNESS (Needed only if signed by mark "X")

DO NOT WRITE BELOW THIS LINE (FOR SSA USE ONLY)
SSN ASSIGNED □□□-□□-□□□□ — DTC — SSA RECEIPT DATE: — NPN — BIC — DOC — NTC — CAN — SIGNATURE AND TITLE OF EMPLOYEE(S) REVIEWING EVIDENCE AND/OR CONDUCTING INTERVIEW.
TYPE(S) OF EVIDENCE SUBMITTED — [ ] MANDATORY IN PERSON INTERVIEW CONDUCTED — DATE — DATE — IDN — ITV — DCL

Form SS-5 (7-82) 3

Administration. You are then assigned one social security number for your lifetime, and are issued a card bearing this number. If the original card bearing the assigned number is lost or destroyed, you can obtain a duplicate without charge.

From time to time—every few years—you should check to see that your earnings have been properly credited to your account. The Social Security Administration in Baltimore provides a handy card for you to complete for this purpose (see Figure 4–3). Within 30 days you should receive a report that lists your income according to the Social Security Administration's records. Any mistakes should be reported immediately.

If you have not yet applied for your social security number, you should do so now, so you will have it handy when you are ready to go to work.

·Check your social
security records
periodically.

FIGURE 4–3
Request for
Social Security
Statement of
Earnings

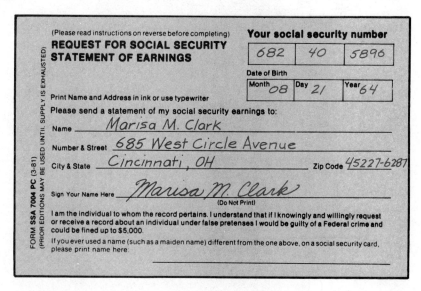

(Please read instructions on reverse before completing)   **Your social security number**

REQUEST FOR SOCIAL SECURITY STATEMENT OF EARNINGS

682   40   5896

Date of Birth
Month 08   Day 21   Year 64

Print Name and Address in ink or use typewriter

Please send a statement of my social security earnings to:

Name _Marisa M. Clark_

Number & Street _685 West Circle Avenue_

City & State _Cincinnati, OH_   Zip Code _45227-6287_

Sign Your Name Here _Marisa M. Clark_
                            (Do Not Print)

I am the individual to whom the record pertains. I understand that if I knowingly and willingly request or receive a record about an individual under false pretenses I would be guilty of a Federal crime and could be fined up to $5,000.

If you ever used a name (such as a maiden name) different from the one above, on a social security card, please print name here:

FORM SSA 7004 PC (3-81)
(PRIOR EDITIONS MAY BE USED UNTIL SUPPLY IS EXHAUSTED)

Work Permit Application

Federal and some state laws require *minors*, persons under the age of legal majority, to obtain a *work permit* before they are allowed to work. The work permit is signed by the parents or legal guardian of persons under 16 years of age. Application for a work permit is obtained from the Department of Labor, a school counseling center, or work experience coordinators. There is usually no charge for obtaining the card, but the applicant will have to provide his or her social security number and proof of birth and have a parent's or legal guardian's signature. Additional information may be required in some states. Figure 4–4 is an example of a work permit application. The form must be filled in completely and

A parent must sign the
work permit
application.

clearly. Processing of the work permit application takes three to six weeks, so early application is advisable.

WORK PERMIT APPLICATION

This Is Not A Permit

| 2 | 5 | 2 | – | 4 | 3 | – | 4 | 5 | 5 | 7 |

SOCIAL SECURITY NUMBER

SEE INSTRUCTIONS

PERMIT WILL NOT BE ISSUED
unless all blanks are carefully filled in and are clearly readable

Mitchell B. Lewin   *M*   *3-28-68*
NAME   SEX   BIRTHDATE

1350 Harrison St.   *272-3485*
MAILING ADDRESS   PHONE NO.

Cincinnati, OH   *45227-6308*
CITY AND STATE   ZIP CODE

Cincinnati   *OH*
BIRTHPLACE (CITY)   STATE

Riverside High School *Cincinnati*   *9*
LAST SCHOOL ATTENDED   LOCATION   GRADE COMPLETED

Janice M. Lewin
PARENT OR GUARDIAN SIGNATURE

1350 Harrison St.   *272-3485*
STREET ADDRESS   PHONE NO.

Cincinnati, OH   *45227-6308*
CITY AND STATE   ZIP CODE

Mitchell B. Lewin
MINOR'S SIGNATURE

Do Not Write Below This Line

Form W-2, Wage and Tax Statement

When you have worked for a business or company during the year, you will receive a *Form W-2, Wage and Tax Statement*, which lists income you earned during the year and all amounts withheld by the employer in your behalf. These amounts include federal income tax, state income tax, and social security tax. Figure 4–5 is a completed W-2 statement. Your W-2 should be compared to payroll slips received with each paycheck to be sure that the right amounts have been reported.

Compare the Form W-2 with your payroll slips.

FIGURE 4–5
Form W-2, Wage and Tax Statement

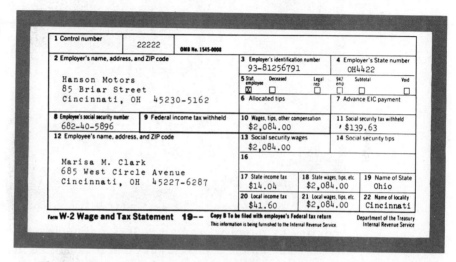

The employer must provide a W-2 form to you no later than January 31 of the year following the one in which you were employed. This is true even if you only worked part of the year and were not working as of December 31. If you do not receive a W-2 from your employer (and all employers you may have worked for during the year) you should contact the employer to get the W-2. Former employers may not have a current address for you.

EMPLOYEE RESPONSIBILITIES

As a new employee, you will want to do the best possible job. In order to be successful, you will have a number of responsibilities to meet.

Responsibilities to Employers

Your employer hires you and pays you at predetermined intervals. In return for this pay and other benefits you may receive, the employer

Plan to meet your job responsibilities.

expects certain things from you.

Competent Work. You should do your best to produce the best possible finished product for your employer. The work needs to be *marketable*; that is, of such quality that the employer can sell it or represent the

ILLUSTRATION 4–1
Responsible employees have a pleasant attitude.

company by use of your product. If, for example, you type a letter that has so many mistakes and erasures that it cannot be mailed, the letter is not a marketable product.

Be thrifty with your employer's supplies.

Thrift. When using an employer's materials, you should be as thrifty as possible, conserving supplies and materials with care and diligence as though they were your own. Supplies and other materials are expensive to an employer.

Punctuality. Workers should consistently arrive at work on time, take allotted breaks, and leave at quitting time. Being punctual means being ready to go to work at the appointed time—not rushing through the door at the last minute.

Pleasant Attitude. On any job, it is important to be pleasant and easy to get along with. You should be willing to follow orders and take directions. Your employer also has the right to expect you to be courteous to customers, since you represent the company or store to others.

Loyalty displays respect for the employer.

Loyalty and Respect. While working for a company, you should never be guilty of spreading rumors or gossiping about your employer or job. As long as you are on the company "team," you are expected to be loyal to the company. Loyalty includes showing respect to the employer and the company on and off the job.

Dependability. When you say you will do something, follow through. The employer should be able to depend on you to do what you are hired to do.

Initiative. You should not have to be told everything to do. Employees who stand idle when a specific job is completed are of very little value to employers. *Initiative* means that you do things on your own without being told to; you're a self-starter.

Interest. It is important for you to show an interest in your job and your company. You should project an attitude of wanting to learn all you can and of giving all tasks your best possible effort. An enthusiastic attitude projects to an employer your sincere interest in being a cooperative and productive worker.

Self-Evaluation. The ability to take criticism and to assess your own progress is important to you and the employer. Everyone has strong points and weak points, but the weak points cannot be improved unless you are willing to admit they exist and begin to work on them. Employers are faced with the task of employee evaluation to determine raises and promotions. Employees should be able to recognize their own strong points and limitations and do a realistic self-evaluation of their job performance.

Be aware of your weak points.

Responsibilities to Other Employees

In addition to the responsibilities that you owe your employer, you also have duties to your fellow workers. These include the following:

Teamwork. You are part of a team when you work with others in a company, and you need to do your share of the work. Employees must work cooperatively in order to produce a quality final product; when friction and personality problems occur, the productivity and efficiency of the whole company decrease.

Do your share of the work.

Thoughtfulness. Be considerate of fellow workers to promote a good work atmosphere for everyone, including customers. Having a pleasant attitude will result in a more enjoyable time for yourself and others. Personal problems and conflicts have no place being displayed at work.

Loyalty. In addition to being loyal to and supportive of your employer, you should also be loyal toward fellow employees. This means not spreading rumors about them. Gossiping leads to a breakdown of teamwork.

Responsibilities to Customers

As an employee, you represent the company. To the customer who walks in the front door, you *are* the company. Thus, your attitude toward a customer often makes the difference in whether he or she returns for future products or services. Therefore, remember that on behalf of your employer you have the responsibility to greet the customer with an attitude of helpfulness and courtesy.

Attitude is very important.

Helpfulness. When customers come to your employer's place of business, they expect to have reasonable help in finding or deciding what to purchase. It is the employee's responsibility to help customers find what they want or to do what is needed. An attitude of helpfulness reflects well on the company and is an important part of any job.

Courtesy. Whether or not you like a customer, that customer actually pays your wages—by keeping your employer in business. Without the customer, the business could not exist. Therefore, your attitude toward the customer should always be respectful and courteous, never hostile or unfriendly. Customer loyalty to a business is often built by friendly, helpful employees.

Being helpful is good for business.

EMPLOYER RESPONSIBILITIES

Employers also have responsibilities to employees. Some responsibilities are required by law, and others are simply good practices to follow for keeping employees happy and on the job. Failure to meet these responsibilities can result in an employer being fined for unfair labor practices or a high turnover rate, higher premiums for unemployment insurance, and costly expenses in connection with the continual need to hire new employees. Some employer duties include adequate supervision, fair personnel policies, safe working conditions, open channels of communication, recognition of achievement, and compliance with civil rights and laws.

Adequate Supervision

Employees need to be properly supervised to be sure they are learning to do a good job on work assigned. Supervision includes providing appropriate instruction in the use of equipment and safety standards, and spending enough time with new employees to adequately train them to do the assigned task.

Fair Personnel Policies

Hiring and firing policies, salary advancement policies, and procedures for recourse for employee disputes are some of the policies that need to be fair and well defined. Employees should know clearly what is acceptable and unacceptable performance, what the standards are for advancements and raises, and what constitutes grounds for suspension or discharge.

Know what is expected of you.

Safe Working Conditions

All employees must be provided safe equipment, a safe working environment, and adequate training for working under dangerous conditions. Special protective equipment and clothing and warning signs must be provided to employees working under dangerous conditions. Minors have stricter working conditions than adults in some industries.

Open Channels of Communication

Employers need to communicate with employees so that all employees have the opportunity to express concerns, ask questions, and make suggestions. Lack of open channels of communication can result in poor morale of workers and low work output. Employees need to know they are an important part of the company and that their opinions are valuable.

Recognition of Achievement

Employers need to provide some form of reward for performance by employees. Merit pay raises, as well as advancement on a regularly established schedule, provide encouragement for workers to do their best possible work. When achievement is not recognized, employees lose the desire to be as productive as possible. All human beings need to be rewarded and encouraged from time to time; a salary bonus or raise is an excellent method of encouragement.

Rewards are work incentives.

Compliance with Civil Rights and Laws

Employers must obey state and federal laws designed to protect workers from discrimination in employment on the basis of race, color, sex,

Employment laws protect workers' rights.

national origin, religion, and, in some cases, age. In the next section we will learn of some of the employment laws enacted to protect workers from unfair labor practices. The employer is responsible for observing workers' rights. Failure to do so can result in severe penalties for the employer. Complaints of discrimination in employment may be filed with the Equal Employment Opportunity Commission.

EMPLOYMENT LAWS

In the last fifty years many laws have been enacted to provide various protections for American workers. Laws enacted are generally enforced by government agencies, such as the Department of Labor or the Social Security Administration.

Major employment acts are called administrative laws. Established by Congress and authorized by the executive branch of government, ***administrative agencies*** are given the power of law to enforce administrative laws. The Department of Labor is responsible for overseeing several important labor acts and their provisions.

All workers receive benefits.

The main provisions of the laws will generally be in one or more of the following areas *for all workers*:

1. To establish a minimum wage
2. To provide regular working hours
3. To provide unemployment, disability, and retirement insurance benefits
4. To provide equal employment opportunities and eliminate discrimination
5. To establish safe working conditions

Other laws have provisions for specific workers that do not apply to all workers. Minors are given several special provisions:

1. Specific safety precautions and working conditions that are more extensive than for adults
2. Maximum number of hours to be worked and times during which minors can work during the school year
3. Requirement for those under age 16 to obtain a work permit

Legal recourse is available.

If any employee believes that he or she has not received benefits as required by law, ***recourse***, or remedy is available. If you think that you have a legitimate complaint, you should call the state Department of Labor, which will assist you without charge. Employers found in violation of labor laws are subject to fine, payment of damages to employees, and other penalties determined by a court of law.

Social Security Act

Originally called the Federal Insurance Contributions Act of 1935, the *Social Security Act* was the first national social insurance program, enacted to provide federal aid for the elderly and for disabled workers. In 1965 the Medicare provision (hospital and medical insurance protection) for elderly retired workers and other qualified persons was added. Five basic types of benefits are paid: (*a*) disability, (*b*) survivor, (*c*) retirement, (*d*) hospital, and (*e*) medical. Benefits received depend on the amount of contributions made. Self-employed workers pay their social security contributions when they pay their income tax. For employees in occupations covered by social security, contributions are mandatory. Social security protection is not yet available for some types of employment. Your local social security office will know if your employment is covered. Social security (FICA) is deducted from your gross pay and sent to the Internal Revenue Service for proper crediting to your social security account.

Benefits depend on contributions.

Unemployment Compensation

An important part of the Social Security Act provides that every state must have an *unemployment insurance* program that provides benefits to workers who lose their jobs through no fault of their own. After a waiting period, laid-off or terminated workers may collect a portion of their regular pay for a certain length of time. Premiums for unemployment insurance are generally paid by employers. Rates vary according to employers' records of turnover, or how often they hire and fire employees. The more often employers let workers go, the higher the premium rate they will pay. Each state has its own regulations as to waiting period, maximum benefits, deadlines for filing claims, and premium rates. Unless otherwise extended by provision of the legislature of the state, benefits are paid for a maximum of 22 weeks, through the local state employment office.

Waiting periods are necessary.

Fair Labor Standards Act

Popularly known as the *Wage and Hour Act*, the Fair Labor Standards Act of 1938 provided that persons working in interstate commerce or a related industry could not be paid less than a minimum wage of 25 cents an hour. A *minimum wage* is the legally established lower limit on wages employers may pay. The minimum wage reached $3.35 an hour in January of 1981. Another provision of the act states that hourly wage workers cannot be employed for more than 40 hours a week. Hours worked in addition to the regular hours are considered *overtime* and must be paid for at one and one-half times the regular rate.

Each state enforces wage and hour laws, which include federal provisions and additional state regulations. These laws, which are regulated by state Departments of Labor, provide that regular paydays must be established and maintained by every employer. Payment of wages to new employees must begin no later than 35 days after the date work has begun. When an employee quits, wages due must be paid within 48 hours of the final day worked. When an employee is discharged, all wages are due immediately. Any employee who requests that his or her paycheck be mailed is entitled to have it mailed to an address designated by the employee. An itemized statement of deductions from wages must be furnished to employees with their regular paychecks. The maximum number of hours that minors may work varies according to state laws. Tips are not considered wages and may not be calculated in the amount of minimum wage due. Any employee who is unduly charged fees or denied any of the preceding legal rights provided by the Fair Labor Standards Act may file an appeal with the nearest office of the Department of Labor. Employees may not be discharged because of a pending wage claim.

Wage laws are enforced.

Tips are not part of minimum wage.

The minimum wage law has an exception—those businesses whose annual sales do not exceed $250,000 are exempt from paying the minimum wage. Also exempt are nonprofit and governmental offices that are providing employment as part of a training program.

Workers' Compensation

Workers' compensation, traditionally called workmen's compensation, is the name for statutes (laws) that give financial security to workers and their families for on-the-job injury, illness, or death that occurs as a result of the job or working conditions. This law is often labeled "liability without fault" because the employer is responsible for employee injuries and illnesses that are the result of employment, even though the employer may have done nothing to cause the injury or illness. Today all 50 states have workers' compensation statutes. In some states, the SAIF (State Accident Insurance Fund), or other designated state agency, collects a premium for each working person. The fee is usually based on the number of days worked during a pay period. Employers pay the workers' compensation premium in most states. However, in some states, employees are required to pay all or a part of the premium. The premiums are used to pay benefits to injured employees. Benefits include payments to doctors and hospitals, payment to the employee for temporary or permanent disability, and payment of benefits to survivors in the event of death.

Employers are responsible for work injuries.

Employers may also elect to maintain their own workers' compensation insurance program, if they qualify. Upon proof that an employer can meet the expenses of such a liability, a private company will establish the fund on behalf of the employer to insure against the loss. Large companies may provide their own workers' compensation insurance program within the company benefits package.

Employers may provide their own insurance.

VOCABULARY

Directions: Can you find the definition for each of the following terms used in Chapter 4?

Form W-4	allowances
exempt	social security number
Form W-2	marketable
initiative	minors
administrative agencies	Social Security Act
unemployment insurance	workers' compensation

1. Persons who are dependent on your income for their support.

2. Your permanent work identification number.

3. A form completed by your employer and mailed to you no later than January 31.

4. Work of such quality that an employer can use it.

5. Persons under the age of legal majority.

6. Authorized by Congress to enforce administrative laws.

7. Enacted in 1935, it was our first national insurance program to provide financial help for elderly and disabled workers.

8. A part of the Social Security Act, ensuring that benefits are paid to workers who lose their jobs.

9. One of the forms you will fill out when you begin working on which you claim a number of allowances to determine taxes withheld from your paycheck.

10. Persons who will not incur any federal tax liability may claim this status on their Form W-4.

11. The ability to do things without being told.

12. Benefits to protect workers from loss due to on-the-job illness or injuries.

ITEMS FOR DISCUSSION

1. What is the purpose of Form W-4?

2. Why do you need to have a social security number before you begin work?

3. Besides retirement income, what other benefits are provided by social security?

4. Why is it important that your employer have your correct social security number?

5. Where can you obtain a work permit application?

6. Besides yourself, who must sign your work permit application if you are under age 16?

7. What information is listed on Form W-2?

8. By what date must your employers for the past year provide you a Form W-2?

9. What should you do if your employer during the past year does not send you a Form W-2?

10. List at least five responsibilities that the employee has to his or her employer.

11. List at least three responsibilities that an employee has to other employees at work.

12. What responsibilities do employees have to the employer's customers?

13. List and describe three responsibilities that employers have to their employees.

14. What is an administrative agency?

15. What were some of the provisions of the Social Security Act?

16. What is unemployment insurance?

17. List the major provisions of the Fair Labor Standards Act.

18. What is meant by the term *liability without fault* ?

APPLICATIONS

1. Obtain a Form W-4 from the closest office of the Internal Revenue Service and complete it properly, claiming exempt status if you are entitled to do so.

2. Obtain an Application for Social Security Number Card from your local Social Security Administration office. Complete the form with the appropriate information.

3. Look up in your telephone directory the address of your nearest Department of Labor office. Go there and pick up a work permit application and fill it in. (Your counseling center or work experience coordinator will probably have work permit forms also.)

4. On a piece of paper list in the order you think most important the responsibilities that employees have to their employers. Then ask your parent or another working person to also list employee responsibilities in order of importance. Compare the two lists. Then, if possible, ask an employer to list in order what she/he considers important responsibilities that employees have to their employers.

5. What responsibilities do you have, as an employee, to customers of your employer?

6. What responsibilities do you think employers should have to employees besides the regular payment of wages you have earned? Interview a person who is working full-time and ask her/him the same question. Compare answers.

7. Look up the Social Security Act in an encyclopedia or historical reference book in your library. Obtain this information: (a) why social security was deemed necessary by the president at the time; (b) who the president at the time was; (c) history of benefits, deductions from paychecks, and purpose of social security.

8. Obtain from your state Department of Labor the provisions of state laws regarding employment of minors. Include: (a) maximum hours per week that can be worked, (b) latest hour in the evening that a minor can work, (c) if a work permit is required for workers under 16, (d) any other provisions to protect you as a minor while working part-time or full-time.

9. From your state Department of Labor or from an employer obtain information as to how workers' compensation insurance is handled in your state. Is it by a state agency or private insurance programs? What types of benefits are available? How much are premiums and who pays them? Since all states have workers' compensation laws, determine all you can about the laws in your state.

CASE PROBLEMS AND ACTIVITIES

1. Your friend Mitch has discovered that the amount of wages paid to him during the year appears to be different from the amount listed on the W-2 sent to him by his employer. He asks you, "What shall I do?" What should you reply?

2. Kris McMahan worked for three employers last year. It is now February 1 of the following year, and she has received Form W-2 from only two of those employers. She asks you what she should do about it. What should you tell her?

3. Because last year Sean did not earn enough money on his part-time job to have to pay any federal taxes, his employer has asked him if this year he would like to claim exempt status on his W-4. Explain to Sean how he can claim to be exempt and what this means to him.

4. Margarita, 14, has decided that she wants to work part-time this summer doing whatever kind of work she can find to earn money to buy school clothes. Tell her what things she should do now, several months before summer, to get appropriate numbers and cards she may need to go to work. Also tell Margarita what forms she may have to complete when she begins work.

5. Karen Jacobs just received her W-2 form from her employer and has noticed that her social security number is wrong on the form. What should she do? What can happen if she does nothing?

6. Clarke Jackson worked for over a year for the same employer, then was laid off because business was slow. He is looking for another job, but is in need of income to make his rent payment. You told Clarke that he may be eligible for unemployment insurance payments. Explain how he could qualify and whom he should see to find out about unemployment benefits.

PART TWO

MONEY MANAGEMENT

5

Employee Pay and Benefits

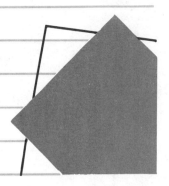

CHAPTER OBJECTIVES

After studying this chapter and completing the activities, you will be able to:

1. Compute payroll deductions and net pay from information and tables provided.
2. Identify optional and required employee benefits and recognize their value as additions to net pay.
3. Understand the role of unions and professional organizations in this country.

GROSS PAY, DEDUCTIONS, NET PAY

Gross pay is the total pay before deductions.

When people work, they agree to perform certain job tasks in exchange for financial remuneration, called gross pay, together with optional and required benefits that go with the employment. ***Gross pay*** is the total or agreed upon rate of pay or salary, before any deductions are made. If a person is working for $800 a month agreed upon salary, that is his or her gross pay. For people who work for an hourly wage or work overtime hours, computations must be made to determine the amount of their gross pay (see Figure 5–1).

Hourly Wage

Perhaps you will be paid for each hour you work. A record is kept of hours worked, and then the number of hours is multiplied by the rate to determine the amount of gross pay. For example, a person working for $3.35 an hour who works 40 hours during the week will earn gross pay of $134 ($3.35 multiplied by 40 hours).

FIGURE 5–1
Paycheck

Marshall Manufacturing Co.
14 Ault Street El Paso, TX 79925-6457

88-0581
1120

PAYROLL CHECK

Co. Code	Department	File No.	Clock No./ID	Social Security No.	TO THE ORDER OF	Pay Date	Check No
R&T	000108	43329	501 A	555 12 3344	M.J. SMITH	02 08 85	BELOW

PAY THIS AMOUNT | NET PAY

ONE HUNDRED FOUR and 41/100THS DOLLARS***** | *****104.41**

M.J. SMITH
1133 ELM STREET
EL PASO, TX 79930-3264

DISBURSING AGENT FOR ABOVE EMPLOYER

EL PASO BANK
EL PASO, TEXAS

AUTHORIZED SIGNATURE

⑆112005812⑆ 010450 001995⑈

Marshall Manufacturing Co.
14 Ault Street El Paso, TX 79925-6457

Co. Code	Department	File No.	Fed. Status	Name	Pay Period	Pay Date
R&T	000108	43329	501 A	SMITH, M.J.	ENDING 02 03 85	02 08 85

Hours/Units	Rate	Earnings	Type	Deduction	Type	Deduction	Type
40 00	3 50	140 00	REG	10 00	CR UN		
5 00	5 25	26 25	OT	14 00	H INS		
				2 50	UN DUES		
				1 20	ACC INS		

	Gross	Fed. With. Tax	Social Security			Net Pay
This Pay	166 25	22 42	11 72			104 41
YTD	836 50	112 80	58 97			

Overtime

Overtime is defined as hours worked in addition to regular hours of work. A standard workday is eight continuous hours with allowed breaks plus an unpaid lunch period. A standard workweek is 40 hours in a five-day period of eight hours each day. According to the Fair Labor Standards Act, overtime is paid at the rate of one and one-half times the regular rate of pay. If the regular rate of pay is $4.00 an hour, the overtime rate is $6.00 an hour ($4.00 times 1 1/2). For example, a person may work a regular workweek of 40 hours at $3.50 an hour, plus one hour overtime each day. Gross pay will be computed as follows:

$$40 \text{ hours} \times \$3.50 \text{ an hour (regular pay)} = \$140.00$$
$$5 \text{ hours} \times \$5.25 \text{ an hour (overtime pay)} = \underline{26.25}$$
$$\text{Gross pay} = \$166.25$$

Monthly Salary

Perhaps you will be paid a set amount per month. In most cases you will work regular hours, but you will not receive additional pay for any overtime work. In the event you work overtime on a regular basis, then your employer could, if he or she wished, pay an agreed upon overtime rate computed from your monthly salary. For example, your salary is $800 a month. The agreed upon rate might be $6.82 an hour for overtime ($800 a month divided by 22 average workdays a month, divided by 8 hours a day, times one and one-half). Thus, if you worked a total of 20 hours overtime in one month, your total gross pay would be $800 plus $136.40 (20 hours times $6.82 an hour).

Overtime pay is added to regular pay.

Annual Salary

Perhaps you will agree to an *annual*, or yearly, salary. Annual pay is usually divided into equal amounts paid each month. For example, you agree to work for $10,800 a year. Your monthly gross pay will be $900 ($10,800 divided by 12).

Deductions

Amounts subtracted from your gross pay are known as *deductions*. Some deductions are required by law, such as social security, federal income tax, and state income tax, if your state has an income tax. Other deductions are optional and you may choose them: an automatic deduction to be sent to your savings account or to your credit union for a car payment.

Records are kept by employers.

Employers are required to keep detailed records of wages earned and hours worked for inspection by the Department of Labor. With each paycheck, you must also receive a detailed list of all deductions taken from your gross pay. Deductions may not, except by court order, be withheld from your pay without your written consent. This, of course, does not apply to taxes, social security, and other deductions required by federal and state laws.

Net Pay

When all deductions are taken out of your gross pay, the amount left is known as *net pay*. This is the amount of your paycheck, or what you can actually spend. Net pay is often called *take-home pay* because it is really what you have left over to do with as you wish.

Regular Wages or Salary + Overtime = Gross Pay
Gross Pay − Deductions = Net Pay

Figure 5–2 is an Employee Withholding Sheet, which lists gross pay, deductions, and net pay. By law, an explanation of the pay computa-

Explanations of with-
holdings are required.

tions—including gross pay, deductions, and net pay—must be provided with each paycheck. It is important to save the Employee Withholding Sheet or other form of itemization of withholdings from your gross pay so that you can check the accuracy of the W-2 your employer gives you the following January for filing your income tax return.

To compute gross pay on the Employee Withholding Sheet, the number of regular hours worked is multiplied by the hourly rate. Any

FIGURE 5–2
Employee
Withholding
Sheet

EMPLOYEE WITHHOLDING SHEET

Employee Name _Shari Gregson_   Social Security Number _898-40-7426_

Pay Period: ☑ weekly   ☐ bi monthly   ☐ monthly

Number of Allowances: __/__   ☐ married   ☑ single

GROSS PAY

   1. Regular Wages: _40_ hours at $ ___ /hr. = $ _160.00_

or

   2. Regular Salary: =   _____

   3. Overtime: _4_ hours at $ _6.00_/hr. =   _24.00_

   GROSS PAY ....$ _184.00_

REQUIRED DEDUCTIONS

   4. Federal Income Tax (use tax tables) ....$ _19.30_

   5. State Income Tax (use tax tables) .... _11.00_

   6. Social Security Tax (use 6.70% times gross pay) .... _12.97_

OTHER DEDUCTIONS

   7. Insurance .... _____

   8. Union Dues .... _8oo_

   9. Credit Union .... _20.00_

   10. Savings .... _____

   11. Retirement .... _____

   12. Charity .... _____

   13. Other: _____ .... _____

   _____ .... _____

   TOTAL DEDUCTIONS (total lines 4 through 14) ....$ _71.27_

   NET PAY (subtract total deductions from gross pay) ....$ _112.73_ overtime hours are multiplied by the overtime rate. Gross pay includes either hourly wages plus overtime, or salary plus overtime.

Required deductions include federal, state, and local taxes, and social security. The tax withholding amounts are determined from tax tables such as those shown in Figures 5–3 through 5–6. The more allowances a person claims on his or her W-4 statement, the less the amount of tax the employer will withhold or deduct from gross pay. The social security deduction is withheld at the rate of 7.05 percent of the first $39,600

Withholding amounts are taken from tables.

Weekly payroll period (Oregon)
Amount of tax to be withheld

WAGE		TWO OR LESS					NUMBER OF WITHHOLDING ALLOWANCES										
		SINGLE			MARRIED		THREE OR MORE SINGLE OR MARRIED										
AT LEAST	BUT LESS THEN	0	1	2	0	1	2	3	4	5	6	7	8	9	10	11	12	13	14+
0--	20	0	0	0	0	0	0	0	0	0	0	0	0	0	0	0	0	0	0
20--	40	1	1	0	1	1	0	0	0	0	0	0	0	0	0	0	0	0	0
40--	60	2	2	1	2	2	1	0	0	0	0	0	0	0	0	0	0	0	0
60--	80	4	3	2	3	3	2	1	0	0	0	0	0	0	0	0	0	0	0
80--	100	6	4	3	4	4	3	2	1	0	0	0	0	0	0	0	0	0	0
100--	120	7	6	4	5	5	4	3	2	1	0	0	0	0	0	0	0	0	0
120--	140	9	7	6	6	6	5	4	3	2	1	0	0	0	0	0	0	0	0
140--	160	10	9	7	8	7	6	5	4	3	2	1	0	0	0	0	0	0	0
160--	180	12	10	9	9	8	7	6	5	4	3	2	1	0	0	0	0	0	0
180--	200	14	12	11	11	9	8	7	6	5	4	3	2	1	0	0	0	0	0
200--	220	15	14	12	13	11	10	8	7	6	5	4	3	2	1	0	0	0	0
220--	240	17	15	14	14	13	11	10	8	7	6	5	4	3	2	1	0	0	0
240--	260	18	17	15	16	15	13	11	10	8	7	6	5	4	3	2	1	0	0
260--	280	20	18	17	18	16	15	13	11	10	8	7	6	5	4	3	2	1	0
280--	300	22	20	19	20	18	16	15	13	12	10	8	7	6	5	4	3	2	1
300--	320	23	22	20	21	20	18	16	15	13	12	10	8	7	6	5	4	3	2
320--	340	25	23	22	23	21	20	18	17	15	13	12	10	8	7	6	5	4	3
340--	360	26	25	23	25	23	21	20	18	17	15	13	12	10	9	7	6	5	4
360--	380	28	26	25	26	25	23	22	20	18	17	15	13	12	10	9	7	6	5
380--	400	29	28	27	28	26	25	23	22	20	18	17	15	14	12	10	9	7	6
400--	420	31	29	28	30	28	27	25	23	22	20	18	17	15	14	12	10	9	7
420--	440	32	31	29	31	30	28	27	25	23	22	20	19	17	15	14	12	10	9
440--	460	34	32	31	33	31	30	28	27	25	23	22	20	19	17	15	14	12	11
460--	480	35	34	32	34	33	31	30	28	27	25	24	22	20	19	17	15	14	12
480--	500	36	35	34	36	34	33	32	30	29	27	25	24	22	20	19	17	16	14
500--	520	38	36	35	37	36	34	33	32	30	29	27	25	24	22	21	19	17	16
520--	540	39	38	36	39	37	36	35	33	32	30	29	27	25	24	22	21	19	17
540--	560	41	39	38	40	39	37	36	35	33	32	30	29	27	26	24	22	21	19
560--	580	43	41	39	42	40	39	38	36	35	33	32	30	29	27	26	24	22	21
580--	600	45	43	41	43	42	40	39	38	36	35	33	32	31	29	27	26	24	22
600--	620	47	45	43	45	43	42	41	39	38	36	35	33	32	31	29	27	26	24
620--	640	50	48	46	46	45	43	42	41	39	38	36	35	34	32	31	29	27	26
640--	660	52	50	48	48	46	45	44	42	41	39	38	36	35	34	32	31	29	28
660--	680	54	52	50	50	48	46	45	44	42	41	39	38	37	35	34	32	31	29
680--	700	56	54	52	53	50	48	47	45	44	42	41	39	38	37	35	34	32	31
700--	720	58	56	54	55	53	51	49	47	45	44	42	41	40	38	37	35	34	32
720--	740	60	58	56	57	55	53	51	49	47	45	44	42	41	40	38	37	35	34
740--	760	63	61	58	59	57	55	53	51	49	47	45	44	43	41	40	38	37	35
760--	780	65	63	61	61	59	57	55	53	51	49	47	45	44	43	41	40	38	37
780--	800	67	65	63	63	61	59	57	55	53	51	49	47	46	44	43	41	40	38
800--	820	69	67	65	65	63	61	59	57	55	53	51	49	47	46	44	43	41	40
820--	840	71	69	67	68	66	64	61	59	57	55	53	51	49	47	46	44	43	41
840-- 860 --		73	71	69	70	68	66	64	62	60	57	55	53	51	49	47	46	44	43
						10.8 PERCENT OF EXCESS OVER 3560 PLUS --												
860--OVER		74	72	70	71	69	67	65	63	61	59	57	54	52	50	48	46	45	44

FIGURE 5–3   State Tax Withholding Table—Weekly Payroll

earned in 1985, and 7.15 percent of the first $40,000 in 1986. This ceiling amount will continue to rise through 1990 because of legislation submitted by President Carter and approved by Congress in 1977.

In addition to required deductions, those which an employee has authorized to have withheld will be subtracted from gross pay. Most common of these deductions are insurance payments, union dues, credit union payments, savings account deposits, retirement contributions, and charity deductions. These types of deductions cannot be withheld from pay without the written consent of the employee.

Additional withholdings may be authorized.

Monthly payroll period (Oregon)
Amount of tax to be withheld

WAGE		NUMBER OF WITHHOLDING ALLOWANCES																	
		TWO OR LESS						THREE OR MORE SINGLE OR MARRIED											
		SINGLE			MARRIED														
AT LEAST	BUT LESS THAN	0	1	2	0	1	2	3	4	5	6	7	8	9	10	11	12	13	14+
0--	40	0	0	0	0	0	0	0	0	0	0	0	0	0	0	0	0	0	0
40--	80	3	0	0	3	0	0	0	0	0	0	0	0	0	0	0	0	0	0
80--	120	5	1	0	5	1	0	0	0	0	0	0	0	0	0	0	0	0	0
120--	160	7	3	0	7	3	0	0	0	0	0	0	0	0	0	0	0	0	0
160--	200	9	5	1	9	5	1	0	0	0	0	0	0	0	0	0	0	0	0
200--	240	11	7	3	11	7	3	0	0	0	0	0	0	0	0	0	0	0	0
240--	280	13	9	5	13	9	5	1	0	0	0	0	0	0	0	0	0	0	0
280--	320	16	11	7	15	11	7	3	0	0	0	0	0	0	0	0	0	0	0
320--	360	19	13	9	17	13	9	5	0	0	0	0	0	0	0	0	0	0	0
360--	400	22	16	11	19	15	11	7	2	0	0	0	0	0	0	0	0	0	0
400--	440	26	19	12	21	17	13	9	4	0	0	0	0	0	0	0	0	0	0
440--	480	29	22	16	23	19	15	11	6	2	0	0	0	0	0	0	0	0	0
480--	520	32	25	19	25	21	17	13	8	4	0	0	0	0	0	0	0	0	0
520--	560	35	29	22	27	23	19	15	10	6	2	0	0	0	0	0	0	0	0
560--	600	38	32	25	29	25	21	17	12	8	4	0	0	0	0	0	0	0	0
600--	640	42	35	28	31	27	23	19	14	10	6	2	0	0	0	0	0	0	0
640--	680	45	38	32	35	29	25	21	16	12	8	4	0	0	0	0	0	0	0
680--	720	48	41	35	38	31	27	23	18	14	10	6	2	0	0	0	0	0	0
720--	760	51	45	38	41	34	29	25	20	16	12	8	4	0	0	0	0	0	0
760--	800	54	48	41	45	38	31	27	22	18	14	10	6	2	0	0	0	0	0
800--	840	58	51	44	48	41	34	29	24	20	16	12	8	4	0	0	0	0	0
840--	880	61	54	48	52	45	38	31	26	22	18	14	10	6	1	0	0	0	0
880--	920	64	57	51	55	48	41	34	28	24	20	16	12	8	3	0	0	0	0
920--	960	67	61	54	58	51	44	37	30	26	22	18	14	10	5	1	0	0	0
960--	1000	70	64	57	62	55	48	41	34	28	24	20	16	12	7	3	0	0	0
1000--	1040	74	67	60	65	58	51	44	37	30	26	22	18	14	9	5	1	0	0
1040--	1080	77	70	64	69	62	55	47	40	33	28	24	20	16	11	7	3	0	0
1080--	1120	80	73	67	72	65	58	51	44	37	30	26	22	18	13	9	5	1	0
1120--	1160	83	77	70	75	68	61	54	47	40	33	28	24	20	15	11	7	3	0
1160--	1200	86	80	73	79	72	65	58	51	44	37	30	26	22	17	13	9	5	1
1200--	1240	90	83	76	82	75	68	61	54	47	40	33	28	24	19	15	11	7	3
1240--	1280	93	86	80	86	79	72	64	57	50	43	36	30	26	21	17	13	9	5
1280--	1320	96	89	83	89	82	75	68	61	54	47	40	33	28	23	19	15	11	7
1320--	1360	99	93	86	92	85	78	71	64	57	50	43	36	30	25	21	17	13	9
1360--	1400	102	96	89	96	89	82	75	68	61	54	46	39	32	27	23	19	15	11
1400--	1440	106	99	92	99	92	85	78	71	64	57	50	43	36	29	25	21	17	13
1440--	1480	109	102	96	103	96	89	81	74	67	60	53	46	39	32	27	23	19	15
1480--	1520	112	105	99	106	99	92	85	78	71	64	57	50	43	36	29	25	21	17
1520--	1560	115	109	102	109	102	95	88	81	74	67	60	53	46	39	32	27	23	19
1560--	1600	118	112	105	113	106	99	92	85	78	71	63	56	49	42	35	29	25	21
1600--	1640	122	115	108	116	109	102	95	88	81	74	67	60	53	46	39	32	27	23
1640--	1680	125	118	112	120	113	106	98	91	84	77	70	63	56	49	42	35	29	25
1680--	1720	127	121	115	123	116	109	102	95	88	81	74	67	60	53	45	38	31	27
1720--	1760	130	125	118	126	119	112	105	98	91	84	77	70	63	56	49	42	35	29
1760--	1800	133	127	121	130	123	116	109	102	95	88	80	73	66	59	52	45	38	31

FIGURE 5–4   State Tax Withholding Table—Monthly Payroll

WAGE-BRACKET WITHHOLDING TABLES

WEEKLY Payroll Period—Employee NOT MARRIED

And the wages are—		And the number of withholding allowances claimed is—										
At least	But less than	0	1	2	3	4	5	6	7	8	9	10 or more
		The amount of income tax to be withheld shall be—										
$0	$27	$0	$0	$0	$0	$0	$0	$0	$0	$0	$0	$0
27	28	.10	0	0	0	0	0	0	0	0	0	0
28	29	.20	0	0	0	0	0	0	0	0	0	0
29	30	.30	0	0	0	0	0	0	0	0	0	0
30	31	.40	0	0	0	0	0	0	0	0	0	0
31	32	.50	0	0	0	0	0	0	0	0	0	0
32	33	.70	0	0	0	0	0	0	0	0	0	0
33	34	.80	0	0	0	0	0	0	0	0	0	0
34	35	.90	0	0	0	0	0	0	0	0	0	0
35	36	1.00	0	0	0	0	0	0	0	0	0	0
36	37	1.10	0	0	0	0	0	0	0	0	0	0
37	38	1.30	0	0	0	0	0	0	0	0	0	0
38	39	1.40	0	0	0	0	0	0	0	0	0	0
39	40	1.50	0	0	0	0	0	0	0	0	0	0
40	41	1.60	0	0	0	0	0	0	0	0	0	0
41	42	1.70	0	0	0	0	0	0	0	0	0	0
42	43	1.90	0	0	0	0	0	0	0	0	0	0
43	44	2.00	0	0	0	0	0	0	0	0	0	0
44	45	2.10	0	0	0	0	0	0	0	0	0	0
45	46	2.20	0	0	0	0	0	0	0	0	0	0
46	47	2.30	0	0	0	0	0	0	0	0	0	0
47	48	2.50	.20	0	0	0	0	0	0	0	0	0
48	49	2.60	.30	0	0	0	0	0	0	0	0	0
49	50	2.70	.40	0	0	0	0	0	0	0	0	0
50	51	2.80	.50	0	0	0	0	0	0	0	0	0
51	52	2.90	.60	0	0	0	0	0	0	0	0	0
52	53	3.10	.80	0	0	0	0	0	0	0	0	0
53	54	3.20	.90	0	0	0	0	0	0	0	0	0
54	55	3.30	1.00	0	0	0	0	0	0	0	0	0
55	56	3.40	1.10	0	0	0	0	0	0	0	0	0
56	57	3.50	1.20	0	0	0	0	0	0	0	0	0
57	58	3.70	1.40	0	0	0	0	0	0	0	0	0
58	59	3.80	1.50	0	0	0	0	0	0	0	0	0
59	60	3.90	1.60	0	0	0	0	0	0	0	0	0
60	62	4.10	1.80	0	0	0	0	0	0	0	0	0
At least	But less than	0	1	2	3	4	5	6	7	8	9	10 or more
62	64	4.30	2.00	0	0	0	0	0	0	0	0	0
64	66	4.60	2.30	0	0	0	0	0	0	0	0	0
66	68	4.80	2.50	.20	0	0	0	0	0	0	0	0
68	70	5.00	2.70	.40	0	0	0	0	0	0	0	0
70	72	5.30	3.00	.70	0	0	0	0	0	0	0	0
72	74	5.50	3.20	.90	0	0	0	0	0	0	0	0
74	76	5.80	3.50	1.20	0	0	0	0	0	0	0	0
76	78	6.00	3.70	1.40	0	0	0	0	0	0	0	0
78	80	6.30	3.90	1.60	0	0	0	0	0	0	0	0
80	82	6.60	4.20	1.90	0	0	0	0	0	0	0	0
82	84	6.90	4.40	2.10	0	0	0	0	0	0	0	0
84	86	7.20	4.70	2.40	0	0	0	0	0	0	0	0
86	88	7.50	4.90	2.60	.30	0	0	0	0	0	0	0
88	90	7.80	5.10	2.80	.50	0	0	0	0	0	0	0
90	92	8.10	5.40	3.10	.80	0	0	0	0	0	0	0
92	94	8.40	5.60	3.30	1.00	0	0	0	0	0	0	0
94	96	8.70	5.90	3.60	1.20	0	0	0	0	0	0	0
96	98	9.00	6.10	3.80	1.50	0	0	0	0	0	0	0
98	100	9.30	6.40	4.00	1.70	0	0	0	0	0	0	0
100	105	9.80	6.90	4.50	2.10	0	0	0	0	0	0	0
105	110	10.50	7.60	5.10	2.70	.40	0	0	0	0	0	0
110	115	11.30	8.40	5.70	3.30	1.00	0	0	0	0	0	0
115	120	12.00	9.10	6.30	3.90	1.60	0	0	0	0	0	0
120	125	12.80	9.90	7.00	4.50	2.20	0	0	0	0	0	0
125	130	13.50	10.60	7.80	5.10	2.80	.50	0	0	0	0	0
130	135	14.30	11.40	8.50	5.70	3.40	1.10	0	0	0	0	0
135	140	15.00	12.10	9.30	6.40	4.00	1.70	0	0	0	0	0
140	145	15.80	12.90	10.00	7.10	4.60	2.30	0	0	0	0	0
145	150	16.50	13.60	10.80	7.90	5.20	2.90	.60	0	0	0	0
150	160	17.70	14.80	11.90	9.00	6.10	3.80	1.50	0	0	0	0
160	170	19.20	16.30	13.40	10.50	7.60	5.00	2.70	.40	0	0	0
170	180	20.70	17.80	14.90	12.00	9.10	6.20	3.90	1.60	0	0	0
180	190	22.20	19.30	16.40	13.50	10.60	7.70	5.10	2.80	.50	0	0
190	200	24.10	20.80	17.90	15.00	12.10	9.20	6.30	4.00	1.70	0	0
200	210	26.00	22.40	19.40	16.50	13.60	10.70	7.80	5.20	2.90	.60	0

WEEKLY Payroll Period—Employee NOT MARRIED

And the wages are—		And the number of withholding allowances claimed is—										
At least	But less than	0	1	2	3	4	5	6	7	8	9	10 or more
		The amount of income tax to be withheld shall be—										
$210	$220	$27.90	$24.30	$20.90	$18.00	$15.10	$12.20	$9.30	$6.50	$4.10	$1.80	$0
220	230	29.80	26.20	22.50	19.50	16.60	13.70	10.80	8.00	5.30	3.00	.70
230	240	31.70	28.10	24.40	21.00	18.10	15.20	12.30	9.50	6.50	4.20	1.90
240	250	33.60	30.00	26.30	22.70	19.60	16.70	13.80	11.00	8.10	5.40	3.10
250	260	35.50	31.90	28.20	24.60	21.10	18.20	15.30	12.50	9.60	6.70	4.30
260	270	37.40	33.80	30.10	26.50	22.80	19.70	16.80	14.00	11.10	8.20	5.50
270	280	39.30	35.70	32.00	28.40	24.70	21.20	18.30	15.50	12.60	9.70	6.80
280	290	41.70	37.60	33.90	30.30	26.60	23.00	19.80	17.00	14.10	11.20	8.30
290	300	44.20	39.50	35.80	32.20	28.50	24.90	21.30	18.50	15.60	12.70	9.80
300	310	46.70	41.90	37.70	34.10	30.40	26.80	23.10	20.00	17.10	14.20	11.30
310	320	49.20	44.40	39.60	36.00	32.30	28.70	25.00	21.50	18.60	15.70	12.80
320	330	51.70	46.90	42.10	37.90	34.20	30.60	26.90	23.30	20.10	17.20	14.30
330	340	54.20	49.40	44.60	39.80	36.10	32.50	28.80	25.20	21.60	18.70	15.80
340	350	56.70	51.90	47.10	42.30	38.00	34.40	30.70	27.10	23.40	20.20	17.30
350	360	59.20	54.40	49.60	44.80	40.00	36.30	32.60	29.00	25.30	21.70	18.80
360	370	61.70	56.90	52.10	47.30	42.50	38.20	34.50	30.90	27.20	23.60	20.30
370	380	64.20	59.40	54.60	49.80	45.00	40.20	36.40	32.80	29.10	25.50	21.80
380	390	66.70	61.90	57.10	52.30	47.50	42.70	38.30	34.70	31.00	27.40	23.70
390	400	69.20	64.40	59.60	54.80	50.00	45.20	40.40	36.60	32.90	29.30	25.60
400	410	71.70	66.90	62.10	57.30	52.50	47.70	42.90	38.50	34.80	31.20	27.50
410	420	74.20	69.40	64.60	59.80	55.00	50.20	45.40	40.60	36.70	33.10	29.40
420	430	76.80	71.90	67.10	62.30	57.50	52.70	47.90	43.10	38.60	35.00	31.30
430	440	79.80	74.40	69.60	64.80	60.00	55.20	50.40	45.60	40.80	36.90	33.20
440	450	82.80	77.10	72.10	67.30	62.50	57.70	52.90	48.10	43.30	38.80	35.10
450	460	85.80	80.10	74.60	69.80	65.00	60.20	55.40	50.60	45.80	41.00	37.00
460	470	88.80	83.10	77.30	72.30	67.50	62.70	57.90	53.10	48.30	43.50	38.90
470	480	91.80	86.10	80.30	74.80	70.00	65.20	60.40	55.60	50.80	46.00	41.20
480	490	94.80	89.10	83.30	77.50	72.50	67.70	62.90	58.10	53.30	48.50	43.70
490	500	97.80	92.10	86.30	80.50	75.00	70.20	65.40	60.60	55.80	51.00	46.20
500	510	100.80	95.10	89.30	83.50	77.80	72.70	67.90	63.10	58.30	53.50	48.70
510	520	103.80	98.10	92.30	86.50	80.80	75.20	70.40	65.60	60.80	56.00	51.20
520	530	106.80	101.10	95.30	89.50	83.80	78.00	72.90	68.10	63.30	58.50	53.70
530	540	109.80	104.10	98.30	92.50	86.80	81.00	75.40	70.60	65.80	61.00	56.20
540	550	113.20	107.10	101.30	95.50	89.80	84.00	78.20	73.10	68.30	63.50	58.70
550	560	116.60	110.10	104.30	98.50	92.80	87.00	81.20	75.60	70.80	66.00	61.20
At least	But less than	0	1	2	3	4	5	6	7	8	9	10 or more
560	570	120.00	113.50	107.30	101.50	95.80	90.00	84.20	78.40	73.30	68.50	63.70
570	580	123.40	116.90	110.40	104.50	98.80	93.00	87.20	81.40	75.80	71.00	66.20
580	590	126.80	120.30	113.80	107.50	101.80	96.00	90.20	84.40	78.70	73.50	68.70
590	600	130.20	123.70	117.20	110.60	104.80	99.00	93.20	87.40	81.70	76.00	71.20
600	610	133.60	127.10	120.60	114.00	107.80	102.00	96.20	90.40	84.70	78.90	73.70
610	620	137.00	130.50	124.00	117.40	110.90	105.00	99.20	93.40	87.70	81.90	76.20
620	630	140.40	133.90	127.40	120.80	114.30	108.00	102.20	96.40	90.70	84.90	79.10
630	640	143.80	137.30	130.80	124.20	117.70	111.20	105.20	99.40	93.70	87.90	82.10
640	650	147.50	140.70	134.20	127.60	121.10	114.60	108.20	102.40	96.70	90.90	85.10
650	660	151.20	144.10	137.60	131.00	124.50	118.00	111.40	105.40	99.70	93.90	88.10
660	670	154.90	147.80	141.00	134.40	127.90	121.40	114.80	108.40	102.70	96.90	91.10
670	680	158.60	151.50	144.40	137.80	131.30	124.80	118.20	111.70	105.70	99.90	94.10
680	690	162.30	155.20	148.10	141.20	134.70	128.20	121.60	115.10	108.70	102.90	97.10
690	700	166.00	158.90	151.80	144.70	138.10	131.60	125.00	118.50	111.90	105.90	100.10
700	710	169.70	162.60	155.50	148.40	141.50	135.00	128.40	121.90	115.30	108.90	103.10
710	720	173.40	166.30	159.20	152.10	144.90	138.40	131.80	125.30	118.70	112.20	106.10
720	730	177.10	170.00	162.90	155.80	148.60	141.80	135.20	128.70	122.10	115.60	109.10
730	740	180.80	173.70	166.60	159.50	152.30	145.20	138.60	132.10	125.50	119.00	112.50
740	750	184.50	177.40	170.30	163.20	156.00	148.90	142.00	135.50	128.90	122.40	115.90
750	760	188.20	181.10	174.00	166.90	159.70	152.60	145.50	138.90	132.30	125.80	119.30
760	770	191.90	184.80	177.70	170.60	163.40	156.30	149.20	142.30	135.70	129.20	122.70
770	780	195.60	188.50	181.40	174.30	167.10	160.00	152.90	145.80	139.10	132.60	126.10
780	790	199.30	192.20	185.10	178.00	170.80	163.70	156.60	149.50	142.50	136.00	129.50
790	800	203.00	195.90	188.80	181.70	174.50	167.40	160.30	153.20	146.10	139.40	132.90
800	810	206.70	199.60	192.50	185.40	178.20	171.10	164.00	156.90	149.80	142.80	136.30
810	820	210.40	203.30	196.20	189.10	181.90	174.80	167.70	160.60	153.50	146.40	139.70
820	830	214.10	207.00	199.90	192.80	185.60	178.50	171.40	164.30	157.20	150.10	143.10
830	840	217.80	210.70	203.60	196.50	189.30	182.20	175.10	168.00	160.90	153.80	146.60
		37 percent of the excess over $840 plus—										
$840 and over		219.60	212.50	205.40	198.30	191.20	184.10	177.00	169.80	162.70	155.60	148.50

FIGURE 5–5 Federal Tax Withholding Tables—Weekly Payroll

WAGE-BRACKET WITHHOLDING TABLES

MONTHLY Payroll Period—Employee MARRIED

And the wages are-		And the number of withholding allowances claimed is—										
At least	But less than	0	1	2	3	4	5	6	7	8	9	10 or more
		The amount of income tax to be withheld shall be—										
$0	$200	$0	$0	$0	$0	$0	$0	$0	$0	$0	$0	$0
200	204	.20	0	0	0	0	0	0	0	0	0	0
204	208	.70	0	0	0	0	0	0	0	0	0	0
208	212	1.20	0	0	0	0	0	0	0	0	0	0
212	216	1.70	0	0	0	0	0	0	0	0	0	0
216	220	2.20	0	0	0	0	0	0	0	0	0	0
220	224	2.60	0	0	0	0	0	0	0	0	0	0
224	228	3.10	0	0	0	0	0	0	0	0	0	0
228	232	3.60	0	0	0	0	0	0	0	0	0	0
232	236	4.10	0	0	0	0	0	0	0	0	0	0
236	240	4.60	0	0	0	0	0	0	0	0	0	0
240	248	5.30	0	0	0	0	0	0	0	0	0	0
248	256	6.20	0	0	0	0	0	0	0	0	0	0
256	264	7.20	0	0	0	0	0	0	0	0	0	0
264	272	8.20	0	0	0	0	0	0	0	0	0	0
272	280	9.10	0	0	0	0	0	0	0	0	0	0
280	288	10.10	.10	0	0	0	0	0	0	0	0	0
288	296	11.00	1.00	0	0	0	0	0	0	0	0	0
296	304	12.00	2.00	0	0	0	0	0	0	0	0	0
304	312	13.00	3.00	0	0	0	0	0	0	0	0	0
312	320	13.90	3.90	0	0	0	0	0	0	0	0	0
320	328	14.90	4.90	0	0	0	0	0	0	0	0	0
328	336	15.80	5.80	0	0	0	0	0	0	0	0	0
336	344	16.80	6.80	0	0	0	0	0	0	0	0	0
344	352	17.80	7.80	0	0	0	0	0	0	0	0	0
352	360	18.70	8.70	0	0	0	0	0	0	0	0	0
360	368	19.70	9.70	0	0	0	0	0	0	0	0	0
368	376	20.60	10.60	.60	0	0	0	0	0	0	0	0
376	384	21.60	11.60	1.60	0	0	0	0	0	0	0	0
384	392	22.60	12.60	2.60	0	0	0	0	0	0	0	0
392	400	23.50	13.50	3.50	0	0	0	0	0	0	0	0
400	420	25.20	15.20	5.20	0	0	0	0	0	0	0	0
420	440	27.60	17.60	7.60	0	0	0	0	0	0	0	0
440	460	30.00	20.00	10.00	0	0	0	0	0	0	0	0
460	480	32.40	22.40	12.40	2.40	0	0	0	0	0	0	0
At least	But less than	0	1	2	3	4	5	6	7	8	9	10 or more
480	500	34.80	24.80	14.80	4.80	0	0	0	0	0	0	0
500	520	37.20	27.20	17.20	7.20	0	0	0	0	0	0	0
520	540	39.60	29.60	19.60	9.60	0	0	0	0	0	0	0
540	560	42.00	32.00	22.00	12.00	2.00	0	0	0	0	0	0
560	580	44.40	34.40	24.40	14.40	4.40	0	0	0	0	0	0
580	600	46.80	36.80	26.80	16.80	6.80	0	0	0	0	0	0
600	640	50.40	40.40	30.40	20.40	10.40	.40	0	0	0	0	0
640	680	55.20	45.20	35.20	25.20	15.20	5.20	0	0	0	0	0
680	720	60.00	50.00	40.00	30.00	20.00	10.00	0	0	0	0	0
720	760	64.80	54.80	44.80	34.80	24.80	14.80	4.80	0	0	0	0
760	800	69.60	59.60	49.60	39.60	29.60	19.60	9.60	0	0	0	0
800	840	75.40	64.40	54.40	44.40	34.40	24.40	14.40	4.40	0	0	0
840	880	82.20	69.20	59.20	49.20	39.20	29.20	19.20	9.20	0	0	0
880	920	89.00	74.80	64.00	54.00	44.00	34.00	24.00	14.00	4.00	0	0
920	960	95.80	81.60	68.80	58.80	48.80	38.80	28.80	18.80	8.80	0	0
960	1,000	102.60	88.40	74.30	63.60	53.60	43.60	33.60	23.60	13.60	3.60	0
1,000	1,040	109.40	95.20	81.10	68.40	58.40	48.40	38.40	28.40	18.40	8.40	0
1,040	1,080	116.20	102.00	87.90	73.70	63.20	53.20	43.20	33.20	23.20	13.20	3.20
1,080	1,120	123.00	108.80	94.70	80.50	68.00	58.00	48.00	38.00	28.00	18.00	8.00
1,120	1,160	129.80	115.60	101.50	87.30	73.10	62.80	52.80	42.80	32.80	22.80	12.80
1,160	1,200	136.60	122.40	108.30	94.10	79.90	67.60	57.60	47.60	37.60	27.60	17.60
1,200	1,240	143.40	129.20	115.10	100.90	86.70	72.60	62.40	52.40	42.40	32.40	22.40
1,240	1,280	150.20	136.00	121.90	107.70	93.50	79.40	67.20	57.20	47.20	37.20	27.20
1,280	1,320	157.00	142.80	128.70	114.50	100.30	86.20	72.00	62.00	52.00	42.00	32.00
1,320	1,360	163.80	149.60	135.50	121.30	107.10	93.00	78.80	66.80	56.80	46.80	36.80
1,360	1,400	170.60	156.40	142.30	128.10	113.90	99.80	85.60	71.60	61.60	51.60	41.60
1,400	1,440	177.40	163.20	149.10	134.90	120.70	106.60	92.40	78.20	66.40	56.40	46.40
1,440	1,480	184.20	170.00	155.90	141.70	127.50	113.40	99.20	85.00	71.20	61.20	51.20
1,480	1,520	191.00	176.80	162.70	148.50	134.30	120.20	106.00	91.80	77.70	66.00	56.00
1,520	1,560	197.80	183.60	169.50	155.30	141.10	127.00	112.80	98.60	84.50	70.80	60.80
1,560	1,600	204.60	190.40	176.30	162.10	147.90	133.80	119.60	105.40	91.30	77.10	65.60
1,600	1,640	212.50	197.20	183.10	168.90	154.70	140.60	126.40	112.20	98.10	83.90	70.40
1,640	1,680	221.30	204.00	189.90	175.70	161.50	147.40	133.20	119.00	104.90	90.70	76.50
1,680	1,720	230.10	211.80	196.70	182.50	168.30	154.20	140.00	125.80	111.70	97.50	83.30
1,720	1,760	238.90	220.60	203.50	189.30	175.10	161.00	146.80	132.60	118.50	104.30	90.10

MONTHLY Payroll Period—Employee MARRIED

And the wages are-		And the number of withholding allowances claimed is—										
At least	But less than	0	1	2	3	4	5	6	7	8	9	10 or more
		The amount of income tax to be withheld shall be—										
$1,760	$1,800	$247.70	$229.40	$211.00	$196.10	$181.90	$167.80	$153.60	$139.40	$125.30	$111.10	$96.90
1,800	1,840	256.50	238.20	219.80	202.90	188.70	174.60	160.40	146.20	132.10	117.90	103.70
1,840	1,880	265.30	247.00	228.60	210.30	195.50	181.40	167.20	153.00	138.90	124.70	110.50
1,880	1,920	274.10	255.80	237.40	219.10	202.30	188.20	174.00	159.80	145.70	131.50	117.30
1,920	1,960	282.90	264.60	246.20	227.90	209.60	195.00	180.80	166.60	152.50	138.30	124.10
1,960	2,000	292.10	273.40	255.00	236.70	218.40	201.80	187.60	173.40	159.30	145.10	130.90
2,000	2,040	302.10	282.20	263.80	245.50	227.20	208.80	194.40	180.20	166.10	151.90	137.70
2,040	2,080	312.10	291.30	272.60	254.30	236.00	217.60	201.20	187.00	172.90	158.70	144.50
2,080	2,120	322.10	301.30	281.40	263.10	244.80	226.40	208.10	193.80	179.70	165.50	151.30
2,120	2,160	332.10	311.30	290.40	271.90	253.60	235.20	216.90	200.60	186.50	172.30	158.10
2,160	2,200	342.10	321.30	300.40	280.70	262.40	244.00	225.70	207.40	193.30	179.10	164.90
2,200	2,240	352.10	331.30	310.40	289.60	271.20	252.80	234.50	216.20	200.10	185.90	171.70
2,240	2,280	362.10	341.30	320.40	299.60	280.00	261.60	243.30	225.00	206.90	192.70	178.50
2,280	2,320	372.10	351.30	330.40	309.60	288.80	270.40	252.10	233.80	215.40	199.50	185.30
2,320	2,360	382.10	361.30	340.40	319.60	298.80	279.20	260.90	242.60	224.20	206.30	192.10
2,360	2,400	392.10	371.30	350.40	329.60	308.80	288.00	269.70	251.40	233.00	214.70	198.90
2,400	2,440	402.40	381.30	360.40	339.60	318.80	297.90	278.50	260.20	241.80	223.50	205.70
2,440	2,480	413.60	391.30	370.40	349.60	328.80	307.90	287.30	269.00	250.60	232.30	214.00
2,480	2,520	424.80	401.50	380.40	359.60	338.80	317.90	297.10	277.80	259.40	241.10	222.80
2,520	2,560	436.00	412.70	390.40	369.60	348.80	327.90	307.10	286.60	268.20	249.90	231.60
2,560	2,600	447.20	423.90	400.50	379.60	358.80	337.90	317.10	296.30	277.00	258.70	240.40
2,600	2,640	458.40	435.10	411.80	389.60	368.80	347.90	327.10	306.30	285.80	267.50	249.20
2,640	2,680	469.60	446.30	423.00	399.60	378.80	357.90	337.10	316.30	295.40	276.30	258.00
2,680	2,720	480.80	457.50	434.20	410.80	388.80	367.90	347.10	326.30	305.40	285.10	266.80
2,720	2,760	492.00	468.70	445.40	422.00	398.80	377.90	357.10	336.30	315.40	294.60	275.60
2,760	2,800	503.20	479.90	456.60	433.20	409.90	387.90	367.10	346.30	325.40	304.60	284.40
2,800	2,840	514.40	491.10	467.80	444.40	421.10	397.90	377.10	356.30	335.40	314.60	293.80
2,840	2,880	526.10	502.30	479.00	455.60	432.30	409.00	387.10	366.30	345.40	324.60	303.80
2,880	2,920	539.30	513.50	490.20	466.80	443.50	420.20	397.10	376.30	355.40	334.60	313.80
2,920	2,960	552.50	525.00	501.40	478.00	454.70	431.40	408.00	386.30	365.40	344.60	323.80
2,960	3,000	565.70	538.20	512.60	489.20	465.90	442.60	419.20	396.30	375.40	354.60	333.80
3,000	3,040	578.90	551.40	523.90	500.40	477.10	453.80	430.40	407.10	385.40	364.60	343.80
3,040	3,080	592.10	564.60	537.10	511.60	488.30	465.00	441.60	418.30	395.40	374.60	353.80
3,080	3,120	605.30	577.80	550.30	522.80	499.50	476.20	452.80	429.50	406.20	384.60	363.60
3,120	3,160	618.50	591.00	563.50	536.00	510.70	487.40	464.00	440.70	417.40	394.60	373.80
At least	But less than	0	1	2	3	4	5	6	7	8	9	10 or more
3,160	3,200	631.70	604.20	576.70	549.20	521.90	498.60	475.20	451.90	428.60	405.20	383.80
3,200	3,240	644.90	617.40	589.90	562.40	534.90	509.80	486.40	463.10	439.80	416.40	393.80
3,240	3,280	658.10	630.60	603.10	575.60	548.10	521.00	497.60	474.30	451.00	427.60	404.30
3,280	3,320	671.30	643.80	616.30	588.80	561.30	533.80	508.80	485.50	462.20	438.80	415.50
3,320	3,360	684.50	657.00	629.50	602.00	574.50	547.00	520.00	496.70	473.40	450.00	425.70
3,360	3,400	697.70	670.20	642.70	615.20	587.70	560.20	532.70	507.90	484.60	461.20	437.90
3,400	3,440	710.90	683.40	655.90	628.40	600.90	573.40	545.90	519.10	495.80	472.40	449.10
3,440	3,480	724.10	696.60	669.10	641.60	614.10	586.60	559.10	531.60	507.00	483.60	460.30
3,480	3,520	737.30	709.80	682.30	654.80	627.30	599.80	572.30	544.80	518.20	494.80	471.50
3,520	3,560	750.50	723.00	695.50	668.00	640.50	613.00	585.50	558.00	530.50	506.00	482.70
3,560	3,600	763.70	736.20	708.70	681.20	653.70	626.20	598.70	571.20	543.70	517.20	493.90
3,600	3,640	776.90	749.40	721.90	694.40	666.90	639.40	611.90	584.40	556.90	529.40	505.10
3,640	3,680	790.10	762.60	735.10	707.60	680.10	652.60	625.10	597.60	570.10	542.60	516.30
3,680	3,720	803.30	775.80	748.30	720.80	693.30	665.80	638.30	610.80	583.30	555.80	528.30
3,720	3,760	816.80	789.00	761.50	734.00	706.50	679.00	651.50	624.00	596.50	569.00	541.50
3,760	3,800	831.60	802.20	774.70	747.20	719.70	692.20	664.70	637.20	609.70	582.20	554.70
3,800	3,840	846.40	815.60	787.90	760.40	732.90	705.40	677.90	650.40	622.90	595.40	567.90
3,840	3,880	861.20	830.40	801.10	773.60	746.10	718.60	691.10	663.60	636.10	608.60	581.10
3,880	3,920	876.00	845.20	814.30	786.80	759.30	731.80	704.30	676.80	649.30	621.80	594.30
3,920	3,960	890.80	860.00	829.10	800.00	772.50	745.00	717.50	690.00	662.50	635.00	607.50
3,960	4,000	905.60	874.80	843.90	813.20	785.70	758.20	730.70	703.20	675.70	648.20	620.70
4,000	4,040	920.40	889.60	858.70	827.90	798.90	771.40	743.90	716.40	688.90	661.40	633.90
4,040	4,080	935.20	904.40	873.50	842.70	812.10	784.60	757.10	729.60	702.10	674.60	647.10
4,080	4,120	950.00	919.20	888.30	857.50	826.70	797.80	770.30	742.80	715.30	687.80	660.30
4,120	4,160	964.80	934.00	903.10	872.30	841.50	811.00	783.50	756.00	728.50	701.00	673.50
4,160	4,200	979.60	948.80	917.90	887.10	856.30	825.40	796.70	769.20	741.70	714.20	686.70
4,200	4,240	994.40	963.60	932.70	901.90	871.10	840.20	809.90	782.40	754.90	727.40	699.90
4,240	4,280	1,009.20	978.40	947.50	916.70	885.90	855.00	824.20	795.60	768.10	740.60	713.10
4,280	4,320	1,024.00	993.20	962.30	931.50	900.70	869.80	839.00	808.80	781.30	753.80	726.30
4,320	4,360	1,038.80	1,008.00	977.10	946.30	915.50	884.60	853.80	823.00	794.50	767.00	739.50
4,360	4,400	1,053.60	1,022.80	991.90	961.10	930.30	899.40	868.60	837.80	807.70	780.20	752.70
4,400	4,440	1,068.40	1,037.60	1,006.70	975.90	945.10	914.20	883.40	852.60	821.70	793.40	765.90
4,440	4,480	1,083.20	1,052.40	1,021.50	990.70	959.90	929.00	898.20	867.40	836.50	806.60	779.10
4,480	4,520	1,098.00	1,067.20	1,036.30	1,005.50	974.70	943.80	913.00	882.20	851.30	820.50	792.30
4,520	4,560	1,112.80	1,082.00	1,051.10	1,020.30	989.50	958.60	927.80	897.00	866.10	835.30	805.50
4,560	4,600	1,127.60	1,096.80	1,065.90	1,035.10	1,004.30	973.40	942.60	911.80	880.90	850.10	819.30
		37 percent of the excess over $4,600 plus—										
$4,600 and over		1,135.00	1,104.20	1,073.30	1,042.50	1,011.70	980.80	950.00	919.20	888.30	857.50	826.70

FIGURE 5–6 Federal Tax Withholding Tables—Monthly Payroll

BENEFITS

A benefit that employers must provide is national holidays. Full-time employees who are receiving a salary are entitled to have off, with pay, those holidays designated as *paid holidays*. These include Christmas, Thanksgiving, Fourth of July, Labor Day, and Memorial Day. Other holidays that are considered paid holidays by many companies include New Year's Day, Veterans' Day, and Presidents' Day. An employee cannot be required to work on a national holiday, and, if he or she does, the compensation is double or more than double the regular rate of pay.

Pay for work on national holidays is usually double.

Many employers provide one or more of the following *optional* (not required) *benefits*.

Profit Sharing

Profit sharing is usually a plan whereby employees are allowed to receive a portion of the company's profits at the end of the corporate year: the more the company makes (profits), the more the company has to share with employees. Most companies who offer profit sharing consider it an *incentive*, which is a way to encourage employees to do more and better quality work.

Incentives encourage better performance.

Paid Vacations

Most businesses provide full-time employees with a set amount of paid vacation time. While you are on vacation, you are paid as usual. It is common to receive a week's paid vacation after a year, two weeks after two years, three weeks after five years' employment, and so on.

Discounts

Many companies offer to their employees discounts on merchandise sold or made by the company. For example, if you work at a clothing store that allows employee discounts, you can purchase your clothing for a reduced price. A usual discount is 10 percent or more.

Sick Pay

Sick pay is available to full-time workers.

Many businesses also provide an allowance of days each year for illness, with pay as usual for full-time workers. It is customary to receive three to ten days a year as "sick days" without deductions from pay.

Leave of Absence

Some employers allow employees to leave their jobs (without pay) for certain events, such as having children or completing education, and return to their jobs at a later time.

Insurance

Most large companies provide group health insurance plans for all employees. Some plans are paid entirely by the employer, as a part of employee compensation, with full family coverage. Other plans require paycheck deductions if employees elect to participate in the plan. Insurance plans typically include hospitalization, major medical, dental, vision, and life insurance. A typical health insurance plan has a $100 deductible (or more for a family), then pays 80 percent of most doctor bills and prescriptions and 100 percent of hospitalization charges and emergency type bills. Many insurance plans will not cover routine physical examinations because they are not classified as illness or injury.

Coverages vary according to plans purchased.

Bonuses

Bonus plans include stock options or salary incentives based on quality of work done, years of service, or company profits.

Retirement Plans

Some employers provide retirement plans whereby employees contribute a percentage of gross pay, which may or may not be matched by the employer. When an employee retires, he or she receives a monthly check that is partially or wholly taxable. In some cases, an employee may draw against the account, withdraw it early in part or in full, or retire early and begin collecting benefits.

Travel Expenses

Companies that require employees to travel in the course of their work often provide a company car or a mileage allowance if they use their own car. Often car insurance, gasoline, and repair and maintenance expenses for the company automobile are also provided. While out of town, employees are paid a daily allowance, or have their motel and meals paid, as well as other travel expenses.

Mileage is allowed when you drive your own car.

Many of these optional benefits are of great value to employees. Optional benefits generally are not taxable to employees (except bonuses and other benefits paid to employees in cash), yet provide valuable coverages and advantages. Generally, large companies provide more extensive optional benefit packages.

LABOR UNIONS AND PROFESSIONAL ORGANIZATIONS

Membership in unions is sometimes required.

Many employment opportunities also involve union membership or participation in a professional organization as a requirement of employment. *Unions* are units or groups of people joined together for a common purpose. *Labor unions* are groups of people who work in the same or similar occupations, organized for the benefit of all employees in these occupations.

History of Unions

Unions were organized in the United States as early as the late 1800s. The first unions were local units organized by skilled craftspeople to protect themselves from competition of untrained and unskilled workers. In 1886 the American Federation of Labor (AFL) was organized by Samuel Gompers, who served as its president for 37 years.

Unions had a slow and painful start.

Early unions had very little power until 1935, when the National Labor Relations Act (Wagner Act) gave unions the right to organize and bargain with employers. In 1938 John L. Lewis became the first president of a new union—the Congress of Industrial Organizations (CIO). Unions continued to grow in number, power, and size until 1947, when Congress passed the Labor Management Relations Act, commonly called the Taft-Hartley Act. The Labor Management Relations Act was passed to limit the powers of unions and to curb strikes. In 1955 the AFL and CIO merged under the leadership of George Meany and became the largest and most powerful union in the United States.

Functions of Unions

The importance of labor unions in American life cannot be measured by the numbers of workers in unions. Many nonunion employers are influenced by the standards set by union agreements with other employers; and many employees reap the benefits of unionization even though they do not belong to a union.

Labor unions have four major functions: (*a*) recruitment of new members; (*b*) collective bargaining; (*c*) support of political candidates who are favorable to the union; and (*d*) provision of support services for members, including employment, job transfer, membership and employment credentials, and education.

Large unions are usually powerful.

Unions exercise power through large numbers of members. Therefore, new employees in occupations that have unions are strongly urged, if membership is not mandatory, to join the union. Political candidates who express opinions favorable to a particular union may receive campaign funds and/or endorsements from union leaders. These endorsements usually mean large numbers of the union members, locally and nationally, will vote for the candidate. Unions provide support for their members by helping to keep their members employed, negotiating job transfers, providing credentials for job-seeking employees, and providing education necessary to obtain and keep jobs held by union members.

Unions negotiate employment contracts.

The major function of unions is *collective bargaining*, which is the process of negotiating the terms of employment for union members. Terms of the agreement are written in an employment contract. The contract is usually quite detailed and is divided into these major sections: wages and supplements; workers' rights on the job; union rights in relation to the employer; management rights in relation to the union; and the grievance procedure when a provision of the contract has not been honored.

Seniority rights are stated in contracts.

The contract stipulates wages to be paid for certain jobs and types of work. Paid holidays, vacations, overtime rates, and hours of work are also specified in the contract. Most contracts also list *fringe benefits*, which are optional or extra benefits provided for union employees. Health insurance, sick leave, and pensions are considered fringe benefits. Union contracts usually provide for *seniority* rights, which state that the last ones hired should be the first ones laid off. In other words, the longer you work, the more job security you are entitled to have. Seniority may be used to determine transfers, promotions, and vacation time according to most union contracts.

When agreement as to meaning of a contract provision cannot be reached between the union and the employer, the dispute must be arbitrated. Through *arbitration*, a decision is made by a neutral third party. When employers and union officials cannot agree on the terms of a new contract, the labor union may make the decision to *strike*, a process whereby the members of the union refuse to work until an agreement is reached.

Types of Unions

Unions are classified into three types: craft unions, industrial unions, and public employee unions.

Craft Unions. Membership in craft unions is limited to those who practice in an established craft or trade, such as bricklayers, carpenters, or plasterers. Major craft unions include those of the building, printing, and maritime trades, and of railroad employees.

Various occupations have different unions.

Industrial Unions. Membership in industrial unions is composed of skilled, semiskilled, or unskilled workers in a particular place, industry, or group of industries. Examples include the AFL-CIO, Teamsters, and United Auto Workers.

Public Employee Unions. Municipal, county, state, or federal employees such as firemen, teachers, and policemen may organize public employee unions.

Unions are self-governing organizations. Major decisions are made by elected leaders. Of the four functions of unions, the most significant is collective bargaining. Many unions have developed a high degree of professionalism and are regarded as powerful. Union leaders often devote full

Powerful unions now exist.

time to their positions. Unions often employ their own lawyers, doctors, economists, educators, and public relations officials; dues collected from members provide the basis for the services of these professionals.

Professional Organizations

Professional organizations also collect dues from members and provide support services. In some cases, membership in a professional organization may be compulsory. Most notable of professional organizations include the American Bar Association (required) for lawyers and the American Medical Association (optional) for doctors. Each state bar association provides the testing procedures by which lawyers who pass are "admitted to the bar." Attorneys who are severely disciplined are "disbarred," which means they can no longer practice law.

Dues are used to fund professional organizations.

Purposes of professional organizations are: (*a*) to establish and maintain professional standards, including procedures for self-improvement; (*b*) to support legislation and political action, known as *lobbying*, that is beneficial to the profession; (*c*) to encourage individual growth and achievement; (*d*) to publish a professional journal or magazine; (*e*) to provide pension, retirement, and insurance benefits for members; and (*f*) to keep members up-to-date on current information and procedures. Because most doctors and lawyers are self-employed, they are not regulated as to professional behavior except through membership in these organizations and/or through court procedures. Exams, accreditations, admission procedures, and other standards are administered through these professional organizations.

Another professional organization, sometimes called a union, is the NEA (National Education Association). Membership is not compulsory, but teachers who choose not to belong pay what is known as a "fair share," which is the same as the deduction for dues paid by members. This payment is justified because the organization benefits all teachers, regardless of membership. There are national, state, and local branches of NEA and other professional organizations. Each branch of the NEA charges dues, just as do the national, state, and county bar associations.

Unions benefit all employees.

VOCABULARY

Directions: Can you find the definition for each of the following terms used in Chapter 5?

gross pay   net pay
deductions   optional or fringe benefits
incentive   collective bargaining
labor unions   seniority
strike   professional organizations
lobbying

1. Similar to labor unions, but membership is required for persons in certain occupations.

2. A process whereby employees refuse to work until an agreement is reached.

3. An effort to support legislation that would be of benefit to a certain group.

4. The total agreed upon salary or pay before deductions.

5. Amounts subtracted from gross pay, some required and some optional.

6. Also known as the amount of the paycheck.

7. Added benefits that are not required by law, but are provided by employers as part of a total wage package.

8. Groups of people in the same or similar occupations, organized for the benefit of all.

9. The process whereby unions and employers negotiate terms of employment.

10. The first hired is the last fired or laid off.

11. Encouragement plan to get employees to do more and better work.

ITEMS FOR DISCUSSION

1. How is gross pay different from net pay?

2. List five optional deductions you may elect to have withheld from your gross pay.

3. How much is the minimum wage?

4. What is required when an employee has worked more than the maximum regular workweek?

5. What is a leave of absence?

6. What are the four major functions of labor unions?

7. What are the three types of labor unions?

8. How are labor unions funded; that is, how are labor unions able to operate—who pays for the services that are provided?

9. What is collective bargaining?

10. What is seniority?

11. What was the significance of the Wagner Act to American labor?

12. What is a strike?

13. Name a professional organization.

14. Explain lobbying.

APPLICATIONS

1. Compute gross pay for these situations:

   (a) Regular hours worked: 40
   Overtime hours worked: 5
   Regular rate of pay: $3.85 an hour

   (b) Regular salary: $800 a month
   Overtime hours agreed upon: 8 a week (four weeks)
   Overtime rate of pay agreed upon: $6.82 an hour

(c) Total hours worked: 43 (in 5 days)
Regular rate of pay: $4.10

(d) Annual salary: $18,000
Compute gross pay (monthly).

2. . Using the payroll income tax withholding tables on pages 74–77, locate the following answers:

(a) For a single person, two allowances, who made $110 last week:

State withholding tax: _____
Federal withholding tax: _____

(b) For a single person, no allowances, who made $222 last week:

State withholding tax: _____
Federal withholding tax: _____

(c) For a married person, two allowances, who made $1,120 last month:

State withholding tax: _____
Federal withholding tax: _____

(d) For a married person, six allowances, who made $1,479 last month:

State withholding tax: _____
Federal withholding tax: _____

CASE PROBLEMS AND ACTIVITIES

1. Mike Martinez, social security number 484-40-9876, works for a weekly paycheck. He is single and claims no allowances. Last week he worked five days, for a total of 44 hours. His regular rate of pay is $6.60 an hour. In addition to federal income tax, state income tax (use tables shown in Figures 5–3 through 5–6), and social security tax, Mike also has insurance of $16 a week withheld and puts 6 percent of his gross pay into a retirement account.

Compute Mike's gross pay, deductions, and net paycheck.

2. Lorraine Wong, social security number 444-33-2121, works for a weekly paycheck. She is single and claims one allowance. Last week she worked five days, for a total of 48 hours. Her regular rate of pay is $6.80 an hour. In addition to required deductions, Lorraine also has $10 a week sent to her credit union account and gives $5 a week to United Fund (charity).

Compute Lorraine's gross pay, deductions, and net paycheck.

3. Willard Weinstein, social security number 644-30-2929, works for a monthly salary. He is married and claims four allowances. Last month Willard worked 22 days. He does not get paid for overtime. His monthly salary is $1,780. In addition to required deductions, Willard also pays insurance premiums of $23 a month and sets aside for retirement 6 percent of his gross monthly pay.

Compute Willard's gross pay, deductions, and net paycheck.

4. Marjorie Wilkinson, social security number 331-84-3139, works for a monthly paycheck. She is married and claims two allowances. Her yearly salary is $14,700. Last month she worked 21 days, without overtime. In addition to required deductions, Marjorie also contributes $14 a week (assume a four-week month) to the Heart Fund and sets aside $50 a month, paid directly to her savings account.

Compute Marjorie's gross pay, deductions, and net paycheck.

5. Jack King, social security number 414-31-3245, works for a monthly salary. He is married and claims no allowances. His monthly salary is $1,500. When Jack works overtime it is at an agreed hourly rate of $12.75. Last month he worked 10 hours that will be paid overtime. He worked 23 days. Jack has only the required deductions.

Compute Jack's gross pay, deductions, and net paycheck.

6
Budgets and Financial Records

```
CHAPTER OBJECTIVES
```
After studying this chapter and completing the activities, you will be able to:

1. Analyze and understand the budgeting process and prepare personal and case study budget problems.
2. Understand the purpose of personal record keeping and be able to prepare a personal net worth statement and personal property inventory.
3. Explain the elements of legal contracts and negotiable instruments and understand consumer rights and responsibilities.

BUDGETING INCOME AND EXPENSES

How would you like to have unlimited resources to buy all the things you want or need? Unfortunately, for most people personal financial management is not that easy. Careful budgeting and planning are needed to enable you to meet your financial goals. That is why you need to study financial planning and budgeting—so that you will learn how to make the most of your financial resources.

Importance of Financial Planning

Your *disposable income* is the money you have to spend as you wish after taxes, social security, and other required and optional deductions have been withheld from your gross pay. In order to use this income to your best ability, you will need to create a financial plan.

ILLUSTRATION 6–1
Budgeting helps you plan your spending.

All the money you receive is spent, saved, or invested. You may spend it for things you need or want, save it for future needs, or invest it to earn more money. *Financial planning* is an orderly program for spending, saving, and investing the money you earn. You may already understand the need to save part of your income for the future. Financial planning is important because it helps you to do the following:

1. Determine and evaluate how wisely you are using your money
2. Get the most from your income
3. Prevent careless and wasteful spending

Eliminate waste through planning.

4. Organize your *financial resources* (sources of income) so that you can maintain a plan of personal financial fitness
5. Avoid money worries and problems by understanding the proper methods of saving, spending, and borrowing money

The first step in financial fitness is to set up a plan. *Budgeting* is an organized plan whereby you match your expected income to your expected outflow. The purpose of budgeting is to plan your spending and saving so that you won't have to borrow money to meet your needs. Careful budgeting will enable you to stretch your money to provide for your present and future needs and satisfy your wants.

Figure 6–1 shows a high school junior's budget plan for one month. This student expects to receive a total of $260, and plans to use the money for certain needs and wants and to save part of it as well.

FIGURE 6–1
Simple Budget

Budget for September	
Income	
Work (part-time)	$230.00
Allowance (household chores)	10.00
Lunch money..	30.00
Total income	$260.00
Expenses	
Savings (monthly)	$195.00
Daily lunches.......................................	20.00
Miscellaneous: supplies............................	12.00
snacks	14.00
other................................	19.00
Total expenses	$260.00

The first step in setting up a budget is to estimate total expected disposable income for a certain time. Include all money you expect to receive. You may wish to use a weekly, biweekly, or monthly budget—whichever best matches how often you expect to receive money.

Set aside for savings each month.

The second step is to decide how much of your income you want to save—to set aside for future needs. Most financial experts advise saving at least 10 percent of your disposable income each pay period. By saving at least 10 percent, you will have money to pay for future needs, both expected and unexpected.

The third step is to estimate your *expenses*, or money you will need for day-to-day purchases; for example, lunches, fees, personal care items, clothing, and so forth.

A Typical Monthly Budget

Figure 6–2 represents the monthly budget of Bill and Mary Anderson, a recently married couple. Bill and Mary have no children, and both are working. The Andersons estimate their expected income by adding together their two take-home incomes (paychecks). They have decided to save at least 10 percent every month, invest some of their income in a home, and use the rest as shown.

To further refine their budget, Bill and Mary could divide their expenses into two groups: fixed expenses and variable expenses.

Fixed expenses are those that remain constant, and to remove them or change them will take a major revision in life-style. Examples are savings, house payments, utilities, car payments, average gasoline and car maintenance costs, and insurance premium payments.

Variable expenses will change according to needs and short-term goals. Sufficient money should be allowed to cover these expenses, since they can change frequently. Examples are telephone, TV cable, groceries, dental or medical bills not covered by insurance, entertainment, recreation, charge account purchases, investments, and miscellaneous purchases.

FIGURE 6–2
Monthly Budget
for Married
Couple

Budget Bill and Mary Anderson	Month	Year
Income (monthly)	$1,800	$21,600
Expenses		
Savings	$ 200	$ 2,400
House payment............................	450	5,400
Utilities (average)........................	80	960
Car payment	150	1,800
Gasoline	100	1,200
Car maintenance	15	180
Insurance		
Car	30	360
Life and Health	50	600
Telephone................................	45	540
Cable television	25	300
Groceries	200	2,400
Entertainment and recreation	100	1,200
Vacation fund	75	900
Charge accounts (clothing)	200	2,400
Miscellaneous	80	960
Total expenses	$1,800	$21,600

PERSONAL RECORDS

Efficient personal records are important. They make planning a budget easier; they assure improved long-range financial planning; and they are a basis for properly completing income tax returns, credit applications, and other needed forms. Basically, there are four types of personal records that most families will want to keep: records of income and expenses, a statement of net worth, a personal property inventory, and tax records.

Keep important records in a safe place.

Records of Income and Expenses

W-2 slips sent by employers each January show money earned and deductions made by the employer during the year. The W-2s prove that you had social security withheld. You may need the W-2s later when you want to collect benefits. Other records of income include statements from banks of interest earned on savings. Expense items include receipts listing charity contributions, medical bills, or work-related expenses. All this information will be needed when preparing budgets and tax returns. These receipts and statements are often referred to as *documents* and can be used as *proof*, or evidence, of income and expenses. These documents should be stored in a safe place for future reference.

Keep receipts for tax return information.

Statement of Net Worth

A net worth statement, such as that shown in Figure 6–3, is a list of items of value, called *assets*, that a person owns; amounts of money that are owed to others, called *liabilities* or debts; and the difference between the two, known as *net worth*. If your assets are greater than your liabilities, you are said to be *solvent*, or in a favorable credit position. But if

FIGURE 6–3
Net Worth
Statement

Net Worth Statement
Wendy Haskins
January 1, 19--

ASSETS		LIABILITIES	
Checking account...	$ 58.00	Loan at bank on car	$ 600.00
Savings account	80.00	Loan from Mother ...	80.00
Car value	1,000.00	Total Liabilities	$ 680.00
Personal property			
(inventory attached)	2,000.00		
		NET WORTH	
		Assets - liabilities....	$2,458.00
Total assets	$3,138.00	Total	$3,138.00

your liabilities are greater than your assets (you owe more than you own), you are said to be *insolvent*, or in a poor credit position.

Net worth information (lists of assets and liabilities) is most often required when you ask for a loan or apply for credit. The bank or other financial institution will want you to be solvent and a good risk who will likely pay back a loan. How does your personal net worth statement compare with the one shown in Figure 6–3?

Personal Property Inventory

An inventory is proof of property ownership.

The personal property inventory is a list of all the personal property a person owns. Personal property is usually all items inside the home—clothing, furniture, appliances, and so forth. A personal property inventory is especially useful in the event of fire, theft, or property damage, as proof of possession and value. As a further safeguard, a person or family may photograph items of value, attach the photographs to the inventory, and keep this information in a safe-deposit box or other safe place to use as evidence in the event the property is damaged, lost, or stolen. As new items are purchased and others disposed of, the inventory should be revised. Figure 6–4 shows the inventory of personal property of Wendy Haskins.

FIGURE 6–4
Personal
Property
Inventory

Personal Property Inventory
Wendy Haskins
January 1, 19--

Item	Year Purchased	Purchase Price	Approximate Current Value
Acme stereo turntable with speakers in cabinet, Model XJ (SN 54J213)	1980	$ 600	$ 600
Bedroom furniture (bed, dresser, lamp, clock)	1971	800	200
Clothing and jewelry	1980-81	app. 2000	1000
Marvel "Cruiser" 10-speed bicycle (SN 5482164)	1983	120	120
TKO microcassette tape recorder, Model II, (SN 81426)	1983	(gift)	80
Total		$3520	$2000
(photographs attached)			

Tax Records

All taxpayers must keep copies of their tax returns, W-2 slips, and other receipts verifying income and expenses listed on tax returns for six years. Information used in preparing tax returns should be kept in a safe place in the event of *audit*, which is the examination of your tax records by the Internal Revenue Service. The IRS has the legal right to examine your tax returns and supporting records for six years from the date of filing the return (longer if fraud or international wrongdoing on your part can be proved).

Your records are subject to IRA audit.

The four types of records discussed are important because they enable you to (*a*) evaluate your family or individual spending; (*b*) provide information for tax returns; (*c*) analyze your financial picture and plan for the future; (*d*) provide a basis for determining future goals; and (*e*) provide a basis for maintaining an effective, updated budget.

LEGAL DOCUMENTS

To manage personal finances, you often need to enter into agreements, fill out forms and applications, and provide personal information and records. It is difficult to function successfully in today's society if you do not master these simple documents.

Contracts and Agreements

A *contract* is a legally enforceable agreement between two or more parties to do or not to do something. We all have many transactions in our daily lives that can be properly classified as contracts or lawful agreements. Contracts are involved in personal business situations even though one may not be aware that contracts exist. If you buy a suit and it needs an alteration, a ticket is filled out by the clerk. What change must be made and when completion is promised are written on the ticket. This ticket is a contract under which you, the consumer, promise to pick up the suit and pay for the alteration when it is completed. The store promises to do the work and present it to you on the agreed upon date for the stated price.

Entering into contracts is a common practice.

Other examples of situations requiring agreements are (*a*) retail credit plans, whereby customers agree to pay for purchases by monthly payments or open a charge account at a store; (*b*) buying a home and paying for it over a number of years by means of mortgage payments; or (*c*) renting an apartment, a duplex, or a house. In each of these cases there is generally an agreement between two or more persons known as an *express*

Written contracts are required for large purchases.

contract. Express contracts can be oral or written: what makes them express is that the terms have been agreed upon between the parties.

Figure 6–5 shows a charge application a retail store may require. In addition to giving certain requested information, you are asked to agree to certain conditions before opening an account. Attached to the application

CHARGE APPLICATION

Please print clearly

ACCOUNT IN NAME OF:
First _Richard_ Initial _J_ Last _Washington_
Address _45 Front Street #8_
City _Portland_ State _OR_ ZIP _97201-1072_

Area Code Number
Phone _(503) 221-1181_ How long at this address? _4 years_

Check one: ☐ Own ☐ Lease ☒ Rent ☐ Live with parents ☐ Other*
*Explain _____

Previous address if less than three years _____ How long? _____

Employer _O'Toole Paper Co._ How long? _4 years_
Employer's Address _Portland, OR 97214-4179_ Phone _221-8342_

Occupation _Administrative Assistant_ Salary _$342_ ☒ Weekly ☐ Monthly

COMPLETE SECTION FOR JOINT ACCOUNT:
Name First _N/A_ Initial ___ Last ___
Employer ___ How long? ___
Employer's Address ___ Phone ___
Occupation ___ Salary ___ ☐ Weekly ☐ Monthly

Other income: Source ___ Amount ___

CREDIT REFERENCES:
Name of Bank _First Bank_ Bank Address _Portland, OR_ ☒ Checking ☒ Savings
Name of Creditor _Meier & Frank_ Account Number _818 424961_ Address _Portland_
Creditor _JC Penney_ Number _489 1248369_ Address _Portland_
Creditor ___ Number ___ Address ___

NEAREST RELATIVE NOT LIVING WITH YOU:
Name _Harry Washington_ Address _614 Chevy St., Portland OR 97216-6172_

I understand the terms and conditions of this credit application, including service charges and fees, which will be charged to this account as explained on the reverse side of this application. I have read it completely and agree to all conditions. I testify that all information contained in this application is true and complete.

APPLICANT'S SIGNATURE _Richard J. Washington_ Social Security Number _481-32-8194_ Date _4/1/--_

FIGURE 6–5 Charge Application

will be an explanation of finance charges and how they are computed. You will sign the application to show that you understand the finance charges and agree to pay them if your balance is not paid in full each month. Be sure you have read everything contained in the agreement *before* you sign it. If something is not clear, be sure to ask for an explanation so that you can understand your rights and responsibilities *before* you enter into the contract.

In addition to written agreements, there are also many unwritten agreements. If you possess a driver's license, a social security card, a work permit, or any of many such items, you have made an ***implied agreement***. Whether or not you realize it, you have agreed to certain things by your acceptance of a license or card. When you are issued a driver's license, you agree to abide by laws, drive in a safe and responsible manner, and have the license with you when driving. A violation of one of these unwritten agreements can result in the loss of your license, a fine, imprisonment, or all these.

By accepting certain items you enter into implied agreements.

Essentials of an Enforceable Contract

To accomplish its purpose, a contract must be binding on all persons who enter into it. Some contracts *must* be in writing and signed by all persons involved in order to be legally binding. Examples of contracts that must be written are contracts for the purpose of sale of real property (homes and land); contracts that cannot be fully performed in less than a year; contracts involving $500 and over; and contracts in which one person agrees to pay the debts of another.

To be enforceable, some contracts must be in writing.

To be legally binding, enforceable agreements, contracts must have all of the following elements:

1. Mutual assent
2. Consideration
3. Competent parties
4. Lawful objective
5. An agreed upon period of time
6. Legal format

Let's examine each of these elements in detail.

Mutual Assent. A contract has ***mutual assent*** when it is offered and accepted. If there is any disagreement, the contract is not legally enforceable. In order to prove mutual assent, two conditions are required by law: a valid offer and acceptance of that exact offer. One person makes the offer, another person accepts the offer. When one person makes an offer and another person changes any part of the offer, the second person making what is known as a *counteroffer*. The counteroffer is a new offer and has to be accepted (or rejected) by the first person.

Consideration. The price involved is called *consideration*. Consideration may be in the form of an object of value, money, a promise, or a performed act. If one person is to receive something but give nothing in return, the contract is not enforceable. The idea of consideration is that each party to the agreement receives something of value. When you buy a pair of shoes, you get the shoes and the store gets your money. The shoes and the money are items of consideration.

Consideration is something of value.

Competent Parties. *Competent parties* are persons who are legally able to give sane and intelligent assent. Those who are unable to protect themselves because of mental deficiency or illness, or who are otherwise incapable of understanding the consequences of their actions, cannot be held to contracts. They are protected from entering into agreements that may prove to be against their best interests. Minors are not considered competent parties and therefore cannot be held to contracts, with exceptions. Generally, any person 18 or older who is not mentally deficient is considered competent. Married persons under age 18 are also considered competent to enter into agreements. Furthermore, all persons 18 or older are considered to be legally competent unless they are declared incompetent by a court of law.

Minors are not considered competent parties.

Lawful Objective. The purpose of a legally enforceable contract must be of a lawful nature. A court of law will not require a person to perform an agreed upon act if it is illegal. Without a lawful objective, the agreement has no binding effect on any person.

Agreed Upon Period of Time. Within the contract, there must be a stated length of time for which the contract is to exist. For example, if the contract is to purchase a home, the agreed upon period of time is so long as money remains due and owing. When the last payment is made, then the contract is considered fulfilled.

Legal Format. State laws provide that contracts must contain the necessary information to be enforceable. The contract may be a printed form, drawn up by attorneys, or it may be in some other readable and understandable form. It must state the date, duration of contract, persons involved, consideration, terms of agreement, and other necessary information to explain the purpose and intentions of the persons entering into the contract. In some cases, the contract, or a memorandum of contract, must be *recorded*. When a contract is recorded it is made a public record, and a

Contracts must be in proper format.

photocopy is stored by the county recorder. Before a document can be recorded, it must meet specific requirements that are set out by state law.

Void and Voidable Contracts

There are basically three types of contracts: valid, void, and voidable.

Valid Contracts. *Valid contracts* are those that contain all of the essential elements—mutual assent, consideration, competent parties, lawful objective, agreed upon period of time, and legal format. They are legally enforceable.

An illegal purpose causes a void contract.

Void Contracts. *Void Contracts* are those that are missing one or more of the essential elements. These contracts are null and void, and are not enforceable in a court of law. An example of a void contract is one that will require doing something illegal. In other words, if you enter into an agreement and later learn that you will be doing something against the law, you cannot be forced to fulfill your part of the contract.

Certain actions can make a voidable contract valid.

Voidable Contracts. *Voidable contracts* contain an element within them that makes them void. If that element is not acted upon by the innocent party, the contract will become valid. An example of a voidable contract is an agreement entered into by a minor. A minor may declare the voidable contract void because contracts with minors do not meet the competent party test of a legally binding contract. However, if the minor continues to make payments on the contract after reaching age 18, he or she has made that contract valid and is legally responsible for fulfilling the contract.

Consumer Responsibilities in Agreements

As a consumer, you have the following responsibilities regarding the contracts and agreements you enter into:

1. Understand all clauses and terms contained in the agreement. Do not sign it until you have read it. By signing, you are acknowledging that you have read and understand the contract.
2. Keep a copy of the agreement. Put it in a safe place. You may need it at a future date.
3. Be sure the agreement is correctly dated.
4. Be sure all blank spaces are filled in or marked out and that no changes have been made after your signature. Your initials at the bottom of each page will prevent subsitution of pages when there is more than one page.

Check a contract carefully before signing.

5. Be sure all provisions agreed upon are clearly written. Because interpretation may vary, vague phrases are often not enforceable.
6. Be sure all dates, amounts, and other numbers are correct and clearly written.
7. Be sure proper disclosure is made by the seller. The buyer is entitled to proper and complete information about the rate of interest, total finance charges, cash payment price, etc.
8. Be sure all cancellations and adjustments are made in accordance with the contract.

Although consumers are protected by numerous consumer protection laws, occasionally specific legal services are required. Legal services, in one form or other, are available to every citizen. But your best protection is to guard yourself in advance by understanding the agreement.

Protect yourself in the beginning.

Negotiable Instruments

The word *negotiable* means legally collectible. A *negotiable instrument* is a document that contains promises to pay moneys and is legally collectible. The kinds of negotiable instruments most people are likely to use are checks (discussed in Chapter 7) and promissory notes. A negotiable instrument is legally collectible if the following conditions are met:

Checks are negotiable instruments.

1. It must be in writing and be signed by the maker (not oral).
2. It must contain an unconditional promise to pay a definite amount of money.
3. It must be payable on demand or on a fixed or determinable future date.
4. It must be payable to the order of a particular person or to the holder of the note.
5. It must be delivered to the payee.

If any one of the above conditions is missing, the document is not a negotiable instrument; it is no longer legally collectible.

A *promissory note* is a written promise to pay a certain sum of money to another person or to the holder of the note on a specified date. A promissory note is a legal document, and payment can be enforced by law. An example of a promissory note is found in Figure 6–6.

The person who creates and signs the promissory note, agreeing to pay it on a certain date, is called the *maker*. The person to whom the note is made payable is known as the *payee*. A promissory note is normally used when borrowing a large sum of money from a financial institution.

In some cases creditors (those extending credit) will require cosigners as additional security for repayment of a note. A *cosigner* is a person who is established (has a good credit rating) and who promises to pay the note

FIGURE 6–6
Promissory Note

PROMISSORY NOTE

$ _400.00_   _January 15_____, 19_--_

I (we) _Marilyn Huykamp_____, jointly and severally, do agree and promise to pay to _Emerald Furniture Co._____ the sum of _Four hundred and °°/100_ ～～～～～dollars with interest at the rate of _18_% from _January 15, 19--_, payable in monthly installments of $ _72.67_ beginning _February 1_____, 19_--_ and on a like day each month until paid in full, the last payment due _July 1_____, 19_--_ Said payment shall include interest. In the event of default, the maker hereof agrees to pay attorneys' fees and court costs in collection of this note.

Marilyn Huykamp
Maker

Cosigners make payments when the debtor fails.

if the maker fails to pay. The cosigner's signature is also on a note. Young people and persons who have not established a credit rating are often asked to provide a cosigner for their first loan.

Warranties

A *warranty*, also called a guarantee, is an assurance of product quality or of responsibility of the seller. The warranty may be in writing or assumed to exist by the nature of the product. However, a warranty is not a safeguard against a poor buying decision.

All products contain implied warranties, and some have written guarantees as well, expressing responsibilities that the manufacturer will strictly enforce. A product is supposed to do that which it is made to do, whether or not standards are expressed in writing. For example, a tennis ball must bounce. If it does not bounce, it is dead. You can return the defective ball, even if there is no written warranty.

Specific written warranties often guarantee that a product will perform to your satisfaction for a certain period of time. Many written warranties state that you may return a product for repair or replacement if it

Read warranties before you buy.

ceases to work because of a defect. Warranties will not protect against normal wear and tear of the product.

Figure 6–7 illustrates a limited warranty that might be found when purchasing a home product. Read it carefully to determine what the manufacturer is and is not guaranteeing.

FIGURE 6–7
Warranty

12 Y 845

Limited Warranty

This product is guaranteed for one year from the date of purchase to be free of mechanical and electrical defects in material and workmanship. The manufacturer's obligations hereunder are limited to repair of such defects during the warranty period, provided such product is returned to the address below within the warranty period.

This guarantee does not cover normal wear of parts or damages resulting from negligent use or misuse of the product. In addition, this guarantee is void if the purchaser breaks the seal and disassembles, repairs, or alters the product in any way.

The warranty period begins on the date of purchase. The card below must be received by the manufacturer within 30 days of purchase or receipt of said merchandise. Fill out the card completely and return it to the address shown.

Owner's Name: _____

Address: _____

City, State, ZIP: _____

Date of Purchase: _____

Store Where Purchased: _____

Return to: ALCOVE ELECTRICAL, INC.
             42 West Cabana
             Arlington, VA 23445-2909

Serial No. **12 Y 845**

A FILING SYSTEM FOR PERSONAL RECORDS

Families often find it to their advantage to keep good records, prepare and file their own tax returns, and plan their own savings and investment strategies. Keeping a good filing system for your personal records will help you organize, store, and retrieve needed information.

A typical home filing system would include manila folders and labels, and a small two-drawer file. The labels might read (alphabetically) as shown in Figure 6–8.

In these files, you would keep records and receipts. For example, in the "automobile" folder, you might want to keep track of mileage, oil changes, tune-ups, repairs, and other expenses. The "insurance" file would include premium due dates, descriptions of coverages, and so on. Original documents, such as insurance policies and wills, would be kept in a safe deposit box, and receipts and records used for income tax purposes should be taken from the home files to the safe deposit box when taxes are filed.

FIGURE 6–8 .
Typical Home
Filing System

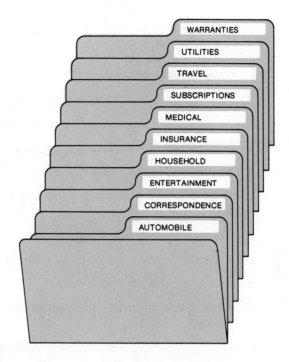

Some of the home files might be in accordion files which allow expansion. You would add to your files as the need arises. Information accumulated in the files would assist in preparing a budget, revising or updating a budget, and writing to companies about problems with products or services. A filing system also helps to keep your personal records in a neat and orderly fashion in your home—easy to find, file, and use when needed.

VOCABULARY

Directions: Can you find the definition for each of the following terms used in Chapter 6?

financial planning	budgeting
disposable income	payee
liabilities	audit
maker	proof
financial resources	assets

recorded   cosigner
mutual assent   warranty
consideration   implied agreement
negotiable instrument

1. Agreement by two or more persons to the terms of a contract.

2. An unwritten statement that nevertheless exists.

3. Evidence that backs up or supports information.

4. Sources of income and money on which you base a budget.

5. A price to be paid, or a promise to pay, or to do something or not do something.

6. Things of value that a person owns.

7. A person who promises to pay a note if the maker fails to pay.

8. An assurance of product quality or of responsibility of the seller.

9. An orderly program for spending, saving, and investing your income.

10. An organized plan of matching income and expenses.

11. Amounts of money that you owe to others, known as debts.

12. Pieces of paper containing written promises to pay.

13. One who signs a note and agrees to pay it on a certain date.

14. One to whom a note is made payable and who will receive its proceeds.

15. An examination of your tax records by the Internal Revenue Service.

16. The money you have left over after required deductions, which you can spend or save as you wish.

17. Made a document, such as a contract, a matter of public record.

ITEMS FOR DISCUSSION

1. Why should consumers prepare a budget and be concerned about financial planning?

2. What is the difference between fixed and variable expenses?

3. Which are the four types of personal records all consumers should prepare and keep in a safe place?

4. Why is it important to maintain these four types of personal records?

5. Besides the obvious use for obtaining credit, what is another good reason for preparing a personal property inventory?

6. Why should taxpayers save copies of their tax returns and supporting receipts and evidence?

7. How is an implied contract different from an express contract?

8. In order to be enforceable in a court of law, contracts must contain six elements. Briefly define each.

9. Give three examples of contracts that must be in writing in order to be enforceable in a court of law.

10. What is the difference between a void contract and a voidable contract?

11. What is the most commonly used form of negotiable instrument.?

12. List the five conditions of negotiable instruments that make them legally collectible.

13. List five consumer responsiblities when entering into contracts.

14. Explain the concept of a filing system for personal records and list what file labels you would choose.

APPLICATIONS

1. Using Figure 6–1 as a model, prepare a simple budget for yourself, listing expected income, savings, and expenses for a month. How much will you set aside for savings?

2. How will your budget change in the next few years? (What are your short-term and intermediate goals?)

3. Using Figure 6–3 as a model, prepare a net worth statement, listing as assets those items of value you possess and any debts for which you are responsible. Compute your net worth. How can you use this information?

4. Using Figure 6–4 as a model, prepare a personal property inventory, listing items of personal property in your room at home. Why should you and your family keep a record such as this?

5. After examining Figure 6–5 (credit application), list the kinds of information requested by a retail store. Why do you think a store needs or wants this type of information?

6. Following the example of Figure 6–6, write out in longhand form a promissory note from you to John Doe, payable in one year of monthly payments, in the amount of $50 with interest at 15 percent and monthly payments of $4.79. Are you the maker or the payee?

7. Bring to class an express warranty from a product you or your family recently purchased. What does the warranty specifically promise to do? List any restrictions (exceptions) that the manufacturer has placed in the warranty.

CASE PROBLEMS AND ACTIVITIES

1. Based on the information given, prepare a monthly and yearly budget for Paul and Peg Jacobsen. Use Figure 6–2 as a model. INCOME: Net paychecks total $1,800 monthly.

   EXPENSES:

Rent payment $350	Savings $150
Utilities 100	Car payment 110
Gasoline 100	Car repairs 30
Insurance 90	Telephone 30
Groceries 200	Entertainment 100
Clothing 100	Vacation fund 100
Investment fund ... 140	Miscellaneous 200

2. Paul Jacobsen has decided to return to college for two years to obtain his degree. He will work part-time instead of full-time, thereby reducing the Jacobsen's take-home pay be $600 a month. Tuition will be $400 each term ($1,200/year); books will cost $300 a year. Revise the Jacobsens' monthly budget.

3. Based on the information given, prepare a monthly and yearly budget for Margarite Brown. Follow Figure 6–2. INCOME: Net monthly paycheck is $1,200.

   EXPENSES:

Rent payment $210	Savings $120
Insurance 60	Telephone 15
Utilities 50	Car payment 150
Gasoline 60	Car repairs 20
Clothing 60	Groceries 150
Entertainment 150	Miscellaneous 155

4. Revise Margarite's budget when she agrees to share her apartment with a friend. Some expenses can be shared; but the car payment, insurance, and car repairs remain fixed. You will need to adjust her other expenses accordingly. What will you have her do with the added funds?

5. Based on the information given, prepare a net worth statement for Bob Engle. Follow Figure 6–3.
   Bob owns a car worth about $3,000, but owes $1,500 to the bank. He has $500 in savings and $100 in checking. His personal property totals $3,000, and he also owes $90 to the credit union.

6. Based on the information given, prepare a personal property inventory for Bob Engle. Follow Figure 6–4.
   Bob has these furnishings in his apartment: JWA stereo system, Model 252, SN 975923, bought last year for $500; still worth $500; sofa, present worth about $800; Bright alarm clock (SN 630AM) and Blare radio (Model 2602, SN 413T) bought years ago, total worth about $200. Bob also has the following personal items: miscellaneous clothing and jewelry, present worth about $800; Quantex wrist watch, present worth about $100; coin collection, valued last year at $600. Bob has photographs of these items.

Banking

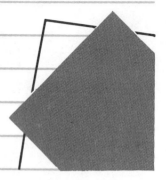

CHAPTER OBJECTIVES

After studying this chapter and completing the activities, you will be able to:

1. Understand and prepare checks, deposit slips, checkbook registers, and bank reconciliations.
2. Define terms used in connection with checking accounts, banking services, and check endorsements.
3. Compare the advantages and disadvantages of the different types of banking services available.

PURPOSE OF A CHECKING ACCOUNT

Financial institutions such as banks, credit unions, and savings and loan associations offer a number of different services. A *checking account* is a banking service wherein you deposit money into an account and write checks, or *drafts*, to withdraw money as needed. This type of account is also known as a *demand deposit*, because you can demand portions of your deposited funds at will. Financial institutions usually charge a fee for checking services, or require that a minimum balance be kept in the account.

Checking accounts are safer than cash.

A checking account can be a useful and convenient tool. Writing a check is often safer than using cash, especially when making major purchases in person, or when paying bills or ordering merchandise through the mail. *Canceled checks* (checks the bank has processed) can be used as proofs of purchase or payment in the event a dispute arises.

Checking accounts also have built-in record keeping systems to help you keep track of money received and spent; thus, they are a great help in personal budgeting and record keeping. Finally, as a checking account customer, you have access to other banking services, such as instant loans and traveler's checks.

In exchange for the convenience of using a checking account, you must accept certain responsibilities. First, you must write checks carefully and keep an accurate record of checks written and deposits made. Second, you must reconcile your account with your bank statement promptly each month. Third, you must keep canceled checks as proofs of purchase or payment and for income tax records. Canceled checks should be kept in a safe place, such as a safe-deposit box.

Safeguard your canceled checks.

In addition, you must not overdraw your account or float a check. An *overdraft* occurs when you, the depositor or *drawer*, write a check that cannot be covered by the funds in your account. The check will bounce—go to your bank and come back to you for payment. *Floating a check* occurs when you realize your account contains insufficient funds, but write a check anyway in the hope that you can make a deposit before the

Intentional overdrafts
are unlawful.

check is cashed. Overdrawing your account and floating a check are illegal practices in most states. In most cases, these acts are felonies that can
result in a fine, imprisonment, or both. In addition, the bank will charge a
fee of $5 to $15 for each *NSF* (not sufficient funds) **check** written.

OPENING YOUR CHECKING ACCOUNT

To open a checking (or savings) account, a depositor must fill out and
sign a signature card, such as the one shown in Figure 7–1. The signature
card provides the bank with important information and an official signature to compare with subsequent checks written.

FIGURE 7–1
Signature Card

In Figure 7-1, Ardys Johnson completed and signed the left side of the
card. The right side is for a joint account holder. Ardys also listed her
mother's full name (including maiden name) for use in identification.
Anyone forging Ardys's signature is not likely to know her mother's
maiden name when questioned by a teller.

USING YOUR CHECKING ACCOUNT

Checking accounts can help you to manage your personal finances—
but only if you use them correctly. Careless or improper use of a checking
account can result in financial losses. Some tips on using a checking
account follow.

Parts of a Check

A check consists of ten parts. Figure 7–2 illustrates these parts.

FIGURE 7–2
Check

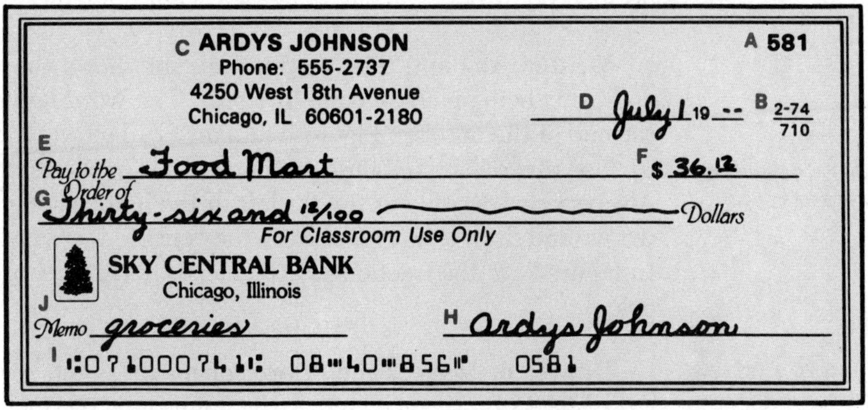

Check Number. Checks are numbered for easy identification. In Figure 7–2, Check 581 has been prenumbered by the bank (see Part A).

ABA Number. The *American Bankers Association number* appears in fraction form in the upper right corner of each check (see Figure 7-2, Part B). The top half of the fraction identifies the location and district of the bank from which the check is drawn. The number on the bottom half of the fraction helps in routing the check to the specific area and bank on which it is drawn.

Maker's Preprinted Name and Address. Most checking account owners prefer to have their name, address, and telephone number preprinted on the top left of each check (see Figure 7–2, Part C). Many stores are reluctant to accept a check unless it is preprinted with this information.

Postdated checks are not held by banks.

Date. The first item to be filled in is the date on which the check is written (see Figure 7–2, Part D). Do not *postdate* checks; that is, do not write in a future date. Most banks process checks when they are presented, or charge a fee for holding them. Checks over six months old may not be honored by the bank.

Payee. The *payee* is the person or company to whom a check is made payable. Food Mart is the payee in Figure 7–2 (see Part E).

Numeric Amount. The numeric amount is the amount of dollars and cents being paid, written in figures (see Figure 7–2, Part F). The amount should be neatly and clearly written, placed as close as possible to the dollar sign, with the dollars and cents distinctly readable. Many people raise the cents above the line of writing, as shown in Figure 7–2, and insert a decimal point between the dollar and cent amounts.

Written Amount. The written amount shows the amount of dollars and cents being paid, written in words. The word *dollars* is preprinted at the end of the line (see Figure 7–2, Part G). The word *and* is handwritten to separate dollar amounts from cents; it replaces the decimal point. Always begin writing at the far left of the line, leaving no space between words, and draw a wavy line from the cents to the word *dollars*, as shown. In Figure 7–2, the fraction *12/100* means that 12 cents out of 100 is to be paid.

The decimal point separates dollars from cents.

Drawer or Maker. The drawer or maker is the person authorized to write checks on the account. Ardys Johnson is the maker of the check in Figure 7–2 (see Part H), because she is the person who opened the checking account and who deposits funds to it. The bank has a copy of Ardys's signature on file so that they can stop someone attempting to forge Ardys's name to one of her checks.

Account Number. The account number appears in bank coding at the bottom of each check. In Figure 7–2 (see Part I), Ardys's checking account number is 08 40 856. The number *581* refers to the preprinted check number at the top of the check.

Memo. A Memo line is provided at the bottom left of each check so that the maker can write the purpose of the check (see Figure 7-2, Part J). This line does not have to be filled in; it is provided for the account holder's convenience.

When writing checks, remember to follow these important guidelines in addition to the hints already given:

Write checks in dark ink.

1. Always use a pen, preferably one with dark ink that does not skip or blot.
2. Write legibly. Keep numbers and letters clear and distinct, without any extra space before, between, or after them.
3. Sign your name exactly as it appears on the check and on the signature card (see Figure 7-1) you signed when you opened the account.
4. Avoid mistakes. When you make a mistake, you should **void** (cancel) the check and write a new one. To cancel a check, write the word

VOID in large capital letters across the check face. Save the voided
check for your records.

5. Be certain adequate funds have been deposited in your account to
   cover each check that you write. A check is a negotiable instrument
   that contains your written promise to pay a certain amount to the
   payee when the check is cashed.

Just as you need a form to withdraw money from your checking
account, you need to complete a form each time you deposit money to the
account. Figure 7–3 illustrates this form, which is called a *deposit slip*.

FIGURE 7–3
Deposit Slip

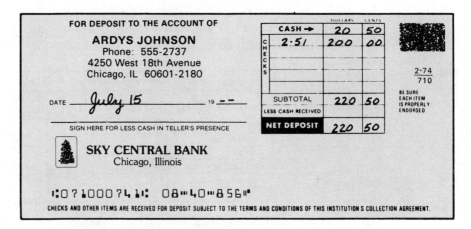

To prepare a deposit slip, follow these guidelines:

1. Insert the date of the transaction.
2. Write in the amount of *currency* (paper money) and coin to be
   deposited.
3. If any checks are being deposited, write in the amount of each
   check, together with the ABA check number.
4. Total the currency, coin, and check amounts. Write this figure on
   the Subtotal line.
5. If you wish to receive some cash at the time of your deposit, you
   should fill in the desired amount on the Less Cash Received line.
   Subtract this amount from the currency, coin, and check total.
   Write your signature on the line above the words *Sign here for less
   cash in teller's presence*.

6. Write the final amount of the deposit on the Net Deposit line.
7. Keep one copy of this deposit slip as proof of the amount of your
   deposit. Financial institutions have been known to make errors in
   crediting an account.

Carefully total your deposit slip.

When writing deposit slips, you should carefully count the currency and coins you are depositing and should recheck all addition and subtraction. Make sure all checks being deposited are properly endorsed (see pages 115-117). Hand the deposit slip to the teller with the currency, coins, and checks you are depositing. Deposits can also be made at automatic teller machines (see page 121).

Using a Checkbook Register

A *checkbook register* is a record of deposits to and withdrawals from a checking account. Figure 7–4 depicts a page from the checkbook register of Ardys Johnson. Through use of her checkbook register, Ardys can keep track of all checks written, service fees paid, interest earned, and deposits made. She can tell at a glance what her present account balance is and whether she needs to make a deposit to her account.

FIGURE 7–4
Checkbook
Register

		PLEASE BE SURE TO <u>DEDUCT</u> ANY PER ITEM CHARGES OR SERVICE CHARGES THAT MAY APPLY TO YOUR ACCOUNT.						
ITEM NO.	DATE	PAYMENT ISSUED TO OR DESCRIPTION OF DEPOSIT	AMOUNT OF PAYMENT	✓	(-) CHECK FEE (IF ANY)	AMOUNT OF DEPOSIT	BALANCE FORWARD	
							800	*00*
581	7/1	To *Food Mart*					Payment or Deposit *-36*	*32*
		For *Groceries*	*36* / *12*		*.20*		Balance *763*	*68*
/	7/15	To *Deposit*					Payment or Deposit *+220*	*50*
		For *Paycheck*				*220* *50*	Balance *984*	*18*
/	7/16	To *Withdrawal*					Payment or Deposit *-20*	*00*
		For *Automatic Teller*	*20* *00*				Balance *964*	*18*
/	7/31	To *Service Charge*					Payment or Deposit *-5*	*00*
		For *Mch. of July*	*5* *00*				Balance *959*	*18*
		To					Payment or Deposit	
		For					Balance	
		To					Payment or Deposit	
		For					Balance	

To fill out a checkbook register, follow these simple guidelines:

1. Write the preprinted check number in the first column. If you are not writing a check, draw a diagonal slash in this column, or use another distinctive notation.
2. Write the month and day of the transaction in the Date column.
3. Enter the name of the payee on the first line of the Description section. On the second line, if one is provided, write the purpose of the check.
4. Enter the amount of the check, service charge, or other withdrawal in the column headed by a minus sign. If the transaction is a deposit, write this amount in the column headed by a plus sign.
5. Transfer the amount deposited or withdrawn to the top line of the Balance column. Add this amount to or subtract it from the previous

Keep the balance column in your checkbook register up-to-date.

balance, then write the new balance on the second line of the column.

6. The column headed by a check mark is provided so that you can check off each transaction when it appears on your monthly bank statement. The check mark shows that the transaction has been cleared by the bank and is no longer outstanding.

Always keep your checkbook register handy so that you can write down the necessary information at the time each transaction is made. Prompt and correct notations will help you keep track of your personal finances.

RECONCILING YOUR CHECKING ACCOUNT

Statements are provided to check your account.

Financial institutions that offer checking accounts provide customers with a regular (usually monthly) *statement of account*. This statement lists checks received and processed by the bank, plus all other withdrawals and deposits made, service charges, and interest earned.

Most financial institutions return your canceled checks with your bank statement. Canceled checks serve as records of purchases and as proofs of payment. *Check safekeeping* refers to the practice of some financial institutions of not returning canceled checks to the customer. Microcopies are made of the processed checks; the checks themselves are then destroyed by the bank. If necessary, copies of canceled checks may be made from the microform for a small fee.

Reconciling is the process of matching.

The process of matching your checkbook register with the bank statement is known as *reconciliation*. The back of the bank statement is usually printed with a form to aid you in reconciling your account. Figure 7-5 represents both sides of a typical bank statement.

On the left in Figure 7–5 is a simple statement of the bank's record of activity in the checking account. Canceled checks and other types of withdrawals are listed and are subtracted from the balance. Deposits are listed and are added to the balance. Bank service charges are subtracted from the balance, and an ending account balance is given.

It is likely that the balance your checkbook register shows will not be identical to the ending balance shown on the bank statement. In this case, you can reconcile your account by following these guidelines:

Follow the directions on the back of the statement.

1. Use the reconciliation form printed on the back of your bank statement, or prepare your own form.
2. Write the ending balance as shown on the front of the statement.
3. List any deposits made that do not appear on the bank statement (they should be listed in your checkbook register).

Bank Statement
SKY CENTRAL BANK

Ardys Johnson
4250 West 18th Avenue
Chicago, Il 60601-2180

For month ended July 31, 19--:

Checks		Deposits	Balance
	7/1		800.00
32.00	7/1		768.00
36.12	7/5		731.88
22.00	7/8		709.88
	7/15	220.50	930.38
40.00	7/20		890.38
10.00	7/25	400.00	1280.38
1.00 SC*			1279.38
Ending balance			1279.38

*Service charge of 20 cents per check processed

Other charges and deductions: none

Bank Reconciliation

1. Write ending balance as shown on bank statement: _1279.38_

2. Add credits or deposits made that do not appear on statement: _100.00_

3. Total lines 1 and 2: _1,379.38_

4. Write total checks outstanding (not processed): _139.90_

Check No.	Amount
586	14 —
591	30 —
602	85 90
604	10 —

5. Subtract line 4 from line 3 and write balance (should agree with checkbook balance): _1,239.48_

FIGURE 7–5 Bank Reconciliation

4. Add the ending bank balance to the deposits made but not yet entered. Write down this subtotal.
5. List all checks you wrote or other withdrawals you made that do not appear on the bank statement.
6. Subtract the total checks outstanding from the subtotal. This should be the same as the balance shown in your checkbook register.

If your attempt at reconciliation is unsuccessful, check your addition and subtraction. Next, go through your checkbook register and check all addition and subtraction for the period covered by the statement. Finally, make certain that you have deducted service charges from your register balance. If you still cannot reconcile your account, report to the bank for help in discovering where the error lies.

Reconciliation must be done immediately upon receipt of the bank statement. Any errors or differences should be reported to the bank as soon as possible. Occasionally the bank does make an error, which it will be happy to correct if you report the error immediately.

ENDORSEMENTS

It is necessary to endorse a check before cashing it.

A check cannot be cashed until it has been endorsed. To *endorse* a check, the payee named on the face of the check simply signs the back of the check across its left end. There are four types of endorsements: the blank endorsement, the special endorsement, the restrictive endorsement, and the joint endorsement.

Blank Endorsement

A *blank endorsement* is simply the signature of the payee written exactly as his or her name appears on the front of the check.

(Note: If Donald's name had been written incorrectly on the face of the check, he would correct the mistake by endorsing the check with the misspelled version first, then with the correct version of his name.)

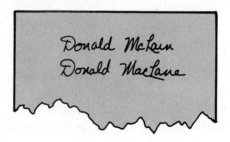

Special Endorsement

A *special endorsement*, or an endorsement in full, is written when the payee signs over a check to a third person. In the following illustration, for example, Donald MacLane uses a check written to him to pay a debt owed to Diana Jones. By using a special endorsement, Donald avoids having to cash the check before repaying Diana. The purpose of the special endorsement, then, is to specifically name the next payee who shall be entitled to cash the check.

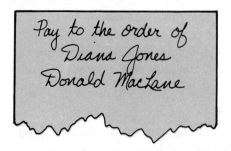

Restrictive Endorsement

A *restrictive endorsement* restricts or limits the use of a check. For example, a check endorsed with the words *For Deposit Only* above the payee's signature can be deposited only to the account specified.

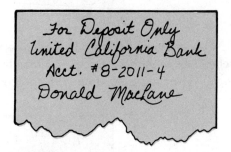

The restrictive endorsement is safer than the blank endorsement for use in mailing deposits, in night deposit systems, or in other circumstances that may result in loss of a check. If a check with a restrictive endorsement is lost, it cannot be cashed by the finder.

Joint Endorsement

A *joint endorsement* is necessary when there is more than one person named as payee on the face of the check. Each payee must endorse the check before it can be cashed.

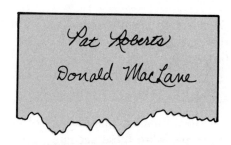

TYPES OF CHECKING ACCOUNTS

There are many types of accounts—both checking and savings—available at banks, savings and loan associations, and credit unions. Savings accounts are discussed in Chapter 9.

Choose your account wisely; costs do vary.

At most financial institutions, you will have a choice between several types of checking accounts. You should carefully study the options, because a wise choice can save you a lot of money. Some current options are the special account, the standard account, the joint account, the interest (NOW) account, the free account, and the share draft account.

Special Accounts

Most banks offer a *special checking account* to customers who will write only a small number of checks each month. No minimum balance is required for this type of account. Service fees may be charged at a low flat rate per month with an additional fee for each check written. These customers also may be charged service fees only when the number of checks written in a month exceeds a set limit. If you write only a few checks each month, this plan might be for you.

Standard Accounts

A *standard account* usually has a set monthly service fee of between $5 and $8, but no per-check fee. Often, if you are able to maintain a minimum balance, you can avoid service fees entirely. Many banks give extra services for this type of account, such as free traveler's checks, a teller machine card, or a free safe-deposit box.

Joint Accounts

A joint account is a survivorship account.

A *joint account* is opened by two or more persons. Such an account is called a *survivorship account* because any person who signs on the account has the right to the entire amount deposited. If one person using the account dies, the other (the survivor) then becomes the sole owner of the funds in the account. All of the accounts discussed in Chapter 7 can be joint accounts.

Interest (NOW) Accounts

Most financial institutions offer what are called *interest checking accounts*. With these accounts, interest is paid if you maintain a certain minimum balance. Minimum amounts may vary greatly among different institutions.

NOW (Negotiable Order of Withdrawal) *accounts* are designed to provide the convenience of a checking account with short-term savings gains. With a NOW account, there are pluses and minuses. This type of account may not be for everyone. While you do receive interest on money deposited in a NOW account, you must put up with certain disadvantages. Minimum balance requirements may be as high as $2,500 or more, for example. If you fall below the minimum balance at any time during the month, you are automatically charged the full service fee, which may be higher than that charged for a standard account. Also, not only are you charged a service fee when your account drops below the minimum balance, but most likely you will not receive any interest for that month.

To earn interest, you need a minimum balance.

Interest rates on NOW accounts, originally set at 5 1/4 percent, are slowly rising to 5 1/2 percent. Keeping money in a low-interest account can cost you money in interest lost because you could have invested elsewhere. NOW accounts vary a great deal among financial institutions; check the options carefully before selecting one.

Free Accounts

Most banks still offer *free checking* (no service fees) if you maintain a minimum balance. These minimum balances may be lower than for NOW accounts, because the bank pays no interest on deposits to free accounts. Free checking is available to senior citizens and to others during special bank promotions, such as the opening of a new bank or branch.

Free accounts are available but limited.

Share Draft Accounts

Most credit unions offer *share draft accounts*. These are checking accounts with no minimum balance requirements, no service fees, and interest payments based on your lowest monthly balance. If you are eligible for credit union membership, this type of account may be the least expensive and most convenient checking method for you.

BANKING SERVICES AND FEES

Many services are
available to depositors.

A *full-service bank* is one that offers every possible kind of service, from checking accounts to credit cards, 24-hour banking machines, safe-deposit boxes, loans, and electronic funds transfers. Some other services commonly offered are certified checks, cashier's checks, money orders, and debit cards. One service that most banks offer is FDIC (Federal Deposit Insurance Corporation) insurance, which protects customers' deposits against loss up to $100,000 per account.

You may choose to deposit your funds—savings or checking—in a full-service bank, a savings bank (such as a savings and loan association), a credit union, or a brokerage account. These are described more fully in Chapter 9 (Saving for the Future).

Checks cashed at banks are cleared through federal reserve banks. A *federal reserve bank* is not open to the public for deposits and transactions—it is a bank for banks. There are 12 federal reserve banks and 25 branches, with approximately 6,000 member banks across the United States. Nearly 80 percent of the nation's demand deposits (checking accounts) are in those banks, which represent less than 50 percent of the total number of banks in the nation. The 12 federal reserve banks are located in San Francisco, Minneapolis, Kansas City, Dallas, Chicago, St. Louis, Cleveland, Atlanta, Boston, New York, Philadelphia, and Richmond. The head offices of the federal reserve banks (the Fed) are in Washington, D.C.

Certified Checks

A *certified check* is a personal check that the bank guarantees or certifies to be good. In effect, the bank puts a hold on that amount in the drawer's account so that the money will be there when the certified check is presented for payment.

Cashier's Checks

A *cashier's check* is a check written by a bank on its own funds. You can pay for a cashier's check through a withdrawal from your savings or checking account, or in cash.

Cashier's checks do
not reveal the identity
of the maker.

Cashier's checks are generally used to pay a person or firm when a cash payment is not desirable. A cashier's check might also be requested instead of a personal check if the payee questions your credit standing. A cashier's check can also be used for transactions in which you wish to remain anonymous, because the bank is listed as the maker of the check, and your identity is not revealed.

Money Orders

Banks sell *money orders* to those who do not wish to use cash or cannot use a check for a transaction. A money order is used like a check, except that it can never bounce. There is a charge for purchasing a money order. This charge ranges from 50 cents to $5 or more, depending on the size of the order.

Debit Cards

Debit cards are like checks—deducted immediately.

Debit cards allow immediate deductions from a checking account to pay for purchases. The debit card is presented at the time of purchase. When the merchant presents the debit card receipt to the bank, the amount of the purchase is immediately deducted from the customer's checking account and paid the merchant. The debit card transaction is similar to writing a check to pay for purchases. The issuing bank may charge an annual fee for the card or a fee for each transaction.

Safe-Deposit Boxes

Guard your valuable documents in a safe-deposit box.

Safe-deposit boxes are available at most financial institutions for a yearly fee that is based on the size of the box. Rental fees may be between $8 and $10 for a small box to $25 or more for a large box. The customer is given two keys for the box and is allowed to store valuables and documents in the box. Private rooms are available for customers to use when opening boxes to add or take away items. Documents commonly kept in safe-deposit boxes are birth certificates, marriage and death certificates, deeds and mortgages, stocks and bonds, contracts, tax returns and receipts, and insurance policies. Jewelry, coin collections, and other small valuables are also commonly stored in safe-deposit boxes. Keeping important papers and other items in a safe-deposit box insures that the items won't be stolen, lost, or destroyed.

Loans and Trusts

Financial institutions also make loans to finance the purchase of cars, homes, vacations, home improvements, and other items. Large banks have loan departments that assist with loans, as well as provide advice for planning estates and trusts. Banks also act as trustees of estates for minors and others.

Bank Credit Cards

You can apply to a full-service bank for a *bank credit card* such as VISA or MasterCard. If you meet the requirements, the card you are issued can be used instead of cash at any business that will accept it. Banks offering national credit cards usually charge an annual fee for use of the card, as well as charge interest on the unpaid account balance.

Electronic Funds Transfers

Cash withdrawals can be done electronically.

Certain transactions, such as the paying of bills, can be made through an *electronic funds transfer*, using an automated teller machine and an automated teller card. Customers may make cash withdrawals from any of their accounts; make cash advances from their bank's VISA or Master-Card account; make deposits to any of their accounts; make payments on loans; and transfer funds from their accounts to pay their credit card, utility, and retail store account bills. With a Touch-Tone telephone, customers can check balances and pay bills from their homes or offices.

Stop Payment Orders

A *stop payment order* is a request that the bank not cash or process a specific check. The usual reasons for stopping payment are that the check has been lost or stolen. By issuing a stop payment order, the drawer can safely write a new check, knowing that the original check cannot be cashed if it is presented to the bank. Most banks charge a fee (usually $5 or more) for stopping payment on a check.

Bank Fees

Banks make loans from customers' deposits.

Customers' savings and deposits are the bank's primary sources of money for loans. Bank assets also come from demand deposits, from stockholders' investments, and from investments made by the bank. In addition, banks charge fees to their customers to cover costs of operation. For example, when you apply for a loan and it is granted, you are charged a loan fee. When a bank acts as a trustee, it charges a fee for this service.

Banks also charge noncustomers for services such as check cashing. If you want to cash a check at a bank where you do not have an account, the bank may charge you a fee for this service. Nondepositors pay for other services that may be free to depositors, such as traveler's checks, certified checks, and notary services.

VOCABULARY

Directions: Can you find the definition for each of the following terms used in Chapter 7?

reconciliation
blank endorsement
restrictive endorsement
payee
drawer, maker
checking account
NSF check (overdraft)
checkbook register
canceled checks

special endorsement (endorsement in full)
stop payment order
federal reserve bank
floating a check
drafts
certified check
demand deposit

1. The person to whom a check is made payable.

2. A banking term to designate that there are insufficient funds to cover a check that has been written.

3. To have payment stopped on a check after the check is lost.

4. To compare your checkbook register with the bank statement each month.

5. Checks that have been processed by the bank and returned to you.

6. An endorsement that consists only of the payee's signature.

7. An endorsement, such as the words *For Deposit Only*, that restricts use of the check.

8. Your personal record of checking account transactions.

9. The person who writes a check, paying money to another person.

10. An endorsement signing a check over to a third party.

11. A check guaranteed by the bank to be good.

12. A type of bank account that allows you to withdraw your money at will.

13. A banking service in which money is deposited and checks written.

14. A form of check for withdrawing money from a demand account.

15. Writing a check on an account that doesn't have enough money in it at the time you write the check.

16. A bank that serves to clear checks for regular banks.

ITEMS FOR DISCUSSION

1. What are reasons for having a checking account?

2. What responsibilities do customers (depositors) have when using a checking account?

3. Why is a checking account called a demand deposit?

4. Explain what is meant by the phrase *floating a check*.

5. What is a canceled check, and why is it important to a depositor?

6. Why do you need to reconcile your checking account promptly when you receive the monthly bank statement?

7. List at least four banking services provided by financial institutions.

8. Why would you be asked your mother's maiden name when opening a bank account?

9. What is a survivorship checking account?

APPLICATIONS

1. List the names, addresses, and telephone numbers of five financial institutions in your geographic location, and list the services provided by each.

2. Using Figure 7–2 (check) as an example and following the rules on pages 110-111, write these checks:
   (a) Check No. 12 to Dennis Apply for $34.44, written today
   (b) Check No. 322 to Save-Now Stores for $18.01, written today
   (c) Check No. 484 to A. P. Smith for $91.10, written today

3. Using Figure 7–3 (deposit slip) as an example and following the rules on page 111, prepare these deposit slips:
   (a) Today's date; currency $40.00; coins $1.44; Check No. 18-88 for $51.00; no cash retained
   (b) Today's date; Check No. 40-22 for $300.00 and Check No. 24-12 for $32.00; $20.00 cash retained

4. Determine your ending reconciled checkbook balance if all of the following six conditions exist:
   (a) Your ending checkbook balance is $311.40 (before the service fee is deducted).
   (b) You made an error, resulting in $30.00 less showing in your account than should be.

(c) The service fee is $6.00.

(d) The ending bank balance is $402.00.

(e) Outstanding deposits total $100.00.

(f) Outstanding checks total $166.60.

5. Determine your ending reconciled checkbook balance if all of the following six conditions exist:

(a) Your checkbook ending balance is $800.40 (before the service fee is deducted).

(b) The service fee is $3.00.

(c) The ending bank balance is $1,100.00.

(d) Outstanding deposits total $50.00.

(e) Outstanding checks total $352.60.

6. List four types of endorsements and give a written example of each.

7. Write out on plain paper the appropriate information needed for a signature card, as shown in Figure 7–1.

8. List the banking services you would like to have when you open a checking account.

9. Which type of account will you choose? Why?

CASE PROBLEMS AND ACTIVITIES

1. Find the errors in the following check:

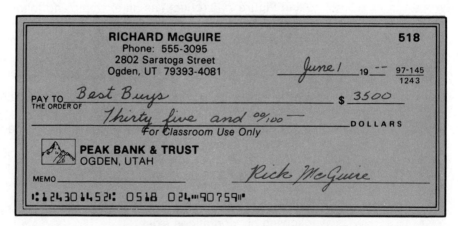

2. A bank reconciliation form and a checkbook register are shown on page 125. Using a separate piece of paper, complete the bank reconciliation form by first finishing the checkbook register and entering the service charge and then computing balances.

ITEM NO.	DATE	PAYMENT ISSUED TO OR DESCRIPTION OF DEPOSIT		AMOUNT OF PAYMENT		✓	(−) CHECK FEE (IF ANY)	AMOUNT OF DEPOSIT		BALANCE FORWARD	
										100	*00*
101	*3/1*	To	*Grocery Mart*	24	75					Payment or Deposit	*24*	*75*
		For	*Groceries*							Balance	*75*	*25*
102	*3/3*	To	*Independent Phone Co.*	13	00					Payment or Deposit	*13*	*00*
		For	*Tel. charges*							Balance		
	3/5	To	*Deposit*					30	00	Payment or Deposit	*30*	*00*
		For								Balance		
103	*3/8*	To	*Local High School*							Payment or Deposit	*10*	*00*
		For	*Band Donation*	10	00					Balance		
104	*3/10*	To	*Alan's Bakery*							Payment or Deposit	*3*	*80*
		For	*Bread*	3	80					Balance		
105	*3/15*	To	*Grocery Mart*							Payment or Deposit	*18*	*20*
		For	*Groceries*	18	20					Balance		
	3/18	To	*Deposit*					42	00	Payment or Deposit	*42*	*00*
		For								Balance		
106	*3/20*	To	*Acme Hardware*							Payment or Deposit	*4*	*18*
		For	*Hammer*	4	18					Balance		

PLEASE BE SURE TO DEDUCT ANY PER ITEM CHARGES OR SERVICE CHARGES THAT MAY APPLY TO YOUR ACCOUNT.

BANK STATEMENT
Hometown Bank

For month ended March 31, 19--

Beginning balance $100.00

Checks cashed		Deposits	Date	Balance
$24.75			3/7	$75.25
13.00		$30.00	3/8	92.25
10.00	$3.80		3/11	78.45
1.20 SC				77.25
Ending balance $77.25				

BANK RECONCILIATION

Ending balance as shown on bank statement $ _____

Add deposits not shown on bank statement $ _____

_____   _____

Subtract checks written but not shown on bank statement   _____

_____   _____

Adjusted balance (should be same as ending balance in checkbook) $ _____

8

Federal Income Tax

CHAPTER OBJECTIVES

After studying this chapter and completing the activities, you will be able to:

1. Understand the purpose of taxes, different types of taxes, and the history of taxes in the United States.
2. Define and show a working knowledge of exemptions, dependents, and taxable and nontaxable income when preparing tax returns.
3. Prepare Forms 1040EZ and 1040A U.S. Individual Income Tax Returns.

OUR TAX SYSTEM

In the democratic, free enterprise society found in the United States, money is collected by the government from citizens and companies in the form of taxes. This money, or *revenue*, is redistributed according to needs and priorities determined by Congress. The largest source of government revenue is income taxes. Other taxes providing government revenue include social security tax, unemployment insurance tax, inheritance and estate tax, automobile license tax, driver's license fees, motel and hotel room tax, long-distance telephone call excise tax, business license tax, import duties, gasoline tax, liquor and tobacco tax, utility tax, and personal property tax.

Income taxes are the largest source of government revenue.

There are three basic types of taxes in the United States. *Progressive taxes* are those that increase in proportion to income. Income taxes are progressive taxes. *Regressive taxes* are those that decrease in proportion to income increases. Sales taxes are regressive taxes, because those who

Income taxes are progressive taxes.

ILLUSTRATION 8–1
Federal taxes collected provide national parks for all citizens.

Credit: Photo courtesy of Ben Humphries.

can least afford to pay the tax (the poor) are assessed the greatest amount in proportion to their income. *Proportional taxes* are those for which the tax rate remains constant, regardless of the amount of income. Property taxes (called ad valorem taxes) are proportional taxes, because all those owning property of a certain value pay the same tax.

Taxes provide services for everyone.

Taxes collected are used to provide services such as education; parks and recreation; streets and roads; and police, fire, and health departments on a local level. On a national level taxes provide salaries for Congress and funds for national defense, highways, parks, welfare, foreign aid, and other services. Most of the services (local, state, and national) are provided for the general welfare of all citizens, although individual citizens may not benefit directly. For instance, through national student loan and grant programs, the entire country benefits because many of its citizens are able to obtain college educations, which increase the quality of the country's work force.

HISTORY OF TAXES

For many years the United States operated without an income tax. Many of the new inhabitants came to America to avoid taxation, and the new society was careful to avoid it. While our country was a colony of England, the British government imposed certain taxes. However, when the Revolutionary War brought independence, there was no direct income tax imposed on citizens. The Constitution drawn in 1787 included the option to tax, but not to tax individuals directly. Excise taxes and customs duties produced enough revenue to meet the nation's needs at that time.

But while taxes were not levied against citizens by the government, the government also did not provide services for the citizens. Such was the case until the mid-1850s.

The Revolutionary War was financed by contributions from sympathetic countries such as France. The War of 1812 brought a temporary income tax; but when the war debts were paid, the tax was dropped.

Temporary income taxes paid for wars.

When the Civil War became an economic burden, the introduction of an income tax to finance the war became necessary. In 1862 President Lincoln signed into law a bill that provided for progressive income taxes on wages earned to pay off war debts; the tax then expired. Congress introduced the first permanent income tax in the form of the 16th Amendment to the Constitution in 1909. The amendment was ratified by three-fourths of the states by 1913. Only nominal taxes were levied as a result of the 16th Amendment.

World War I (1917) cost $35 billion, paid for by taxes. The country prospered until the Great Depression of 1929. At that time the government was providing few services, and many people suffered badly without help from the government. But President Roosevelt's New Deal again brought prosperity through taxation and redistribution of income. In 1935 the Social Security Act was signed into law, creating the *Internal Revenue Service* (IRS). The IRS was designed to collect taxes and turn them over to the government for the payment of debts, commitments, and benefits. Money withheld from wages for social security is deposited with the U.S. Department of the Treasury.

During World War II taxes were increased to finance the war. This increase set a precedent for the increasing tax rates we know today. Rates are increased to pay for the growing services and needs of the government.

The IRS

The Internal Revenue Service is an administrative agency of the Department of the Treasury. The IRS has its headquarters in Washington, D.C., with seven regional offices throughout the country. Each regional office is a major data processing center that oversees at least ten district and local offices. The main functions of the IRS are to collect income taxes and enforce tax laws.

The IRS collects taxes.

In addition to collecting income taxes, the IRS performs a number of other services. In local offices, IRS employees assist taxpayers in finding information and forms. The IRS prints brochures and pamphlets to aid taxpayers in preparing their returns. Tax information and instruction booklets are furnished free to schools and colleges by the IRS. Auditors employed by the IRS examine returns selected for audit based on a computer check procedure.

The Power to Tax

Congress has the power to raise taxes.

The power to levy taxes rests with the Congress of the United States. The Constitution provides that "all bills for raising revenue shall originate in the House of Representatives." Proposals to increase or decrease taxes may come from the president, the Department of the Treasury, or from a congressman representing the interests of a geographic group of people. The House Ways and Means Committee studies the proposals and makes recommendations to the full House. Revenue bills must pass a vote in both the House and the Senate and then be signed by the president before they become law.

The Presidential Election Campaign Fund was established by Congress so that all taxpayers could share equally in the costs of election campaigns. This method of campaign financing makes it possible for all presidential candidates to compete for votes without taking large donations from minority interests, such as large corporations, unions, or wealthy individuals. When a taxpayer wishes to contribute $1 to the Presidential Election Campaign Fund, the dollar comes from taxes already withheld. Income taxes are not increased for the individual. You can elect to contribute to the Presidential Election Campaign Fund by checking the appropriate box on your tax return.

Paying Your Fair Share

Income taxes are based on ability to pay

The ability to pay is the basic principle behind the tax laws of this country. Our income tax is a graduated rate—the more income you receive, the more income tax you pay. Tax rates range from 14 to 50 percent of net income for individuals.

Our income tax system is based on *voluntary compliance*, which means that all citizens are expected to prepare (or have prepared) and file income tax returns. Taxes owed are due on or before the deadline of April 15 of each year. Responsibility for filing a tax return and paying taxes due rests with the individual. Failure to do so can result in penalty, interest charges on the taxes owed, fine, and/or imprisonment. Willful failure to pay taxes is called *tax evasion*, which is a felony.

The Federal Debt

In 1980 the federal government spent $60.9 billion more than it collected. **Deficit spending** occurs when the government spends more money than it collects. To pay for the deficit, the government borrows money. Corporations and individuals buy bonds (such as U.S. savings bonds) or Treasury bills, which are, in effect, loans to the government. In 1980 the total federal debt passed the $1 trillion mark. The national debt continues to grow by approximately $200 billion a year.

Government bonds are loans to the government.

DEFINITION OF TERMS

Before you can understand how to prepare tax forms, you need a working knowledge of the tax vocabulary. The terms described in the following paragraphs are found on income tax returns, in IRS instruction booklets, and on forms and schedules you will work with.

Filing Status

There are four different ways to file a tax return: (*a*) as a single person (not married), (*b*) as a married person filing a joint return (even though only one spouse may have earned income), (*c*) as a married person filing a separate return, or (*d*) as a "head of household." (A person may qualify as a head of household whether married or single if certain conditions are met in providing a residence for persons dependent on the taxpayer.) You mark your filing status on the front of the tax form. Tax rates vary according to the status claimed (see the tax tables). A more complete description of these classifications is found in IRS instruction booklets. After you file your first tax return, you will automatically receive these information and form booklets in the mail each year for use in preparing your tax returns.

Filing status determines which tax table is used.

Exemptions

An *exemption* is an allowance a taxpayer claims for each person dependent on the taxpayer's income. Each taxpayer is automatically allowed one exemption for self, an additional exemption if over age 65, and an additional exemption if blind. The same exemption allowances may be taken for spouses of taxpayers.

Each exemption claimed on the income tax form excludes a certain amount ($1,000 in 1984; $1,040 in 1985) from a person's taxable income. You cannot claim an exemption on your tax return for a person claimed on another tax return. For example, two children may share the expense for taking care of an aging parent. Only the child who contributed more

The amount of personal exemption changes occasionally.

than half for the parent's care may claim the exemption. The only exception to the rule is for a student attending school full-time, until age 22.
Students may claim themselves, and the students' parents may claim
them as well.

Dependents other than the spouse and children in the household may
include children from a previous marriage. The taxpayer claiming exemption for children from a previous marriage must have contributed more
than half of the funds for their support. The parent who contributes $100
a month or more per child (or by written decree or agreement) claims the
exemption. The burden is on the custodial parent to prove that he or she
spent $1,200 or more a year for each child's support in order to claim the
exemption.

Other persons who qualify as dependents of a taxpayer include parents, grandparents, stepchildren, or other relatives who did not have
income of over $1,000 during the year. To qualify as dependents, these
people must receive more than half their support from the taxpayer.

Gross Income

Gross income is all the taxable income you receive, including wages,
tips, salaries, interest, dividends, unemployment compensation, alimony,
and so forth. Certain types of income are not taxable and are not reported
as income, such as child support, gifts, inheritances, scholarships, social
security payments received, life insurance benefits, veterans benefits,
and workers' compensation benefits.

Wages, Salaries, and Tips. These items are moneys received through
employment, as shown on the Form W-2, Wage and Tax Statement supplied by the employer each year.

Interest Income. Interest earned on savings accounts, certificates of
deposit, and loans to others is taxable. This income must be included on
your tax return.

Dividend Income. Dividends are moneys paid from profits to stockholders of a corporation. Dividends are taxable, although on certain qualifying dividends there is an *exclusion* of $100 for single taxpayers or $200
for married taxpayers filing jointly (1984). Exclusion means the first $100
or $200 of dividends received during the year is not taxable (with certain
exceptions explained in the tax instruction booklets).

Unemployment Compensation. Payments you receive while unemployed may be partly taxable. If you receive $12,000 (single status) or

Unemployment compensation may be taxable.

$18,000 (married filing jointly), which includes some unemployment compensation payments, you must fill out a separate schedule to compute your tax liability.

Social Security. Beginning in 1984, some social security benefits become taxable income. If social security benefits are taxable, the taxpayer must use Form 1040 (long form). If you are single and your adjusted gross income, plus any interest income that is exempt from federal tax, plus one half of your net social security benefits, is more than $25,000, you must pay taxes on one half of your social security benefits. (If you are married, it becomes $32,000.) Social security recipients receive Form SSA-1099 reporting total benefits paid during the year. This form needs to be attached to the income tax return.

Child Support. Money paid to a former spouse for support of dependent children is called *child support*. This income is not taxable for the one receiving it, nor is child support deductible for the one paying it.

Alimony. Money paid to support a former spouse is called *alimony*. It is taxable for the person receiving it and deductible for the person paying it. (The long Form 1040 is required.)

Deductions

Keep receipts for your deductions.

Deductions are expenses the law allows the taxpayer to subtract from gross income. The full dollar amount may be deducted for medical expenses, state and local taxes, property taxes, interest on home mortgages and credit purchases, union dues, and casualty and theft losses. For contributions to charities and religious organizations, you are limited to a deduction of 25 percent of the amount given or a maximum of $75. When subtracted from gross income, deductions reduce taxable income. Personal deductions are listed on Schedule A of Form 1040. Persons who file the short Form 1040A or 1040EZ cannot itemize deductions. You can, however, take advantage of some deductions, as will be shown later in this chapter.

Zero Bracket Amount

The *zero bracket amount* is the minimum dollar amount of deductions you need before it is worth it to you to itemize your deductions. Single persons should not itemize unless their deductions total more than $2,300 in 1984 and $2,390 in 1985; married persons, $3,400 in 1984 and

There are different tax forms to choose from.

$3,540 in 1985; and married persons filing separately, $1,700. Because tax tables begin at these zero bracket amounts, the standard deduction automatically allows for these amounts. In other words, if you file a short Form 1040A or 1040EZ, these minimum deduction amounts are automatically included. Only if your deductions exceed these minimum amounts is it profitable to itemize.

PREPARING TO FILE

Once income and expense records are ready, you can rough draft your tax return. You should also study the tax booklet that accompanies the printed tax forms. The booklet gives you the latest tax information, tax laws that have passed, and new information you may need to prepare your tax return. Read the tax return carefully to be sure you are taking advantage of every possible deduction and are reporting all taxable income. A simple 1040EZ tax return may require only 15 minutes to prepare; the long form 1040 may require several days after all information has been gathered. In addition to a federal tax return, you may have to file a state income tax return.

Who Must File

You must file a tax return if:

You must file if you earn a certain amount.

1. You are single, under age 65, and earn at least $3,300. You are single, age 65 or older, and earn at least $4,300.
2. You are married, filing a joint return, both you and your spouse are under age 65, and together you earn at least $5,400.
   You are married, filing a joint return, you or your spouse is age 65 or older, and together you earn at least $6,400.
   You are married, filing a joint return, both you and your spouse are 65 or older, and together you earn at least $7,400.
3. You are married, filing a separate return, and earn at least $1,000.
4. You were claimed as a dependent on your parents' tax return, but you had dividends, interest, or other unearned income of at least $1,000.
5. You are self-employed and earn at least $400.
6. You owe taxes, such as social security, that were not withheld during the year.

Persons who did not earn enough to owe taxes, but who had taxes withheld from their paychecks, should file a return to reclaim moneys withheld. If you do not file, you will not get a refund.

When to File

You must file no later than April 15 of the year after you earned income. If April 15 falls on a weekend or holiday, your tax return is due on the next regular weekday. If you file late, you are subject to penalties and interest charges.

Short Form or Long Form

You must decide whether to fill out a short form (1040A or 1040EZ) or to itemize your deductions, using the long form (1040).

Most students use
Form 1040EZ.

1. *Use Form 1040EZ* if you are single; you have only your own exemption; you have no dependents; your income is from wages, salaries, and tips; your interest income is $400 or less; you have no dividend income; and your taxable income is less than $50,000. You can claim a partial charitable contributions deduction, but no tax credits.

2. *Use Form 1040A* if your deductions do not exceed zero bracket amounts; your income is from wages, salaries, tips, interest and dividends (no maximums), and unemployment compensation; and your taxable income is less than $50,000. You can claim a partial charitable contributions deduction, IRA payments, the marital deduction, partial credit for political contributions, credit for child and dependent care expenses, and earned income credit. You may file under any of the four filing statuses, claim all exemptions you are entitled to, and claim all qualified dependents.

3. *Use Form 1040* if you wish to itemize deductions; you can claim adjustments to income (such as alimony or business expenses); you claim credits not available on 1040EZ or 1040A; you have income such as capital gains, self-employment income, or other business income that cannot be listed on short forms; you need to fill out any other forms or schedules that must be attached to your return; or you have taxable income of $50,000 or more.

Where to Begin

Everyone who works
must pay social secu-
rity taxes.

During the year, save all receipts and proofs of payment for your itemized deductions. You will need these receipts to prove the accuracy of your tax return if you are audited. Save all employee withholding records. When you receive your Form W-2, Wage and Tax Statement from each of your employers (by January 31), compare it with your records and check it for accuracy. Any discrepancy between the Form W-2 and your records should be reported immediately to the employer and corrected. Social security tax withholding rates are scheduled as follows:

YEAR	MAXIMUM AMOUNT OF EARNINGS	RATE	MAXIMUM TAX
1984	$37,500 (employer)*	7.00%	$2,646.00
	37,800 (employee)*	6.70	2,532.60
1985	39,600	7.05	2,791.80
1986	40,800**	7.15	2,917.20
1987	42,900**	7.15	3,067.35
1988	45,300**	7.51	3,402.03
1989	48,000**	7.51	3,604.80
1990	51,000**	7.65	3,901.50

*Employers paid the full 7.0 percent in 1984; employees paid 6.7 percent.
**Estimated.

It is wise to prepare your tax return early—as soon as you receive your Form W-2 (Wage and Tax Statement), 1099-INT (Statement for Recipients of Interest Income) forms from banks and savings institutions, 1099-UC (Statement for Recipients of Unemployment Compensation Payments) forms, and can gather all other necessary information. If you owe additional taxes, mail your return and the amount due in sufficient time to have the envelope postmarked by April 15. If you have a refund coming, the sooner you file, the sooner you will receive it. If you wait until April, your refund may be delayed for months. You will not receive interest on refunds.

Mail your tax return no later than April 15.

Once you have gathered all your information, prepare both the short and the long form to determine whether you can save money by itemizing deductions. Read all directions carefully and fill out all schedules completely.

If you do not have enough taxes withheld during the year, and you owe the government more than $100 when taxes are due, you may be subject to a penalty and have to increase withholdings for the next year. If you receive a large refund, you should increase your exemption status to have less withheld during the year.

You can amend your tax return.

If you discover you made an error in a tax return after it has been filed, you may file an amended return (Form 1040X) in order to claim a refund or credit, or to pay additional tax due.

Save copies of the tax returns you file, together with all supporting evidence (receipts) for six years. Tax returns should be kept in a safe-deposit box, together with copies of W-2s and other supporting information.

PREPARING INCOME TAX RETURNS

The federal income tax return must be completed in ink or typed with no errors or omissions. The booklets provided by the IRS have line-by-line instructions that explain each section and type of income or deduction. The preparation of tax returns is a simple process of following directions and inserting appropriate information. An unsigned tax return will be returned to the taxpayer before a refund is issued. If a joint return is prepared, both spouses must sign it.

Form 1040EZ

Line-by-line instructions for filling out the 1984 Form 1040EZ are given on the back of the form. Highlights of the instructions are described in the following paragraphs.

Step 1: Name and Address. Fill in your name, address, and social security number. Check the Yes box if you want $1 to go to the Presidential Election Campaign Fund.

Step 2: Tax Computation. On line 1 enter your total wages, salaries, and tips, as shown on your W-2 form(s). On line 2 enter interest earned on savings accounts (cannot be more than $400). Add lines 1 and 2, and enter the total on line 3.

Some deductions are allowed on the 1040EZ.

Line 4 is for your charitable contributions. Your deduction is limited to 25 percent of your contributions to qualified organizations. The amount on line 4 may not be more than $75 ($37.50 for a married couple filing separately). Line 4 is subtracted from line 3, and the difference is entered on line 5.

Your personal exemption (line 6) is $1,000 for 1984. Subtract $1,000 from the amount on line 5. The result is your taxable income (line 7).

On line 8 enter the total federal tax withheld (as shown on your W-2 forms). On line 9 enter the tax you owe based on your taxable income. Look up the amount of your taxable income and the amount of tax you owe in the tax tables.

Step 3: Refund or Amount You Owe. If the amount of federal taxes withheld (line 8) is larger than the amount of tax you owe shown on line 9, you will receive a refund. Enter the amount due you on line 10. If you owe more tax than was withheld (line 9 is greater than line 8), you must pay the difference. Enter the amount you must pay on line 11. Write a check to the Internal Revenue Service and attach it to your return.

Tax returns must be
signed.

Sign your return. Make sure your W-2 form(s) and check (if applicable) are attached to the completed return, and mail the return to the nearest regional IRS office.

Form 1040A

Form 1040A is printed on four pages. Line-by-line instructions for completing the 1984 1040A are available in the booklet "Instructions for Preparing 1984 1040EZ and 1040A." Instructions as to who may and may not use the form are also in the booklet. The following steps will guide you through the completion of Form 1040A.

Step 1. Name and Address. The first section requires writing in the name, address, social security number, and occupation of persons filing the return. Each person filing can elect to give or not to give to the Presidential Election Campaign Fund.

Use the preprinted
label.

Step 2. Filing Status. In this section, you select your tax filing status. Choices of filing status are: single, married filing jointly, married filing separately, or unmarried head of household.

Step 3. Exemptions. Lines 5a through 5e provide space to declare your exemptions. You claim yourself and your spouse if you are filing jointly. If you or your spouse is over 65 and/or blind, you may take additional exemptions (up to six). Names of your dependent children who live with you are entered on line c. Other dependents are listed on line d. Persons listed as other dependents must meet these tests for dependency: must not earn over $1,000; must receive more than half of their support from you; and must be related to you. The total number of exemptions is entered on line e.

Step 4. Total Income. Lines 6 through 10 are used for listing income. On line 6, you enter wages, salaries, tips, and other income as shown on a Form W-2 which you will attach to the tax return. Line 7 is used for interest income on savings. If you have over $400 in interest, you must list the name of each payer and the amount on Schedule 1. Line 8 is used for income from stock dividends. Again, if you have over $400 in dividends, each source must be listed separately on Schedule 1. The total dividend income is entered on Line 8a. The exclusion (amount not subject to tax) entered on line 8b is a maximum of $100 for single taxpayers, and $200 for married filing jointly (regardless of which spouse owned the stock). When line 8b is subtracted from 8a, the result is entered on line 8c.

Line 9 is used for unemployment compensation income. Form 1099-G which shows the amount of unemployment compensation received during the year must be attached. Some or all of the unemployment compensation earnings may be taxable. On line 9b you enter the amount of unemployment compensation that is taxable (the instruction booklet provides a worksheet). Basically, if your income exceeds $12,000 (single) or $18,000 (married filing jointly), you will be taxed. The total income is entered on line 10.

Step 5. Adjusted Gross Income. On line 11a, you can deduct contributions to an IRA. Each employed worker who earns at least $2,000 can contribute up to $2,000 toward an IRA. A spouse not working can add $250 to the couple's IRA for a total of $2,250. A married couple, both employed, can contribute a maximum of $4,000. On line 11b, you must report IRA contributions made in 1985 (up to April 15). Line 12 is used for the marital deduction for couples in which both spouses work. The marital deduction allows a couple to deduct 10 percent of the lesser of the two incomes. Part III of Schedule 1 is completed, and the total is entered on line 12. Line 13 is the total of these adjustments to income. Line 13 is then subtracted from line 10. The difference is your *adjusted gross income*.

Married couples get a tax break.

Step 6. Taxable Income. Lines 15 to 19 are used for computing taxable income. First, the adjusted gross income (from line 14) is brought forward to line 15. Then you enter the amount of your allowable charitable contributions and subtract. Line 17 is the net amount. The number of exemptions you claimed on line 5e is multiplied by $1,000. This total is entered on line 18 and subtracted from line 17. Your adjusted gross income minus charitable contributions and exemptions is your *taxable income*. Enter this amount on line 19.

Step 7. Figuring Taxes, Credits, and Payments. This section is used for entering the amount of *tax liability* which is the amount of taxes due from you based on your taxable income, and credits due you. To find the amount of tax due, consult the tax tables in the instructions booklet and enter on line 20. On line 21a you may claim any credit due for child care expenses. Complete Part IV to determine the credit amount. On line 21b, you get partial credit for political contributions (maximum of one half of your contribution but not more than $50 for single taxpayers and $100 for marrieds filing jointly). Lines 21a and b are added and entered on line 22. Then subtract line 22 (credits) from line 20 (tax liability) and enter your total tax on line 23.

Tax liability is based on taxable income.

On line 24a enter the amount of federal income tax withheld shown on your W-2 form which you will attach to the tax return. Line 24b is used for earned income credit (EIC) for people who have a child, but income of less than $10,000. EIC can be as much as $500. Lines 24a and b are added together. This amount is your total payment and is entered on line 25.

Step 8. Refund or Amount Owed. If line 25 is larger than line 23, then the difference is your refund, and it is entered on line 26. But if line 23 is larger than line 25, you owe money to the government. Enter this amount on line 27. The check for the amount owed must be attached to your tax return.

Each taxpayer must sign the return.

Step 9. Signature. In this section, taxpayer and spouse must both sign a joint return even though only one may have earned or received income. Anyone who was paid to prepare your tax return for you also signs and dates the return.

Sample Tax Returns

Figure 8-1 shows John Calhoun's Form W-2, Wage and Tax Statement. Figure 8-2 shows his completed Form 1040EZ tax return. Mr. Calhoun is single and claims one exemption. His wages are found on the W-2 slip, which he previously checked for accuracy. John earned $134 in interest on his savings account and gave $100 in charitable contributions.

FIGURE 8-1
Sample W-2
Wage and Tax
Statement

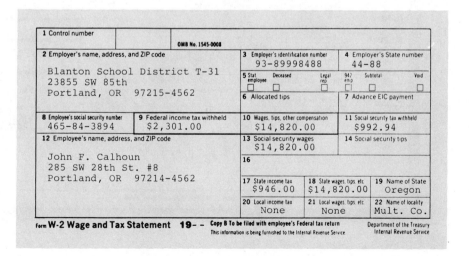

Department of the Treasury · Internal Revenue Service
Form 1040EZ Income Tax Return for
19--   **Single filers with no dependents**   OMB No. 1545-0675

Name & address

Use the IRS mailing label. If you don't have one, please print:

Please print your numbers like this.

| 1 | 2 | 3 | 4 | 5 | 6 | 7 | 8 | 9 | 0 |

▶ John F. Colhoun
Print your name above (first, initial, last)

285 SW 28th St. Apt. 8
Present home address (number and street)

Portland, OR 97214-4562
City, town, or post office, State, and ZIP code

Social security number

| 4 | 6 | 5 | 8 | 4 | 3 | 8 | 9 | 4 |

Presidential Election Campaign Fund
Check box if you want $1 of your tax to go to this fund. ▶

[✓]   **Dollars   Cents**

Figure your tax

1   Total wages, salaries, and tips. This should be shown in Box 10 of your W-2 form(s). (Attach your W-2 form(s).)   1   **14,820.00**

2   Interest income of $400 or less. If the total is more than $400, you cannot use Form 1040EZ.   2   **134.00**

Attach Copy B of Form(s) W-2 here

3   Add line 1 and line 2. This is your **adjusted gross income.**   3   **14,954.00**
4   Allowable part of your charitable contributions. Complete the worksheet on page 21 of the instruction booklet. Do not enter more than $75.   4   **25.00**

5   Subtract line 4 from line 3.   5   **14,929.00**

6   Amount of your personal exemption.   6   **1,000.00**

7   Subtract line 6 from line 5. This is your **taxable income.**   7   **13,929.00**

8   Enter your Federal income tax withheld. This should be shown in Box 9 of your W-2 form(s).   8   **2,301.00**
9   Use the **single** column in the tax table on pages 31-36 of the instruction booklet to find the **tax** on your taxable income on line 7. Enter the amount of tax.   9   **1,786.00**

Refund or amount you owe

10 If line 8 is larger than line 9, subtract line 9 from line 8. Enter the **amount of your refund.**   10   **515.00**
11 If line 9 is larger than line 8, subtract line 8 from line 9. Enter the **amount you owe.** Attach check or money order for the full amount, payable to "Internal Revenue Service."   11

Attach tax payment here

Sign your return

I have read this return. Under penalties of perjury, I declare that to the best of my knowledge and belief, the return is true, correct, and complete.

Your signature   Date

John F. Calhoun   4/15/--

For IRS Use Only—Please do not write in boxes below.

| 1 | 2 | 3 | 4 | 5 |

For Privacy Act and Paperwork Reduction Act Notice, see page 41.

FIGURE 8-2   Sample 1040EZ Return

On the tax tables, John locates $13,929 (taxable income–line 7) in the Single column. His tax liability, based on his taxable income, is $1,786. When John's tax liability is subtracted from taxes withheld (line 8), the difference is $515. The amount of tax withheld is greater by $515 than John's tax liability; so he should receive a refund for that amount.

Married persons filing jointly may choose to file Form 1040A or Form 1040. Figures 8-3A and 8-3B show the Wage and Tax Statements for Michael J. and Melissa B. Anderson. Figure 8-4 is their joint return (1040A). The Andersons could not file 1040EZ because they are married.

FIGURE 8-3A
Sample W-2 Wage and Tax Statement, Michael J. Anderson

1 Control number	OMB No. 1545-0008	
2 Employer's name, address, and ZIP code A Art Studios 48 East 11th Street Des Plaines, IL 60601-3132	3 Employer's identification number 91-4813141	4 Employer's State number .33-261
	5 Stat. employee / Deceased / Legal rep. / 942 emp / Subtotal / Void	
	6 Allocated tips	7 Advance EIC payment
8 Employee's social security number 323-40-6128 / 9 Federal income tax withheld $1,591.00	10 Wages, tips, other compensation $11,028.60	11 Social security tax withheld $738.92
12 Employee's name, address, and ZIP code Michael J. Anderson 312 East 34th Street Chicago, IL 60604-5214	13 Social security wages $11,028.60	14 Social security tips
	16	
	17 State income tax / 18 State wages, tips, etc.	19 Name of State
	20 Local income tax / 21 Local wages, tips, etc.	22 Name of locality

Form W-2 Wage and Tax Statement 19-- Copy B To be filed with employee's Federal tax return
This information is being furnished to the Internal Revenue Service.
Department of the Treasury
Internal Revenue Service

FIGURE 8-3B
Sample W-2 Wage and Tax Statement, Melissa B. Anderson

1 Control number	OMB No. 1545-0008	
2 Employer's name, address, and ZIP code A & W Welding Supply 85 West Bensington Blvd Chicago, IL 60615-2358	3 Employer's identification number 92-186848	4 Employer's State number 33-261
	5 Stat. employee / Deceased / Legal rep. / 942 emp / Subtotal / Void	
	6 Allocated tips	7 Advance EIC payment
8 Employee's social security number 411-86-3214 / 9 Federal income tax withheld $1,611.00	10 Wages, tips, other compensation $12,811.40	11 Social security tax withheld $858.38
12 Employee's name, address, and ZIP code Melissa B. Anderson 312 East 34th Street Chicago, IL 60604-5214	13 Social security wages $12,811.40	14 Social security tips
	16	
	17 State income tax / 18 State wages, tips, etc.	19 Name of State
	20 Local income tax / 21 Local wages, tips, etc.	22 Name of locality

Form W-2 Wage and Tax Statement 19-- Copy B To be filed with employee's Federal tax return
This information is being furnished to the Internal Revenue Service.
Department of the Treasury
Internal Revenue Service

Department of the Treasury — Internal Revenue Service

19-- **Form 1040A US Individual Income Tax Return**   OMB No. 1545-0085

Step 1
Name and
address

Use the IRS mailing label. If you don't have one, print or type:

Your first name and initial (if joint return, also give spouse's name and initial)	Last name	Your social security no.
Melissa B and Michael J	*Anderson*	*411-86-3214*

Present home address (number and street)   Spouse's social security no.
312 East 34th Street   *323-40-6128*

City, town or post office, State, and ZIP code
Chicago IL 60604-5214

Presidential Election Campaign Fund
Do you want $1 to go to this fund?. . . . . ☑ Yes   ☐ No
If joint return, does your spouse want $1 to go to this fund? ☑ Yes   ☐ No

Step 2
Check your
filing status
(Check only one)

1 ☐ Single (See if you can use Form 1040EZ.)
2 ☑ Married filing joint return (even if only one had income)
3 ☐ Married filing separate return. Enter spouse's social security number above
     and spouse's full name here. _____
4 ☐ Head of household (with qualifying person). If the qualifying person is your unmarried child
     but not your dependent, write this child's name here. _____

Step 3
Figure your
exemptions

Always check the exemption box labeled Yourself. Check other boxes if they apply.
5a ☑ Yourself   ☐ 65 or over   ☐ Blind   Write number of boxes checked on 5a and b   **2**
  b ☑ Spouse   ☐ 65 or over   ☐ Blind
  c First names of your dependent children who lived with you   *Amy*   Write number of children listed on 5c   + **1**

Attach Copy B of
Form(s) W-2 here

d Other dependents:

1. Name	2. Relationship	3. Number of months lived in your home.	4. Did dependent have income of $1,000 or more?	5. Did you provide more than one-half of dependent's support?
Billy	*son*	*1*	*no*	*yes*

                                                             Write number of other dependents listed on 5d   + **1**
                                                             Add numbers entered on lines above   - **4**

e Total number of exemptions claimed. (Also complete line 18.)

Step 4
Figure your
total income

6 Total wages, salaries, tips, etc. This should be shown in Box 10
   of your W-2 form(s). (Attach Form(s) W-2.)   6   *23,840. —*

7 Interest income. (If the total is over $400, also complete and attach
   Schedule 1 (Form 1040A), Part I.)   7   *284. —*

Attach check or
money order here

8a Dividends. (If the total is over $400, also complete
   and attach Schedule 1 (Form 1040A), Part II.)   8a   *368. —*

  b Exclusion. See the instructions on page 16.   8b   *200. —*

  c Subtract line 8b from line 8a. Write the result.   8c   *168. —*

9a Unemployment compensation (insurance), from
   Form(s) 1099-G. Total received.   9a   *0. —*

  b Taxable amount, if any, from the worksheet on page 17 of the instructions.   9b   *0. —*

10 Add lines 6, 7, 8c, and 9b. Write the total. This is your **total income.**   10   *24,292 —*

Step 5
Figure your
adjusted
gross
income

11a Individual retirement arrangement (IRA)
    deduction, from the worksheet on page 19.   11a   *4,000. —*
  b Write IRA payments made in 1985 that you
    included on line 11a: ($ *0. —*   )
12 Deduction for a married couple when both
    work. Complete and attach Schedule 1
    (Form 1040A), Part III.   12   *902.86*

13 Add lines 11a and 12. Write the total. These are your **total adjustments.**   13   *4,902.86*
14 Subtract line 13 from line 10. Write the result. This is your **adjusted**
    gross income.   14   *19,389.14*

FIGURE 8-4 Sample 1040A Return

19- -   **Form 1040A**   Page 2

Step 6

Figure your taxable income

15	Write the amount from line 14.	15	19,389.14
16	Allowable part of your charitable contributions, from the worksheet on page 21 of the instructions.	16	75.—
17	Subtract line 16 from line 15. Write the result.	17	19,314.14
18	Multiply $1,000 by the total number of exemptions claimed on line 5e.	18	4,000.—
19	Subtract line 18 from line 17. Write the result. This is your **taxable income**.	19	15,314.14

Step 7

Figure your tax, credits, and payments

If You Want IRS to Figure Your Tax, See Page 21 of the Instructions.

20	Find the tax on the amount on line 19. Use the tax table, pages 31–36.	20	1,633.—
21a	Credit for child and dependent care expenses. Complete and attach Schedule 1 (Form 1040A), Part IV. 21a 0.—		
b	Partial credit for political contributions for which you have receipts. See page 24 of the instructions. 21b 100.—		
22	Add lines 21a and 21b. Write the total.	22	100.—
23	Subtract line 22 from line 20. Write the result (but not less than zero). This is your **total tax.**	23	1,533.—
24a	Total Federal income tax withheld. This should be shown in Box 9 of your W-2 form(s). (If line 6 is more than $37,800, see page 24 of the instructions.) 24a 3,202.—		
b	Earned income credit, from the worksheet on page 26 of the instructions. See page 25 of the instructions. 24b 0.—		
25	Add lines 24a and 24b. Write the total. These are your **total payments.**	25	3202.—

Step 8

Figure your refund or amount you owe

26	If line 25 is larger than line 23, subtract line 23 from line 25. Write the result. This is the **amount of your refund.**	26	1669.—
27	If line 23 is larger than line 25, subtract line 25 from line 23. Write the result. This is the **amount you owe.** Attach check or money order for full amount payable to "Internal Revenue Service." Write your social security number and "1984 Form 1040A" on it.	27	

Step 9

Sign your return

Under penalties of perjury, I declare that I have examined this return and accompanying schedules and statements, and to the best of my knowledge and belief, they are true, correct, and complete. Declaration of preparer (other than the taxpayer) is based on all information of which the preparer has any knowledge.

Your signature	Date	Your occupation
X *Melissa B. Anderson*	2/15/--	*Welder*
Spouse's signature (if joint return, both must sign)	Date	Spouse's occupation
X *Michael J. Anderson*	2/15/--	*Photographer*
Paid preparer's signature	Date	Preparer's social security no.
X		
Firm's name (or yours, if self-employed)		Employer identification no.
Address and ZIP code		Check if self-employed ☐

For **Privacy Act and Paperwork Reduction Act Notice, see page 41.**

FIGURE 8-4   Sample 1040A (continued)

To claim the marital deduction on line 12, Melissa and Michael Anderson had to complete Schedule 1, Part III (see Figure 8-5). The marital deduction allows the couple to deduct 10 percent of the lesser of the two incomes. The lesser income may not exceed $30,000.

The Andersons' charitable contribution deduction of $75 is entered on

FIGURE 8-5
Sample Schedule 1 (Form 1040A)

19--   **Schedule 1 (Form 1040A)**   OMB No. 1545-0085

Part I—Interest Income
Part II—Dividend Income
Part III—Deduction for a Married Couple When Both Work
Part IV—Credit for Child and Dependent Care Expenses

Name(s) as shown on Form 1040A.   Your social security number

You MUST complete and attach Schedule 1 to Form 1040A if you:

- Have over $400 of interest income (complete Part I)
- Have over $400 of dividend income (complete Part II)
- Claim the deduction for a working married couple (complete Part III)
- Claim the credit for child and dependent care expenses (complete Part IV)

Part I   **Interest Income** (See page 15)
Complete this part and attach Schedule 1 to Form 1040A if you received over $400 in interest income. If you received any interest from an All-Savers Certificate (ASC), use Form 1040 instead of Form 1040A.

1 List name of payer   Amount
                                                   $.
                                                   $.
                                                   $.
                                                   $.
                                                   $.
                                                   $.
                                                   $.
                                                   $.
                                                   $.
                                                   $.
2 Add amounts on line 1. Write the total here and on Form 1040A, line 7.   2   .

Part II **Dividend Income** (See page 16)
Complete this part and attach Schedule 1 to Form 1040A if you received over $400 in dividends.

1 List name of payer   Amount
                                                   $.
                                                   $.
                                                   $.
                                                   $.
                                                   $.
                                                   $.
                                                   $.
                                                   $.
2 Add amounts on line 1. Write the total here and on Form 1040A, line 8a. 2   .

Part III **Deduction for a married couple when both work** (See page 20)
Complete this part to figure the amount you can deduct on Form 1040A, line 12.
Attach Schedule 1 to Form 1040A.

		(a) You	(b) Your spouse
1 Wages, salaries, tips, etc., from Form 1040A, line 6.	1	_12,811.40_	_11,028.60_
2 IRA deduction, from Form 1040A, line 11a.	2 —	_2,000.—_	— _2,000.—_
3 Subtract line 2 from line 1. Write the result.	3 =	_10,811.40_	= _9,028.60_
4 Write the amount from line 3, column (a) or (b) above, whichever is smaller.	4		_9,028.60_
5 Percentage used to figure the deduction (10%).	5		× .10
6 Multiply the amount on line 4 by the percentage on line 5. Write your answer here and on Form 1040A, line 12.	6 =		_902.86_

line 16. Michael and Melissa gave $200 in political contributions; $100 is entered on line 21b.

The Andersons' tax liability is smaller than taxes withheld by $1,669. They are due a refund in that amount.

Federal tax tables, which taxpayers use to determine the amount of their income tax, are shown in Figure 8-6, pages 146-148.

FIGURE 8-5
Sample Schedule 1 (Form 1040A, continued)

19 - -   **Schedule 1 (Form 1040A)**   OMB No. 1545-0085

Name(s) as shown on Form 1040A. (Do not complete if shown on other side.)   Your social security number

Part IV   **Credit for child and dependent care expenses** (See pages 22-24)
Complete this part to figure the amount of credit you can take on Form 1040A, line 21a. Attach Schedule 1 to Form 1040A.

1 Write the number of qualifying persons who were cared for in 1984. (See the instructions for the definition of a qualifying person.)   1 _____

2 Write the amount of expenses you incurred and actually paid in 1984, but DO NOT write more than $2,400 ($4,800 if you paid for the care of two or more qualifying persons).   2 _____ .

3 ● If **unmarried** at the end of 1984, write your earned income on line 3, OR
● If **married**, filing a joint return for 1984,
    a. Write your earned income $_____ . ___ , and
    b. Write your spouse's earned income $_____ . ___ , and
    c. Compare the amounts on lines 3a and 3b, and write the **smaller** of the two amounts on line 3.   3 _____ .

4 Compare the amounts on lines 2 and 3. Write the **smaller** of the two amounts here.   4 _____ .

5 Write the percentage from the table below that applies to the amount on Form 1040A, line 15.

If line 15 is:		Percentage is:	If line 15 is:		Percentage is:
Over—	But not over—		Over—	But not over—	
0—$10,000		30% (.30)	$20,000—22,000		24% (.24)
$10,000—12,000		29% (.29)	22,000—24,000		23% (.23)
12,000—14,000		28% (.28)	24,000—26,000		22% (.22)
14,000—16,000		27% (.27)	26,000—28,000		21% (.21)
16,000—18,000		26% (.26)	28,000		20% (.20)
18,000—20,000		25% (.25)			

5   × .

6 Multiply the amount on line 4 by the percentage on line 5. Write the result here and on Form 1040A, line 21a.   6 = _____ .

19-- Tax Table

Based on Taxable Income

For persons with taxable incomes of less than $50,000

Example: Mr. and Mrs. Green are filing a joint return. Their taxable income on line 19 of Form 1040A is $23,270. First, they find the $23,250–23,300 income line. Next, they find the column for married filing jointly and read down the column. The amount shown where the income line and filing status column meet is $3,174. This is the tax amount they must write on line 20 of Form 1040A.

Tax Table (Continued)

Continued on next page

FIGURE 8-6 Selected Tax Tables

1994 Tax Table (Continued)

Tax Table (Continued)

FIGURE 8-6 Selected Tax Tables (continued)

Tax Table (Continued)

If 1040A, line 19, OR 1040EZ, line 7 is— At least	But less than	And you are— Single (and 1040EZ filers)	Married filing jointly	Married filing separately	Head of a household
		Your tax is—			
32,000					
32,000	32,050	6,802	5,385	8,435	6,322
32,050	32,100	6,819	5,399	8,456	6,338
32,100	32,150	6,836	5,413	8,477	6,354
32,150	32,200	6,853	5,427	8,498	6,370
32,200	32,250	6,870	5,441	8,519	6,386
32,250	32,300	6,887	5,455	8,540	6,402
32,300	32,350	6,904	5,469	8,561	6,418
32,350	32,400	6,921	5,483	8,582	6,434
32,400	32,450	6,938	5,497	8,603	6,450
32,450	32,500	6,955	5,511	8,624	6,466
32,500	32,550	6,972	5,525	8,645	6,482
32,550	32,600	6,989	5,539	8,666	6,498
32,600	32,650	7,006	5,553	8,687	6,514
32,650	32,700	7,023	5,567	8,708	6,530
32,700	32,750	7,040	5,581	8,729	6,546
32,750	32,800	7,057	5,595	8,750	6,562
32,800	32,850	7,074	5,609	8,771	6,578
32,850	32,900	7,091	5,623	8,792	6,594
32,900	32,950	7,108	5,637	8,813	6,610
32,950	33,000	7,125	5,651	8,834	6,626
33,000					
33,000	33,050	7,142	5,665	8,855	6,642
33,050	33,100	7,159	5,679	8,876	6,658
33,100	33,150	7,176	5,693	8,897	6,674
33,150	33,200	7,193	5,707	8,918	6,690
33,200	33,250	7,210	5,721	8,939	6,706
33,250	33,300	7,227	5,735	8,960	6,722
33,300	33,350	7,244	5,749	8,981	6,738
33,350	33,400	7,261	5,763	9,002	6,754
33,400	33,450	7,278	5,777	9,023	6,770
33,450	33,500	7,295	5,791	9,044	6,786
33,500	33,550	7,312	5,805	9,065	6,802
33,550	33,600	7,329	5,819	9,086	6,818
33,600	33,650	7,346	5,833	9,107	6,834
33,650	33,700	7,363	5,847	9,128	6,850
33,700	33,750	7,380	5,861	9,149	6,866
33,750	33,800	7,397	5,875	9,170	6,882
33,800	33,850	7,414	5,889	9,191	6,898
33,850	33,900	7,431	5,903	9,212	6,914
33,900	33,950	7,448	5,917	9,233	6,930
33,950	34,000	7,465	5,931	9,254	6,946
34,000					
34,000	34,050	7,482	5,945	9,275	6,962
34,050	34,100	7,499	5,959	9,296	6,978
34,100	34,150	7,517	5,973	9,317	6,995
34,150	34,200	7,536	5,987	9,338	7,012
34,200	34,250	7,555	6,001	9,359	7,030
34,250	34,300	7,574	6,015	9,380	7,047
34,300	34,350	7,593	6,029	9,401	7,065
34,350	34,400	7,612	6,043	9,422	7,082
34,400	34,450	7,631	6,057	9,443	7,100
34,450	34,500	7,650	6,071	9,464	7,117
34,500	34,550	7,669	6,085	9,485	7,135
34,550	34,600	7,688	6,099	9,506	7,152
34,600	34,650	7,707	6,113	9,527	7,170
34,650	34,700	7,726	6,127	9,548	7,187
34,700	34,750	7,745	6,141	9,569	7,205
34,750	34,800	7,764	6,155	9,590	7,222
34,800	34,850	7,783	6,169	9,611	7,240
34,850	34,900	7,802	6,183	9,632	7,257
34,900	34,950	7,821	6,197	9,653	7,275
34,950	35,000	7,840	6,211	9,674	7,292
35,000					
35,000	35,050	7,859	6,225	9,695	7,310
35,050	35,100	7,878	6,239	9,716	7,327
35,100	35,150	7,897	6,253	9,737	7,345
35,150	35,200	7,916	6,267	9,758	7,362
35,200	35,250	7,935	6,282	9,779	7,380
35,250	35,300	7,954	6,299	9,800	7,397
35,300	35,350	7,973	6,315	9,821	7,415
35,350	35,400	7,992	6,332	9,842	7,432
35,400	35,450	8,011	6,348	9,863	7,450
35,450	35,500	8,030	6,365	9,884	7,467
35,500	35,550	8,049	6,381	9,905	7,485
35,550	35,600	8,068	6,398	9,926	7,502
35,600	35,650	8,087	6,414	9,947	7,520
35,650	35,700	8,106	6,431	9,968	7,537
35,700	35,750	8,125	6,447	9,989	7,556
35,750	35,800	8,144	6,464	10,010	7,572
35,800	35,850	8,163	6,480	10,031	7,590
35,850	35,900	8,182	6,497	10,052	7,607
35,900	35,950	8,201	6,513	10,073	7,625
35,950	36,000	8,220	6,530	10,094	7,642
36,000					
36,000	36,050	8,239	6,546	10,115	7,660
36,050	36,100	8,258	6,563	10,136	7,677
36,100	36,150	8,277	6,579	10,157	7,695
36,150	36,200	8,296	6,596	10,178	7,712
36,200	36,250	8,315	6,612	10,199	7,730
36,250	36,300	8,334	6,629	10,220	7,747
36,300	36,350	8,353	6,645	10,241	7,765
36,350	36,400	8,372	6,662	10,262	7,782
36,400	36,450	8,391	6,678	10,283	7,800
36,450	36,500	8,410	6,695	10,304	7,817
36,500	36,550	8,429	6,711	10,325	7,835
36,550	36,600	8,448	6,728	10,346	7,852
36,600	36,650	8,467	6,744	10,367	7,870
36,650	36,700	8,486	6,761	10,388	7,887
36,700	36,750	8,505	6,777	10,409	7,905
36,750	36,800	8,524	6,794	10,430	7,922
36,800	36,850	8,543	6,810	10,451	7,940
36,850	36,900	8,562	6,827	10,472	7,957
36,900	36,950	8,581	6,843	10,493	7,975
36,950	37,000	8,600	6,860	10,514	7,992
37,000					
37,000	37,050	8,619	6,876	10,535	8,010
37,050	37,100	8,638	6,893	10,556	8,027
37,100	37,150	8,657	6,909	10,577	8,045
37,150	37,200	8,676	6,926	10,598	8,062
37,200	37,250	8,695	6,942	10,619	8,080
37,250	37,300	8,714	6,959	10,640	8,097
37,300	37,350	8,733	6,975	10,661	8,115
37,350	37,400	8,752	6,992	10,682	8,132
37,400	37,450	8,771	7,008	10,703	8,150
37,450	37,500	8,790	7,025	10,724	8,167
37,500	37,550	8,809	7,041	10,745	8,185
37,550	37,600	8,828	7,058	10,766	8,202
37,600	37,650	8,847	7,074	10,787	8,220
37,650	37,700	8,866	7,091	10,808	8,237
37,700	37,750	8,885	7,107	10,829	8,255
37,750	37,800	8,904	7,124	10,850	8,272
37,800	37,850	8,923	7,140	10,871	8,290
37,850	37,900	8,942	7,157	10,892	8,307
37,900	37,950	8,961	7,173	10,913	8,325
37,950	38,000	8,980	7,190	10,934	8,342
38,000					
38,000	38,050	8,999	7,206	10,955	8,360
38,050	38,100	9,018	7,223	10,976	8,377
38,100	38,150	9,037	7,239	10,997	8,395
38,150	38,200	9,056	7,256	11,018	8,412
38,200	38,250	9,075	7,272	11,039	8,430
38,250	38,300	9,094	7,289	11,060	8,447
38,300	38,350	9,113	7,305	11,081	8,465
38,350	38,400	9,132	7,322	11,102	8,482
38,400	38,450	9,151	7,338	11,123	8,500
38,450	38,500	9,170	7,355	11,144	8,517
38,500	38,550	9,189	7,371	11,165	8,535
38,550	38,600	9,208	7,388	11,186	8,552
38,600	38,650	9,227	7,404	11,207	8,570
38,650	38,700	9,246	7,421	11,228	8,587
38,700	38,750	9,265	7,437	11,249	8,605
38,750	38,800	9,284	7,454	11,270	8,622
38,800	38,850	9,303	7,470	11,291	8,640
38,850	38,900	9,322	7,487	11,312	8,657
38,900	38,950	9,341	7,503	11,333	8,675
38,950	39,000	9,360	7,520	11,354	8,692
39,000					
39,000	39,050	9,379	7,536	11,375	8,710
39,050	39,100	9,398	7,553	11,396	8,727
39,100	39,150	9,417	7,569	11,417	8,745
39,150	39,200	9,436	7,586	11,438	8,762
39,200	39,250	9,455	7,602	11,459	8,780
39,250	39,300	9,474	7,619	11,480	8,797
39,300	39,350	9,493	7,635	11,501	8,815
39,350	39,400	9,512	7,652	11,522	8,832
39,400	39,450	9,531	7,668	11,543	8,850
39,450	39,500	9,550	7,685	11,564	8,867
39,500	39,550	9,569	7,701	11,585	8,885
39,550	39,600	9,588	7,718	11,606	8,902
39,600	39,650	9,607	7,734	11,627	8,920
39,650	39,700	9,626	7,751	11,648	8,937
39,700	39,750	9,645	7,767	11,669	8,955
39,750	39,800	9,664	7,784	11,690	8,972
39,800	39,850	9,683	7,800	11,711	8,990
39,850	39,900	9,702	7,817	11,732	9,007
39,900	39,950	9,721	7,833	11,753	9,025
39,950	40,000	9,740	7,850	11,774	9,042
40,000					
40,000	40,050	9,759	7,866	11,795	9,060
40,050	40,100	9,778	7,883	11,816	9,077
40,100	40,150	9,797	7,899	11,837	9,095
40,150	40,200	9,816	7,916	11,858	9,112
40,200	40,250	9,835	7,932	11,879	9,130
40,250	40,300	9,854	7,949	11,900	9,147
40,300	40,350	9,873	7,965	11,921	9,165
40,350	40,400	9,892	7,982	11,942	9,182
40,400	40,450	9,911	7,998	11,963	9,200
40,450	40,500	9,930	8,015	11,984	9,217
40,500	40,550	9,949	8,031	12,005	9,235
40,550	40,600	9,968	8,048	12,026	9,252
40,600	40,650	9,987	8,064	12,047	9,270
40,650	40,700	10,006	8,081	12,068	9,287
40,700	40,750	10,025	8,097	12,089	9,305
40,750	40,800	10,044	8,114	12,110	9,322
40,800	40,850	10,063	8,130	12,131	9,340
40,850	40,900	10,082	8,147	12,152	9,357
40,900	40,950	10,101	8,163	12,173	9,375
40,950	41,000	10,120	8,180	12,194	9,392

Continued on next page

Tax Table (Continued)

If 1040A, line 19, OR 1040EZ, line 7 is— At least	But less than	And you are— Single (and 1040EZ filers)	Married filing jointly	Married filing separately	Head of a household
		Your tax is—			
41,000					
41,000	41,050	10,139	8,196	12,215	9,410
41,050	41,100	10,158	8,213	12,236	9,427
41,100	41,150	10,177	8,229	12,257	9,445
41,150	41,200	10,196	8,246	12,278	9,462
41,200	41,250	10,215	8,262	12,299	9,480
41,250	41,300	10,234	8,279	12,320	9,497
41,300	41,350	10,253	8,295	12,341	9,515
41,350	41,400	10,272	8,312	12,362	9,532
41,400	41,450	10,291	8,328	12,383	9,550
41,450	41,500	10,310	8,345	12,404	9,567
41,500	41,550	10,330	8,361	12,425	9,585
41,550	41,600	10,351	8,378	12,446	9,602
41,600	41,650	10,372	8,394	12,467	9,620
41,650	41,700	10,393	8,411	12,488	9,637
41,700	41,750	10,414	8,427	12,509	9,655
41,750	41,800	10,435	8,444	12,530	9,672
41,800	41,850	10,456	8,460	12,551	9,690
41,850	41,900	10,477	8,477	12,572	9,707
41,900	41,950	10,498	8,493	12,593	9,725
41,950	42,000	10,519	8,510	12,614	9,742
42,000					
42,000	42,050	10,540	8,526	12,635	9,760
42,050	42,100	10,561	8,543	12,656	9,777
42,100	42,150	10,582	8,559	12,677	9,796
42,150	42,200	10,603	8,576	12,698	9,812
42,200	42,250	10,624	8,592	12,719	9,830
42,250	42,300	10,645	8,609	12,740	9,847
42,300	42,350	10,666	8,625	12,761	9,865
42,350	42,400	10,687	8,642	12,782	9,882
42,400	42,450	10,708	8,658	12,803	9,900
42,450	42,500	10,729	8,675	12,824	9,917
42,500	42,550	10,750	8,691	12,845	9,936
42,550	42,600	10,771	8,708	12,866	9,952
42,600	42,650	10,792	8,724	12,887	9,970
42,650	42,700	10,813	8,741	12,908	9,987
42,700	42,750	10,834	8,757	12,929	10,005
42,750	42,800	10,855	8,774	12,950	10,022
42,800	42,850	10,876	8,790	12,971	10,040
42,850	42,900	10,897	8,807	12,994	10,057
42,900	42,950	10,918	8,823	13,016	10,075
42,950	43,000	10,939	8,840	13,039	10,092
43,000					
43,000	43,050	10,960	8,856	13,061	10,110
43,050	43,100	10,981	8,873	13,084	10,127
43,100	43,150	11,002	8,889	13,106	10,145
43,150	43,200	11,023	8,906	13,129	10,162
43,200	43,250	11,044	8,922	13,151	10,180
43,250	43,300	11,065	8,939	13,174	10,197
43,300	43,350	11,086	8,955	13,196	10,215
43,350	43,400	11,107	8,972	13,219	10,232
43,400	43,450	11,128	8,988	13,241	10,250
43,450	43,500	11,149	9,005	13,264	10,267
43,500	43,550	11,170	9,021	13,286	10,285
43,550	43,600	11,191	9,038	13,309	10,302
43,600	43,650	11,212	9,054	13,331	10,320
43,650	43,700	11,233	9,071	13,354	10,337
43,700	43,750	11,254	9,087	13,376	10,355
43,750	43,800	11,275	9,104	13,399	10,372
43,800	43,850	11,296	9,120	13,421	10,390
43,850	43,900	11,317	9,137	13,444	10,407
43,900	43,950	11,338	9,153	13,466	10,425
43,950	44,000	11,359	9,170	13,489	10,442
44,000					
44,000	44,050	11,380	9,186	13,511	10,460
44,050	44,100	11,401	9,203	13,534	10,477
44,100	44,150	11,422	9,219	13,556	10,495
44,150	44,200	11,443	9,236	13,579	10,512
44,200	44,250	11,464	9,252	13,601	10,530
44,250	44,300	11,485	9,269	13,624	10,547
44,300	44,350	11,506	9,285	13,646	10,565
44,350	44,400	11,527	9,302	13,669	10,582
44,400	44,450	11,548	9,318	13,691	10,600
44,450	44,500	11,569	9,335	13,714	10,617
44,500	44,550	11,590	9,351	13,736	10,635
44,550	44,600	11,611	9,368	13,759	10,652
44,600	44,650	11,632	9,384	13,781	10,670
44,650	44,700	11,653	9,401	13,804	10,687
44,700	44,750	11,674	9,417	13,826	10,707
44,750	44,800	11,695	9,434	13,849	10,728
44,800	44,850	11,716	9,450	13,871	10,749
44,850	44,900	11,737	9,467	13,894	10,770
44,900	44,950	11,758	9,483	13,916	10,791
44,950	45,000	11,779	9,500	13,939	10,812
45,000					
45,000	45,050	11,800	9,516	13,961	10,833
45,050	45,100	11,821	9,533	13,984	10,854
45,100	45,150	11,842	9,549	14,006	10,875
45,150	45,200	11,863	9,566	14,029	10,896
45,200	45,250	11,884	9,582	14,051	10,917
45,250	45,300	11,905	9,599	14,074	10,938
45,300	45,350	11,926	9,615	14,096	10,959
45,350	45,400	11,947	9,632	14,119	10,980
45,400	45,450	11,968	9,648	14,141	11,001
45,450	45,500	11,989	9,665	14,164	11,022
45,500	45,550	12,010	9,681	14,186	11,043
45,550	45,600	12,031	9,698	14,209	11,064
45,600	45,650	12,052	9,714	14,231	11,085
45,650	45,700	12,073	9,731	14,254	11,106
45,700	45,750	12,094	9,747	14,276	11,127
45,750	45,800	12,115	9,764	14,299	11,148
45,800	45,850	12,136	9,782	14,321	11,169
45,850	45,900	12,157	9,801	14,344	11,190
45,900	45,950	12,178	9,820	14,366	11,211
45,950	46,000	12,199	9,839	14,389	11,232
46,000					
46,000	46,050	12,220	9,858	14,411	11,253
46,050	46,100	12,241	9,877	14,434	11,274
46,100	46,150	12,262	9,896	14,456	11,295
46,150	46,200	12,283	9,915	14,479	11,316
46,200	46,250	12,304	9,934	14,501	11,337
46,250	46,300	12,325	9,953	14,524	11,358
46,300	46,350	12,346	9,972	14,546	11,379
46,350	46,400	12,367	9,991	14,569	11,400
46,400	46,450	12,388	10,010	14,591	11,421
46,450	46,500	12,409	10,029	14,614	11,442
46,500	46,550	12,430	10,048	14,636	11,463
46,550	46,600	12,451	10,067	14,659	11,484
46,600	46,650	12,472	10,086	14,681	11,505
46,650	46,700	12,493	10,105	14,704	11,526
46,700	46,750	12,514	10,124	14,726	11,547
46,750	46,800	12,535	10,143	14,749	11,568
46,800	46,850	12,556	10,162	14,771	11,589
46,850	46,900	12,577	10,181	14,794	11,610
46,900	46,950	12,598	10,200	14,816	11,631
46,950	47,000	12,619	10,219	14,839	11,652
47,000					
47,000	47,050	12,640	10,238	14,861	11,673
47,050	47,100	12,661	10,257	14,884	11,694
47,100	47,150	12,682	10,276	14,906	11,715
47,150	47,200	12,703	10,295	14,929	11,736
47,200	47,250	12,724	10,314	14,951	11,757
47,250	47,300	12,745	10,333	14,974	11,778
47,300	47,350	12,766	10,352	14,996	11,799
47,350	47,400	12,787	10,371	15,019	11,820
47,400	47,450	12,808	10,390	15,041	11,841
47,450	47,500	12,829	10,409	15,064	11,862
47,500	47,550	12,850	10,428	15,086	11,883
47,550	47,600	12,871	10,447	15,109	11,904
47,600	47,650	12,892	10,466	15,131	11,925
47,650	47,700	12,913	10,485	15,154	11,946
47,700	47,750	12,934	10,504	15,176	11,967
47,750	47,800	12,955	10,523	15,199	11,988
47,800	47,850	12,976	10,542	15,221	12,009
47,850	47,900	12,997	10,561	15,244	12,030
47,900	47,950	13,018	10,580	15,266	12,051
47,950	48,000	13,039	10,599	15,289	12,072
48,000					
48,000	48,050	13,060	10,618	15,311	12,093
48,050	48,100	13,081	10,637	15,334	12,114
48,100	48,150	13,102	10,656	15,356	12,135
48,150	48,200	13,123	10,675	15,379	12,156
48,200	48,250	13,144	10,694	15,401	12,177
48,250	48,300	13,165	10,713	15,424	12,198
48,300	48,350	13,186	10,732	15,446	12,219
48,350	48,400	13,207	10,751	15,469	12,240
48,400	48,450	13,228	10,770	15,491	12,261
48,450	48,500	13,249	10,789	15,514	12,282
48,500	48,550	13,270	10,808	15,536	12,303
48,550	48,600	13,291	10,827	15,559	12,324
48,600	48,650	13,312	10,846	15,581	12,345
48,650	48,700	13,333	10,865	15,604	12,366
48,700	48,750	13,354	10,884	15,626	12,387
48,750	48,800	13,375	10,903	15,649	12,408
48,800	48,850	13,396	10,922	15,671	12,429
48,850	48,900	13,417	10,941	15,694	12,450
48,900	48,950	13,438	10,960	15,716	12,471
48,950	49,000	13,459	10,979	15,739	12,492
49,000					
49,000	49,050	13,480	10,998	15,761	12,513
49,050	49,100	13,501	11,017	15,784	12,534
49,100	49,150	13,522	11,036	15,806	12,555
49,150	49,200	13,543	11,055	15,829	12,576
49,200	49,250	13,564	11,074	15,851	12,597
49,250	49,300	13,585	11,093	15,874	12,618
49,300	49,350	13,606	11,112	15,896	12,639
49,350	49,400	13,627	11,131	15,919	12,660
49,400	49,450	13,648	11,150	15,941	12,681
49,450	49,500	13,669	11,169	15,964	12,702
49,500	49,550	13,690	11,188	15,986	12,723
49,550	49,600	13,711	11,207	16,009	12,744
49,600	49,650	13,732	11,226	16,031	12,765
49,650	49,700	13,753	11,245	16,054	12,786
49,700	49,750	13,774	11,264	16,076	12,807
49,750	49,800	13,795	11,283	16,099	12,828
49,800	49,850	13,816	11,302	16,121	12,849
49,850	49,900	13,837	11,321	16,144	12,870
49,900	49,950	13,858	11,340	16,166	12,891
49,950	50,000	13,879	11,359	16,189	12,912
50,000 or over—use Form 1040					

FIGURE 8-6 Selected Tax Tables (concluded)

VOCABULARY

Directions: Can you find the definition for each of the following terms used in Chapter 8?

A revenue
B progressive
C regressive
D proportional
E Internal Revenue Service
F child support
G deductions
H taxable income
I tax liability

J voluntary compliance
K deficit spending
L exemption
M gross income
N exclusion
O alimony
P zero bracket amount
Q tax evasion

1. Money collected by the government through taxes. A

2. A tax based on the more income earned, the more tax paid. B

3. A tax wherein the rate remains constant, regardless of the amount of your income. D

4. A tax that decreases in proportion to income increases. C

5. An agency of the U.S. Department of the Treasury charged with collecting federal income taxes. E

6. A system whereby citizens are expected to prepare and file appropriate tax returns. J

7. Willful failure to pay taxes. Q

8. A condition wherein the government spends more money than it collects. K

9. An allowance for each person dependent on the taxpayer's income. L

10. All the taxable income received during the year, including wages, tips, salaries, interest, dividends, alimony, and unemployment compensation. M

11. Money that is exempt from taxation. N

12. Money paid to a former spouse to support dependent children of a previous marriage. F

13. Money paid to support a former spouse. O

14. Expenses allowed by law that are subtracted from gross income to obtain the amount of taxable income. G

15. The minimum amount of deductions needed before a taxpayer can itemize deductions. P

16. The amount remaining when deductions have been subtracted from adjusted gross income. H

17. The actual or total amount of taxes due, based on taxable income.

          I

ITEMS FOR DISCUSSION

1. What is the United States government's largest source of revenue?

2. List the three types of taxes and define each.

3. List five other taxes besides the three listed in No. 2.

4. List at least five services the government provides for all citizens from taxes collected.

5. When was the first permanent income tax ratified?

6. When was the Internal Revenue Service created?

7. List three services provided by the IRS.

8. Who has the ability to levy taxes on the citizens of the United States?

9. What is meant by a tax system based on voluntary compliance?

10. What can happen to you if you deliberately do not file your tax return and pay taxes due?

11. What type of dependent can be claimed on two tax returns?

12. List five types of income that are taxable.

13. List five types of income that are not taxable.

14. How is child support different from alimony in terms of taxation?

15. Explain the zero bracket amount.

16. When must you file your federal tax return? Why?

17. What should you do if you discover an error after you have filed your tax return?

18. Under what circumstances would you file the long Form 1040 tax return?

19. Why should you file your tax return early when you expect a refund?

20. Explain the purpose of the Presidential Election Campaign Fund. If you check the Yes box on your return, does it increase your taxes by $1?

APPLICATIONS

1. Explain the need for taxes in this country. How does everyone benefit from taxes?

2. Summarize how taxing income came about in this country. Do you think that the time will ever come when taxation will no longer be needed? Explain.

3. Explain how new federal taxes are imposed.

4. How does your filing status affect the amount of taxes you will pay?

5. How does the number of exemptions claimed affect the amount of taxes you will pay?

6. What are deductible expenses?

7. When should you file the short Form 1040EZ? 1040A?

8. How many exemptions would you have if you were over 65, married, and your spouse, under 65, were legally blind?

9. What is the maximum credit for a donation to a candidate for public office made by a single person? by married persons filing jointly?

10. What should you do if more than $2,532.60 in FICA taxes was withheld from your paychecks in 1984?

CASE PROBLEMS AND ACTIVITIES

1. Using Figure 8-2, Form 1040EZ, prepare a tax return for Brian Reid on plain paper. Use the following information:

   Brian Reid (541-33-9892)
   54 Center Street
   San Francisco, CA 96214-3627

   Brian is a carpenter. He wants $1 to go to the Presidential Election Campaign Fund. He is single and claims only himself as an exemption. Brian's salary is $14,200, plus interest of $155. He gave $150 to charitable organizations and had $2,186 in federal taxes withheld from his paychecks.

2. Using Figure 8-4, Form 1040A, and the tax tables given on pages 146-148, compute the tax liability of Tony Martin. Tony's adjusted gross income was $14,000. He gave $150 to candidates for public office and had $2,004 in federal taxes withheld from his wages. He is

single and is entitled to one exemption. Based on this information, how much does Tony owe, or how much is his refund?

3. Using Figure 8-4 (Form 1040A) and the tax tables (Figure 8-6), compute the tax liability of Angela Olinger. Angela's wages totaled $16,201; interest income, $190; and dividends, $200 ($100 can be excluded). She gave $75 to candidates for public office, and had $2,408 in federal taxes withheld from her wages. She is single and is entitled to one exemption. How much does Angela owe in taxes, or how much is her refund?

4. Using Figure 8-4 (Form 1040A) prepare a joint tax return for Alex and Marilyn Harris on plain paper.

Alex K. and Marilyn J. Harris
(895-10-9008, 485-01-9089)
2450 West 18th Avenue
Dallas, TX 75201-7242

Alex is an architect, and Marilyn is a teacher. They both want to contribute $1 to the Presidential Election Campaign Fund. Married, filing jointly, Alex and Marilyn have two dependent children, Valerie and Carole. They both contributed $2,000 to IRAs.

Alex's and Marilyn's combined incomes totaled $38,400 (the lesser is $18,400). They contributed $500 to candidates for political office and had a total tax of $4,800 withheld from their wages.

Alex and Marilyn had interest income of $1,400: First Interstate Bank, $300; private loan to J. Smith, $600; time certificate at State Savings & Loan, $500.

Dividend income amounted to $1,100: $411 from CDK stock, $621 from Investors' Mutual Fund, Inc., and $68 from I.P.Q. Manufacturing Co. These dividends are subject to exclusion.

PART THREE
ECONOMIC SECURITY

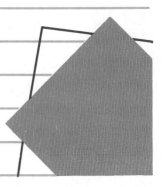

9

Saving for the Future

CHAPTER OBJECTIVES

After studying this chapter and completing the activities, you will be able to:

1. Understand the need for and purpose of savings.
2. List and compare the types of savings options available and the financial institutions where they can be obtained.
3. Compute interest on savings accounts with monthly, quarterly, semiannual, and annual interest rates.

WHY YOU SHOULD SAVE

The chief reason for saving money is to provide for future needs, both expected and unexpected. When nothing is set aside for these certain-to-happen needs, families experience frustration, financial troubles, and even bankruptcy.

Short-Term Needs

Often short-term needs arise that require money above what is normally allowed for by a budget. These needs typically are paid for out of savings. Some short-term needs you might encounter include the following:

Savings provide for sudden emergencies.

1. Emergencies—such as unemployment, sickness, accident, or death in the family
2. Vacations—short weekend trips and leisure activities
3. Social events—such as weddings, family gatherings, and other potentially costly special occasions

ILLUSTRATION 9-1
A savings plan can help you meet your future needs.

4. Major purchases—such as a car, major appliances, remodeling, or other expense that becomes necessary as time goes by (Things do wear out and have to be replaced, repaired, or remodeled.)

You can probably think of other short-term needs for which you should save. If you anticipate having to pay for part of your college education, for example, a regular savings plan could make it easier when the time comes to go to school.

Long-Term Goals

Large purchases require savings plans.

Many individuals and families anticipate some major purchases in the future and save to make these purchases possible. These long-term goals include outlays for such things as home ownership, children's education, retirement, and investments.

Home Ownership. A down payment on a house amounts to thousands of dollars. The larger the down payment you can make, the smaller your monthly payments will be.

Children's Education. Many couples begin a savings plan when their children are very young. Then when the time comes for college, the necessary money is waiting.

Retirement. Most people should not depend on social security payments to be sufficient support in their old age. Other plans should be made for financial security after retirement.

Investment. To provide a hedge against inflation or make money for future use, people may invest in a business, real estate, insurance, stocks, collectibles, or a number of other alternatives. Because investments are often risky in nature, they should be made only *in addition to* regular savings.

Investments should be made only in addition to savings.

Financial Security

Probably the best reason to save is to provide peace of mind in knowing that when short-term needs arise there will be adequate money to pay for them. Another reason to save is to ensure that upon retirement enough money will be available to live comfortably. Persons who set aside money each pay period experience the security of knowing that there is money available if and when it is needed.

The amount of money you save will vary according to several factors: (*a*) the amount of your **discretionary income** (what you have left over when the bills are paid); (*b*) the importance you attach to savings; (*c*) your anticipated needs and wants; and (*d*) your willpower, or ability to forego present spending in order to provide for your future.

You must forego purchases today to save for tomorrow.

HOW YOUR MONEY GROWS

Money grows when it is saved and invested. We will examine how money grows in a savings account.

Compounding Interest

The amount of money deposited by the saver is called the **principal**. Money paid by the financial institution to the saver for the use of his or her money is called **interest**. When interest is computed on the sum of the principal plus interest already earned it is **compound interest**. Figure 9-1 illustrates how annual interest is compounded.

FIGURE 9-1
Compounding
Interest Yearly

Year	Beginning Balance	Interest Earned (5%)	Ending Balance
1	$100.00	$5.00	$105.00
2	105.00	5.25	110.25
3	110.25	5.51	115.76

To compound interest, you add interest on interest.

The more often interest is compounded, the greater your earnings. Figure 9-2 illustrates what happens when 5 percent interest is compounded quarterly (every three months) and is added to the principal before more interest is calculated. You will notice that more interest is earned if interest is compounded quarterly than if it is compounded annually.

FIGURE 9-2
Compounding Interest Quarterly

Year	Beginning Balance	First Quarter	Second Quarter	Third Quarter	Fourth Quarter	Ending Balance
1	$100.00	$1.25	$1.27	$1.28	$1.30	$105.10
2	105.10	1.31	1.33	1.35	1.36	110.45
3	110.45	1.38	1.40	1.42	1.43	116.08

True daily interest is computed on each day of deposit. Banks and financial institutions can rapidly compute the interest compounding daily with computers.

Percentage Rates

The effective rate is the rate you receive when interest is compounded.

The *nominal rate* of interest is calculated on the principal amount only and does not include compounding. The *true annual percentage rate* is the effective rate you will receive when the money is compounded and you receive interest on interest earned. Often when you see advertisements for interest offered at financial institutions, you see these two different rates offered, as depicted in Figure 9-3.

FIGURE 9-3
Interest Rates

INTEREST OFFERED

12-month time certificates
Minimum deposit of $500.00

Nominal rate: 13.89%

Effective yield: 15.58%

While some time certificates allow the interest to accumulate and compound, others require that interest earned be paid into a regular passbook account where much lower interest rates are paid. This fact is an important one to know before you buy a time certificate.

WHERE YOU CAN SAVE

The main financial institutions found in most cities include commercial banks, savings banks, savings and loan associations, credit unions, and brokerage firms.

Commercial Banks

Commercial banks are very convenient.

Many people prefer to keep their checking and savings accounts in the same bank for ease in transferring funds and making deposits and withdrawals. Commercial banks offer much convenience to customers in the form of services that may go along with accounts. Services may include automatic cash transfer accounts, bank cards, use of 24-hour teller machines, overdraft protection, and other free services. Ninety-seven percent of banks are insured by the FDIC. Most large commercial banks in states where branch banking is legal have many branches for ease of deposits and withdrawals. Commercial banks may be either nationally chartered or state chartered. Large banks are able to offer more services to customers, but generally minimum deposits and fees are higher. Rates offered on savings accounts will vary among commercial banks, as well as between commercial banks and savings banks, savings and loan associations, and credit unions.

Savings Banks

Savings banks are state chartered.

Savings banks are usually referred to as mutual savings banks. These financial institutions are few in number—about 500 of them in roughly a dozen states, mostly throughout New England and the Northeast—but they are substantial in size, having nearly $150 billion in assets. Savings banks are state chartered and are insured by FDIC. A major business of savings banks is savings plans and loans on real property, including mortgages and home-improvement loans. Because of deregulation of the banking industry (1980), savings banks also offer checking accounts and other types of consumer loans.

Savings and Loan Associations

Savings and loan associations are organized primarily to handle savings and lend money: these associations make over 80 percent of all home mortgage loans. Money deposited in savings accounts is loaned to people purchasing homes or making home improvements. Generally, savings and loan associations are able to offer slightly higher interest rates on savings accounts (passbook and certificate) than commercial banks. Eighty percent of all savings and loan associations are insured by *FSLIC* (Federal Savings and Loan Insurance Corporation), which, like FDIC, insures individual accounts up to $100,000.

Slightly better rates are available at savings and loans.

Savings and loan associations offer many of the conveniences and services of commercial banks. NOW accounts and money market accounts are available at savings and loan associations. Some savings and loans even offer major credit cards and 24-hour teller machines. Few, however, have safe-deposit boxes, automatic cash transfers, and instant loans. It is because they specialize that savings and loans are able to offer higher interest rates than banks. Rates vary among savings and loan associations—check around before depositing your money.

Credit Unions

Credit unions are not-for-profit organizations established by groups of workers in similar occupations who pool their money. Credit unions generally offer higher interest rates on savings and lower interest rates on loans. They are insured through membership in *NCUA* (National Credit Union Administration) so that deposits are insured up to $100,000 in each account. Savings accounts at a credit union are often called *share accounts*, because deposits entitle the saver to shares of interest. Credit unions also offer IRA accounts, share draft accounts (checking accounts), consumer loans, certificates of deposit, and many other services. Credit unions are offering more diversified services and are growing rapidly in most parts of the country.

Brokerage Firms

Cash management accounts or money market accounts offer less convenience and involve more risk than other types of accounts, but offer high rates of return to savers. Money you deposit is invested in your behalf, and you share in the profits earned. Generally, however, large minimum deposits are required, and your check-writing privileges are restricted. Another disadvantage of these accounts is that they often are not very liquid. Savers sometimes find it inconvenient to withdraw money and make deposits.

More risk often means higher returns.

Brokerage investment firms do not have insurance on deposits, but they do offer the advantage of *diversification*—purchasing a variety of investments to protect against large losses and increase the rate of return.

The investment firm buys different types of securities and investments, from common stock and Treasury bills to government bonds. Consequently, brokerage firms are able to offer higher interest rates than commercial banks, savings banks, savings and loan associations, or credit unions.

SAVINGS OPTIONS

Once you have determined to establish a savings program for yourself or your family, you need to know about different options available to you. Money that is set aside for future needs can be deposited in a number of different savings plans. Options include regular passbook savings accounts, certificates of deposit, government savings bonds and Treasury bills, cash management accounts, and IRA accounts.

Explore the options in your area.

Regular Passbook Savings Accounts

A regular passbook savings account has a major advantage of high liquidity. *Liquidity* is the quality of being easily converted into cash. A regular passbook account is said to be liquid because you can withdraw your money at any time without penalty. However, of all savings plans, a regular passbook account probably pays the least amount of interest. Interest is money paid for the use of money: the bank pays you interest on your deposits. Once you have opened the passbook account, you are free to make withdrawals and deposits. Some financial institutions charge service fees when you make more than a maximum number of withdrawals in a certain period of time. Other institutions charge a monthly fee if your balance falls below a set minimum.

Savings accounts may have minimum balance requirements.

Certificates of Deposit

A *certificate of deposit*, or time certificate, represents a sum of money deposited for a set length of time—for example, $500 for six months. A certificate of deposit is less liquid than a regular passbook account, and sometimes requires that a minimum amount be deposited. The rate of interest is generally higher by several percentage points than on passbook accounts. But, if you withdraw your money before the deposit time is up, you will be penalized; that is, you will receive less interest. A certificate of deposit has a set *maturity date*—the day on which you must renew the certificate, cash it in, or purchase a new certificate. Some financial institutions offer certificates of deposit that allow the interest to accumulate to maturity. Other financial institutions send you a check for the interest or deposit the interest in a separate passbook account. The interest earned

A certificate of deposit is less liquid.

is placed in a passbook account to earn interest at a lower rate; that is, you do not receive interest on the interest earned.

Government Savings Bonds and Treasury Bills

U.S. savings bonds are loans to the government.

When you buy a savings bond, you are, in effect, lending money to the United States government. A Series EE savings bond is known as a *discount bond* because you buy it for less than its cash-in value. At maturity, you receive the full value of the bond. The difference between the purchase price and the cash-in value is considered interest earned. For example, a $50 bond may be purchased at a discount for $25. A $100 bond may be purchased for $50. The interest grows through periodic increases in redemption value and is paid at the time a bond is cashed. Interest earned is then taxable. The maturity date for Series EE bonds is ten years; but a bond may be held longer, with interest continuing to build until the bond is cashed. Interest rates on Series EE bonds are variable, but 7 1/2 percent is the minimum guaranteed five-year yield.

A Series HH savings bond pays interest semiannually at 7 1/2 annual percent (the government sends a check). The bond is purchased at face value (a $500 bond sells for $500) and is redeemed at face value. Series HH bonds may be redeemed at any time after six months, but mature in ten years.

Interest is not taxable until the bonds are cashed.

Savings bonds may be purchased over the counter or by mail at most financial institutions, and the bond certificates should be kept in a safe-deposit box. The advantage of the Series EE bond is that interest is not taxed until the bond is cashed. So if you are saving for a child's college education, there is no tax until the child cashes the bond. Your child will probably have a low income when he or she is ready to enter college and will have no tax liability. Bonds are also a good investment because they are considered very safe. Bonds can be quickly and easily converted to cash; their interest is not subject to state or local taxes (only federal taxes); and if they are lost, stolen, or destroyed they can be replaced without cost.

Treasury bills are auctioned weekly.

U.S. Treasury bills are available in denominations of $10,000, then in increments of $5,000. A Treasury bill is for one year or less; that is, the bill is usually a three-month, six-month, or one-year government obligation. Treasury bills are auctioned weekly for three- and six-month maturities, and monthly for one-year maturities. Treasury bills are purchased for individuals by investment companies, mutual funds, stock brokerage firms, cash management accounts, banks, and other agents who have a pool of money for such purchases. Rates for these sales are often used as the basis for rates paid on certificates of deposit, IRAs, money market funds, etc.

Cash Management Accounts

Offered at stock brokerage companies and investment service firms, *cash management accounts*, also called money market accounts, are available for persons wishing to invest their money at higher rates of return, but with less liquidity. The minimum balance in these types of accounts is $1,000, $5,000, or $20,000, depending on the account. Interest (often called dividends) is computed monthly, and earnings sometimes are not taxable. A person saves money and deposits it in this account, and the company invests the money in stocks and bonds. Based on the return earned by the company, a dividend is paid. The dividend is usually much higher than with other savings methods. The investor is given checks, but there are frequently minimum amounts for which the checks can be written and limitations on how often withdrawals can be made.

Risk is a disadvantage.

Cash management accounts are not insured by the FDIC or other government service. However, these accounts are safe because the securities purchased are very stable. Managers of these accounts purchase government bonds and securities issued by the United States Treasury. Therefore, the risk of losing your money is low.

IRA Accounts

An IRA (individual retirement account) is a savings plan whereby an individual (or couple) sets aside a certain amount of money (up to a specified maximum) each year for retirement. Although an individual may be enrolled in a retirement plan with his or her employer, an IRA can also be opened. The advantage of an IRA over other savings plans is that amounts put into the IRA account can be subtracted from annual taxable income. You will pay taxes on the IRA when you begin withdrawing funds and will probably be in a lower tax bracket. Interest rates paid on IRA accounts vary; some are equal to Treasury bill rates, while others are set individually by the different financial institutions holding the accounts. Most financial institutions have IRA accounts available. The disadvantage of an IRA is that you cannot remove part or all the money set aside before age 59 1/2 without severe penalty. This makes it a very illiquid savings plan.

IRAs are tax-deferred savings plans.

FACTORS IN SELECTING A SAVINGS ACCOUNT

There are a number of important factors to consider in selecting a savings account and a savings institution. These factors include (*a*) safety, (*b*) liquidity, (*c*) convenience, (*d*) purpose, (*e*) interest-earning potential, and (*f*) early withdrawal penalties.

Safety

Most financial institutions are insured.

You want your money to be safe from loss. Most financial institutions are insured by agencies such as the *FDIC* (Federal Deposit Insurance Corporation). Accounts protected by this insurance are safe up to $100,000 per account. You should check on the type of regulations and insurance the financial institution of your choice has to be certain of the safety of your deposit.

Liquidity

Liquidity, or how quickly you can get your cash when you want it, may be important to you. Some types of deposits may be obtained instantly; others may take weeks or even months to withdraw.

Convenience

People often choose their financial institution because of convenience of location and services offered. Interest rates on various savings accounts and certificates may vary only slightly. Fees charged are often very similar, while minimum deposits required may give preference to a certain type of account.

Many banks have several branches within a geographic area, which makes it convenient to do your banking after work or on the way home. If there is only one branch located several miles away, it is more expensive and inconvenient for you to bank at that financial institution. A very large bank may have branches in other states and parts of the country, giving you check-cashing privileges away from home.

Many banks offer drive-up windows that open at 7:30 A.M. on weekdays and are open for a few hours on Saturday. Day-and-night teller machines may be installed at all branches, offering an added convenience on weekends, holidays, and evenings.

Interest-Earning Potential

Little risk means little return.

Interest earnings on your deposit should be as great as possible—that is, your savings should be placed in the institution that offers the highest interest returns. Usually, the more liquid your deposit, the less interest it will earn; and the more risk you are willing to take, the higher the rate of return. The account that involves the least risk, the regular passbook account, pays the lowest interest.

Figure 9-4 is an example of interest rates being paid on Dec. 10, 1984. As you can see from the illustration, interest earned depends both on the type of financial institution in which you choose to save your money and on the type of account you open.

FIGURE 9-4
Current Interest
Rates As
Reported Weekly

> ### INTEREST RATES
> ### FOR CONSUMERS
>
> for the week ended Dec. 10, 1984 (Rates change each Tuesday. Treasury bills are sold Mondays.)
>
> **PASSBOOK SAVINGS:**
> Commercial banks 5.25%
> Savings and loans 5.50%
>
> **MONEY MARKET CERTIFICATES:**
> 3-month 9.0%
> 6-month 9.9%
>
> **TREASURY SECURITIES:***
> 3-month Treasury bills 9.0%
> 6-month Treasury bills 9.2%
>
> **OTHER:**
> Tax-exempt bonds 9.84%
> Daily money market funds 8.65%
>
> **HOME MORTGAGES:**
> FHA or GI 11.00%
> Conventional 11.75%
>
> *Most variable rate accounts are based on Treasury bill rates (Treasury bills are auctioned each Monday).

Purpose

Your purpose for saving money may greatly affect your choice of financial institution. Savings for a down payment on a home might best be placed at the savings and loan association that would someday make the loan to you for the home. You would establish credit with that institution and enhance your opportunities for securing the financing at a later date.

Consider how much money you can put away.

Early Withdrawal Penalties

Early withdrawal penalties should be considered when you are choosing a savings plan. If you need to withdraw all or some of your money before the maturity or withdrawal date, you may be charged a penalty.

Regular passbook accounts have no withdrawal penalties. You may make deposits or withdrawals at your convenience.

Depositors who withdraw time certificates before the maturity date are penalized. Three months' interest is lost on a six-month certificate. Six months' interest is lost on time certificates of over six months.

An IRA account either partially or fully withdrawn before age 59 1/2 will have an interest loss of six months, plus a 10 percent penalty. In addition, all income previously set aside in the IRA will become taxable immediately (you will recall it was subtracted from taxable income on tax returns).

Cash management and money market accounts usually do not carry early withdrawal penalties. Money may be withdrawn in full or in part at any time, provided the rules are met.

Each type of account at each institution is controlled by different rules. Before you open any account, be' sure to read carefully the minimum deposit and withdrawal restrictions, and other special conditions that may exist.

Early withdrawal penalties can be substantial.

THE IMPORTANCE OF SAVING REGULARLY

It is important not only that you save, but also that you save *regularly*. By saving regularly in accounts that accumulate interest and pay interest on interest, you can greatly increase your earnings. Figure 9-5 illustrates the effect of compounding when regular deposits are made to savings.

FIGURE 9-5
Compounding Interest and Making Additional Deposits

Year	Beginning Balance	Deposits	Interest Earned (5%)	Ending Balance
1	$ 0.00	$100.00	$ 5.00	$105.00
2	105.00	100.00	10.25	215.25
3	215.25	100.00	15.76	331.10
4	331.01	100.00	21.55	452.56

Obviously no savings plan is effective unless you have the willpower to set aside money—to forego purchases now in order to provide for them in the future. There are ways to make regular saving easier, however, including automatic payroll deductions, savings clubs, and automatic checking account deductions.

Automatic Payroll Deductions

Pay yourself first.

It is often possible to have money withheld from your paycheck and sent directly to your savings account. Before any other bills or expenses are paid, you "pay yourself." If the money is set aside before it reaches your checkbook, it is easier to forget about, and you can budget your expenses around the remainder with less difficulty.

Savings Clubs

Many banks and other institutions offer savings clubs, such as a Christmas club. You make regular payments into a special account and agree not to touch these funds before a specified date. In this way you are forcing yourself to save for some event or need, and when the time comes you know you will have the money. Interest paid on savings clubs may vary substantially among different financial institutions.

Automatic Checking Account Deductions

Automatic deductions are forced savings plans.

You may authorize an automatic deduction from your checking account each month. In this way you are also forcing yourself to save. You must remember to enter the automatic deduction in your checkbook register so that your checkbook will balance each month.

Figure 9-6 illustrates what a person could have saved for retirement, assuming he or she could save $2,000 a year at an average of 12 percent interest a year, beginning at age 20, 25, 30, or 35. You can see the compounding effect of saving. In addition, if the $2,000-a-year savings were placed in an IRA (individual retirement account), a tax advantage would result, because the full $2,000 could be subtracted from taxable income each year.

FIGURE 9-6
Saving for
Retirement

Beginning Age	No. of Years Saved	Amount Saved Each Year	Annual Interest Rate	Money at Retirement
20	45	$2,000	12%	$2,716,400
25	40	2,000	12%	1,534,182
30	35	2,000	12%	863,326
35	30	2,000	12%	482,665

VOCABULARY

Directions: Can you find the definition for each of the following terms used in Chapter 9?

liquidity	diversification
interest	principal
maturity date	compound interest
FDIC	true annual percentage rate
FSLIC	share account
NCUA	

1. Measure of how easily a deposit can be converted into cash.

2. An ending date on which a certificate or note is due (must be renewed or otherwise dealt with).

3. Money paid for the use of money.

4. Insurance company of the federal government that insures your deposit with a savings and loan association.

5. Insurance company of the federal government that insures your deposit with a commercial bank.

6. Insurance company that insures deposits kept at credit unions.

7. The type of account offered to a saver (regular savings plan) at a credit union.

8. A feature of a cash management account whereby the brokerage company buys many different types of investments.

9. A sum of money in a savings account on which interest accrues.

10. Interest computed on the sum of the principal plus interest already earned.

11. The effective yield on a deposit when compounding of interest is considered.

ITEMS FOR DISCUSSION

1. List several short-term needs that you may experience in the next few months or years.

2. List any long-term plans you may have that will require money in the next five years or more.

3. What four personal factors determine the amount of money you will save?

4. Why does a regular passbook savings account pay less interest than a certificate of deposit?

5. What are the tax advantages of owning a Series EE savings bond?

6. What is an IRA?

7. Explain how a cash management account works.

8. What things should you consider when choosing a financial institution for your savings?

9. Why might people choose to save their money in a commercial bank when they could receive higher interest rates at some other type of financial institution?

10. What is the main purpose of savings and loan associations?

11. How much is an account insured for by the FDIC?

12. What is diversification?

13. List three ways you can force yourself to save every pay period.

14. What types of penalties might you face for early withdrawal of all or part of your savings?

APPLICATIONS

1. Write out your savings plans, listing short-term and long-term goals you want to meet and how you plan to achieve those goals (how much money you will save to meet them).

2. What is discretionary income and what does it have to do with saving?

3. Which of the following is the least liquid?

    (a) regular passbook savings   (d) Treasury bill
    (b) certificate of deposit   (e) IRA account
    (c) savings bond

4. What happens if you need to withdraw all or part of your time certificate before its maturity date?

5. Why is a Series EE bond called a discount bond?

6. List a significant advantage of saving by purchasing savings bonds.

7. List one disadvantage for each of the following savings plans:

   (a) regular passbook account   (d) cash management account
   (b) certificate of deposit   (e) IRA account
   (c) savings bond

8. What major advantage is gained by saving at a commercial bank?

9. Why should you join a credit union when you have the opportunity?

10. Is it safe to invest your money with a brokerage firm in a cash management account that is not insured?

CASE PROBLEMS AND ACTIVITIES

1. Compute the interest compounded for Harriet Burke, assuming she deposits $1,000 in a time certificate that compounds interest every six months at the rate of 11 1/2 percent. It is a three-year time certificate. Use these column headings:

Year	Beginning Balance	First-Half Interest	Second-Half Interest	Total Interest	Ending Balance
1	$1,000				
2					
3					

2. Marsha Olson wishes to save $100 a month. Her bank computes interest and compounds it monthly. The current rate for a passbook account is 5 1/2 percent. Compute the interest compounded for Marsha. Use this format:

Month	Beginning Balance	Deposit	Total	Interest	Ending Balance
1	0	100	100	5.50	105.50
2	105.50	100	205.50		
3					
4					
5					
6					
7					
8					
9					
10					
11					
12					

3. Compute the interest compounded quarterly on a deposit of $500 for three years at 12 percent. Use the following column headings:

| | | INTEREST | | | | | |
| | | First | Second | Third | Fourth | Total | Ending |
Year	Beginning Balance	Quarter	Quarter	Quarter	Quarter	Interest	Balance
1	$500						
2	___	___	___	___	___	___	___
3	___	___	___	___	___	___	___

4. Compute your total savings if you keep $1,000 in a regular passbook account at 5 1/4 percent, compounded quarterly, for two years and if you put $1,000 in a two-year time certificate at 11.89 percent, compounded semiannually. Use these column headings:

REGULAR PASSBOOK

| | | INTEREST | | | | | |
| | | First | Second | Third | Fourth | Total | Ending |
Year	Beginning Balance	Quarter	Quarter	Quarter	Quarter	Interest	Balance
1	$1,000						
2	___	___	___	___	___	___	___

TIME CERTIFICATE

Year	Beginning Balance	First-Half Interest	Second-Half Interest	Total Interest	Ending Balance
1	___	___	___	___	___
2	___	___	___	___	___

5. Suppose you need to have the money from the time certificate in No. 4 before the two years are up. What is the penalty? What is the penalty for withdrawing all or part of your passbook savings account?

10
Investment Choices

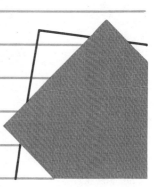

CHAPTER OBJECTIVES

After studying this chapter and completing the activities, you will be able to:

1. Understand the need for and purpose of investments and describe the criteria for choosing investments.
2. List and compare investment options available and make investment decisions.
3. Give examples of fixed- and variable-income investments and describe the advantages and disadvantages of each.

INVESTMENT ESSENTIALS

Investment is the outlay of money in the hope of realizing a profit. Money is usually invested for a long term to meet future needs and goals. Good investments provide long-term protection of income.

Good investments protect income.

There are numerous investment alternatives; some of the more common investment choices will be discussed in detail in this chapter. These alternatives include real estate, collectibles, business ventures, municipal bonds, preferred stocks, corporate bonds, common stocks, mutual funds, investment clubs, commodities, money market funds, and precious metals and gems.

The Investment Environment

Stock market is a general term that describes the securities market—the place where supply and demand for investment alternatives meet.

**ILLUSTRATION
10-1**
Stocks and
bonds are
bought and sold
at a stock
exchange.

Credit: Photo
courtesy of the
American Stock
Exchange/
James McGoon

Stocks of larger companies are listed with a specific *stock exchange*, where stocks and bonds are bought and sold. The largest organized stock exchange in the United States is the New York Stock Exchange. The smaller American Stock Exchange is also in New York City. Ten other regional exchanges are located throughout the country.

The New York Stock Exchange is a big building at the corner of Wall and Broad Streets in New York City. The trading floor (where stocks are bought and sold) is about two-thirds the size of a football field. Around the edge of the trading floor are teletype booths that are open at both ends, with room inside for a dozen or more brokers. *Brokers* do the buying and selling of stocks and bonds on the exchange. Only brokers who are members of the exchange may do business at the exchange.

Brokers must be members to be at the exchange.

Spaced at regular intervals around the trading floor are trading posts, which are horseshoe-shaped counters, each occupying about 100 square feet on the floor. Behind each counter are a dozen or more specialists and employees of the exchange. All buying and selling is done around the trading posts. About 90 different stocks are assigned to each post. Placards above each counter show which stocks are sold in each section, the last price of that stock, and whether that price represents an increase or a decrease from the previous price.

Buyers and sellers
make offers through
brokers.

Orders received at a brokerage firm are phoned or teletyped to that firm's teletype booth at the exchange. A clerk writes out the order and hands it to the floor broker to carry out. When the transaction is completed, the clerks for the brokers who bought and sold the stock report back to their respective home offices. The buyer and seller can then be advised that the transaction has been concluded and can be told the final price. Stocks listed with the exchange may be traded only during official trading hours—10 A.M. to 4 P.M., New York time, Monday through Friday (except holidays).

You can follow the progress of a stock by looking at the latest closing stock prices in your daily newspaper. *The Wall Street Journal*, published daily in a number of regional editions, also provides up-to-date financial and business news.

Unlisted securities can
be bought privately.

Stocks not listed with an exchange are called ***unlisted securities***. Individual brokers working directly with the corporation issuing stock may purchase and sell unlisted securities. An individual may buy and sell unlisted securities with another individual. When securities are bought and sold through brokers, but not through a stock exchange, the transaction is called an ***over-the-counter exchange***. Government and municipal bonds are traded over the counter. Generally, unlisted securities are those small companies well known locally but not nationally. Because prices for unlisted securites are not set by auctioning at a large exchange and their value is more difficult to determine, they are more risky.

Reasons for Investing

There are four basic reasons to invest money: (*a*) to provide supplemental income, (*b*) to make profits, (*c*) to provide a hedge against inflation, and (*d*) to provide income for retirement.

Money should be used for investment only in addition to savings. Money invested in stocks that provide dividends can provide a person with extra income to meet monthly expenses. Because there is more risk involved in investing, there is also a possibility of making large profits. Investors must be willing to gamble—to take chances that could mean big profits or big losses.

Investments protect you
from the effects of
inflation.

Inflation refers to the increased cost of living. A hedge against inflation is a way to make your money earn more than the rate of inflation. For example, if the annual inflation rate is 8 percent, you would want to invest your money to make more than 8 percent. A savings account would pay 5 to 6 percent. Therefore, a regular savings account would be worth less to you because it would represent less purchasing power.

At retirement, most people need to have more income than social security payments provide. Investments provide retirement income for security when earning power is diminished, and the desire to earn money through employment is low.

INVESTMENT COUNSELORS

Suppose you have just decided that, in addition to your savings, you have some money to invest. What next? You might go to your local banker and ask advice. You would then know of some investment firms in your local area and some of your options. But your banker may also try to convince you to buy your investments through the bank—bonds or securities that are very safe, yet provide a reasonable return. You may also get investment information from your lawyer or friends who have invested their money.

Trained professionals help you with investments.

The people best qualified to advise you about investments, however, are the professional investment planners, advisers, and brokers. These people are trained to give you intelligent overall advice, based on your goals, age, net worth, occupation, investment experience, life-style, family responsibilities, and other factors. The investment planner, broker, or adviser usually receives a fee for services rendered, although some mutual fund firms do not charge a commission for investing. You can purchase directly in many cases and pay no commissions, but you may not make wise investments because you are not an expert.

If you don't know a planner, adviser, or broker, perhaps a friend, associate, lawyer, or banker can recommend one to you. You may also see advertisements for investment and brokerage firms in the paper and make your own choice. Many people hesitate to use planners, advisers, or brokers because they are embarrassed about the small amount of money they have to invest—only a few hundred dollars or less a month. In this case, a broker can advise you of your options and some good investment clubs.

Don't be embarrassed to ask questions.

Some people are well informed and know what they want to buy and sell on the stock market. For these people, there is a service available called *discount brokerage*. Discount brokers buy and sell stocks for individuals for a reduced fee. The fee can be half as much as the one ordinarily charged by a full-service stockbroker who gives competent investment advice. But the discount broker gives no service other than to buy and sell stock in behalf of the customer. Large banks and savings and loan associations now have discount brokers to perform this service for customers. In most cases, you will be required to have an account at that bank so that money can be transferred from your account to pay for any stocks and bonds you purchase. For an annual fee, the bank will also keep a brokerage account for you, keep your stock certificates in the bank, and send you monthly or quarterly statements of value (showing the current value of your securities). A phone call from you to the discount broker is all that is needed to buy and sell stocks and bonds.

FIXED-INCOME AND LOW-RISK INVESTMENTS

There are a number of relatively safe investments that provide fixed income or have other safety features. These investments include notes and debentures; corporate and municipal bonds; preferred stocks; and mutual funds, investment clubs, and money market funds. Many conservative investors think these investments provide the best return for a relatively reasonable risk.

Corporate Notes and Debentures

A *corporate note* is an investment wherein you loan money to a corporation or other business and receive a note, or written promise to repay the loan plus interest, as evidence of the debt. A corporate note may be *secured*, which means payment is guaranteed by a pledge of property or other assets. If your note is not repaid, you can then claim the property pledged and sell it. An unsecured note, or *debenture*, is an investment

Interest on corporate notes is taxable.

made on the credit of the corporation only. Because the companies and corporations that borrow your money have good credit ratings and the purposes for borrowing money are good, notes and debentures are generally considered safe investments.

Interest rates and maturity dates for notes are determined at the time of purchase. You know how much you will receive on your investment and when you will receive it. Notes and debentures can be short-term (for six months or less) or long-term (for over a year).

Corporate and Municipal Bonds

Municipal bonds are issued by a government division, such as a city or county, and are guaranteed by the property owners within that tax district. Before these bonds are issued, they must be approved by voters. Municipal bonds have a major advantage: you pay no federal income tax

Interest on municipal bonds is not taxable.

on interest earned on them. Because they are tax free, municipal bonds do not carry a high interest rate.

Corporate bonds may be of four types. Secured bonds are those that are guaranteed by a pledge of property or other assets. A *bond indenture* is a written proof of the debt; the bonds are secured by the pledge of corporate assets. Unsecured bonds are those issued on the general credit of a corporation, and they do not involve a pledge of property. *Registered bonds* are those for which the corporation keeps a record of names of bonds and their owners; a change in ownership requires a change in records. *Coupon bonds* have individual coupons attached for each interest payment. The coupons are in the form of a check payable to the *bearer*, or anyone who presents them to the bank for payment on the date of the coupon (usually semiannual).

Bonds are issued in various denominations—from $1,000 to $10,000 or more. Most bonds are considered very safe investments with little risk of loss. You know when you purchase the bond exactly how much interest will be earned and when you will receive it.

Bond coupons can be cashed by anyone.

Preferred Stocks

Stocks on which dividends are paid first and whose holders are paid first in the event of company liquidation are called *preferred stocks*. There is little risk in preferred stock because dividends are predetermined. The four different classes of preferred stock are cumulative, noncumulative, participating, and nonparticipating.

There are four classes of preferred stock.

Cumulative. Cumulative stock is the most common type of preferred stock. For this type of stock, dividends not paid the year before because there were no profits must be paid this year before common stock dividends are paid.

Noncumulative. For noncumulative preferred stock, dividends not paid in previous years will not be made up when there is a profit to be distributed.

Participating. Stockholders holding participating preferred stocks are paid a set dividend. Common stockholders then receive a share of the profits. Any additional profits are shared proportionately by the two groups of stockholders.

Nonparticipating. Those holding nonparticipating preferred stock receive only the predetermined dividend. They do not receive any dividend above that declared for the year.

A cumulative, participating preferred stock would be an expensive stock to purchase, but a very safe investment with a solid rate of return. Dividends not paid one year would be made up when profits allowed, plus any excess profits would be shared with stockholders.

**ILLUSTRATION
10-2**
One way to
invest your
money is to buy
stocks.

Preferred stock has
less risk than common
stock.

Preferred stock is typically much more expensive than common stock because it has a high, set return of investment (interest) and involves little risk. Corporations must pay dividends to preferred stockholders before they can pay common stockholders, so dividends are virtually guaranteed.

Mutual Funds, Investment Clubs, and Money Market Funds

A *mutual fund*, also called a stock fund, is an investment wherein someone else is paid to choose and buy various stocks, bonds, money market investments, etc. Many individual investors deposit their money in a mutual fund, the money is invested by chosen experts, and a dividend is paid based on how well the investments perform.

An *investment club* is similar to a mutual fund. A group of people organize to pool their money, vote on how to spend their finances, purchase the desired investments, and share the profits made. There may be twenty people, each with $1,000 to invest. This $20,000 is used to buy selected investments that meet the overall goals of the club.

Diversification is
spreading the risk.

Mutual funds and investment clubs have the advantage of diversification. The investor is not dependent on the rise or fall of one or two stocks, because he or she has bought shares in a company that has invested in many different stocks, bonds, and other securities. The main advantage for you as an investor in a mutual fund is that you can invest with a relatively small amount of money. Combining your money with that of many other investors in the mutual fund company or investment club enables you to purchase stocks that you as an individual would not be able to afford, and thus increases your investment earnings. Between 1976 and 1981, some mutual funds advanced by more than 300 percent, for example.

Small investors should consider a money market fund.

For small investors, the **money market fund** has proved to be an excellent investment. Money market funds invest in short-term government, bank, and corporate notes. Interest rates on these investments have been consistently higher than on savings accounts.

The fund approach to investment is usually relatively safe; however, the rate of return is often low when there is less risk involved. The more aggressive the fund or club with which you invest, the more you stand to gain—or lose.

VARIABLE-INCOME AND ILLIQUID INVESTMENTS

Investments that involve greater risk also provide greater returns. However, in many cases such investments become *illiquid*, which means they are not easily converted into cash. High-risk investments are not easily sold, and the market to sell them is very small. Variable-income investments include common stocks, real estate, precious metals and gems, commodities, collectibles, and business ventures.

Common Stocks

Corporate stocks may be in the form of preferred stock, discussed earlier, or common stock. **Common stock** is a security representing a share in the ownership of a company. Common stockholders share in the profits of a corporation, elect a board of directors, vote in stockholders' meetings, and take the greatest investment risk. Common stock does not carry a fixed dividend as does preferred stock. Dividends on common stocks are based on corporate profits: the better the company does, the more common stockholders stand to make. Directors of the corporation declare a dividend out of the profits of the corporation, and common stockholders receive a dividend for each share of common stock owned.

Common stock is risky.

Real Estate

To purchase **real estate** is to purchase land and anything attached to it. The single largest real estate investment most people make during their lives is the purchase of their home.

Buying your own home is a large but relatively safe investment.

While real estate is generally considered very illiquid, buying your own home is regarded as a safe investment. Homes are purchased by making a **down payment**, which in most cases is 10 percent or more of the purchase price of the home, and financing the balance with a mortgage or trust deed. Therefore, if you buy a home costing $60,000, your down payment would be about $6,000 or more. You would pay the rest in monthly payments for the next 30 years. At 12 percent interest, your payments would be about $690 a month.

Both new and used homes have held their value over the past ten years, according to the National Association of Realtors. The average used home valued at $25,000 in 1970 more than doubled in value by 1980. The average new home built in 1970 increased in value 15 percent more than a used house by 1980. By 1985, home values seemed to stabilize from the decreasing values of the early 80s.

True, big investors have made fortunes in real estate. But as a general rule, real estate investment (other than investment in your own home) is not wise unless you are in the 50-percent tax bracket. Other real estate investments include apartment buildings, duplexes, commercial buildings, and rental homes. But to buy these types of real estate requires a large sum of cash and often more money annually to make repairs and keep the investment going. Real estate investments provide tax advantages for those with large incomes to shelter; others would find owning rental property a financial strain.

Buying real estate other than your home can be a financial strain.

Precious Metals and Gems

Gold, silver, and platinum are examples of *precious metals*—tangible, beautiful, desirable substances of great value. Precious metals are said to be the best hedge against inflation; but in times of low inflation rates, values of precious metals are also low.

The price of gold fluctuates with world economic conditions. The reason for this fluctuation is that gold is rare, yet a basis for money, which is always of value and universally acceptable. Figure 10-1 shows how gold and silver prices have fluctuated in recent years.

FIGURE 10-1
Gold and Silver Prices

	Dec. 1984	June 1983	June 1982	June 1967
Gold (troy oz.)	$327.00	$437.50	$318.50	$35.00
Silver (troy oz.)	6.98	11.80	10.50	1.80

Precious metals earn no interest or dividends for their owners. The profit is realized when they are sold. Gold and silver may be purchased in the form of coins, but coins present a problem of storage and safekeeping

Profits on precious metals are realized at sale.

because of their bulk. Gold and silver can also be purchased in the form of a certificate that states how much gold or silver bullion is being held in storage. However, for banks to hold gold or silver in storage, a minimum investment of $1,000, a commission of 4 percent, and storage fees are usually required.

Gems are natural precious stones such as diamonds, rubies, sapphires, and emeralds. Diamond prices are high and are subject to drastic change. Prices have fluctuated rapidly in recent years. A flawless, Grade D, one-carat diamond valued at $50,000 in 1980 dropped to $27,500 in 1981. But in 1971, the same diamond could have been purchased for $1,900. Likewise, rubies, sapphires, and emeralds increased in value greatly between 1971 and 1980, but decreased by 1981. By 1985, gem values had stabilized. When investments such as real estate become more expensive and less profitable because of high interest rates, many investors turn to precious stones. But when economic conditions are more favorable, precious stones lose their investment value.

Precious metals and gems have their greatest value as jewelry. Stones that are one carat or more are rare and are much more valuable than smaller stones. *Semiprecious stones*, such as garnets, spinels, and opals, often are a good investment. A one-carat semiprecious stone might cost between $1,000 and $2,000. Cultured pearls, however, are a poor choice for the average investor. The demand for pearl jewelry has increased over the past several years, but so has the supply of the most popular sizes of pearls. Consequently, only perfectly round black or rose pearls of a certain diameter are rare enough to be considered good investments—and these pearls are much too expensive for the average investor to consider.

Jewelry is a risky investment.

The biggest disadvantage of investing in metals and gems is, of course, that the market to sell them is often unpredictable. If you are eager to sell, you may face a loss. When purchasing metals and gems for investment, be aware of the markup. When buying from a jewelry store, the profit to the store is 50 to 100 percent of the actual value, so you should get several quotes before buying.

Commodities

Commodities, such as livestock, crops, or copper, are quantities of goods or interests in tangible assets. You can purchase the commodity itself or what is called a *futures contract*—a contract to buy or sell a commodity on a specified date at a specified price. You could, for example, contract to buy a certain commodity at what you consider its lowest price. You would buy on credit, putting up 8 to 10 percent of the value of the contract. You would then attempt to sell the contract for a higher price before the date on which delivery of the commodity must be made. Thus you can buy on paper without ever having to take possession of the actual goods. Enormous profits can be made in this way.

You rarely take possession of commodities.

Unfortunately, speculation in commodities is also much more risky than speculation in stocks. More people lose money than make money. If you buy a commodity at what you think is its low price, and the price either remains the same or drops lower, you lose your original investment. For this reason, investment in the commodities market should be limited to those with a great deal of excess money, financial wisdom, and the ability to take a big risk.

If, for example, you invest in cattle futures, you are buying cattle by the pound and expecting the price to rise before you sell it. In 1981 the average price per pound for live cattle was 69 cents. That is double the price of ten years earlier, but a mere penny more than the price in 1980. Soybean prices may fluctuate by only a few cents to as much as 15 cents or more. From 1971 to 1981, soybean prices rose 140 percent. Between 1981 and 1985, prices dropped slightly but regained their original 1981 prices. Timing is the crucial ingredient of effective investment in futures—knowing when to buy, how long to hold, and when to sell.

Collectibles

Collectibles are valuable or rare items, from antiques and coins to comic books and art pieces. They are valuable because they are old, no longer made, unusual, irreplaceable, or of historic importance.

Coins are the most common collectible.

Coins are perhaps the most commonly collected items. Coins that are silver (rather than an alloy) are worth more than 20 times their face value. For example, a fifty-cent piece dated before 1964 contained almost pure silver and is worth at least $10, depending on year and condition. A $20 gold piece, worth $50 in 1971, was worth $825 in 1980. By 1985 collectibles seemed to be holding value but not picking up increases.

People like to collect favorite items and hope someday their collection will be valuable. An advantage of collectibles is that you can start small and buy in small quantities. Unfortunately, collectibles are very illiquid, as a ready buyer for your collection is often difficult to find. The trick to collecting wisely is to buy only the highest quality of anything you are fond of collecting.

Business Ventures

Many a quick and tidy profit has been made by a person or group who invests in a *business venture*—the creation of a business to sell a specific idea, product, or service. The business venture is a riskier type of investment. If the idea, product, or service catches on, it will be very profitable; but if it fails it can represent a large financial loss. The manufacturing and selling of the hula hoop, for example, was a risky venture in which to invest several years ago. However, the hula hoop was very popular for a few years, and the original investors made large profits before the hula hoop declined in popularity. Fortunes can, then, be made and lost through investment in a business venture. In general, the best business ventures are those that offer a service that is needed but is not otherwise available.

Investment in a business venture can be very profitable.

INVESTING WISELY

A wise investment is one that results in the greatest financial gain available for your money; a poor investment is one that results in financial loss. Investing wisely is a difficult task, as you may have gathered from your reading thus far. The hints that follow, however, may make this task easier for you.

Criteria for Choosing an Investment

Some investments rise in value at a rate higher than inflation; some do not. Some investments provide retirement income that is tax sheltered; some do not. Some investments provide for increases in value that do not show up as taxable income for many years; some do not. The ideal investment would fulfill *all* of these criteria:

Some investments are tax shelters.

1. Complete safety from loss
2. High liquidity
3. High interest return
4. Growth in value that exceeds the rise in cost of living
5. Reasonable purchase price

Obviously, you may not find all of these elements in any single investment. However, all your investments should fulfill as many of these criteria as possible. The more elements fulfilled, the more desirable the investment.

Wise Investment Practices

People commonly make one or more serious mistakes in connection with their investment practices. Some mistakes are minor and can be corrected easily; others will cause serious financial damage. If you wish to

Mistakes cause finan-
cial damage.

avoid investment disaster, follow the wise investment practices described below.

Define Your Financial Goals. In Chapter 5, you were introduced to the importance of setting short- and long-term goals. If these goals are not clearly defined, you will not know which investments can best serve to meet them.

Follow Through. Putting off plans and never taking action will lead to failure in meeting your financial goals. If a goal is important, it should be worked on in the present, not put off until some never-to-come future day.

Keep Good Records. In order to be aware of your future needs and goals, you need to keep good financial records. Your personal inventory and net worth statement, plus lists of insurance policies and investments, balances and locations of bank accounts, and contents and location of your safe-deposit box, etc., are essential pieces of information. Unless you know where you have been and where you are, it is difficult to plan where you are going.

Personal records must
be complete.

Seek Good Investment Advice. Many people think they can make wise investments without seeking and paying for advice from an expert. In the long run, these investments may prove expensive, because poor investments can cost a great deal. In general, it is wise to seek competent advice from a trained professional before making any investment decisions.

Keep Current Your Knowledge of Investments. You should be aware of what is new in the financial market, what is or is not a good investment, when to sell and when to buy. The economy is a major consideration in making investment decisions. Although you should seek advice before making an investment move, it is your responsibility to know when to ask questions and to make any final decisions about the handling of your investment portfolio.

Remain informed about
the financial market.

Investment decisions become very complicated when even the best economists and advisers cannot agree. Nevertheless, making a thorough analysis of economic trends—past, present, and future—and carefully planning and following through on your financial goals will help you to make wise investment choices.

VOCABULARY

Directions: Can you find the definition for each of the following terms used in Chapter 10?

inflation	unlisted securities
broker	stock market
corporate note	real estate
preferred stock	precious metals
mutual fund	gems
money market funds	commodities
illiquid	futures contract
common stock	

1. Agreement to buy or sell a commodity on a specified date at a specified price.

2. The increased cost of living.

3. Livestock, crops, or copper—quantities of goods or interests in assets.

4. A person who buys and sells stocks and bonds on the exchange.

5. The written promise of a corporation to pay a debt.

6. Stock for which dividends are paid first but which confers no voting rights on the holder.

7. Many people invest their money in funds with an expert who makes the decisions.

8. A type of investment fund that purchases short-term government, bank, and corporate notes.

9. A type of stock that represents a share of ownership in a company.

10. Investments that are not easily converted to cash.

11. The place where supply and demand for investment alternatives meet.

12. Stocks that are not listed with an exchange.

13. Property such as land and buildings.

14. Natural precious stones, including diamonds, rubies, and sapphires.

15. Gold, silver, and platinum—tangible substances of great value.

ITEMS FOR DISCUSSION

1. List the basic reasons for investing.

2. What is inflation? How has inflation affected you?

3. List the characteristics of the ideal investment.

4. List the five wise investment practices.

5. List ten investment alternatives.

6. What are secured and unsecured notes?

7. What is the major advantage of purchasing municipal bonds rather than corporate bonds?

8. List the four classes of preferred stock.

9. Describe how an investment club works.

10. What are unlisted securities?

11. Give examples of precious metals.

12. Give examples of gems.

13. What are commodities?

14. What is a broker?

15. Why should you invest money (in addition to savings)?

APPLICATIONS

1. List your top five choices of investment alternatives, and give an advantage and disadvantage of each.

2. Assuming you have $5,000 to invest as you wish, describe your investment choices.

3. From the financial section of your newspaper listing stock exchange closing prices, select five stocks. Make a list of the five stocks and record their closing prices for five days. The illustration in Case Problem No. 1 explains how to read the columns.

4. Explain the difference between common stocks and preferred stocks.

5. Explain the meaning of the following statement: A buyer purchased 500 shares of cumulative, nonparticipating preferred stock.

6. Why is a mutual fund or investment club a good idea for people with small sums to invest?

7. Explain the meaning of this statement: The investment was good but very illiquid.

8. The market for precious metals and gems is described by investment experts as very volatile (subject to drastic and sudden changes). Explain why precious metals and gems are good investments and why they can be poor investments.

CASE PROBLEMS AND ACTIVITIES

1. The financial section of your newspaper generally has a listing of the closing prices of the daily stock market. The daily newspaper reports the weekday closing prices; the weekend newspaper reports a summary of the week's trading activities. The following is a clipping from the *Eugene Register-Guard* showing the closing prices for 2 P.M., April 29, 1982:

On this partial listing, there are five columns of stock listings. Beginning at the left of each column of stock listings and proceeding to the right, there are five important columns: (*a*) stock name; (*b*) price-earnings (PE) ratio; (*c*) sales; (*d*) last; and (*e*) change. Names of companies are abbreviated and listed alphabetically. The PE ratio is determined by dividing the current price of the stock by the earnings (dividends) for the past 12 months. The higher the ratio, the more desirable the stock for price increase profits. Sales indicates the number of shares sold during the day in hundreds. The last column lists the last or closing price for that day. Changes from the previous day's closing price are shown in the final column. Dividends are listed between the stock name and PE columns. Dividends listed are in relation to every $10 worth of stock owned.

In the clipping, look at the first stock listed: AAR. It is down about 12.5 cents in the day's trading, as shown by the −1/8. Closing price was 6 7/8, or $6.785 a share. One hundred shares of stock were sold that day. The price-earnings ratio is 15 (the price is 15 times last year's earnings), and possibilities of making a profit because value of the stock will go up are good. A dividend is paid, but only 44 cents for every $10 of stock owned, which is considered to be low.

Refer to the newspaper clipping above and fill in the information requested below.
(a) What is the daily change for AMD?
(b) What is the closing price of that stock?
(c) How many shares of AMD were sold that day?
(d) What is the daily change for PSA?
(e) What is the closing price of that stock?
(f) How many shares were sold that day?
(g) What is the price-earnings ratio for PSA?
(h) What is the dividend for every $10 of PSA stock owned?

6. Using the financial section of your daily newspaper, keep track of the progress of five different stocks for five consecutive days. List for each stock the closing price and net change for each day. On a piece of paper, prepare a form to record your information.

NAME OF STOCK	CLOSING PRICE					NET CHANGE				
	Day 1	2	3	4	5	Day 1	2	3	4	5
1.										
2.										
3.										
4.										
5.										

11

Insurance

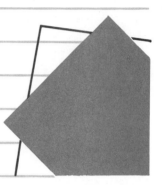

CHAPTER OBJECTIVES

After studying this chapter and completing the activities, you will be able to:

1. Identify types of insurance protection and the benefits of the major types of insurance available.
2. Understand the terms used to describe insurance policies and coverages.
3. Determine your insurance needs and make choices of insurance programs to meet various needs.

INSURANCE TERMINOLOGY

To understand insurance, you must understand the basic vocabulary. Here are some typical words that relate to insurance:

1. *Actuarial table*—a table of premium rates based on ages and life expectancies
2. *Actuary*—one who calculates insurance and annuity premiums, reserves, and dividends; a specialist on insurance statistics
3. *Agent*—a trained professional acting for the insurance company in negotiating, servicing, or writing a policy
4. *Beneficiary*—a person named on an insurance policy to receive the benefits (proceeds) of the policy
5. *Benefits*—sums of money to be paid for specific types of losses under the terms of an insurance policy
6. *Cash value*—the amount of money payable to a policyholder upon discontinuation of a life insurance policy

7. *Claim*—a demand for payment for a loss under the terms of an insurance policy
8. *Coverage*—protection provided by the terms of an insurance policy
9. *Deductible*—a specified amount subtracted from covered losses; the insurance company pays only the amount in excess of the amount subtracted
10. *Exclusions*—circumstances or losses that are not covered under the terms of an insurance policy
11. *Face amount*—the death benefit of a life insurance policy
12. *Grace period*—the period following the due date of an unpaid premium during which the policy is still in effect (usually 30 days)
13. *Insurable interest*—a condition required of the insured in nearly all insurance contracts, wherein the insured must be in a position to sustain a financial loss if the event insured against occurs
14. *Insurance*—a cooperative system of sharing the risk of financial loss
15. *Insured*—the person, partnership, or corporation protected against loss (not always the owner of the policy)
16. *Loss*—an *unexpected* reduction or disappearance of an economic value; the basis for a valid claim for repayment under the terms of an insurance policy
17. *Peril*—an exposure to the risk of loss
18. *Premium*—the sum of money the policyholder agrees to pay to an insurance company periodically (monthly, quarterly, annually, or semiannually) for an insurance policy
19. *Proof of loss*—the written verification of the amount of a loss that must be provided by the insured to the insurance company before a claim can be settled
20. *Risk*—the chance of loss
21. *Standard policy*—a contract form that has been adopted by many insurance companies, approved by state insurance departments, or prescribed by law (modifications can be made to suit the needs of the individual)
22. *Unearned premium*—the portion of the original premium that has not been earned by the insurance company and is returned to the policyholder when a policy is canceled

LIFE INSURANCE

Insurance protects the survivors.

The main reason families need life insurance is that the survival of the family usually depends on the income of one or two people. If a family wage earner dies uninsured, financial disaster could result for the remaining family members. A family that has no life insurance protection sometimes has to change its life-style drastically to survive when its primary wage earner dies—even to the point of moving from its home and giving

**ILLUSTRATION
11-1**
Life insurance
helps guarantee
a child's educa-
tion after a wage
earner's death.

up many things. *Life insurance* protects a family from the financial disaster that might otherwise result when a primary wage earner dies.

Financial Needs for Life Insurance

Life insurance needs are often hard to measure. One approach to determining the importance of life insurance coverage is to consider the financial needs that will exist for the family after the death of its primary wage earner. These needs typically include funds for last expenses, funds to support dependents, money to maintain a home, and funds for ongoing monthly expenses.

There are many ongoing expenses to consider.

Funds for Last Expenses. Death-related costs that survivors often must pay include medical bills from a last illness, funeral expenses, and burial costs. Funeral expenses of more than $5,000 are common.

Funds to Support Dependents. If the head of a household dies, his or her dependents will still need income. In the case of small children, much insurance is needed to provide support for many years until they are able to support themselves. Insurance coverage of $100,000 or more on the life of a wage earner is common.

Money to Maintain a Home. Mortgage payments on the family home must continue each month. Otherwise, the remaining family members will be forced to sell the home and lower the family's living standard in order to reduce housing payments.

Funds for Ongoing Monthly Expenses. Outstanding debts must be paid. Food, clothing, education, utilities, and other fixed and variable expenses continue.

Term Life Insurance

One type of life insurance, known as **term life insurance**, protects you for a set period of time—five, ten, or twenty years, or until you reach a certain age. Term insurance is death protection for a number of years only. There is no savings or cash value on a term life policy. For this reason, term insurance is the least expensive of all types of life insurance.

Term life insurance is temporary insurance only.

When a term life insurance policy is written, the insured names a beneficiary to receive the benefits of the policy if the insured dies during the term of the policy. The insured then pays the premiums, which are based on his or her approximate life expectancy as computed by an actuary. Premiums vary with the age of the insured and the amount of coverage. For example, at age 25, a person can purchase $100,000 of term insurance for about $250 a year. At age 30, the same term insurance will cost closer to $300 a year.

Decreasing Term. *Decreasing term* life insurance policies are those in which the coverage value decreases each year while the premium remains the same. A 20-year decreasing term policy, for example, decreases in value each year until the value reaches zero at the end of 20 years. If the insured dies during the first year of the policy, the policy pays $100,000. If the insured dies during the second year, death benefits decrease to $95,000. The value of the policy decreases each year thereafter.

There is no value at the end of the policy.

Level Term. *Level term* life insurance (also called renewable term) is renewable yearly, every five years, or every ten years. Evidence of insurability is not required for renewal. When a level term policy is renewed, premiums go up while the face amount of the policy remains the same. Therefore, when a $100,000 policy is first purchased, the premium may be about $240 a year. When the policy is renewed five years later, the premium may be about $280 a year. The face amount of $100,000 remains the same, however.

Premiums go up on level term insurance.

Some term insurance policies have additional features, such as optional conversion to a whole life policy, or automatic renewal. These additional features, however, raise the premiums. Also, at age 55 or 60 a term life insurance policy cannot be renewed. Therefore, term insurance is temporary protection for the wage earner while the family needs ongoing income.

Whole Life Insurance

Another major type of life insurance is *whole life insurance*, which pays the face amount to the beneficiaries on the death of the insured. The policyholder has the option of buying a straight life or a limited-payment life contract.

Straight Life. A type of whole life policy on which premiums are paid throughout life and the face value is paid at death is called *straight life*. When a policyholder stops making payments (paying premiums), she or he may choose to receive (a) a cash settlement of a guaranteed amount (less than face value), (b) income for a period of time, (c) full protection for a period of time, or (d) continued protection at a reduced amount.

These policies represent permanent insurance.

Limited-Payment Life. *Limited-payment life* is a type of whole life insurance on which premiums are higher because the payment period is limited to a specific number of years, such as 20 years, or until age 65. At the end of the established payment period, the policy is considered paid up.

Both types of whole life insurance build cash value. Money can be borrowed from the insurance company at low interest rates against policies carrying a cash value. If the loan is not repaid, that amount is subtracted from the face value of the insurance policy.

Endowment Insurance

Endowment insurance is an expensive type of life insurance policy that functions primarily as a savings contract. Premiums accumulate as a sum of money to be paid the insured on a specified date. If the insured does not die, the lump sum is paid to the policyholder at maturity of the policy. A policyholder may choose to receive a regular income after the policy matures, instead of a lump sum payment. If the insured does die before the savings plan is completed, the insurer completes the plan and pays the accumulated sum to the beneficiaries of the policy.

Endowment insurance is a savings plan.

Proceeds from life insurance policies are not taxable to a beneficiary. However, interest earned on the proceeds of life insurance policies is taxable to the policyholder.

Purchasing Life Insurance

When purchasing life insurance, keep in mind these two important facts:

Life insurance premiums are based on risk.

1. Life insurance contracts are based on the assumption that the insured is of average health and physical condition for his or her age. A person with a serious health problem, such as a heart condition, may be uninsurable (unable to get insurance).
2. Life insurance premiums are low for young people because their death risk is less.

Figure 11-1 is an actuarial table of premiums for a $10,000 term insurance policy (nonsmoker rates).

FIGURE 11-1
Actuarial Table

$10,000 Term Policy		
Age	1-Year Renewable*	10-Year Renewable
15	$ 28/year	$ 48/year
20	36	56
25	44	64
30	52	72
35	60	80
40	70	90
45	82	102
50	95	120
55	110	138
60	140	180

*Each year premiums go up by a few dollars.

Actuarial tables are based on risk. Females have lower premiums than males because the life expectancy for females is longer than for males. According to the National Center for Health Statistics (1983), a female born in 1980 can expect to live 77.7 years, while a male born the same year can expect to live only 70 years. In 1970 life expectancy was 74.7 years for females and 67.1 years for males; in 1900 it was 48.3 and 46.3, respectively.

HEALTH INSURANCE

Health care expenditures totaled $315.6 billion in 1983. Of this amount, private health insurance paid $78 billion, government (federal, state, and local) paid $132.5 billion, private individuals paid $173.1 billion, and the rest was paid by industry and donations.

In 1970, health care expenditures totaled $69.3 billion, up from $11.7 billion in 1950. In the 10 years between 1970 ($69.3 billion) and 1980 ($249 billion), health care expenses rose 259 percent.

In the last ten years, medical costs in this country have skyrocketed and continue to rise sharply. In 1983, the United States spent $355 billion on health care. This is an increase of 10.3 percent over 1982 health-care costs. The average annual amount of health-care costs for every man, woman, and child is $1,459. Spending for physicians' services in 1983 was $69 billion or nearly 20 percent of all health-care costs. Much of this expense is covered by health insurance companies.

Health insurance costs have risen sharply.

Several factors are responsible for the continued increase in costs to the public for medical care. Advances in technology and discoveries of new treatments for diseases result in a continuous need for expensive equipment and specially trained, highly paid personnel. The high cost of medical schooling, the increasing shortage of medical doctors, the increasing malpractice insurance premiums, and the rising cost of overhead and office operations are also factors that contribute to the increase in medical expenses paid by the public.

Health insurance is a plan for sharing the risk of financial loss due to accident or illness—of avoiding financial disaster in the event of large medical bills. Over 70 percent of all health insurance is issued in the form of **group health insurance** plans. Group plans provide coverage for

Most people have group health insurance.

employees or other large groups of people; all those insured have the same coverage and pay a set rate for the insurance. Pooling of resources results in greater coverage for lower premiums on group policies than could be obtained through individual policies. **Individual health** insurance plans are expensive because only a single person or household is insured under one policy. There is no pooling or grouping of financial resources to allow lowering of premiums.

Medicare and Medicaid Programs

For persons over age 65, the federal government has a medical and hospital insurance program under social security called **Medicare.** A monthly premium is charged for each type of coverage (medical and hospital). Medicare hospital insurance covers hospitals and nursing home facilities. Hospital insurance pays for all covered hospital services from the first through the sixtieth day in each benefit period, except for the first $304. From the 61st through the 90th day in each pay period, hospital insurance pays for all covered services except for $76 a day.

For a monthly charge, social security recipients may add benefits to help pay costs of doctors' fees, office calls, and other medical services not covered by Medicare. For the elderly, group or individual health insurance policies supplement Medicare and offer additional coverage for retired persons. The supplemental or added coverage usually pays the deductible, or first $75 that Medicare will not pay, plus other expenses not covered by Medicare. Aged persons receive benefits under this supplementary program only if they sign up for the program and pay the monthly premium ($15.50 as of Jan., 1985). The plan pays for 80 percent of doctors' visits, health services, and tests, as well as physical therapy and outpatient services.

Medicare is health insurance for the elderly.

Another government program, called **Medicaid**, is provided for indigent persons, regardless of age, who do not qualify for Medicare. Medicaid benefits are paid through welfare offices and are designed for those persons who cannot pay their regular medical expenses. There is no deductible. Those who qualify to receive welfare payments generally qualify to receive Medicaid benefits as well for medical care.

Medicaid is for those who can't pay medical expenses.

Hospital and Surgical Insurance

Hospital and surgical insurance benefits pay for all or part of hospital bills, surgeons' fees, and the expenses connected with certain in-hospital services such as anesthesia, laboratory work, X rays, drugs, and other care items. Usually a maximum dollar amount is allowed for each day a patient is in the hospital, for a maximum number of days. The greater the number of days and the larger the amount per day, the higher the premiums. Group policies will generally pay 100 percent of these medical costs.

Most hospital bills have full coverage (no deductible).

Medical Expense Insurance

Medical expense insurance pays for doctors' fees for office visits and for routine services other than those connected with hospital care. Most policies have a deductible. Typically, in a group policy, the deductible is the first $100 for a single person, and $100 a person on a family policy. After the deductible is met (paid by the insured), the insurance company begins paying 80 percent of qualifying medical expenses.

Major Medical Insurance

Major medical insurance applies to both hospitalization and medical services and may be purchased as a separate policy. Most major medical policies have high limits—$250,000 to $1,000,000. Major medical insurance provides the type of coverage necessary to protect individuals and families from financial ruin as a result of prolonged hospitalization or

Major medical protects against catastrophic illness or injury.

other medical care. For example, being hospitalized for a month or longer could cost $50,000 or more, depending on services provided. Accidents or illness can happen to anyone, and large medical bills can devastate a family without adequate health insurance coverage.

Disability Income Insurance

Disability income insurance helps to replace the income of a wage earner who cannot work for a prolonged period of time because of an illness or injury. There are many different types of disability income available to workers and their families.

Short-Term Disability Policies. A short-term disability policy provides income protection for the worker who is unable to work for six months or less. Under this type of policy, the worker must wait two to three weeks before claiming benefits—usually until the regular sick pay time has expired. Then, the benefits may or may not be retroactive to the first day of absence not covered by sick pay. The benefits last as long as six months, or until the worker returns to work, whichever comes first. Usually, the employee pays the premium for this type of insurance, and the benefits payable are about 50 percent of the worker's regular pay.

Long-Term Disability Policies. For the worker who becomes permanently unable to return to work in his or her usual occupation, this type of protection is best. An injury or illness may prevent a worker from returning to work for such a long period of time that returning would no longer be reasonable. For example, a severe back injury could prevent a person from returning to work where heavy lifting was a requirement. Under a long-term disability policy, the worker must wait 60 to 90 days before benefits begin. The longer the waiting period, the lower the premium. Again, the maximum benefits are no more than 50 to 75 percent of an individual's regular wages. The worker is free to return to other types of work in most cases. Employers often provide this type of coverage to employees as a part of their benefit program.

Annuities. Company-held and private annuities are savings programs which are set aside monthly to provide benefits for workers who need emergency or retirement funds. Company-held annuity programs are often called ***tax-sheltered annuities*** because (a) the money withheld from employees' wages is not taxed until the annuity is paid out, and (b) matching funds paid by the employer are not taxed to the employee until paid out. In this way, you can set aside part of your pay now, and pay taxes on it when you withdraw it later. Your tax rate will be lower because you are retired.

You can set up your own annuity program through a bank, credit union, savings and loan, or insurance company. You pay a set amount into the account each month. It gathers interest or dividends which accumulate in your account. As an individual, you may still be qualified for some tax-shelter provisions, depending on your occupation. The money is paid back to you in monthly payments at a predetermined retirement age, or when you become disabled, or when you can show your need. Early withdrawal of funds (when one of the predetermined conditions is not met) can result in lower monthly income payments to you.

Government Assistance Programs. Disability income is available to you as a worker under the social security program and under the workers' compensation program in your state. Social security pays disability income benefits to workers who qualify (have worked a minimum length of time) and can prove permanent total or partial disability that prevents them from returning to their regular work. Workers' compensation benefits are available under your state's accident insurance program and will pay your medical costs and lost wages due to job-related injury or illness. To file workers' compensation claims, you might need the services of an attorney. The attorney can advise you on how to establish your medical condition and needs and that the cause of the accident or illness is directly related to your employment.

Dental Insurance

Most ***dental insurance*** is written under group insurance plans to cover such expenses as repair of damage to teeth, examinations, fillings, extractions, inlays, bridgework, dentures, oral surgery, and root canal work. Most dental insurance policies have a deductible, in addition to restrictions on the types of dental work covered and maximum amounts payable (the usual limit is 80 percent of dental bills). Orthodontic work (correction of irregularities of the teeth with braces) is rarely covered, or if it is covered, a set maximum amount is paid. The high cost of individual dental policies makes group policies most feasible.

Dental insurance has many exclusions.

A single person or a family should have adequate health insurance coverage so that unforeseen medical and dental expenses do not cause

National health insurance has been proposed many times.

financial ruin. Although a form of national health insurance may be legislated in the United States at some future time so that all citizens have coverage (as in Canada), it is more likely that the individual family will continue to determine its own health insurance needs and provide for them.

AUTOMOBILE INSURANCE

In most states, automobile insurance is required for operation of a motor vehicle. Automobile insurance provides protection to owners and operators of motor vehicles. It is designed to cover the costs of damage to a motor vehicle, its owner, and any passengers. Auto insurance also covers the cost of repairs to other vehicles and medical expenses of occupants in other vehicles with which you are involved in an accident.

Automobile insurance rates are based on many variables.

Automobile insurance is expensive. Premium rates are based on (*a*) driving record; (*b*) driver's education and training; (*c*) model, style, and age of car; (*d*) age and sex of driver; (*e*) location (city, county) of driver and car; (*f*) distances driven; (*g*) whether or not car is used for work; and (*h*) age and sex of other regular or part-time drivers. The driving record includes number and type of tickets received and accident record. Arrests for driving under the influence, speeding, or driving without a valid license are also part of the driving record. Driver's education courses will reduce premiums. Except for vintage models, the older the car, the less insurance required, because the car is worth less. Expensive and new cars cost more to insure because they are worth more. Sports cars, for example, are more expensive to insure than family automobiles. Young single

Young drivers pay more for automobile insurance.

drivers pay more for insurance than those who are over age 25 and married. Male drivers pay more than females. Certain locations are considered to be more hazardous because of narrow roads, country roads, the number of licensed drivers in the area, and the accident rate in the area: if you live in one of these locations, your rates will be higher. The farther you drive on a regular basis (such as to work), the higher your premiums. Who will be driving your car, primarily and occasionally, will also be a factor in determining insurance cost. Adding a teenage driver to a car insurance policy will increase premiums.

There are four basic types of automobile insurance. These include liability, collision, comprehensive, and personal injury protection. All four types of insurance purchased in one policy is known as *full coverage*.

Liability Insurance

Liability coverage is required in most states. Liability protects the insured against claims for personal injury or damage when the insured is

Liability insurance is
required in most states.
driving his or her car or someone else's car. However, the insured receives nothing for his or her personal losses. Payments under liability coverage are for injuries and damages caused to others.

Liability insurance coverage is described using a series of figures, such as 100/300/10. The figures mean the insurance will pay up to $100,000 for an injury to one person, $300,000 for injury to two or more persons (total), and $10,000 for property damage. Premiums charged for liability insurance vary according to amounts of coverage.

Collision Coverage

Most automobile policies provide *collision coverage*—coverage of the insured's own car in the event of an accident. *No-fault insurance* laws provide for the repair or replacement of your car by your insurance company, regardless of who is at fault at the scene of an accident. Payment for repairs is made by each insurance company to its own client. Repairs are made and paid for; then the insurance companies settle the costs later, based on which driver is at fault.

Most collision insurance has a deductible: the policyholder pays the first $50 or $100 (or any amount specified in the policy) for repairs, and the insurance company pays the rest. Because many minor traffic accidents involve minimum damage that is less than most deductibles, it is wise to have a deductible and pay low premiums. In other words, paying the first $100 for each accident is less expensive than having no deductible and paying high insurance premiums.

The higher the deductible, the lower the premium.

Comprehensive Coverage

Comprehensive insurance covers damage to your car from events other than collision or upset. Events other than collision include fire, theft, tornado, hail, water, falling objects, acts of God, accidental acts of man, and acts of vandalism. If your car is scratched while parked in a parking lot, or it receives a dent in the hood or trunk from a flying rock, your insurance will pay for all the cost of repairs. There is usually no deductible for comprehensive coverage.

Comprehensive coverage usually has no deductible.

Personal Injury Protection (PIP)

Commonly known as medical coverage, *personal injury protection* (PIP) pays for medical, hospital, and funeral costs of the insured and his or her family and passengers, regardless of fault. If the insured is injured as a pedestrian, automobile insurance personal injury protection will pay the medical expenses. Another option, sometimes called **uninsured motorist coverage**, protects you as a pedestrian when hit by a car that is uninsured.

In many states proof of insurance is required in order to obtain a current vehicle registration. Liability insurance (to protect others in the event of your negligence) is the minimum requirement. Most lenders who finance the purchase of a new or used automobile require full insurance coverage (all four types of insurance combined in one policy)

Figure 11-2 shows a comparison of coverages for automobile insurance.

FIGURE 11-2
Automobile
Insurance

AUTOMOBILE INSURANCE		
	WHO IS PROTECTED:	
	Policyholder	Other Persons
Liability insurance:		
Personal injuries	No	Yes
Property damage	No	Yes
Collision coverage:		
Damage to insured vehicle	Yes	No
No-fault provision	Yes	No
Comprehensive coverage:		
Damage to insured vehicle	Yes	No
Personal injury protection:		
Bodily injury	Yes	Yes
Uninsured motorist coverage	Yes	Yes
Medical payments	Yes	Yes
Pedestrian coverage	Yes	No

PROPERTY INSURANCE

When you rent an apartment or other space or buy a home, you will need property insurance to protect your personal possessions (contents). You will need property insurance on the structure if you own the property. An apartment or house landlord can insure the building, but cannot insure personal possessions of tenants. Therefore, tenants must insure the contents of their apartment or rented house. As a homeowner, you will want to insure the building in addition to having the added protection of liability insurance. The basic types of property insurance are fire insurance, loss or theft insurance, liability insurance, and homeowners insurance.

Fire Insurance

More than a billion dollars is lost each year because of fires that destroy buildings and their contents. *Fire insurance* will reimburse you for fire damage to your home and possessions. Generally, insurance for contents is half the value of the building. If the building is insured for $50,000, the contents would be covered for $25,000.

Fire insurance protects the homeowner against damages that are caused by fire and lightning. Damages to a home and its contents by smoke and water as a result of the fire are also covered by fire insurance.

Overinsuring property (buying more insurance than the amount necessary to cover the value) is unwise because the insurance company will pay only the true value. Therefore, if a home valued at $40,000 with contents of $20,000 is totally destroyed, the insurance company will pay no more than $60,000, even if the owner carries $75,000 insurance. Carrying extra insurance only causes higher premiums.

When buying fire insurance for a home, remember that the lot or land will not burn. Only the part of the structure that will burn or can be destroyed needs to be insured.

For a small additional premium, the property owner can extend coverage to add an endorsement for loss caused by windstorm, hail, riot, civil commotion, vehicles and aircraft, smoke and explosion. This is called *extended coverage* to a basic policy. Instead of adding separate coverages, the homeowner may wish to purchase a package homeowners policy, which contains all the coverages mentioned.

Loss or Theft Insurance

Loss or theft insurance coverage applies to personal property, whether it is at home or with you. Valuables are insured in the event of burglary, robbery, or damage. A *personal property floater* may also be purchased to protect certain specified items of property (such as a 35-mm camera). Under a floater policy, property is protected without regard to its location at the time of loss or damage. Rates are reasonable. For example, a camera worth $500 can be insured for about $12 a year.

Liability Insurance

Property liability insurance protects the property owner against legal claims by persons injured while on the insured's property. For instance, if a guest in your home slips and falls on your front steps, you may be held liable for medical expenses for his or her broken leg.

Homeowners need lia-
bility coverage.

All homeowners and landlords should carry liability insurance, since they are responsible for acts occurring on their property, even acts involving uninvited persons. If you own a dog, you are responsible for the acts of the dog. If the dog bites someone, your liability insurance will cover the expenses of treating the injury. Except in the case of an attractive nuisance, when someone trespasses on private property, a homeowner will not be held liable for damages, unless a trap was set with the intent to harm trespassers.

An attractive nuisance
applies to all minors.

An *attractive nuisance* is a dangerous place, condition, or object that is particularly attractive to children. A swimming pool is an example of an attractive nuisance. If a child sneaks into a private pool, without permission, and is hurt, the homeowner will be held liable for damages and injuries. This is true even if steps had been taken to prevent entry into the pool.

Homeowners Insurance

Homeowners insurance combines fire, loss and theft, and liability coverage into one comprehensive policy. Generally, homeowners policies provide coverage at a lower cost than would be available if the coverages were purchased separately. A minimum amount of coverage must be purchased, but this minimum is usually an amount that will meet the needs of most people. The minimum liability for most homeowners policies is $25,000, with $50,000 or $100,000 being more common limits.

Figure 11-3 shows what coverages are included under a homeowners insurance policy.

DETERMINING INSURANCE NEEDS

It is important to have adequate insurance coverage, yet insurance premiums can be expensive. In order to manage your personal finances wisely, therefore, you must determine your insurance needs carefully to avoid paying premiums for coverage you do not require. Use the following step-by-step list as an aid in determining your insurance needs.

1. Determine your most important needs (they should be covered first).
2. Determine other types of insurance that may be needed, and list them by priority and cost.

Determine your insur-
ance needs carefully.

3. Decide how much money is available in the family budget to meet these insurance needs.

FIGURE 11-3
Homeowners
Policy

HOMEOWNERS INSURANCE

Properties covered:	Home	Personal property at or away from home
Perils normally covered:	Fire	Fire or lightning
	Lightning	Windstorm or hail
	Windstorm	Explosion
	Hail	Riot or civil commotion
	Explosion	Aircraft
	Riot	Vehicles
	Civil commotion	Smoke
	Aircraft	Vandalism
	Vehicles	Theft
	Smoke	Falling objects
	Vandalism and malicious mischief	Weight of ice, snow, or sleet
	Theft	Collapse of a building or any part of a building
	Breakage of glass	Accidental discharge or overflow of water or stream
		Sudden and accidental tearing asunder, cracking, burning, or bulging
		Freezing
		Artificially generated electrical current
Liability:	Bodily injury	Damage to property of others
	Cost of legal defense	Medical payments

4. Based on needs, shop around and ask questions. Check out the insurance companies you are considering to be sure they are sound and reputable. Discuss options and prices with agents. Take enough time to consider the options thoroughly so that you make the right decision.

5. Read and understand all policies—what is included and what is excluded—before signing and paying premiums. Know exactly what coverage you have, what is not covered, and how to file claims.

6. Periodically review your insurance program and compare it with your family's changing needs. Be sure that you and your family are adequately protected at all times.

VOCABULARY

Directions: Can you find the definition for each of the following terms used in Chapter 11?

16 agent
19 beneficiary
15 benefits
5 Medicare
2 no-fault insurance
10 term life insurance
18 tax-sheltered annuity
20 coverage
6 health insurance
3 full coverage
14 exclusions

13 insurance
12 loss
21 premium
17 disability income insurance
11 proof of loss
22 unearned premium
9 whole life insurance
8 cash value
4 deductible
1 extended coverage
7 endowment insurance

1. A feature added to a standard fire insurance policy that covers additional hazards such as windstorm, hail, riot, and other perils.

2. A type of auto insurance that eliminates the need to establish fault before payment is made to cover damages.

3. All types of automobile coverage combined into one policy.

4. The amount of damages you must pay before the insurance company begins paying.

5. A federal health insurance program for the elderly.

6. A plan of sharing the risk of financial loss due to illness or injury requiring medical treatment.

7. The most expensive type of life insurance because it combines a savings plan with insurance and pays whether or not the insured dies.

8. The amount of money paid to a policyholder if he or she elects to give up a policy and no longer make premium payments.

9. Life insurance that pays the face value to beneficiaries upon the death of the insured.

10. Life insurance that pays the face value to beneficiaries only if the insured dies during the term of the policy, while premiums are being paid.

11. A formal written statement by the insured to the insurance company to request repayment for a loss.

12. The basis of a valid claim for repayment under the terms of a policy.

13. A cooperative system of sharing the risk of a financial loss.

14. Circumstances or losses that are not covered under the terms of an insurance policy.

15. Sums to be paid for specific types of losses under the terms of an insurance policy.

16. A trained professional acting for the insurance company in negotiating, servicing, or writing an insurance policy.

17. A policy to replace the income of a wage earner who cannot work for a prolonged period due to an illness or injury.

18. An income security program that allows you to defer taxes on income until a later date.

19. The person named in an insurance policy to receive the proceeds (benefits) of the policy.

20. Protection provided by the terms of an insurance policy.

21. The amount of money a policyholder agrees to pay to an insurance company for an insurance policy.

22. The portion of the original premium that has not been earned by the company and is returned to the policyholder when an insurance policy is canceled.

ITEMS FOR DISCUSSION

1. Why do families need life insurance?

2. What are some of the financial needs to be considered following the death of the primary wage earner?

3. How does an insurance company determine the amount of premiums on insurance?

4. What are the three main types of life insurance?

5. Which type of life insurance is the least expensive? the most expensive?

6. Why has the cost of health insurance risen so drastically in the last several years?

7. Who is eligible to receive Medicare? Medicaid?

8. List five major types of health insurance coverage.

9. What type of automobile insurance coverage is required in most states? Who is protected under this type of insurance?

10. On what factors are the insurance premiums for automobile insurance based?

11. List the four types of automobile insurance coverage.

12. Explain the concept of no-fault insurance.

13. Why should renters have property insurance?

14. List the three major types of property insurance.

15. What type of policy protects a valuable item of personal property regardless of its location at the time of loss?

APPLICATIONS

1. What are your life insurance needs at this time in your life? What are the life insurance needs of your family?

2. Assume that you are married, have two small children, and you and your spouse have either part-time or full-time jobs. What type of life insurance should you have? How much should you have?

3. Contrast and compare these three major types of life insurance: term insurance, whole life insurance, and endowment insurance.

4. Why should families have some type of health insurance or major medical insurance coverage?

5. Why are automobile insurance premiums higher for a new car than for an older model?

6. Explain which types of coverage are included with full coverage automobile insurance.

7. Which type of automobile insurance is required to pay for damage to a car from a falling object such as a tree branch?

8. What type of automobile insurance is required in your state? How does your state ensure that this requirement is met?

9. Does your state have no-fault insurance laws? Explain the provisions of no-fault insurance in your state.

10. List several ways you can reduce the amount of your automobile insurance premiums.

11. Why should you not have more fire insurance coverage on your home than the home and its contents are actually worth?

12. Why is it necessary for homeowners to have some type of liability insurance?

CASE PROBLEMS AND ACTIVITIES

1. Judy Seubert, a friend of yours, is thinking about putting an in-ground swimming pool in her backyard. Explain to Judy the dangers of having a pool and the type of insurance coverage needed.

2. The local department store delivers a couch to your home, and your dog bites the delivery person, who demands that you pay the medical bills. You had a sign warning "Beware of Dog" posted on your front door. What responsibilities do you have, and what type of insurance coverage do you need?

3. Interview an employee who has a group health insurance plan. Discuss what types of expenses are covered, what deductibles are applied, how much of the premium is paid by the employer and how much by the employee, and what the maximum benefits are.

4. Call a private health insurance carrier (company) and ask for information about an individual major medical insurance policy. What types of coverages are available and what are the premiums for individuals?

5. Why is it necessary for families to have life insurance on wage earners? How much coverage do you think is necessary if each wage earner makes $15,000 a year and there are children under age five?

PART FOUR
CREDIT MANAGEMENT

12

Credit in America

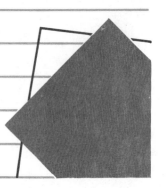

CHAPTER OBJECTIVES

After studying this chapter and completing the activities, you will be able to:

1. Define *credit* and describe the history of credit in America.
2. List advantages and disadvantages of the use of credit by the American consumer.
3. Briefly describe the kinds and sources of credit available in the United States.

HISTORY OF CREDIT

Most purchases are made on credit.

When you borrow money or use a charge account to pay for purchases, you are taking advantage of the most commonly used method of purchase in the United States: credit. When you buy something now, but agree to pay for it later, or borrow money and promise to pay it back later, you are using **credit**. For the privilege of charging purchases or accepting a loan, you will usually pay an interest or finance charge. It is estimated that over 80 percent of all purchases made in the United States are made through the use of credit.

The need for credit arose in the United States when the country grew from a bartering and trading society to a currency exchange economy. Most historians credit this transition to the time of the Industrial Revolution. During that period items were first manufactured for sale—everyone did not produce everything for their own use any longer.

Americans began to be dependent on one another. Instead of each family being wholly self-supporting, growing its own food and providing

210

When you buy something now, but pay for it later, you are using credit.

Lack of self-sufficiency created a need for credit.

its own clothing and shelter, family heads began to work for others to earn wages. Soon the need developed for sources of credit to help families meet their financial needs. Consumer credit had begun.

One of the earliest forms of credit was the account at the local mercantile or general store. The wage earner or farmer would pick up supplies and put the amount due "on account." Accounts would accumulate for a month, for a season, or even for a year. When a paycheck was received or a crop was harvested, the account would be paid in full, and the charging process would begin again. Interest was rarely charged. But only those customers who were well known to the business owner were offered credit.

Banks loaned farmers lump sums of money as large as $500 at the start of the planting season to put in crops. The loans were repaid after the harvest. This type of credit was very expensive, however. In the 1800s, interest rates were very high, and loans were generally made only in emergency situations. Most people, including bankers, knew very little about credit and how it worked. Consequently, bankers and others making loans charged high interest rates and were very reluctant to loan large sums of money.

The first loans were expensive.

Early 1900s

Since 1900 interest rates have dropped. The decrease is mainly a result of a new awareness and understanding of the advantages—especially the financial rewards—of loaning money. Lending institutions

Since 1900 rates have dropped.

began to ask for security on loans (the pledging of property and income); consequently, they became more willing to make loans.

As the use of credit expanded, individual purchasing power also expanded. Because more people were willing and able to buy more goods and services, the American economy grew at a healthy pace. Conveniences as well as necessities were purchased with the help of credit, and the standard of living of the average American rose. Businesses and consumers benefited from credit. New jobs were created, and the economy grew until World War I, which created a significant debt. The war debt was paid off, however, and the United States entered the 1920s in a secure position with credit stronger than ever.

The Next 50 Years

Credit flourished after World War I.

Between 1920 and 1970, buying on credit became the American way of life. No longer was credit saved for emergencies. Many different forms of credit developed to meet changing consumer needs and wants.

In 1929 when the stock market crashed, many Americans lost their savings. Banks went bankrupt, and loans were defaulted. It took almost a decade to bring back confidence in credit and investments. But recovery was followed by war again, and World War II proved costly. The federal government went heavily into debt and was no longer able to balance its budget. However, consumer credit continued to grow and flourish. Interest rates were low, and inflation rates were stable and under 10 percent. All seemed well until the 1970s brought unusually rapid economic growth, overuse of credit, and high inflation rates.

Credit Today

Overuse of credit causes problems.

In the last 25 years, the amount of consumer credit has greatly increased. The widely accepted use of credit has created many jobs, but it has also caused problems. Many consumers at all income levels have found themselves in financial trouble with credit.

Lenders are now more willing to make loans to consumers considered high risk—those who have poor credit records or little capital to ensure their ability to repay debt. Credit cards have been generally easy to obtain for nearly all consumers who have earning ability and the desire to use credit. But the last decade has shown that, as more people borrow and use credit, the interest rates charged also rise, bringing the cost of credit to a new high.

Consumer protection interests grew in the 1970s.

The 1970s brought the first powerful consumer credit protection legislation. No longer was "buyer beware" the rule in credit transactions. Laws were enacted to protect consumers from fraudulent practices. Both government and private agencies were formed to assist consumers with their rights and responsibilities.

The late 1970s brought a new occupation—credit counseling. Credit counselors advise others on how to use credit wisely, pay bills, and get out of trouble with credit; when to seek legal advice; and how to avoid damaging their credit ratings.

Loans on real estate purchases were at 6 percent and lower until 1970. By 1980 that rate had more than tripled. Department stores began charging 18 to 24 percent by 1981. By 1985 this rate had decreased but only moderately with 18 percent still common. Consumer credit reached an all-time high in the early 1980s. A corresponding record number of bankruptcies by people who could not manage credit wisely followed this growth.

CREDIT VOCABULARY

To understand credit fully, you must understand certain terms. These words are commonly used to describe credit, its availability, or its cost.

1. *Balance due*—the total amount that remains due on a loan, including both principal and interest
2. *Billing (closing) date*—the last date of the month that any purchase you made with your credit card or any payment you made on your account is recorded in the account
3. *Borrower*—the person who borrows money or uses another form of credit (When you charge something, you are, in effect, borrowing.)
4. *Capital*—the property you possess that is worth more than your debts (one of the requirements for credit)
5. *Collateral*—personal property (bonds, stocks, automobiles, livestock, proceeds from an insurance policy) pledged to a lender to secure a loan
6. *Creditor*—person to whom one owes money or goods
7. *Due date*—the date on or before which payment is due (typically 25 to 30 days after the billing date)
8. *Finance charge* (handling charge)—the interest or money charged the borrower for the use of credit
9. *Installment contract*—a written agreement to make regular payments on a specific purchase
10. *Prorate*—divide, as to divide the interest or handling charge, proportionately over a period of time
11. *Secured loan*—a loan wherein the borrower pledges property or other assets to assure the creditor of repayment
12. *Service charge* (carrying charge)—the amount charged to borrowers (customers) by merchants or banks for servicing an account or loan

ADVANTAGES OF CREDIT

The wise consumer can gain many advantages from the use of credit. Used correctly, credit can greatly expand a family's purchasing potential and raise its standard of living in many ways.

Credit is handy for emergencies.

Credit can, for example, provide emergency funds—a sudden need for cash can be solved with a credit card. Budgeting and increased buying power can be achieved through the use of credit. Major purchases may be paid for over a period of time, and establishing a good credit record by the early use of credit makes future use of credit for major purchases easier.

Credit is convenient and easy to use.

Credit is convenient. Credit customers often get better service because they can withhold payment until a problem is resolved. The proof of purchase provided by a charge slip is sometimes more descriptive than a cash register receipt and helps in making adjustments when merchandise is returned. Finally, shopping is made safer with the use of credit. Carrying a credit card or store charge card makes for faster shopping and is safer than carrying large sums of cash.

DISADVANTAGES OF CREDIT

There are many disadvantages associated with the use of credit. For instance, credit purchases generally cost more than cash purchases. An item purchased on credit and paid for with monthly payments costs more than the price marked on the tag, because interest is charged for the use of credit. An interest rate of 18 percent a year is 1 1/2 percent a month. On a $100 purchase, the interest would be $1.50 a month. The larger the purchase and the longer the period of time taken to pay the balance due, the greater the interest charges.

Credit can be expensive.

Using credit reduces the amount of comparative shopping. Many consumers shop only in stores where they have credit. Comparing prices and quality at several different stores can save money.

Credit ties up future income.

Future income is tied up when credit is used. Buying something that will require payments for several years reduces funds available for items that may be needed in the months to come. This situation can put a strain on the budget that may be discouraging.

Credit can lead to overspending. People get into trouble with credit when they buy more than they can pay back comfortably. At the end of the month, when the bills come in, they realize how much they have really spent.

These disadvantages can be avoided by the wise use of credit. Consumers who start out slowly and plan their credit purchases can avoid credit problems. Credit is a privilege that must be earned and responsibly maintained—it is not a right. Use this privilege wisely and you will find credit to be a good friend.

Credit is a privilege, not a right.

KINDS OF CREDIT

There are many different credit opportunities to explore. An awareness of the kinds of credit available and sources of credit will help you to make wise choices when you make credit purchases. Most credit purchases or uses can be divided into these major categories: charge and other credit card accounts, layaway plans, installment purchase agreements, and service credit accounts.

Charge and Other Credit Card Accounts

Charge and other credit card accounts are open-ended forms of credit. *Open-ended credit* is credit wherein the lender places a limit on how much a qualifying customer can borrow during a given period. The borrower usually has a choice of repaying the entire balance within 30 days or repaying over a number of months or years.

Regular Charge Accounts. A regular charge account (open account) provides credit for an open period, usually 30 days. Normally, full payment is expected at the end of each period, and no interest is charged. If full payment is not made, however, a finance charge is added. A charge plate may be provided by large retailers to identify customers with valid accounts. Clothing is commonly purchased on a regular charge account.

Full payment is expected on open accounts.

Revolving Charge Accounts. A revolving charge account allows you to extend repayment of charges. There is usually a limit on the amount you can owe at one time and a minimum monthly payment that must be made. If the balance due is paid in full within 30 days or before the next billing cycle begins, finance charges are not included. If the balance due is not paid in full, a finance charge is added to the unpaid balance.

Other Credit Card Accounts. Bank credit cards such as VISA or MasterCard, oil company credit cards, and entertainment and travel credit cards operate on the same basis as the revolving charge account. The bank or other creditor charges your account for all purchases made during a month and bills you at the end of the month. Usually you do not pay a

Bank credit cards operate like a revolving charge account.

finance charge if you pay the total bill each month. However, a finance charge will be added to your bill if you pay only a portion of the unpaid balance and allow your account to accumulate. An annual fee may be charged for the use of the credit card.

Layaway Plans

Many retail businesses offer *layaway* plans. Merchandise may be laid away in your name; you make regular payments and claim the merchandise when it has been paid for in full. Most merchants require 25 percent or more of the total price as a down payment, with regular payments to be made monthly or twice monthly. A service fee, ranging from $1 to 5 percent of the purchase price, is usually charged. A coat purchased for $100 on layaway, for instance, might require a deposit of $26 (25 percent plus a $1 fee). Then three monthly payments of $25 each would pay off the balance, and you would receive the coat. You would receive a receipt when the coat is selected and as regular payments are posted to the account.

If you change your mind about a layaway purchase, a portion of the payments already made may be forfeited. The merchant has provided a service—credit and storage of the merchandise—and is entitled to payment for that service.

Layaways provide credit for a service.

Because layaway account terms vary among merchants, it is wise to compare service fees, down payment requirements, and penalties. The advantage of layaway credit is that payment can be made over a period of time. Layaway credit is available to most customers whether or not they have any other form of credit with a particular merchant.

Installment Purchase Agreements

Installment purchase agreements, also called installment loans, are contracts defining the repayment of the purchase price plus finance charges in equal regular payments (installments). For example, if an item with a purchase price of $800 is purchased on a two-year payment plan with a 15 percent annual finance charge, the total installment price of the item becomes $1,040 ($800 plus $240). Regular monthly payments of $43.34 include both principal and interest. More purchases cannot be added to an installment purchase agreement. When the balance is paid off, another agreement can be drawn up.

Installment payments include principal and interest.

Some businesses carry their own financing, and monthly payments are made directly to them. Other businesses require that customers get outside financing for installment purchases. Such financing may be obtained from a bank, credit union, or finance company. By requiring the customer to borrow money to cover the purchase, the merchant is assured of immediate payment in full. Installment payments are then made to the lender.

Installment purchase agreements generally are used for large purchases such as automobiles, appliances, furniture, or cash loans. A signed contract is usually required. The purchased item serves as collateral and will be repossessed if the agreed upon payments are not made. In the case of an automobile or mobile home, the lender retains the title until the full purchase price is paid. Large purchases such as this often require signing of a promissory note. As a consumer it is your responsibility to read and understand any contract or note before signing it.

Large purchases often require a promissory note.

Service Credit Accounts

Almost everyone uses some type of *service credit* by having a service performed and paying for it later. Your telephone and utility services are provided for a month in advance, then you are billed. Many businesses—including doctors and dentists, dry cleaners, repair shops, and others—extend service credit. Terms are set by the individual businesses. Most doctors do not charge interest on unpaid account balances, but they do expect that regular payments will be made until the bill is paid in full. Utility and telephone companies expect payment in full within a set time limit; however, they usually offer a budget plan as well, which allows you to average bills to get lower rates. Service credit accounts are usually offered by businesses whose services are considered necessary to the average consumer.

Service credit is available when needed.

SOURCES OF CREDIT

There are many sources for consumer credit. Some of the major sources are retail stores, commercial banks and credit unions, finance companies, pawnshops, and private lenders.

Retail Stores

Retail stores include department stores, drug stores, clothing stores, hardware stores, and all types of service businesses. Retailers purchase from wholesalers, who purchase from manufacturers and producers. Consumers buy directly from the retailers.

Retail stores take advantage of credit because customers like to shop where they have credit established. Most retail stores offer their own accounts, both regular and revolving. Many retail stores also accept bank credit cards and other well-known national cards, such as American Express or Diners Club. Charge customers receive advance notice of special sales, discounts, and other privileges not offered to cash customers. For example, some large department stores offer a deferred billing plan for charge customers. Upon request, merchandise charged between November 1 and December 25 is not billed to the customer's account until February. No finance charges are added unless the balance is not paid by the next closing date.

Commercial Banks and Credit Unions

Commercial banks and credit unions make loans to individuals and companies based on collateral, capital, and credit records. Interest rates vary with location or financial institution and according to what is being purchased. Good reasons for a loan, such as the need to purchase a car or home or the desire to take a vacation, are required. Banks generally charge the maximum loan interest rates allowed by law. Regular bank customers who have established credit are able to get loans at their banks more easily than noncustomers. Noncustomers may be required to open an account before a loan will be considered. Banks also offer credit cards, teller machines, and other services discussed in Chapter 7.

Banks require good
reasons for loans.

Credit unions make loans available to their members only. Interest rates are generally lower than those charged by banks because credit unions are nonprofit and are organized for the benefit of members. Credit unions are more willing to make loans because the members who are borrowing also have a stake in the credit union.

Finance Companies

Often called *small loan companies*, finance companies usually charge high rates of interest for the use of their money. The reason for the high rates is that finance companies are willing to take risks that banks and credit unions will not take. In many cases, people who are turned down by banks and credit unions can get loans at small loan companies.

Small loan companies
take more risk than
banks.

Finance companies are called small loan companies because the maximum amount that can be loaned to one person or business is set by the state. This maximum is usually small in comparison to what banks and credit unions can lend. For example, most finance companies are limited to a maximum loan amount. The loan limit may be established by the home office of the finance company or by the state in which the company is operating. It is common practice for large banks to loan over a million dollars at a time to a commercial customer.

Small loan companies take more risk than banks. Therefore, they must be more careful to protect their loans. When payment is not received when due, an officer calls the customer for an explanation. Constant contact is kept to make sure payments are made as agreed. Phone calls, letters, and personal visits are to be expected if the customer deviates even slightly from the agreed upon payment schedule. High interest rates are also another form of protection for the small loan company. In states where **usury laws** exist (laws setting maximum interest rates that may be charged), finance companies charge the maximum. Where no usury laws exist, finance companies charge as much as the customer is willing to pay. When an emergency or other extreme need arises, consumers often feel forced to pay these higher rates of interest to get the money they need.

Usury laws protect consumers from high rates of interest.

Pawnshops

A **pawnshop** is a legal business where loans are made against the value of specific personal possessions. Merchandise that is readily salable, such as guns, cameras, jewelry, radios, TVs, and coins, is usually acceptable. The customer brings in an item of value to be examined and appraised. A loan made against the property is considerably less than the appraised value of the item. Some pawnshops give only 10 to 25 percent of the value of the article; most give no more than 50 or 60 percent. For example, if you have a ring appraised at $500, you will probably be loaned between $50 and $250. You will be given a receipt for the ring and a certain length of time—from two weeks to six months—to redeem the ring by paying back the loan plus interest. If you do not pay back the loan and claim the ring, it will be sold. Merchandise taken in a pawnshop is considered collateral for the loan because it is something of value that may be sold if you fail to pay off the loan. Prices charged for the used merchandise in a pawnshop are generally lower than actual value. Sometimes you can find a bargain, and the pawnbroker still makes a profit.

Pawnshops make loans based on appraised value.

Private Lenders

The most common source of cash loans is the private lender. Private lenders include an individual's parents, other relatives, friends, etc. Interest may or may not be charged on loans made by private lenders.

Other Sources of Consumer Credit

Life insurance policies can be used as an alternate source of consumer credit. As a life insurance policy builds up a cash value, the policyholder can borrow at low rates of interest against his or her policy. The loan does

Your life insurance pol-
icy may have loan
value.

not have to be paid back, but interest on the loan will be charged to the policyholder, and the amount of the loan will reduce the face value (amount) of the life insurance policy.

If you have a certificate of deposit with a bank, credit union, or savings and loan association, you can borrow money against the certificate. The certificate is used as collateral, and the interest rate charged you is usually only 2 to 5 percent above the interest rate being paid on the certificate. If you cash in the certificate, you incur interest penalties; but if you borrow money using the certificate as collateral, you get a moderate rate of interest, plus the certificate retains its full value.

VOCABULARY

Directions: Can you find the definition for each of the following terms used in Chapter 12?

4. balance due
9. revolving account
5. borrower
15 layaway
3. credit
14 service credit
2. creditor
13. retail stores
7. capital

1. finance charge (handling charge)
16 small loan companies
12 usury laws
17 pawnshop
6. prorate
8. service charge (carrying charge)
10. collateral

1. The interest or money charged the borrower for the use of credit.

2. One who lends money or the use of goods and services for payment at a later date.

3. Paying at a future date for the present use of money, goods, or services.

4. The total amount that remains due on a loan, including both principal and interest.

5. The person who borrows money or uses credit.

6. To divide proportionately over a period of time.

7. Property possessed that is worth more than debts.

8. The amount charged by merchants or other creditors to borrowers for servicing or maintaining an account.

9. An account that is not assessed a finance charge unless the balance is not paid in full by the due date.

10. Property or possessions that can be mortgaged or sold, which are used as security for payment of a debt.

11. A type of installment account that has a maximum amount of credit, and payments made include a finance charge (interest) in each regular installment.

12. Laws setting maximum interest rates that may be charged.

13. Businesses offering goods and services to consumers, including department stores, drug stores, clothing stores, etc.

14. Having a service performed and paying for it at a later date.

15. A plan whereby merchandise is set aside in a customer's name until it is paid for in full.

16. Finance companies that make relatively small loans, take more risk, and generally charge higher rates of interest.

17. A legal business where loans are made based on the value of merchandise pledged as collateral.

ITEMS FOR DISCUSSION

1. What is credit?

2. What is collateral?

3. When credit first began in this country, did loans have high interest rates or low rates?

4. Why, when credit began, were bankers and merchants reluctant to loan money and give credit?

5. How has credit affected the American economy?

6. What kinds of jobs are created by credit?

7. List four advantages of using credit.

8. List four disadvantages of using credit.

9. What are three major kinds of credits?

10. How is a regular charge account different from a revolving charge account?

11. Explain how layaway credit operates. Why is it a good way to begin to establish credit?

12. Give three or four examples of service credit.

13. List the five major sources of credit for consumers.

14. Why do retail stores accept VISA and MasterCard in addition to their own credit cards?

15. Why do credit unions offer lower interest rates on loans than do commercial banks?

16. Why do small loan companies charge higher rates of interest on their loans?

17. Explain how a pawnshop operates.

APPLICATIONS

1. Give an example of a situation in which you would use collateral when making a purchase on credit.

2. How does your family make use of credit? Do you see credit use in your family as a good thing or a bad thing? What advantages of credit do you use?

3. List retail stores in your area that:

    (a) Extend credit by accepting credit cards.

    (b) Accept VISA, MasterCard, and other major credit cards.

    (c) Offer regular charge accounts and installment credit.

4. List several businesses in your area that offer layaway plans. Choose one such plan and list the following:

    (a) Name of store

    (b) Amount of down payment required

    (c) Layaway fee

    (d) Penalty for failure to complete payments

    (e) Maximum amount of merchandise that may be purchased on layaway

    (f) Frequency of and amount of payments needed

5. List five sources of service credit that most families use. Of these sources, do any charge a fee or interest rate if the payment is not made in full?

6. List four commercial banks and credit unions in your area. Write down their addresses and telephone numbers.

7. List four finance companies (small loan companies) in your area, together with addresses and phone numbers. (Hint: The Yellow Pages of your telephone book will list them by subject, such as under the heading "finance.")

8. List four pawnshops in your area; include addresses and phone numbers.

9. Does your state have usury laws? You can find out by consulting your library (the current *World Almanac & Book of Facts*). List some of the finance rates that states allow, including your state and neighboring states.

CASE PROBLEMS AND ACTIVITIES

1. Friends of your grandparents have never used credit. Having lived through the Great Depression, when they lost their life savings, they have never trusted others enough to pay for anything except with cash. What types of problems can result from not using credit? What would be your advice to them, knowing that they have a good income from investments and have no need to buy on credit?

2. Interview three or four adults about credit. Ask them the following questions. Prepare a short report.

   (a) How do you feel about credit in America?

   (b) Do you use credit cards, such as store credit cards or bank credit cards?

   (c) Do you think the rates of interest charged by stores and banks on unpaid balances are reasonable?

   (d) What rate of interest is charged by some creditors?

   (e) How would you advise a young person just starting out about credit?

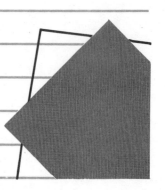

13
Buying on Credit

CHAPTER OBJECTIVES

After studying this chapter and completing the activities, you will be able to:

1. Understand the importance of credit records and summarize how and why records are compiled.
2. Explain the qualifications needed to obtain credit and list the types of questions usually asked on credit applications.
3. Outline the contents of a credit report.
4. List the provisions of the major credit laws.

CREDIT RECORDS

In determining your credit worthiness, a creditor will ask about past credit performance: were bills paid on time? were bills paid off as agreed? how much total credit was given? what is the credit that appears to be outstanding at this time? Your **credit history**, the complete record of your credit performance, will provide answers to these questions and thus help the creditor to gauge your ability to pay back new debts.

Credit File

Every person who uses credit has a credit file. The **credit file** is a summary of a person's credit history. Each time credit is used and reported, information on the transaction will appear in the credit file.

Most people have credit files.

Maintaining credit files is a big business. A company that operates for profit in the business of accumulating, storing, and distributing credit

ILLUSTRATION 13–1
Every time you use credit, the transaction will appear in your credit file.

information is called a *credit bureau*. There are an estimated 2,500 credit bureaus in the United States, supplying 125 to 150 million credit reports a year. TRW Credit Data, a major credit bureau, reports having files on 40 million consumers and supplying 15 million credit reports a year to 26,000 creditors.

Some credit bureaus still keep records in handwritten form and post new information by hand as it is received. Most larger bureaus, however, use computerized clearinghouses that can search and retrieve a file in seconds to give information to potential creditors. Thus, your credit file can be a folder with your name on the tab, or it can be on microfilm, or stored in a central computer. Information is stored on a local level, and when you purchase through national companies or mail-order houses you also establish a file with national bureaus. You may have a file in three or more places, depending on the sources and types of credit used.

Modern methods of storage make credit information readily available.

How Information Is Gathered

Credit bureaus gather information from creditors, called *subscribers*. A subscriber pays dues or an annual fee to the credit bureau. Each subscriber supplies information to the credit bureau about its accounts—

Businesses support the
credit bureaus.

names, addresses, credit balances, how payments are being handled, and so forth. Credit bureaus also gather information from many other sources. Articles about consumers found in local newspapers are clipped and added to the files. Public records are searched for information to add to a consumer's file. When someone applies for credit from a subscriber, a credit report showing all accumulated data on the applicant is requested by the subscriber. Information in the credit report is then used as the basis for granting or denying credit. Because the credit report shows the credit history of an applicant, risks to a creditor in granting credit are lowered when that creditor makes use of credit reports.

Types of Information Kept

All public information
may be included in
credit files.

Any public information becomes a part of your credit record. For instance, if you fail to pay your property taxes, file bankruptcy, file for a divorce, or apply for a marriage license, this information will be recorded in your file. Birth announcements published in newspapers, job promotions, lawsuits, and other visible activities are recorded. When you fill out a credit application, information requested such as occupation, length of employment, spouse's name and occupation, residence, length of occupancy, number of children and other dependents, and so forth is sent to the credit bureau by the subscriber. Facts supplied in this way can give future creditors sufficient information to make a wise decision about granting or denying credit to you.

FACTORS IN DETERMINING CREDIT WORTHINESS

Before potential creditors will grant credit to you, they must determine whether you are a good risk—whether you are credit worthy. If you meet certain standards that creditors feel are important, you will usually qualify for the credit you desire.

The Six Cs of Credit

Your qualifications
determine your credit
rating.

A person who is considered a good credit risk usually meets six basic qualifications. These qualifications include character, capacity, capital, conditions, collateral, and common sense.

Character. A person with a good character is one who willingly and responsibly lives up to agreements. One distinctive sign of a good character is a responsible attitude toward paying bills and meeting obligations on time.

Capacity. The ability to repay a loan or make payments on merchandise with present income is known as capacity. Creditors want to make certain that you will have enough money left over each month after other fixed expenses have been met to pay your credit debts.

Capital. Property and other assets that total more than debts are known as capital. In other words, when you add up all that you own (assets) and subtract all that you owe (liabilities), the difference (your net worth or capital) should be sufficient to ensure payment of another bill.

Conditions. All other existing debts, stability of employment, personal factors, and other factors that might affect a person's ability or desire to meet financial obligations are important conditions to be considered. For example, a person who has moved six times during the past year might not be considered a good risk because of living conditions that indicate some type of problem.

Stability is important to your credit rating.

Collateral. Property or possessions that can be mortgaged or used as security for payment of a debt are known as collateral. If a debt is not paid as agreed, the collateral is repossessed and sold to pay the debt.

Common Sense. A person's inner ability to make wise decisions is often referred to as common sense. A loan officer or credit manager would determine that you have good common sense based on how you answer questions (either orally or in writing). Good decisions are reflected in answers such as reasons for leaving employment, number and types of credit cards and balance outstanding, or references listed on an application.

Your ability to handle credit shows in your decisions.

If a credit applicant meets all six of the above qualifications, he or she is considered worthy of credit. The applicant has shown a willingness and ability to pay bills in an acceptable and responsible manner.

Procedures for Obtaining Credit

Everyone has to get started in credit sometime. As soon as you can begin these steps to establishing a good credit rating, the better for you and your financial future. It is a slow procedure, and depending on your age, can take several years to get well established.

Begin with a Savings Account. Open an account at your credit union if you are eligible; if not, open a savings account at a savings and loan association or bank. You will want to start at a financial institution that has full services available to you as you prove yourself: checking account, loans, and credit cards.

Each month or pay period, make a deposit to your savings account. Keep your account growing through regular savings, as discussed in Chapter 9.

Open a Checking Account. As soon as you have enough money in your savings account to allow you a little "cushion," open a checking account. This will allow you a method of paying your bills when you have accounts and provide a record keeping system for your budget. Many different kinds of checking plans are available to you; choose the one that is the least expensive and most convenient for you (See Chapter 7).

Maintain your checking account diligently. Do not write checks when there are insufficient funds to cover them. Bouncing checks causes a negative reflection on your creditworthiness. Fulfill all your responsibilities in maintaining your checking account; balance your checkbook as soon as you receive the statement.

Use Parents to Get Started. You may need your parents' assistance in opening the first account or two. They may need to act as cosigners, or you may rely on their credit rating at first. Many department stores and local merchants will allow you to open a small account ($100 limit) with your parents' signature, or based on your own accounts and your parents' permission.

Make small purchases on your new account(s) and pay them as soon as they are due, using your checking account. If you need to make monthly payments to pay off a larger charge purchase, be sure each month's payment is received on or before the due date—never late. This will give you a good credit record as you are beginning.

Get a Small Loan. From the credit union, savings and loan, or bank where you have your checking and savings accounts, take out a small loan. Even though you may not need the cash and can wait, borrowing will establish your credit with the bank. Pay back the loan as agreed; make early payments if possible. A six-month loan is sufficient. Again, you may need to rely on parents or a cosigner to get your first loan.

Apply for a Check Guarantee. After you have had your checking account for at least a year, apply for the bank's check guarantee card. This card will allow you to make instant cash loans, use day and night teller machines, and have access to other credit. Use it wisely because it is a privilege rather than a right, and the bank can revoke the guarantee card if it is not used properly.

Apply for a Bank Credit Card. With credit established for a couple of years, a part-time job, and a couple of other credit references, you might now be eligible for a VISA or MasterCard account. Check the application carefully and ask about the income limit. If you do not make enough money to qualify for the card, do not apply for it until you do. In some cases you will have to be working full time and for the same employer for three years. Once you have the bank credit card, you will find it very easy to obtain all the additional credit cards you want.

When applying for any kind of credit card, list your bank checking and savings accounts, small loans you have established, charge accounts, and your parents' or cosigners' names. Start small and slowly build a solid credit foundation.

Credit Records and Credit Worthiness

Your credit record will reveal to a potential creditor whether you have the character, capacity, capital, conditions, collateral, and common sense necessary to gain access to additional credit. Information in your file concerning your income, payment record, employment record, and various personal factors will affect the potential creditor's decision.

Part-time workers may not qualify for credit.

Income. On an application for credit, you will be asked how much your gross or net pay is each pay period. Part-time employees who earn only a few hundred dollars a month generally will not qualify for credit. Unless you can show that your expenses are so low that you have enough money left over to pay extra bills adequately, part-time jobs are not enough. Many credit card companies, such as American Express and VISA, require an annual income of $12,000 to $15,000 or more before they will grant credit to an applicant. Income other than regular pay may be listed, such as interest income, child support or alimony, spouse's income, or dividend income (unearned income). It is wise not to apply for credit until you are earning enough income to afford the payments.

Paying your bills responsibly will result in more credit.

Payment Record. Your payment record is a list of your previous credit accounts and how you paid off those debts. Based on your payment record, the credit bureau will assign you a credit rating (credit ratings will be discussed later in this chapter). If you have paid your bills on time, your credit rating will be favorable. Consequently, potential creditors will be more likely to grant you additional credit, based on the character, capacity, and common sense you have exhibited through your responsibility in paying your bills.

Employment Record. Many creditors require a credit applicant to have worked steadily at one job for at least six months or longer before they will extend credit. If your work history shows that you switch jobs several times a year, you will not be considered a good risk. Creditors will assume that at some future time you may be unemployed and unable to make your credit payments. You are considered stable in your employment if you have worked for a number of years for one company, or in one particular job. The longer you work consistently, the better your stability rating.

Employment history is part of your credit rating.

Personal Factors. Personal factors that are often considered by creditors include such things as occupation, geographic area, type of residence (renting or owning), age or age group, bank affiliations (types of accounts), and purpose for the credit (a good reason).

Denial of Credit

There are many legitimate reasons for which an applicant may be denied credit. Some reasons used for denying credit, however, are considered discriminatory. The Equal Credit Opportunity Act of 1975 was designed to prevent such discrimination in judgments of credit worthiness. The act provides that:

Some reasons for denying credit are discriminatory.

1. Credit may not be denied solely because you are a woman, single, married, divorced, separated, or widowed.
2. Credit may not be denied specifically because of religion, national origin, race, color, or age (except as age may affect your physical ability to perform, or your ability to enter into contracts; i.e., minors cannot be held liable for their contracts because they are not considered competent parties).
3. Credit may not be denied because you receive public assistance (welfare), unemployment, social security, or retirement benefits.
4. Credit applications may be oral or written. However, a creditor is prohibited from asking certain questions either orally or in writing.
5. A creditor may not discourage you, in writing or orally, from applying for credit for any reason prohibited by the act (such as being divorced).

In addition to these prohibitions, the act states that creditors must notify you of any action taken on your credit application within 30 days of submittal. If you are denied credit, the denial must be in writing and

You can appeal if
credit is denied.

must list a specific reason for the denial. After a denial of credit, the creditor must keep for 25 months all information used to determine the denial and any written complaint from you regarding the denial. You have the right to appeal, and the creditor must give you the name and address of the state or federal agency that enforces credit laws for his or her type of business (there are numerous agencies).

It is lawful and proper for creditors, in determining your credit worthiness, to ask you for the following personal information: name; age (provided it is not used as the basis for denying credit); source of income; number of dependents, their ages, and other obligations to them; obligations to pay alimony, child support, or other such payments; permanent residence and immigration status; a list of assets; amount of income; place of employment; length of employment; history of employment; outstanding debts; telephone number (or whether you have a telephone); whether you rent or own your home; length of residence at present address; residence history; savings and checking accounts in your name. A creditor may ask about your marital status only if you are making a joint application, or if your spouse will be an authorized user. If you reside in a community property state, marital status is important. (Community property states are Arizona, California, Idaho, Louisiana, Nevada, New Mexico, Texas, and Washington.) In any case, a creditor may ask only whether you are married, unmarried, or separated.

Community property
states have different
credit laws.

The Equal Credit Opportunity Act is a federal law. Many states also have similar laws; these laws vary widely from state to state and are changing rapidly. Many state laws are stricter than federal laws. You would be wise to be knowledgeable of those laws when applying for credit.

CREDIT RATINGS

Many different systems are used nationwide in rating consumers' credit worthiness. In a *point system*, you are given points for employment, amount of income, length of residence, type of residence, etc. If your points total a certain number, you are given credit. But if you don't have enough points, then your personal factors don't total enough to warrant the risk of extending credit to you.

A point system may be
used to determine
credit worthiness.

A rating system, which is fairly well accepted by most creditors, rates consumers according to how they pay back money borrowed or pay off amounts charged. Consumers may earn a rating of excellent, good, fair, or poor.

To earn an *excellent credit rating*, sometimes called an *A* rating, a customer must pay bills before the due date. If a payment is due on the fifth of the month, it must be received *before* the fifth. An excellent rating also means that the customer has not missed any payments and has attempted to make a larger payment than the minimum amount required.

To earn a *good credit rating*, which is designated a *B* rating, a customer must pay bills on the due date or within a five-day grace period. That is, if the payment is due on the first of the month, it must be received by the fifth, but no later than the tenth, of the month. (When a bill is paid within 10 days of its due date, this is considered an automatic grace period.) A good customer pays around the due date, but never outside the grace period, and does not miss any payments.

A *fair credit rating* is earned by a customer who usually pays all bills within the grace period, but occasionally takes longer. Late charges are sometimes necessary, but normally no reminder is necessary. This person is often described as slow in paying, but fairly dependable.

A person with a *poor credit rating* is usually denied credit because payments are not regular—months are often missed in making payments, and frequent reminders must be sent. In many cases, this person has failed entirely to pay back a debt, has filed bankruptcy, or has otherwise shown that he or she is not a good credit risk.

In establishing a rating for a consumer, many credit bureaus ask their subscribers to rate their own customers. Then, based on other information gathered, such as total credit outstanding, job stability, and other personal factors, a composite rating is determined. Some credit bureaus merely supply credit files to their subscribers and allow the subscribers to make their own rating decisions. Because different credit bureaus use different systems of compiling information and ratings, you should check in your local area to be familiar with the system used for your credit file.

It is important to pay your bills on time.

Ratings are often determined by creditors.

CREDIT REPORTS

A *credit report* is a written report issued by a credit bureau. This report contains relevant information about a person's credit worthiness. A separate file is kept for each person, although spouses are listed on each report. Reports are usually in the form of a computer printout, called an automated credit file. Each report is divided into sections: Identification, Summary of Information, Public Records or Other Information, Inquiries, and Trade.

The *Identification section* is the first part of the report, and it identifies the subject. Included is such information as full name of consumer,

Credit reports contain several types of information.

spouse's name, how long the file has been active, last file activity date, present address, previous addresses, any nicknames, marital status, number of dependents, date of birth, social security number, and social security number of spouse.

Following the personal information is the employment information. Dates and types of employment; salary; spouse's employment, dates, and salary; and other household income sources are listed.

The *Summary of Information section* may show total credit rating points, if a point system is used; newest and oldest reporting dates; and whether public records or foreign (out-of-area) information is included. This section may also show the number of active accounts the consumer has and the credit ranges of those accounts, plus any statements added to the file by the consumer.

Active credit accounts are part of your record.

In the *Public Records and Other Information section*, there may be information about filing for bankruptcy—court and case number, liabilities, assets, exemptions, and how filed (individual, joint, or business). Also in this section is information about loan repayment or default and balance owing. Any other court proceedings against the consumer with regard to debt payment are reported in this section.

The *Inquiries section* shows the number of inquiries made by subscribers to the credit bureau within the last six months. The inquiries are listed by name, number, and date of inquiry.

The *Trade section* shows the consumer's present credit status. Companies reporting credit information and dates of their reports are listed. Dates accounts were opened, credit limits, amounts of monthly payments, number of years or months paying or left to pay, balances owing, and any amounts past due are listed here. Account types (joint or individual) and account numbers, number of months the accounts were late, and previous high ratings are also shown. Any out-of-area (foreign) information would be reported in this section, along with the reporting bureau, in-file date, and date given to local bureau.

Types of accounts are listed and rated.

All information included on the credit report is written in abbreviated form. A listing of key words and abbreviations is necessary for understanding information included on the report. Files are updated daily, and information stays in the file for seven years. In bankruptcy cases, information stays in the file for ten years.

Credit reports legally may be requested for investigations of credit applications, employment applications, and insurance matters. Anyone making unauthorized use of a credit report is liable for a $5,000 fine and/ or one year in jail. You may see your own credit report, in person, for a small fee of under $10.

Certain uses of credit reports are lawful.

CREDIT LAWS

A number of credit laws have been enacted in recent years, primarily for consumer protection purposes and to provide assistance to consumers using credit. Several of these laws are summarized in the following paragraphs.

Fair Credit Reporting Act

If you are denied credit based on a credit bureau report, inaccurate information in your file may be the cause of the denial. Under the Fair Credit Reporting Act, you have a right to know what is in your file and who has seen your file. A listing of requests made for your file for credit purposes in the last six months, and for employment purposes in the last two years, must be available to you. You may see your credit file at no charge within 30 days of a credit denial. A small fee may be charged in the event you want to see your file at any other time for any reason. You have the right to have inaccurate information investigated, corrected, and deleted from your file and have a new report furnished to creditors. Or, if the information is essentially correct, you can write your own statement giving your side of the story. Your statement will be added to the file.

You can see your file for a small fee.

Fair Credit Billing Act

Under the Fair Credit Billing Act, creditors must resolve billing errors within a specified period of time. A *statement* is an itemized bill showing charges, credits, and payments posted to your account during a billing period. Suppose your monthly statement shows purchases you did not make, or that you were charged for items you returned. Perhaps you are billed for merchandise you ordered but have not received. Creditors are required to have a written policy for correction of such errors.

If you believe there is an error on your bill, you should act immediately. Do not write on the bill that has been sent to you. On a separate piece of paper, write a letter explaining what you believe the problem to be. Write clearly and give a complete explanation of why you believe there is an error. Be specific about the amount in dispute, when you noticed the error, and any details relevant to the disputed amount. For example, you might say

Write immediately when you discover an error.

> I have just received my December bill. I noticed today that there is a charge dated November 24, for Wyatt's Department Store in Calooga, Wisconsin, in the amount of $42. I have never shopped at Wyatt's, and I have never been to Calooga, Wisconsin. I have not lost my credit card,

nor have I authorized anyone else to use it. Therefore, I would appreciate your looking into this matter at your earliest convenience.

Your complaint must be in writing and mailed within 60 days after you receive the statement. The error or amount disputed must be dealt with by the company in a reasonable manner and within a reasonable period of time. The creditor must acknowledge your complaint within 30 days. Within 90 days after receipt of your letter, the creditor must either correct the error or show why the bill is correct. Customers are still liable for amounts not disputed while the error dispute is being settled.

You are responsible for amounts not in dispute.

Figure 13-1 is an example of one company's written policy for handling billing errors.

Equal Credit Opportunity Act

Discrimination on the basis of sex or marital status in granting or denying credit is prohibited under the Equal Credit Opportunity Act (see also pages 230 and 231). According to the U.S. Department of Labor, Bureau of Labor Statistics:

More women are in the labor force.

1. Women make up over 40 percent of the labor force.
2. Fifty-four percent of all women between 18 and 64 are in the labor force.
3. Thirty-two percent of mothers with children under three are working.
4. Forty percent of all working women are single, divorced, or separated and qualify for head-of-household status.
5. The employment life expectancy of a single woman is 45 years—two years longer than a man's.
6. More young single women between the ages of 18 and 24 are entering the labor force than ever before, pursuing careers that will be continued regardless of marriage and childbearing.

As a result of the act, new accounts must reflect the fact that both husband and wife are responsible for payment. In this way, both spouses establish their own credit histories. Existing accounts should be changed to assure that the wife, as well as the husband, is being given credit for the payment record.

Fair Debt Collection Practices Act

The Fair Debt Collection Practices Act was designed to eliminate abusive collection practices by debt collectors. A ***debt collector*** is a person or company hired by a creditor to collect the balance due on an

FIGURE 13–1
Error Policy

IN CASE OF ERRORS OR INQUIRIES ABOUT YOUR BILL:

The Fair Credit Billing Act requires prompt resolution of errors. To preserve your rights, follow these steps:

1. Do not write on the bill. On a separate piece of paper write a description as shown below. A telephone call will not preserve your rights.
   (a) Your name and account number.
   (b) Description of the error and your explanation of why you believe there is an error. Send copies of any receipts or supporting evidence you may have; do not send originals.
   (c) The dollar amount of the suspected error.
   (d) Other information that might be helpful in resolving the disputed amount.
2. Mail your letter as soon as possible. It must reach us within 60 days after you receive your bill.
3. We will acknowledge your letter within 30 days. Within 90 days of receiving your letter, we will correct the error or explain why we believe the bill is correct.
4. You will receive no collection letters or collection action regarding the amount in dispute; nor will it be reported to any credit bureau or collection agency.
5. You are still responsible for all other items on the bill and for the balance less the disputed amount.
6. You will not be charged a finance charge against the disputed amount, unless it is determined that there is not an error in the bill. In this event, you will be given the normal 25 days to pay your bill from the date the bill is determined to be correct.

---

account. The fee charged by the debt collector is often half of the amount collected. The use of threats, obscenities, and false and misleading statements to intimidate the consumer into paying when there is a legitimate reason for nonpayment, such as an error, is prohibited. Time and frequency of collection practices, such as telephone calls and contacts at place of employment, are restricted. Debt collectors are required to verify the accuracy of a bill and give the consumer the opportunity to clarify and dispute the bill.

Debt collectors' actions are limited.

Consumer Credit Protection Act

The Consumer Credit Protection Act of 1968, known as the Truth in Lending Act, requires that consumers be fully informed about the cost of a credit purchase before an agreement is signed. Regulation Z of this act provides that the creditor (lender) must disclose all of these facts, in writing, to a debtor (borrower):

You must be informed of credit charges.

1. Cash price
2. Down payment and/or trade-in price
3. Amount financed
4. Insurance costs, filing costs, and other miscellaneous added costs of any kind
5. Finance charge
6. Annual percentage rate of the finance charge
7. Deferred payment price
8. Amount(s) and date(s) of payment
9. Description of security interest (item being purchased)
10. Method of computing unearned finance charge (in case of early payoff)
11. Any other information that may be applicable or necessary

The Truth in Lending Act also limits your liability to $50 after your credit card is reported lost or stolen. There is no liability at all if the card is reported lost prior to its fraudulent use.

VOCABULARY

Directions: Can you find the definition for each of the following terms used in Chapter 13?

statement	credit file
credit history	fair rating
point system	credit report
credit bureau	subscriber
Summary of Information section	good rating
Identification section	poor rating
excellent rating	debt collector
	Trade section

1. A summary of a person's credit history that is kept at a credit bureau and from which a credit report is made.

2. Past credit performance in paying debts, amount of credit outstanding, and credit worthiness based on facts of previous credit experience.

3. A business that accumulates, stores, and distributes credit information to members.

4. A member of a credit bureau who pays fees or dues to the bureau in exchange for credit information collected and compiled into reports.

5. A credit rating based on payment of bills on the due date or within a few days (but never outside the grace period).

6. A credit rating given a person who pays during the grace period, but occasionally takes longer, incurring some late charges.

7. A credit rating earned when bills are paid before due dates and extra effort is shown in paying debts.

8. A credit rating likely to harm chances for further credit because it shows that past payments were irregular and that frequent problems arose in the credit accounts.

9. A written statement about a person's credit worthiness, issued by a credit bureau, which summarizes credit history, present indebtedness, public records, and other information available.

10. An itemized list of purchases charged, credits, and payments made on a credit account during a billing period.

11. A person or company who is hired by a creditor to collect the balance due on an account that has not been paid by a customer.

12. A type of rating used by credit bureaus in determining a person's general credit worthiness.

13. The part of a credit report that gives name, address, and other personal information.

14. The part of a credit report that gives the subject's present credit status.

15. The part of a credit report that gives the number of active accounts a subject has, with credit ranges.

ITEMS FOR DISCUSSION

1. What does a credit bureau do to earn money? Who pays for its services?

2. What is the advantage for businesses of becoming members of (subscribers to) credit bureaus?

3. What types of public records become a part of your credit record?

4. Why is it important to pay your bills when they are due, rather than a few days late?

5. Why do creditors care about how long you have worked at your present job and about how many jobs you have had?

6. List personal factors that are often considered by creditors.

7. What types of discrimination are unlawful when considering personal factors in granting or denying credit?

8. What types of personal information can lawfully be asked of credit applicants?

9. What is the name of the federal law enacted in 1975 to protect consumers from unlawful discrimination in credit?

10. How long are bankruptcy records kept in a credit file? How long are other records kept on file?

11. What is the possible penalty for unauthorized use of a credit report?

12. Do you have a right to see your own credit file?

13. What should you do if you are denied credit based on your credit file? What can you do if information in your credit file is basically correct, but damaging to you as is?

14. What is the purpose of the Fair Credit Reporting Act?

15. What should you do if there is an error on your statement from a creditor?

16. What was the purpose of the Truth in Lending Act?

APPLICATIONS

1. Go to a local credit bureau and see what type of system is being used for locating, storing, and using credit information. Write a one-page report describing the process. Be sure to include the credit rating system used and explain how customers are rated and by whom (the creditor or the credit bureau). Before visiting the credit bureau, prepare a list of questions to ask and call first to make an appointment.

2. You have filled out an application for credit at a local department store. The store has notified you that they cannot give you credit because you have a poor credit rating. What are your rights, and what are some things you should do? You really have no bad payment records, and you have paid previous debts as agreed. Sup-

pose there is an error; what responsibilities to you does the credit bureau have?

3. What types of personal information are likely to appear in the Information section of a credit report? Where would a credit bureau get this information?

4. Summarize the basic provisions of the following laws:

   (a) Fair Credit Reporting Act

   (b) Fair Credit Billing Act

   (c) Equal Credit Opportunity Act

   (d) Fair Debt Collection Practices Act

   (e) Consumer Credit Protection Act

5. Describe what you must do if you believe a statement you receive from a creditor contains an error. Describe the process for error correction, including your responsibilities and time limits and the responsibilities and time limits of your creditor.

6. List the five main sections contained in a credit report, and summarize the information that would be contained in each section.

7. What kinds of credit do you think you will be using in five years? How will you establish a good credit rating?

CASE PROBLEMS AND ACTIVITIES

1. Obtain a credit application form from a local merchant or national credit card company. On a separate piece of paper, list each question on the form in a column on the left. To the right of the column of questions, make another column. Indicate beside each question whether it is a(n) (a) personal question, (b) payment record question, (c) employment stability question, or (d) income question.

2. You have just received your monthly VISA bill. There is a charge on your bill of $42, but you have a receipt showing the amount should have been $24. The purchase was made at a local clothing store (you supply the name and address) one month ago. Write a letter to the bank that issued the VISA (choose a local bank) and explain the error.

14

Cost of Credit

RESPONSIBILITIES OF CONSUMER CREDIT

Credit must be used wisely and carefully. Failure to do so can result in having credit limited or, in some cases, withdrawn. For this reason, credit users must understand their responsibilities to their creditors and themselves, and creditors must understand their responsibilities to credit users.

User's Responsibilities to Creditors

All credit users have the responsibility to limit spending to amounts that can be repaid according to the terms of their credit agreements. By signing a credit agreement, the consumer agrees to make all payments promptly, on or before the due date.

You make many agreements to use credit.

In addition, the credit user has a responsibility to read and understand the terms of all agreements signed, including finance charges, what to do

241

ILLUSTRATION 14–1
Credit users must understand their responsibilities.

in case of error, how to return items, and any other provisions of the agreement. The consumer must contact the creditor or merchant immediately when there is a problem with a bill or merchandise is discovered to be defective. In an emergency situation, when a payment cannot be made, the consumer must contact the creditor to make arrangements for payment at a later date.

User's Responsibilities to Self

Be responsibile when using credit.

Credit users' most important responsibility is to themselves: they are responsible for using credit wisely. This responsibility includes checking out businesses and companies before making credit purchases. Better Business Bureaus and Chambers of Commerce have information about businesses and complaints that have been filed against them.

Another important aspect of the credit user's responsibility is to do comparative shopping. A wise buyer does not make a purchase the first time an item is inspected, nor does the buyer limit his or her shopping to one store because that store offers credit. Before making a major budget expenditure, the wise buyer comparison shops and thinks about the purchase for at least 24 hours.

To use credit privileges wisely and to best advantage, the consumer should be familiar with billing cycles, annual percentage rates, and any added charges related to each credit account. Credit users should understand state and local laws regarding the use of credit. Finally, the credit user must have the right.attitude about borrowing and using credit. This means entering into each transaction in good faith and with the full expectation of meeting the obligations and upholding a good credit reputation.

Enter into transactions in good faith.

Creditor's Responsibilities to Credit Users

Creditors, including banks, retail stores, small loan companies, credit unions, and private individuals, also have responsibilities when extending credit to individuals and businesses. Some of these responsibilities include:

1. Assisting the consumer in making wise purchases by clearly representing goods and services, with all their advantages and disadvantages.

Creditors have well-designed credit policies.

2. Informing customers about all rules, regulations, charges, fees, and interest rates.

3. Cooperating with established credit reporting agencies, making credit records available to the consumer, and promptly discussing and clearing mistakes in records when they occur.

4. Establishing and carrying out sound lending and credit extension policies that do not overburden or deceive customers. (Setting reasonable guidelines and standards for credit helps to ensure that more credit will not be extended to customers who cannot financially afford it.)

5. Establishing and maintaining fair and reasonable credit charges and methods of contacting customers who fail to meet their obligations, assisting whenever possible with payment schedules and other means for solving credit problems.

Joint Responsibilities—Credit Card Fraud

Both creditors and credit users have a responsibility to prevent credit card fraud. The most common type of credit card fraud is the illegal use of a lost or stolen card. While the credit card holder's liability is limited to $50, the merchant is not protected from losses. Consequently, merchandise prices must be raised to cover such losses.

Protect your credit cards from loss.

It is your responsibility to protect your credit cards from loss. Carry only the cards you need. Keep a list of credit and charge cards and their numbers in a safe place. Notify issuers immediately when a loss occurs. Keep a copy of all sales receipts. Put your cards in your wallet immediately after completing a credit purchase. Sign newly issued cards immediately and completely destroy (cut) expired cards.

Use your credit or charge cards carefully. Giving credit card numbers over the telephone or sending them through the mails increases the risk of fraudulent use. Know the creditor before you purchase with a credit card.

Merchants should check credit cards against lists of lost or stolen cards, make authorization calls for large purchases, and ask for identification when accepting credit cards. New cards should be sent to customers by registered mail. When creditors promptly prosecute persons who use a lost or stolen credit card, fraudulent practices are discouraged.

Expect to have your credit card number checked.

CREDIT CAN BE EXPENSIVE

To fully understand and appreciate the use of credit in your daily life, it is important to be aware of the total cost of credit. All transactions involving credit should be fully understood. Total cost, annual percentage rate, monthly payments, and all information available should be clear before a decision is made to enter into a credit agreement.

Vocabulary of Credit Costs

When you borrow money or purchase goods or services for payment at a future date, you will want to know the meaning of the terms that appear most frequently in credit agreements. Understanding the meaning of these words before entering into a credit agreement can help you to avoid problems later.

Special credit terms are widely used.

1. *Add-on interest*—interest that is added to the principal; equal payments are made each month that include both principal and interest
2. *Annual percentage rate*—the true annual rate of interest
3. *Deferred payment price*—the total amount, including principal and interest, that will be paid under a credit agreement
4. *Full disclosure*—to reveal to a purchaser (borrower), in complete detail, every possible charge or cost involved in the granting of credit
5. *Interest*—the amount paid for the use of credit
6. *Principal*—the total amount that is financed or borrowed and on which interest is computed

Why Credit Costs So Much

How much you will pay for the use of credit is determined by several factors. When each factor is considered carefully, the best possible credit agreement can be reached. These important factors include the following:

The cost of credit varies with the conditions.

1. Source of credit
2. Total amount of money borrowed

3. Length of time for which money is borrowed
4. Ability of the borrower to repay the loan
5. Type of credit selected
6. Collateral or security offered
7. Costs other than finance charges (such as delivery charges)
8. Method used in computing interest
9. Current rate of interest
10. Amount of money the lender has available to loan, and business and economic conditions that affect the lender's willingness to loan

As stated in Chapter 12, the source of credit is important; some financial institutions and lenders are able to offer lower rates of interest and better credit plans than others. The more money you borrow, and the longer you take to pay it back, the more interest you will pay. Your ability to repay the loan also affects the total cost of the loan. The greater your ability to repay and, consequently, the less risk to the lender, the better the rate of interest you will be able to get. The type of credit selected—whether a charge account, a bank loan, or a bank credit card—will vary according to the amount and rate of interest and repayment plans available. The more secure your collateral, the lower the rate of interest you will have to pay. Real estate and real property are often considered to be the most solid collateral; personal property, such as automobiles, and income are often considered unreliable. Additional costs that may be involved with credit include service or delivery fees, license or title fees, filing fees for security documents such as mortgages or liens, inspection or credit check fees, and so forth. Total cost, including principal, interest, and any other expenses involved in the purchase, is known as the deferred payment price.

Consider how long you need to pay off a debt.

Collateral will help you get a better interest rate.

To get an accurate picture of the total cost of credit, add up all the costs. Then subtract the original purchase price of the item. The difference is the dollar cost of credit.

TOTAL PRICE (including all finance charges)

— CASH PRICE (what you would have to pay if you paid in
_____ full, in cash, at the time of purchase)
COST OF CREDIT

The current rate of interest is often affected by the *prime rate*, which is the rate of interest lenders offer to their best commercial (business) customers. Private individuals pay more than the prime rate because the risk is greater to the lender.

Individual loans are riskier than business loans.

The *discount rate* is the rate of interest that banks are charged to borrow money from the Federal Reserve System. The prime rate is usually at least three percentage points above the discount rate, a difference that allows the banks to make a reasonable profit on loans. Therefore, when the discount rate is 8 percent, the prime rate is about 11 percent, and consumers can expect to pay about 14 percent for consumer loans.

When business conditions and interest rates call for tight lending policies, consumer loans become more expensive and difficult to get.

COMPUTING THE COST OF CREDIT

There are several methods for computing the cost of credit.

Easy computations can be made to determine the cost of credit, using the formula for simple interest, or the formula for calculating the total installment interest. The cost of a revolving charge account can be calculated using the previous balance method, the adjusted balance method, or the average daily balance method.

Simple Interest

Simple interest is computed on the principal only. The result is the total amount to be paid to the lender, usually in equal monthly portions for a set length of time. The formula for computing simple interest is

$$\text{Interest (I)} = \text{Principal (P)} \times \text{Rate (R)} \times \text{Time (T)}$$

The amount borrowed is called the principal.

Principal. The amount borrowed, or original amount of debt, is called the principal. When you ask for a loan, the principal is the amount loaned to you, before interest is added (add-on interest) or subtracted (discount interest). For example, if you borrow $5,000 to buy a car, that $5,000 is the principal, or amount of the loan.

Rate. The interest rate is expressed as a percentage. The higher the rate, the less desirable the loan for the consumer.

Time. The length of time the borrower will take to repay a loan is expressed as a fraction of a year—12 months, 52 weeks, or 360 days (in most business transactions, the standard practice is to use 360 as the number of days in a year). For example, if a loan is taken for six months, the time is expressed as 1/2. If money is borrowed for three months, the time would be expressed as 1/4. When a loan is for a certain number of days, such as 90, the time would be expressed as 90/360, or 1/4.

A simple interest problem is shown in Figure 14-1. In this problem, a person has borrowed $500 and will pay interest at the rate of 12 percent a year. The loan will be paid back in four months.

FIGURE 14–1
Simple Interest

$I = P \times R \times T$	To multiply by a percent, first change it to a decimal: drop the percent sign, then move the decimal point two places to the left.
$I = ?$	
$P = \$500$	
$R = 12\%$	
$T = 4$ months	
$I = 500 \times .12 \times 4/12$	(Four months is 4/12 or 1/3 of a year.)
$\quad = 500 \times .12 \times 1/3$	
$\quad = 60 \times .3333$	
$\quad = \$20$	

The simple interest formula can also be used to find principal, rate, or time when any one of these factors is unknown. For example, in Figure 14-2 the rate of interest is 18 percent, and the loan was repaid in 18 months. What was the principal?

FIGURE 14–2
Simple Interest
(Principal)

$I = P \times R \times T$	(or change the formula to read:
$I = \$26$	$P = \dfrac{I}{R \times T}$
$P = ?$	
$R = 18\%$	
$T = 18$ months	$= \dfrac{\$26}{.18 \times 1.50}$
$26 = P \times .18 \times 18/12$	
$\quad = P \times .18 \times 3/2 \ (1.50)$	$= \dfrac{\$26}{.27}$
$\quad = P \times .27$	
$P = 26 \div .27$	$= \$96.30)$
$\quad = \$96.30$	

To find the missing rate, again the formula may be used. See Figure 14-3 for an illustration.

FIGURE 14–3
Simple Interest
(Rate)

$I = P \times R \times T$	(or change the formula to read:
$I = \$18$	$R = \dfrac{I}{P \times T}$
$P = \$300$	
$R = ?$	$= \dfrac{18}{300 \times 2/3}$
$T = 240$ days	
$18 = 300 \times R \times 240/360$	$= \dfrac{18}{200}$
$\quad = 300 \times 2/3 \times R$	
$\quad = 200 \times R$	$= .09$ or $9\%)$
$R = 18 \div 200$	
$\quad = .09$ or 9%	

As shown in Figures 14-2 and 14-3, you can either plug the numbers into the existing formula, or rearrange the formula. Either way, you can find the unknown amount by simple mathematics.

Installment Interest

As you have just learned, simple interest is calculated on the basis of one year of time. However, lenders may charge a monthly interest rate on unpaid balances. On installment loans, charge accounts, and credit card accounts, interest may be charged only on the amount that is unpaid at the end of each month. When you borrow money from a bank, the amount of interest is added to the principal amount. This total, or installment, price is also part of the deferred payment price.

Interest is often charged on the unpaid balance.

The down payment is often called a deposit, or amount given as security to ensure that other payments will be made. When you buy a car, the car you traded in is often considered a down payment because the older car is worth money. The down payment is part of the deferred payment price because it is part of the total amount needed to purchase the good or service desired. Many merchants require that the down payment be at least 10 percent or more of the purchase price.

The rate of interest charged on installment contracts is called the annual percentage rate (APR). By law, installment contracts must reveal the finance charge, the amount financed, and the annual percentage rate. The formula for calculating the annual percentage rate is presented in the Appendix.

The annual percentage rate must be revealed.

In Figure 14-4, the annual percentage rate is calculated on an installment purchase in which a down payment was made. The total number of payments is multiplied by the amount of each payment to determine how much, in addition to the down payment, will be paid for the merchandise. Each payment includes principal and interest. The deferred payment price is the total of all the payments added to the amount of the down

FIGURE 14–4
Annual
Percentage Rate

The Kramers are buying a new sofa. The cash price is $800. The installment terms are $100 down and the balance in 12 monthly payments of $66 each.

1.   Down payment $100
    + Payments (12 × 66)   + 792
    = Installment price $892
2. − Cash price   − $800
3. = Finance charge $ 92
4. APR (divide finance
    charge by cash price:
    92 ÷ 800 = APR)   11.5%

The finance charge is the cost of credit.

payment. When the cash price is subtracted from the deferred payment price, the difference is the amount of the finance charge. When the amount of the finance charge is divided by the cash price, the result is the annual percentage rate.

Interest on Revolving Charge Accounts

The cost of using a revolving charge account varies with the method the merchant uses to compute the finance charge. Merchants use the method that will bring the highest amount of interest. Interest is usually calculated by computer and is based on the monthly billing cycle. Purchases made up to the closing date are included in the monthly bill. Finance charges are computed on the unpaid balance after the billing date. Merchants may calculate finance charges on revolving charge accounts using the previous balance method, the adjusted balance method, or the average daily balance method.

Previous Balance Method. When the *previous balance method* is used, the finance charge is added to the previous balance. Then the payment made during the last billing period is subtracted to determine the new balance in the account. Figure 14-5 shows how a $500 balance at 18 percent interest (1 1/2 percent a month) would be computed using the previous balance method.

FIGURE 14–5
Previous
Balance Method

BALANCE	+	FIN. CHG.	=	BALANCE	–	PMT.	=	NEW BALANCE
$500.00		$ 7.50		$507.50		$50.00		$457.50
457.50		6.86		464.36		50.00		414.36
414.36		6.22		420.58		50.00		370.58
		$20.58						

To compute the finance charge, the balance is multiplied by .015 (18 percent divided by 12). The finance charge is then added to the balance before the payment is subtracted to determine the new account balance.

Adjusted Balance Method. When the *adjusted balance method* is used, the monthly payment is subtracted from the balance due before the finance charge is computed. As you can see in Figure 14-6, using $500 at 18 percent with $50 payments, the total finance charge is less than when the previous balance method is used.

FIGURE 14–6
Adjusted
Balance Method

BALANCE	–	PAYMENT	=	BALANCE	+	FIN. CHG.	=	NEW BALANCE
$500.00		$50.00		$450.00		$ 6.75		$456.75
456.75		50.00		406.75		6.10		412.85
412.85		50.00		362.85		5.44		368.29
						$18.29		

Average Daily Balance Method. Many large department stores and creditors use the *average daily balance method* of computing finance charges. The finance charge is based on the average outstanding balance during the period. This average daily balance is computed by adding together all daily balances and dividing by the number of days in the period (usually 25 or 30). Payments made during the billing cycle are used in figuring the average daily balance, as of the date received. Since payments made during the period reduce the average daily balance, the finance charge using this method is often less than when the previous balance method is used. The minimum finance charge is 50 cents to $1 if the account is not paid in full, regardless of the amount of the balance.

Unearned interest means less interest paid.

When an installment agreement or loan is paid off before it is actually due, the result is unearned interest. If you agree to an installment loan that will take two years to pay off, but you pay it off in less than two years, you will pay less total interest. Therefore, the sooner you pay off a loan, the more you save in interest charges. Various methods of calculation are used to determine how much interest is saved. One method, called the Rule of 78, is presented in the Appendix.

AVOIDING UNNECESSARY CREDIT COSTS

Credit can be very advantageous to the consumer when it is used wisely. Most credit costs can be avoided or minimized if the following simple guidelines are followed:

Unused credit can work against you.

1. Don't accept more credit than you need. Although having credit there when you need it may seem comforting, unused credit can count against you, too. *Unused credit* is the amount of credit above what you owe that you could charge, to a maximum amount (credit limit). For example, if the maximum credit limit on your VISA account is $1,000 and you owe $200, your unused credit is $800. Other creditors may be reluctant to loan money to you because you could at any time charge that other $800, thereby reducing your ability to pay back another loan. Potential creditors, then, may view you as a bad risk because of your unused credit. Unused

credit accounts are also temptations for you to use more credit than you need.

2. Don't increase credit spending when your income increases. Instead of spending or tying up that increase in income, put it into savings or invest it. This way you can avoid the trap of being totally dependent on your income. Other costs of living will rise also; therefore, that increase in pay should not be spent so readily. It is wiser to reduce existing debt or save the additional income for future use.

3. Keep credit cards to a minimum. Most credit counselors recommend carrying only two or three credit cards. The more credit cards you have, the more temptation you have to buy. A bank credit card is often good at many places, and many individual accounts are not needed.

4. Don't charge amounts under $25. If you make yourself pay cash for small purchases, you won't be surprised with a big bill at the end of the month. Having to pay cash will make you realize the extent of the purchase; consequently you will buy less, and only when you really need an item.

5. Understand the costs of credit. You should compute for yourself the total cost, payment, length of time you will make payments, total finance charges, and so on, for any credit purchase, if this information is not provided in writing. Study the figures carefully and consider the commitment of future income you are making, and how this commitment will affect your budget in the months to come.

6. Shop for loans. The type and source of your loan will make a big difference in cost. The costs from three different sources should be compared. Decisions to make major purchases should be planned carefully—never made on the spur of the moment. Don't sit and figure costs in a lender's office. Go home, figure all costs, and consider the purchase carefully without the presence of third persons.

Major credit purchases should be planned carefully.

7. Use credit to beat inflation. With the help of credit, you can often purchase needed items on sale that you could not purchase if cash were your only payment option. In this way, you can avoid price increases and save dollars.

8. Let the money you save by using credit work for you. When you purchase on credit, rather than spending cash, you can put your cash into savings or investments that will earn you interest or dividends. Many people find it very difficult to save any money at all. But by putting aside some money in this way, you not only provide funds for later use, but you also earn more money to help pay for the cost of the credit.

9. Time your credit purchases carefully. By purchasing after the closing date of the billing cycle, you can delay your payment for two

months rather than one month. Your repayment time is usually 25 to 30 days. You can extend your time to repay for 60 days, interest free, if your timing is right. Know the closing dates and billing cycles for all your credit accounts and use them to your advantage.

Through credit, you can have use of your money longer.

10. Use service credit to the best advantage. Don't pay bills that will be covered by insurance. If your medical or dental insurance will pay for 80 percent or more of a claim, do not pay your share until the insurance company has been billed and has paid their portion. In this way, you will have full use of your money and will not over-pay a bill and have to wait for a refund. Hospitals, doctors, and others often take weeks or months to refund overpayments. Service credit, which is available to most consumers, should be used wisely.

11. Keep track of all interest paid on credit purchases. Interest you pay can be deducted from your federal income tax liability using Schedule A. Keep track of interest paid and compare your total with year-end statements provided by creditors.

VOCABULARY

Directions: Can you find the definition for each of the following terms used in Chapter 14?

simple interest	average daily balance method
adjusted balance method	unused credit
previous balance method	annual percentage rate
deferred payment price	principal
interest	time
rate	full disclosure
discount rate	prime rate
add-on interest	

1. The total amount borrowed, on which interest is charged.

2. The total amount, including principal, interest, and down payment, that will be paid for merchandise in an installment purchase agreement.

3. The amount of credit available, above what you owe, up to your maximum credit limit.

4. A short and easy method of computing interest on short-term loans that have no down payment.

5. To reveal to a borrower in complete detail every possible charge or cost involved in the granting of credit.

6. An installment plan whereby interest is added to principal, then equal payments of principal and interest are made monthly until the balance is paid in full.

7. The true annual rate of interest.

8. The dollar cost of credit.

9. Stated as a percentage that represents interest.

10. Written as a fraction of a year and used to compute interest charged in payment of a loan.

11. A method of computing finance charges whereby the interest is first added to the amount due, then the amount of payment is subtracted to get the new balance.

12. A method of computing the finance charge whereby the monthly payment is first subtracted from the balance, then the finance charge is computed and added to get the new balance.

13. A method of computing the finance charge that is based on the average of balances during the month.

14. The rate of interest bank lenders offer to their best commercial (business) customers.

15. The rate of interest banks are charged to borrow money from the Federal Reserve System.

ITEMS FOR DISCUSSION

1. How is a loan with add-on interest different from a loan that has discount interest? Which is probably better, and why?

2. Describe how the cost of credit is determined.

3. List ten factors that affect the cost or rate of interest a customer will have to pay to get a loan.

4. What is the prime rate?

5. List ten things you can do to avoid unnecessary credit costs.

6. What is meant by "timing your purchases" to your advantage?

7. What is the formula for computing simple interest?

8. Why is the down payment added to the total amount of payments made to determine the deferred payment price (installment price)?

9. What is included in the deferred payment price?

10. How can unused credit work against you when you are applying for a new loan?

11. What is meant by the word *time* used in computing simple interest?

12. What is your liability and responsibility if your credit card is lost or stolen?

13. What kinds of things can you do to protect yourself from losing your credit cards and having large purchases made with your credit cards?

14. What kinds of things can merchants do to protect themselves from losses due to fraudulent credit card use?

APPLICATIONS

1. Using the formula for simple interest (I = PRT), solve the following problems, rounding to the nearest penny:

   (a) I = ?
       P = $500
       R = 18 percent
       T = 6 months

   (b) I = ?
       P = $1,000
       R = 13.5 percent
       T = 8 months

   (c) I = ?
       P = $108
       R = 21.6 percent
       T = 3 months

   (d) I = ?
       P = $89.50
       R = 16 percent
       T = 9 months

2. The following simple interest problems have different elements missing. Either change the formula to find the missing element, or insert the given elements into the formula and solve as shown in this chapter. Round to the nearest penny. Use the formula I = PRT.

   (a) I = $8
       P = ?
       R = 12 percent
       T = 60 days (60/360)

   (b) I = $54
       P = ?
       R = 18 percent
       T = 18 months (18/12)

   (c) I = $510
       P = $2,100
       R = ?
       T = 2 years (24/12)

   (d) I = $36
       P = $108
       R = ?
       T = 18 months (18/12)

3. Using the procedure illustrated in Figure 14-4, determine the annual percentage rates for the following problems:

    (a) The purchase of an item requiring a down payment of $60, with the balance to be paid in 12 equal payments of $60 each. The cash price is $700.

    (b) The purchase of an item that has a down payment of $100 and 24 equal payments of $90. The cash price is $2,000.

    (c) The cash price of an item is $200. The down payment is $20, and 10 equal payments of $22 each are to be made.

    (d) The cash price of an item is $895. With $95 down, the balance is payable in 15 payments of $60 each.

4. The previous balance method of computing interest is determined by first calculating interest, then subtracting the monthly payment to determine the new balance. Complete the following chart, using a calculator and rounding to the nearest penny. The interest rate is 12 percent. What is the total interest paid?

BALANCE	+	FINANCE CHARGE	=	BALANCE	− PAYMENT	=	NEW BALANCE
$100.00		————		————	$20.00		————
————		————		————	20.00		————
————		————		————	20.00		————

5. With the adjusted balance method of computing interest, the monthly payment is subtracted before interest is calculated. The amount of interest is then added to get the new balance. Complete the following chart, using a calculator and rounding to the nearest penny. The interest rate is 18 percent. What is the total interest paid?

BALANCE	−	PAYMENT	=	BALANCE	−	FINANCE CHARGE	=	NEW BALANCE
$500.00		$50.00		————		————		————
————		50.00		————		————		————
————		50.00		————		————		————

CASE PROBLEMS AND ACTIVITIES

1. Your friend Barry is unable to determine whether he is getting a good deal on a loan of $100 for 6 months when he pays back $114. What is the simple interest rate he is paying? (Use I = PRT.)

2. You are considering buying a piano. The cash price of the piano is $600. The company selling the piano is willing to sell it to you for $50 down and 12 equal payments of $50. What is the installment price? What is the amount of interest?

3. If you were to purchase a major appliance and pay for it this year, borrowing $800 at 18 percent for 8 months, how much total interest would you pay?

4. What is the annual percentage rate when you buy a car that would sell for $8,000 cash by trading in your used car for a down payment of $2,000 and paying the balance at $195 a month for 36 months?

15
Personal Decision Making

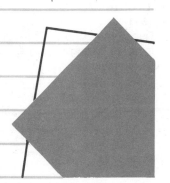

CHAPTER OBJECTIVES

After studying this chapter and completing the activities, you will be able to:

1. Demonstrate an understanding of the decision-making process by applying it to a real or hypothetical problem.
2. List and describe factors that influence consumer decision making.
3. Analyze and compare advertising gimmicks and promotional devices used to induce consumer spending.

THE CONSUMER DECISION-MAKING PROCESS

Decisions should be carefully planned.

Buying decisions play an important role in your efforts to manage your personal finances. Good decisions can save you money; bad decisions can be expensive. For this reason, your decision to purchase a product or service should always be based on careful consideration of available information and alternatives. The five-step consumer decision-making process presented in this chapter is a logical plan to use in solving problems caused by wants, needs, and goals. By following this process, you can make wise and economical buying decisions.

Define the Problem

First, you must define the problem.

The first step in the consumer decision-making process is simple: define the need or want to be satisfied and state it in a short, concise sentence. Then when your want or need has been pinpointed, you can proceed to the goal of satisfying the need or want in a manner that fits your

**ILLUSTRATION
15–1**
Decision making
involves finding
a way to fulfill a
need or want.

financial resources. For example, you and your roommate have just moved into an apartment complex that offers no laundry facilities. Your problem is that you want and need clean clothes; your goal is to find a way to satisfy this need in an economical fashion. The problem, when solved, will achieve your goal of finding laundry facilities and will satisfy the need for clean clothes in a way that will give you the most value for the money you spend. This first step in the consumer decision-making process is an important one, because it is at the problem level of satisfying needs and wants that you make decisions concerning the purchase of products and services.

Obtain Accurate Information

Once you have determined the problem, you must then gather information relating to your problem. List all alternative solutions to the problem and the cost of each. In the laundry problem example, there are three basic solutions:

List all possible solutions to the problem.

1. Use a laundromat.
2. Buy a new washer and dryer.
3. Buy a used washer and dryer.

In order to make a wise decision regarding your problem of obtaining clean clothes, you will need to know what products and services are available and how much it will cost you to use or purchase them. For instance, you will need to know where laundry facilities are located. The cost of use will include the price for each washer and dryer load as well as mileage for driving to and from the laundry and the time involved. For the possible purchase of new appliances, you will need to list desired features and then visit various appliance stores, department stores, and discount stores for the purpose of comparative shopping. At each location, you should list the brands available, features available, costs, and warranties. The classified ads are a good source for used washers and dryers.

Comparison shopping provides alternatives.

Whenever possible, keep a written record of the information you collect on choices of products and services. By doing so, you can make comparisons of alternatives and costs more easily. Figure 15-1 shows information collected for comparison in the laundry problem.

Compare Alternatives

When comparing total costs, you must consider time and convenience factors as well as dollar amounts. In some cases, convenience may be more important than cost, as long as the cost is reasonable. Using the previous example, you may decide that the convenience of having a washer and dryer in your apartment is worth the extra dollar cost. You may also decide to buy a new washer and dryer, even though the cost will be greater, because you prefer to avoid the expense of possible repairs. Purchasing used rather than new appliances results in greater risks because previous owners may or may not have cared for and maintained the appliances properly.

Convenience may be more important than cost.

On the other hand, if your housing situation is temporary, and you and your roommate anticipate that you will share the apartment for less than a year, going to the nearest laundromat and sharing the expenses may be the best choice. These are just a few of the factors you must consider in this step of the consumer decision-making process.

Consider how long you will live in the apartment.

Select an Alternative

If you follow the steps outlined in the preceding paragraphs, the decision you make will be based on a careful analysis of the problem, thorough information gathering, and analysis of that information. In our example, the decision is to determine whether to use a laundromat or to buy a washer and dryer. The cost is the price you will pay for what you decide to do. All choices have prices, because to choose one thing is not to choose another. The wise decision in this or in any situation is the one that is within your budget and that gives you the most value for your dollar investment.

You should be satisfied with your decision.

FIGURE 15–1
Information for
Comparison

COST COMPARISON

	Per Month	Per Year
Option 1: Use a Laundromat		
Time: about 4 to 6 hours each weekend spent at laundromat	20 hrs.	250 hrs.
Gasoline: 6 miles round trip, once each weekend, 52/year	$ 3.00	$ 36.00
Washer, 75 cents each load, 6 loads a weekend	18.00	216.00
Dryer, 50 cents each load, 6 loads each weekend	12.00	144.00
	$35.00	$396.00
Option 2: Buy New Machines		
Average quality machines, on sale (washer/dryer)	$600.00 one-time cost	
Monthly payments (2 years to pay off, 13 percent interest)	$26.63	$319.50

Costs of repair, upkeep, service contract, etc., are additional.
There is no time expense, because other things can be done while
machines are running.
Machines should last 5 to 10 years.

Option 3: Buy Used Machines		
Average quality used washer/dryer at garage sale	$300.00 one-time cost	
Monthly payments (usually have to pay cash; borrow money from bank for 1 year at 13 percent interest)	$28.25	$339.00

Costs of repair and upkeep are additional.
Machines should last 3 to 5 years.

Take Action

After you have selected the best alternative, you must take action to
accomplish the goal of satisfying your need. Because you have made a

thorough analysis of information necessary to solve your problem, you can be sure that you have made a wise decision.

PERSONAL FACTORS THAT INFLUENCE SPENDING DECISIONS

There are many personal factors that influence consumer spending decisions. *Personal factors* are those influences in a person's or family's life that determine spending patterns, preferences, and choices. Some persons and families may be influenced greatly by one or more of the following factors: personal resources; position in life; customs, background, and religion; and values and goals.

Personal Resources

Your *personal resources* include your time, money, energy, skills and abilities, and available credit. The greater the quantity and the higher the quality of any one of these factors, the greater your purchasing power. Generally speaking, the more resources you have available to you, the greater your earning potential and the greater your buying capacity.

Your personal resources affect your choices.

Position in Life

Your position in life includes such factors as age, marital status, sex, employment status, and life-style. At different times in your life, your needs and wants are different. Within each of life's stages, your spending patterns will also vary. Spending patterns of single people are different from those of married couples and families. Spending patterns at age 40 are different from those at age 30. Right now your spending patterns are probably different from those of your parents, and your parents' patterns differ from your grandparents' patterns because of age differences alone. If you have been working for 20 years, your spending patterns are different from the person who just started working three months ago.

Customs, Background, and Religion

A *custom* is a long-established practice that may be considered an unwritten law. Families may be dedicated to traditions that have been followed for generations. This is particularly true of religious groups or of cultures in which strict rules and policies are followed. Persons in these religious or cultural groups may observe special holidays and occasions

Customs can be strong motivating influences.

that are not observed nationally. Buying patterns of these groups are greatly influenced by the values and priorities in their lives. In many cases, custom overshadows all other buying preferences.

Values and Goals

Values are expressed through choices.

Values, which lie at the base of all our purchasing decisions, are slow to change. Goals change often. You accomplish goals and move on to others. Your total value system may change as your goals in life are met, or not met. Individual and family values and goals are expressed through choices of entertainment, literature, sports, luxuries, and so on. These choices are reflected in decisions to purchase goods and services, use of time and energy, and attitudes toward possessions and their accumulation.

OUTSIDE FACTORS THAT INFLUENCE SPENDING DECISIONS

To understand how the world in which you live plays a role in your decision-making process, you must consider the following: the economy, technological advances, the environment, and social pressures.

The Economy

Inflation causes loss of purchasing power.

The *economy* is the system or structure of economic life in a country. This term describes the financial well-being of the nation as measured by economists. The general condition of the economy affects every one of us, and we react to it accordingly. For example, in a period of high inflation, when prices are rising rapidly, people tend to buy more and save less. Prices rise so rapidly that money purchases less each day. There is little incentive to save because the rate of interest on savings is much less than the rate of inflation, and to save money is to lose money. When the rate of inflation is low, the economy is slow, and interest rates are high. When interest rates on automobile loans are high, fewer people are able to buy new cars. Consequently, older cars are kept longer. In these times, people save more and buy less (or buy less expensive items) because they do not want to pay the high rates of interest, but they do want high interest rates paid on their savings accounts.

Technological Advances

You may be fascinated or even obsessed with new electronic games. Or you may be interested in the world's first water-powered automobile.

Faster, better ways of doing things are important to us.

Perhaps you want to add a new solar heating device to your home to make it more energy efficient. In America, a high value is placed on new technological advances. Many people want to have the newest, most convenient, modern, and interesting gadgets. As new goods and services are created to increase our level of comfort and standard of living, we willingly purchase them. These types of purchases, whether large or small, are important to the emotional well-being of the consumer who needs to have the latest gimmick to feel a part of what is going on in the world.

The Environment

Conservation is a high priority in America.

Concern for the environment can affect consumer buying decisions to a great extent. The physical environment and quality of life are very real concerns today. Our natural resources are scarce and are disappearing rapidly. Air quality, of vital importance to our health and well-being, is a problem individuals and the government spend much time and money to solve. In addition, millions of dollars are spent each year to help preserve the natural beauty, landscape, waterways, wildlife, and other natural resources of our country. Citizens find themselves concerned with home projects, community activities, and statewide programs to beautify and preserve, recycle, and protect existing resources and environment. Thus, this interest in the environment affects consumers' actions and also their product preferences because products purchased must be ecologically safe and biodegradable (or otherwise recyclable) to meet present and future environmental standards.

Social Pressures

Advertising appeals to hidden fears and desires.

Social pressures often induce consumers to buy goods and services beyond their real wants and needs. People can be influenced to make purchases by their friends, relatives, and co-workers. The media (radio, television, newspapers) also act as sources of social pressure for consumers. Through advertising, the media convince consumers to buy goods and services designed to keep them young, good looking, healthy, and appealing to the opposite sex. America is a country obsessed with youth, beauty, physical fitness, and material comforts. We are easily enticed into buying merchandise we do not need—status symbols, such as a second car or designer clothes that are beyond our budget, rather than necessities. The list is endless. Understanding how outside factors such as the economy, technological advances, the environment, and social pressures influence our spending patterns can help us to make wise consumer decisions.

PLANNING FOR MAJOR PURCHASES

Because major purchases generally tie up future income or take a big bite out of accumulated savings, carefully consider your needs and wants before committing to a large purchase. Ask yourself these questions, think about it for at least 24 hours, and then make a final decision based on a rational–not emotional–perspective.

1. Why do I need/want this purchase?
2. How long will this product last?
3. What substitutes are available and at what cost?
4. By postponing this purchase, is it likely that I will choose not to buy it at a later date?
5. What types of additional costs are involved, such as supplies, maintenance, insurance, and financial risks?
6. For what other purposes might I use the money spent or committed for this purchase?
7. What is the total cost of this product (cash price, deferred price, interest, shipping charges, etc.)?

Once you have made a decision that you will purchase the good or service, then you need to determine whether to pay cash or use credit. Even though you may have the cash available, you should not automatically pay cash for all purchases. If you do, your cash reserves will dwindle, or you may do without many conveniences you could have now with wise use of credit. Figure 15-2 is a comparison of various options available, with positive and negative consequences.

Comparison shopping will allow you to determine whether you are getting the best quality for the price you are paying. Name brands often sell at considerably different prices; by shopping various retail outlets you may be able to save money. In addition, many stores offer sale prices at various times of the year, or at regular intervals. Before making a major purchase, ask if and when the merchandise will be placed on sale.

Because you are paying a high price does not necessarily mean you are getting the best quality merchandise. It pays to be aware of what is good quality and what you need and expect from the merchandise. Magazines such as *Consumer Reports* make quality comparisons of products. Yearly buying guides that show quality comparisons for almost all major purchase items, from electric mixers to air humidifiers, are also available. You can do a similar comparison while doing your own comparison shopping. Figure 15-3 is an illustration of how to compare cost with quality and utility (usefulness) of product selections.

FIGURE 15–2
Cash or Credit
Purchase

ITEM	CASH	CREDIT
Refrigerator Price	$800 + $15 delivery charge	$50/month ($900 total) + $15 delivery charge
Total cost	$815	$915
Substitutes Used refrigerator Price	$400 + $15 delivery charge	$30/month for 15 months + $15 delivery charge
Total cost	$415	$465
Considerations	Ties up cash; cannot make other purchases. No monthly payments. Reduces savings balance. No interest charges.	Allows for budgeting; ties up future income. Can make other purchases. Establishes credit.

FIGURE 15–3
Cost Analysis

ITEM	COST	QUALITY	UTILITY
Product A Hair Dryer	$25.00	High; Five-Year Warranty; Metal	3 Speeds 3 Attachments
Product B Hair Dryer	$18.75	Good; Two-Year Warranty; Plastic	3 Speeds 2 Attachments
Product C Hair Dryer	$15.00	Good; No Warranty; Plastic	1 Speed 1 Attachment

Considering the cost difference for quality and usefulness, the buyer would probably buy either Product A or B because quality and utility make them more reasonable for the price paid.

MARKETING STRATEGIES THAT INFLUENCE SPENDING DECISIONS

Numerous marketing strategies lure us into stores to buy goods and services. Many of these strategies are subtle, and we are often unaware of

Marketing strategies are designed to sell products.

their impact on our buying patterns. Some frequently used marketing strategies explained in this chapter are advertising, pricing, sales, and promotional techniques.

Advertising

The primary goal of all advertising is to create within the consumer the desire to purchase a product or service. Some advertising is false and misleading; other advertising is informational and valuable.

A variety of media are available for advertising—billboards, television, radio, newspapers, magazines, leaflets, balloons, and T-shirts—all carefully coordinated to reach specific consumer groups. Advertising agencies create colorful and attractive campaigns: They compose jingles and catchy tunes, develop slogans and trademarks, design colorful logos, and choose mascots to identify their products. There are three basic types of advertising: product, company, and industry.

Product Advertising. Advertising to convince consumers to buy a specific good or service is called *product advertising*. The name of the advertised product is repeated several times during radio and television commercials. Testimonials from people who have used the product, giveaways, promotional gimmicks, and other clever and catchy methods are used to persuade consumers to purchase products and services. Advertisements are carefully planned to appeal to specific types of consumers.

Advertising is directed to a target audience.

A *target audience* is a specific consumer group to which the advertisements for a product are directed. Research has revealed specific characteristics of people who will probably be interested in a given product or service. Day of the week, time of day, and type of program are taken into consideration by television advertisers. All these factors are important when trying to reach a target audience. Products advertised during football games differ from products advertised during daytime television because the target audiences are different.

Companies advertise to promote a good image.

Company Advertising. Advertising to promote the image of a store, company, or retail chain is known as *company advertising*. Usually price is not a consideration, and specific products are not mentioned. Emphasis is placed on the quality of the products or services the company sells, warranties and/or guarantees offered, or social and environmental concerns of the company. In a store advertisement, you may hear or read about the company's friendly employees, its wide selection of products or services, or its claim that you can find everything you want in one place. These advertisements are designed to prompt a favorable attitude toward the company so that you develop a loyalty to the store and will not shop anywhere else. Company advertisements may be accompanied by catchy slogans and tunes, happy cartoons, or pleasant scenes to which products of this company make a contribution.

Industry Advertising. Advertising to promote a general product group, without regard to where these products are purchased, is called *industry advertising*. For example, the dairy industry emphasizes the nutritional value of milk and other natural dairy products. Consequently, the whole dairy industry benefits when people drink more milk and eat more dairy products. Oil industry advertisements stress concern about energy conservation, environmental protection, and the search for new alternative forms of fuels. The automobile industry gives safe-driving tips and reasons for buying American-made cars. General health and safety advertisements are often presented in industry advertising campaigns, such as the Smokey the Bear fire safety commercials and the stop-smoking ads.

Industry advertising is general and many retailers benefit.

Pricing

The price of merchandise depends on several factors. Supply and demand determine what will be produced and the general price range. The cost of raw materials and labor, competitive pressures, and the seller's need to make a reasonable profit are some of the factors that determine the price of a product. But there is more to pricing than adding up the production costs and including a profit. Retailers understand the psychological aspects of selling goods and services and use pricing devices to persuade consumers to buy. For example, if buyers believe they are getting a bargain, or are paying a lower price, they are more inclined to buy a product or service. *Odd-number pricing* is the practice of putting odd numbers on price tags—99 cents instead of $1.00. Because the price is under a dollar, it appears to be a bargain. By paying $5.98 instead of $6.00 the customer is happy because he found a sound buy; the retailer is happy because she has made a profitable sale.

Discounts or low unit prices are often available for buying in large sizes or quantities. However, you cannot assume that because you are buying the large economy size you are actually paying less per ounce than if you bought a small size. Compare unit prices on all sizes.

There are psychological aspects of selling products.

Sales

Stores advertise end-of-month sales, anniversary sales, clearance sales, inventory sales, holiday sales, preseason sales, and so on. Merchandise may be marked down substantially, slightly, or not at all. In order to be sure that you are actually saving money by buying sale items, you must do comparative shopping and know the usual prices. When an advertisement states that everything in the store is marked down, check carefully for items that only appear to be marked down in price.

A *loss leader* is an item of merchandise marked down to an unusually low price, sometimes below the store's actual cost. The store may actually lose money on every sale of this item because the cost of producing the item is higher than the retail price. However, the loss leader is used to get customers into the store to buy other products as well. Sales on other items are expected to make up for the loss sustained on the loss leader. There is nothing illegal or unethical about a loss leader as long as the product advertised is available to the customer on demand. A customer who buys only loss leaders and super sale items is called a *cherry picker*. Retailers rely on customers to buy other products to make up for the loss caused by sales of the loss leader. Consequently, cherry pickers are not highly favored by retailers.

Promotional Techniques

In order to get customers into stores, retailers may use one or more promotional techniques: displays, contests and games, trading stamps, coupons, packaging, and sampling.

Displays. Retail stores often use window displays, special racks of new items, or sampling promotions to entice customers. Products are arranged attractively, and the promotion may carry a theme centered around the nearest holiday—Halloween, Thanksgiving, Christmas, Valentine's Day, Mother's Day, Father's Day, or the Fourth of July. Color schemes, decorations, music, and special effects often set off the products being offered to appeal to consumers' ego needs.

Contests and Games. Grocery stores, department stores, fast food restaurants, and other retail stores that depend on repeat customers often use contests and games to bring customers into the store. Individual product packages, such as cereal boxes, may contain game cards. The possibility of winning something or getting something for nothing appeals to many people. Large and small prizes are offered with the intention of getting customers to come back and buy more so that they can get more game cards, have more chances to win, and receive some of the minor prizes. Careful reading of the rules on the reverse side of the game card or other token reveals the customer's chances of winning. Usually, the chances of winning a major prize are small.

Know product prices when shopping sales.

Loss leaders are used to draw you in to buy other things, too.

Contests and games lure in new customers and keep old ones interested.

Trading stamps are still popular in some areas.

Trading Stamps. The trading stamp is a promotional gimmick that is still popular in some parts of the country. Some stores give trading stamps based on the total dollar amount of individual purchases. These stamps are collected and redeemed for prizes, reduced prices on special purchases, or other types of rewards. This type of promotion is designed to maintain customer loyalty—the more customers shop in the same store, the more stamps they can collect. Many customers think that they are getting more for their money or are getting something for nothing when they receive trading stamps.

Coupons. Manufacturer coupons offer cents off on specifically described products from a specific manufacturer and may be redeemed wherever the product is sold. Store coupons offer discounts on specific products, usually for a short period of time, and only at a specific store. Manufacturer and store coupons may be inside a package, on the outside of the package, in newspapers or magazines, or on a store shelf. Coupons may not be redeemed for cash, but may be used to give cents off on the product promoted on the coupon. The effect of the coupon is to lower the price of the product in an attempt to lure customers to choose that product or the store offering the bargain over its competitors. Stores that accept manufacturer coupons return the coupons to the manufacturer for a refund in the amount given to the customer. Figure 15-4 shows coupons issued by a manufacturer and a store.

Coupons offer discounts on merchandise.

Packaging. Packages are designed to appeal to the eye with the necessary information correctly and attractively arranged. Distinctively designed packages are used to attract the customer's attention away from competitive products. Company logos, brightly colored designs, pictures

FIGURE 15–4A Manufacturer Coupon

FIGURE 15–4B Store Coupon

of people promoting or using the product, and other attention getters may appear on product boxes. Special features are emphasized, such as: sugar free, no saccharin, fortified with eight vitamins and minerals, new and improved, safe for children, and many others. Manufacturers know that the package or container must be attractive because it plays such an important role in inducing purchases. Size and shape of packages are significant. Containers that appear to hold more of the product and containers that are reusable as storage devices also attract consumers. Often, a game or prize inside the box is also shown on the outside, or coupons are contained inside the package or on the package. A cents-off price means that the price on the package is reduced by a discount amount usually shown in big letters.

Sampling. Many companies use direct advertising of their products through sampling. Small sample-size free packages of a product may be sent directly to households. Or company representatives may give out samples, free drinks, or tastes of products in selected stores, in shopping centers, or on street corners. Usually when a new product is first introduced into the marketplace, sampling allows potential customers to try the new product. Some companies advertise in magazines and newspapers, with offers for free samples by mail. All you have to do is fill out the coupon with your name and address and mail it in. In addition to a sample of the product, you may receive a coupon to be used on future purchases of the new product.

VOCABULARY

Directions: Can you find the definition for each of the following terms used in Chapter 15?

define the problem	industry advertising
personal resources	loss leader
target audience	personal factors
custom	company advertising
economy	odd-number pricing
product advertising	cherry picker

1. To state what specific want or need must be satisfied.

2. A customer who buys only loss leaders and super sale items.

3. An item of merchandise marked down to a very low price, often below actual cost.

4. The practice of putting uneven price numbers on merchandise to make the price appear low.

5. Factors present in one's life that influence spending patterns.

6. Time, money, energy, skills, abilities, and credit—the more you have, the more you can spend.

7. A long-established practice that is the same as an unwritten law.

8. A system or structure of life in a country that describes its financial well-being.

9. Advertising that attempts to convince you to buy a certain good or service.

10. Technique used to promote and maintain customer loyalty.

11. A specific consumer group.

12. A type of promotion that attempts to sell a general product group, without regard to where it is purchased.

ITEMS FOR DISCUSSION

1. List the five steps in the consumer decision-making process. Briefly describe each.

2. What are some personal factors that influence a person's or a family's spending patterns?

3. What are some outside factors that determine a person's or family's spending patterns?

4. List six different advertising media. Which one(s) do you see most frequently?

5. What is a target audience?

6. What is odd-number pricing? Is it used frequently in the advertising that you see most often?

7. Why don't retailers like to see cherry pickers?

8. On what theme do promotional displays often center?

9. What types of businesses often offer contests and games to attract customers?

10. What types of trading stamps are available in your community?

11. What is a store coupon?

12. What is a manufacturer coupon?

APPLICATIONS

1. Using the steps in the consumer decision-making process, make a decision that will satisfy your need for a piano.

2. How do your spending patterns differ from those of your parents? What things do you buy that your parents also purchase? Can you trace any of these purchases to strong family custom, background, or religion?

3. How are you or the members of your family affected when interest rates are very high? Do you benefit, or are you hurt? How? Can you think of anyone who is affected in an opposite way from you? Why is this so?

4. What community-centered and national environmental concerns do you have? What can you do as a single concerned citizen to help preserve the quality of the environment?

5. Spend an evening viewing television or listening to the radio. List the jingles, tunes, key words, phrases, and slogans used in each commercial. How many commercials can you automatically sing along with?

CASE PROBLEMS AND ACTIVITIES

1. Watch a television program for one hour any time during the day. Determine the target audience (teenagers, children, homemakers, sports fans, families, adults only) of the program. Pay close attention to all commercials shown during the hour. Write your answers to the following questions on a separate piece of paper.

    (a) List all the commercials. Categorize them as either product, company, or industry advertising. (Public service advertisements and political campaigns are industry advertisements.)

    (b) Rate each commercial as good, fair, or poor, depending upon how well it is directed to the television program's target market.

    (c) Rate each commercial according to tastefulness (either good taste or poor taste). Do you find it offensive, degrading, insulting? Explain why you liked or disliked the commercial.

2. Bring to class an advertisement insert from a newspaper. It should be from a department store, local discount store, or grocery store. Write your answers to these questions on a separate piece of paper:

    (a) How many advertisements show odd-number pricing?

    (b) How many individual advertisements mention how much money will be saved or what the regular price is?

    (c) Are there any coupons or references to coupons?

    (d) Are trading stamps, games, or special incentives mentioned in the advertisement?

    (e) Is the advertisement insert attractively arranged?

    (f) Is the insert in color or black and white?

    (g) Rate the advertisement insert as to quality, attractiveness, and readability.

    (h) Do you see any loss leaders or super buys?

Attach the advertisement insert to your paper. On the insert, write comments next to items to identify them as examples of loss leaders, odd-number pricing, etc.

3. Describe a store display built around the theme of the most recent major holiday. Describe colors used, products displayed, product arrangement, location in the store, etc. Were there any actual price reductions?

4. List any stores in your area that use one or more of the following promotional techniques. Beside each store name, describe the specific techniques used.

    (a) Contests and games   (d) Sampling

    (b) Trading stamps   (e) Other

    (c) Coupons

16
Personal Economic Decisions

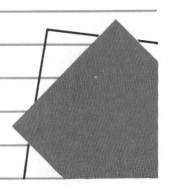

CHAPTER OBJECTIVES

After studying this chapter and completing the activities, you will be able to:

1. Identify individual and societal needs and wants and define the term *economics.*
2. List the four factors of production and describe them in economic terms.
3. Outline types of production decisions that must be made and list factors contributing to those decisions.

WHY STUDY ECONOMICS?

Before we can begin our study of economics, we must understand the meaning of the word and the importance of the subject. *Economics* is the study of human efforts to solve the problem of making scarce resources meet the unlimited needs and wants of society. When we study economics, we study human behavior in producing, exchanging, and consuming material goods and services to satisfy needs and wants. Specifically, we study a diverse array of topics from balancing household budgets to labor disputes, farm surpluses and taxes, debt, inflation, and unemployment—all vital issues.

Well-informed consumers know basic economics.

No one can escape the principles of economics—the study of scarcity. As we will discuss later, society's needs and wants are always increasing, and there is no way our existing resources could possibly meet all our present needs and wants, nor the continuing and unknown needs and wants

ILLUSTRATION 16–1
We choose which needs and wants to fulfill.

of the future. As a result, consumers must make choices concerning which needs and wants to fulfill and how best to fulfill them. We study economics to learn how to make wise and responsible choices, for our individual good and for the good of society.

Benefits to Society

An informed citizen has an understanding of economics.

Consumers who are well informed and knowledgeable about economics make wise decisions that determine the courses of their own lives and contribute to the destiny of their country's economic future. By giving you a better understanding of the world in which you live, economics can help you to be a more productive, responsible, and effective citizen who is a part of the positive changes in society. One major function of an informed citizen—that of voting—depends a great deal on a good understanding of important social and economic issues.

Consumers who are knowledgeable about economics can help to conserve the country's resources. Wise economic decisions facilitate the use of resources to their maximum potential (conservation), while unwise choices lead to waste and mismanagement of scarce resources, to the detriment of society as a whole. Because natural, human, and human-made resources are limited in supply and quality, consumers have a responsibility to future generations to make good decisions now.

Personal Benefits

Understanding economics is a personal benefit.

The study of economics is of practical value in our daily lives, both personally and professionally. As an academic subject, economics can be used as an aid in making good decisions that will allow us to enjoy effective, productive, and rewarding lives. For instance, a citizen who understands such concepts as inflation and unemployment (their causes and cures) is better able to survive personally during periods of inflation, recession, or even depression. In studying economics, we learn not only how and why such things happen, but also how to deal with such problems and bring about solutions.

As a vocational subject, economics is also valuable. Many persons choose economics careers. Big businesses, labor unions, and government offices hire economic specialists, counselors, and advisors; every successful business person relies on dependable interpretation of economic indicators. Although economics may not specifically teach you how to make more money, it can give you insight into ways to make your money do more for you. Once you have a good basic understanding of economics, you will be better equipped to survive in a world that can be very threatening and unsympathetic and that is constantly changing.

ECONOMIC NEEDS AND WANTS

Our needs and wants can be divided into two groups. We have basic survival needs and other life-improving or fulfilling wants and needs.

Basic Needs

Basic needs must be met first.

Basic survival needs include (*a*) food and water, (*b*) shelter, and (*c*) clothing. As you can see, **basic needs** are those ingredients necessary for maintaining physical life. Some authors would add safety and security to this list, because until these basic needs are met, there is little necessity for any of the other things life has to offer. Many people do not have these basic needs met in their lives. Daily they struggle to remain alive in the midst of war and conflicts, and they have little concern for other needs besides safety and food.

Other Needs and Wants

Life-improving or fulfilling wants and needs include the following:

1. Food, clothing, and shelter beyond what is necessary for biological survival.

2. Medical care to improve the quality and length of life.
3. Education to achieve personal goals, both social and economic.
4. Travel, vacations, and recreation to improve personal enjoyment of life.
5. Gadgetry or extra items to make life more fun and give it extra excitement, challenge, or meaning.

You may have decided that many of the life-improving needs and wants are necessary for your happiness. But you must admit, they are not absolutely necessary to your physical survival—you may simply have become used to them and, therefore, expect to have them.

Our needs and wants are unlimited.

Two important concepts can be drawn from this information: (*a*) material wants and needs are virtually unlimited, and (*b*) economic resources to meet those needs and wants are limited (scarce). Humanity's material desires for goods and services cannot be satisfied; we always want more than we can have! It can safely be said that at any point in time, society has unfulfilled wants and needs—biological needs (food, clothing, shelter) plus other wants and needs that are socially oriented or involve learned responses (cars, vacations, luxuries).

Individual Needs and Wants

What each of us decides we need and want depends on a number of individually unique factors. These factors are different among individuals and different among societies. All factors may change at different points in our lives. Individual factors include personal style, income, education, security level, and leisure time.

Our choices are based on our tastes and styles.

Personal Style. Each person has his or her own set of values and personal preferences. Personal taste may be formal or informal, flashy or subdued, dominating or easygoing. One person may prefer dark colors; another may choose pastels. One person may enjoy a weekend alone in the mountains hiking, while another would choose a visit to Disneyland. Based on those personal tastes, style, and preferences, we make choices; we fulfill our wants and needs according to those personal values.

Your career meets or fails to meet your wants and needs.

Income. What a person is able to earn and spend will greatly influence the type of consumer choices she or he can make. The more disposable income—money left over after expenses are paid, which you can spend as you wish—the higher the quality and quantity of your selections. Whether or not a person can afford to buy goods and services to fulfill the wants and needs she or he considers important will affect his or her satisfaction or dissatisfaction with employment, personal life, goals, and other personal factors such as self-worth or self-esteem. Figure 16-1 shows the average per capita (per person) personal income, by region, for 1983. The median personal income in 1983 was $11,685. The *median* income is the statistical middle of the list of incomes. In a list of statistics, the same number of statistics is positioned above the median as is positioned below the median. In 1983, the state of Texas had the same per capita personal income as the U.S. average.

FIGURE 16–1
Per Capita Personal Income, by Region

New England	$13,005	Southwest	$11,330
Mideast	12,794	Rocky Mountain	11,069
Great Lakes	11,517	Far West	11,069
Plains	11,322		
Southeast	10,216	Texas	$11,685
		U.S. average	11,685

Source: Bureau of Economic Analysis, U.S. Commerce Department (Washington: U.S. Government Printing Office, 1985).

Nationwide, the median family income is $23,838. If your total family income (in your household) is more than $75,000, you would be in the top 2 percent of the nation. If you earned $50,000 or more, you would be in the top 10 percent. Those earning $25,000 or more, per household, make up the top 45 percent of the U.S. population.

Women's wages have remained fairly constant over the past 30 years, at 58-62 percent of men's wages. As income levels in some professions are lower, the gap between men's and women's wages is even wider. Women's wages are as low as 38 percent of men's wages in some service industries.

You can evaluate the career you are considering from the standpoint of the income it provides. For example, you might be considering a career as a systems analyst. By researching the average earnings of a person in this type of work, you might find that in your area, the level of pay you could expect is $23,000. In this position you would be in about the middle of the wage scale, and you would find that about half the labor force would be earning more than you, and half would be earning less. You need to evaluate how well the $23,000 salary will be able to meet your needs and wants as well as fulfill your status attainment, social standing, and prestige requirements.

Education. *Formal education* is knowledge gained through attending formal institutions of learning. The end result is a diploma or degree, which is evidence that the recipient has accomplished a certain educational goal and has met the standards for graduation. The level of education achieved will influence a person's needs and wants and his or her methods of fulfilling them because it will affect income. A person who has earned a college degree is likely to make different choices (based on greater earning power) than a person who dropped out of high school at age 16. Figure 16-2 illustrates how the level of education attained directly affects income.

FIGURE 16–2
Education and Income

	Lifetime Earnings (40 years)	
Educational Level	**Men**	**Women**
4-Year College Degree	$1.3 Million	$848,000
1-3 Years of College	1 Million	626,000
High School Graduate	926,000	575,000
1-3 Years of High School	620,000	359,600
Grade School Graduate	424,000	202,000

Source: Bureau of the Census, U.S. Commerce Department (Washington: U.S. Government Printing Office, 1983).

Security Level. A person acts and reacts in accordance with the degree of safety, security, and peace he or she enjoys. These factors include personal safety as well as personal freedoms and fears for life, liberty, and property. Being secure from physical harm—whether from civil conflicts or robbery and property damage—influences our perceptions and, therefore, our needs and wants. Job security is another important factor. If you feel secure and satisfied in your employment, your choices will be different from those you make when you feel threatened or dissatisfied.

Leisure Time. Individual needs and wants are often satisfied in our choices of pleasure and recreational activities. All of us have time after our work and chores are done. Those who are retired or not employed have more leisure time to allocate. Wise choices in this area can make life rewarding and satisfying. Wasting and making poor use of leisure time results in frustation, loneliness, and depression.

Leisure time needs careful planning.

Collective Values

Collective values are those things important to society as a whole; all citizens share in their costs and in their benefits. The society in which you live influences your values, goals, and choices because it demands from citizens and provides for citizens legal protection, employment, progress, quality environment, and public and government services.

Legal Protection. One of the first needs of the individual that is met by society is preservation of legal and personal rights, and protection from others who would deny you those rights. Law enforcement is the result of society's value of protection for citizens and property. Although it may not be often used directly by citizens, law enforcement is always made available. Laws are passed to protect freedoms and rights guaranteed by the Constitution or by local, state, and federal governments.

Legal and personal rights are important to society.

Employment. Society as a whole expects that its able members will be productive members. Employment is an acceptable measure of that productivity. Most people who are able will work in their lifetimes because it is expected and demanded in order to survive in the society. Most of us are aware of this subtle, yet very real, pressure to perform in the work arena. Therefore, we strive to do the best we can—to get a job that pays us well for the effort we put forth. In this way, we can be personally satisfied with our productivity and can, at the same time, satisfy society's demand for citizens who contribute.

Progress. The relative state of the country in which you live—its technological advances and feelings about their importance—will affect your personal goals. Our society is technologically advanced and places a high value on positive innovations. *Innovations* are new ideas, methods, or devices that bring about changes. Positive innovations, such as more efficient equipment or machinery, timesaving devices, or new solutions to old problems, bring about progress. Because we, as a society, place a high value on progress, we strive to achieve and discover new and more efficient methods and products. Discovery of new ideas, methods, or devices pays off, both financially and emotionally, because we are encouraged by our society to be innovative. A by-product of this encouragement is that citizens seek higher education and academic achievement to enhance their positions in society.

High value is placed on progress and innovation.

Quality Environment. Natural resources are of great value and concern to society as a whole because they are very limited, and some cannot be replaced. Because of our priority of preserving a quality environment for ourselves and future generations, we concentrate on activities such as land-use planning, preserving natural beauty and wildlife, and establishing air pollution standards. We also place a great importance on the environmental effects of a given product or service. Environmental quality is of great importance to society as a whole, and individuals respond to this concern by acting and purchasing accordingly.

Quality of environment is a collective value.

Public and Government Services. Our country is organized to be "of the people, by the people, and for the people." We have a highly advanced and intricate system of government made up of the people, performing services for the people, with money contributed (through taxes) by the people. Our system of taxation takes money from those who earn it and redistributes this money to those who need it. High value is placed on providing services for all citizens—from police protection to public parks. Services, such as roads and highways, are provided for all citizens, regardless of how much the citizens are able to contribute to society. Most citizens have come to expect public goods and services automatically—as a right rather than a privilege. What is often forgotten or ignored is that these goods and services are provided because of taxation of productive workers, and that no one can be excluded from receiving their benefits.

Citizens receive all public services.

You may be able to identify other collective or societal values that influence your personal choices—each person has a different perception and reacts accordingly.

FACTORS OF PRODUCTION

Factors of production are necessary for producing goods and services to meet consumer wants and needs. The quantity and quality of these factors determines a country's productive capacity. Effective use of factors of production determines a country's ability to meet the needs and wants of its own citizens and of others in the world. There are four factors of production that a firm uses to produce goods and services: land, labor, capital, and entrepreneurship.

A nation's productivity depends on the factors of production.

Land

Land is the factor of production that represents resources that are fixed or nonrenewable. Land includes water, climate, minerals, quantity of soil, and quality of soil. None of these resources can be easily changed or altered by humans. Natural resources either exist or do not exist in a given geographic area. *Rent* is the price paid for land.

Land is our most limited productive resource.

Humans can use up natural resources, but only limited circumstances allow complete replacement of what has been used. Reforestation is one example of replacing a resource (our forests) that has been used. Once a resource such as oil is used up, there is no way to remake it. Consequently, increased usage of alternative sources of energy to decrease the dependence on oil is necessary. Once land and other natural resources have been used up, they cannot be replaced. Land is scarce and very valuable because it exists in limited quantities and qualities and cannot be replaced.

Labor

Labor is the human factor of production. The labor force is the human resources available within a country to work and produce the necessary goods and services. The labor force in the United States numbers slightly less than half of the total population, estimated to be 226 million (1980 census). All persons ages 16 to 70 who are regularly employed for 35 hours or more a week (not including temporary or part-time employment) are considered to be in the labor force. Persons under age 16 are not considered a part of the labor force because they are required to attend school until age 16.

The labor force directly affects a country's productivity. When the labor force changes in quantity or quality, its productivity changes proportionately. For example, women are now entering into the labor force in large numbers. Almost half of the total number of American households are two-income families; most women work outside the home at some time during their lives. There are more than 3 million women business owners and sole proprietors now in the U.S. The largest increase in new workers to the labor force is caused by women entering into paid employment. Labor statistics from 1981 show that 52.3 percent of all women, age 16 and over, are in the work force. Figure 16-3 illustrates the unemployment rates for men and women between 1964 and 1982. By 1985, the national unemployment figure became 7.5 percent for men and 7.2 percent for women. For the first time, in 1982 unemployment rates for men exceeded those for women.

The quality of the work force is affected by such things as level of education attained. An increased standard of living is directly related to a higher educational level. The nation as a whole is affected when we do or do not educate our citizens. Education, from the standpoint of labor productivity, is for the benefit of all, not just those currently receiving an education.

Another factor affecting the quality of the work force is the general health of the nation. Whether or not national health insurance is the solution, all persons need good medical care and services. The reason is clear: when people do not feel well, they do not work well.

Motivation can make a great deal of difference in productivity, too Factors that motivate workers include rate of pay, working conditions, performance incentives, and fair labor agreements. In a "work ethic" society such as ours, productive employment is considered a positive goal.

Payment for the labor force is in the form of wages. *Wages* are total compensation for employment and include gross pay, insurance, sick pay,

The quantity and quality of the labor force determines its productivity.

Public education benefits everyone.

FIGURE 16-3
Unemployment
Rates for Men
and Women,
1964-1982

Source:
*Monthly Labor
Review*
(November,
1984), p. 9.

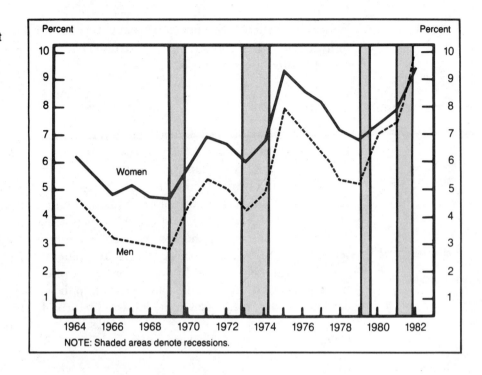

fringe benefits, and all other types of direct or indirect compensation.

Employment is viewed as a positive contribution to society.

Wage level acts as an indication to the employee of his or her worth and value to the employer in terms of quality and quantity of work performed. Wage increase is the greatest incentive for higher productivity.

Capital

Capital is the factor of production that represents the durable, but depreciable, input in the production process. Machines, tools, and buildings are capital. Capital is used to make the investment in equipment, raw materials, and human resources needed to produce necessary goods and services. The price paid for using capital is *interest.*

Capital is an economic term.

Money is a *measure* of the productivity of capital. Money is NOT capital. In order to produce goods and services, all factors of production—land, labor, capital (natural and human resources, tools and machines, etc.), and entrepreneurship—are necessary. Capital is not wanted for its own use; it is used to invest in factors necessary for production.

The United States has great capacity for generating capital and productive capital equipment (machinery, factories, tools) and the knowledge to use them both effectively. Capital is also used in our personal lives.

Home devices that save time and money, such as washing machines and dishwashers, office computers, and communication systems are examples of capital investments.

Entrepreneurship

Entrepreneurs take the risk of ownership.

Entrepreneurship is the factor of production that represents management, innovation, and risk-taking. The entrepreneurs are the owners or persons who are taking the risk of loss for owning land, investing in capital equipment, or hiring labor. The return for entrepreneurship is *profit.* If a profit is made, the entrepreneur knows he or she has an effective combination of land, labor, and capital to produce a product or service. The profit is the excess income received from the sale of a product or service over the cost of the land, labor, and capital used to make the product or provide the service. In other words, sale price less cost of production equals profit. Profit is the compensation to the owner for the risk that has been taken. Businesses sometimes refer to profit as "net profit" or "net income" because it represents what is left over after all income is collected and all expenses have been paid.

PRODUCTIVITY ANALYSIS

Production is the result when the factors of production (land, labor, capital, and entrepreneurship) are effectively combined into one successful venture. Entrepreneurs must use internal controls and external controls in order to make wise decisions that result in a profit.

Internal Controls

Decision making is responsibility for success or failure.

The entrepreneur collects data and is responsible for the decisions that ultimately lead to the success or failure of a company or business. The entrepreneur must decide the following:

1. What and how much should be produced (product/quantity decision)
2. How production should take place (production decision)
3. How what is produced should be distributed among the population (distribution decision)

If the entrepreneur's decisions are accurate and well planned, the result is success and profit.

External Controls

To make the preceding decisions, the entrepreneur must also consider the following:

1. Laws that may prohibit and dictate production or nonproduction, quantities, qualities, or other decision factors
2. Customs that dictate that some things are necessary while others are luxuries

(margin note: Owners do not have total power to make decisions.)

3. Government restrictions, controls, guidelines, or standards to be met
4. Amount, quality, and cost of available resources
5. Company goals and plans as well as profitability requirements (Generally, that which will generate the greatest profit will be produced.)
6. Economic concerns and stability of the nation, including interest rates and loan costs, times of peace or conflict, and issues of importance to citizens

Failure to consider one of these important items may cost a company in the salability of a product. Therefore, all of these considerations must be weighed carefully by the entrepreneur before a decision is made.

Time

Time is the element of production that refers to the crucial timing of production so that a product or service is available for consumption when it is desired by the consumer. Time has three significant characteristics that affect production decisions:

1. Once time has been invested, it cannot be recaptured. Time is money; once it has been used (spent), it is gone.
2. Time cannot be stored.
3. Time is limited in quantity and, therefore, is very valuable in terms of production.

(margin note: Time is an important factor to consider.)

Time is an important part of production. Once a decision has been made and time is invested, then the decision has incurred a cost that cannot be recovered. That is, it is too late to make a change. Perhaps the most important decisions an entrepreneur makes relate to time because it is the one element of production that is unchanging in relation to other conditions.

Space

Space is the physical attribute of production that is concerned with dimensional, geographic, and measurable commitments of productive

Space is limited and expensive.

resources. Space is also very limited in quantity and must be considered in the following arenas:

1. Amount of living or producing space that is available to the citizen or to the entrepreneur
2. Population of the area in which production is being considered (Is it large enough to pay the costs of production? Will enough be purchased to make production worthwhile?)
3. Distances to be traveled in the process of production or distribution

The entrepreneur must decide issues that involve wise use of the available space in relation to cost, projected profit, storage, and many other areas of concern. Space, like time, is expensive in terms of production.

VOCABULARY

Directions: Can you find the definition for each of the following terms used in Chapter 16?

economics	basic needs
formal education	median
innovations	collective values
land	factors of production
labor	rent
capital	wages
interest	entrepreneurship
profit	time
space	

1. The study of human efforts to solve the problem of making scarce resources meet the unlimited needs and wants of society.

2. The physical attribute of production that relates to dimensional, geographic, or measurable commitments of productive resources.

3. The element of production referring to the crucial planning of production to assure that a product is available for sale when it is demanded.

4. Ingredients necessary for maintaining physical life.

5. The excess amount earned by the entrepreneur over the cost of production.

6. The price paid for using capital.

7. A statistical middle amount.

8. Knowledge gained through attending formal institutions of learning, such as colleges and universities.

9. Things that are important to society as a whole; all citizens share in their benefit and in their cost.

10. New ideas, methods, or devices that bring about changes.

11. Ingredients necessary to produce goods and services.

12. A factor of production that is provided by nature, such as water, climate, and soil.

13. A factor of production that is the human work force necessary to work and produce within a country.

14. The factor of production necessary to produce other goods and services.

15. The price paid for land.

16. The return or payoff to those who make up the labor force.

17. The factor of production that represents management, innovation, and risk-taking.

ITEMS FOR DISCUSSION

1. What are the basic needs for survival?

2. List five life-improving wants and needs.

3. Of the life-improving needs and wants, how many are met in your life?

4. If your family income is $40,000 or more, into what income range do you fall?

5. How does level of income relate to amount of education attained?

6. Why are natural resources expensive and valuable?

7. List the factors of production.

8. Who makes the decisions about what and how much is to be produced, and for whom?

9. What types of external controls affect production decisions?

10. What three important facts about time must be considered in production?

11. What are the three space considerations in production?

APPLICATIONS

1. Why is it important for everyone to have a good basic understanding of economics?

2. List the life-fulfilling and improving needs and wants that you have now and expect to have in the future. Prioritize them, placing a numeral *1* by very important wants and a *5* by your least important wants. How do you expect that each of these needs and wants will be met in your life (by self, parents, government, others)?

3. Explain what your achieved level of education has to do with the amount and the types of wants and needs you will have and will be able to meet.

4. As a citizen, what types of societal values do you consider important? List them and prioritize them, giving very important values a *1* and least important values a *5*. How are these societal values provided?

5. What types of things are being done in your local area and state to preserve natural resources, land use, and air quality?

6. What types of public goods and services do you expect to receive as a citizen? Are most of these taken for granted? How are these goods and services provided for all?

7. Most countries that are in deep poverty lack one major productive resource—capital. How can American entrepreneurs assist these countries? (Send them money? Send them food? Help them to be productive?)

CASE PROBLEMS AND ACTIVITIES

1. An innovation is a new idea, method, or product. As an inventor who has a great idea for a new product or service, what things do you have to consider before implementing a plan to produce your innovation and sell it to consumers?

2. When a farmer sells fresh corn in a vegetable stand at the side of the road, he or she sells what was planted, raised, and harvested. To do this, farm labor is hired during the summer growing months. In addition, farm equipment and tools, sprinklers, and fertilizers are purchased at the store. Yearly, the farmer plants crops, and when there is a good crop and expenses are low, the farmer makes a good profit. But when expenses of production are too high, labor costs too much, or bad weather causes a poor crop, the farmer is likely to lose money.

   Identify the factors of production the farmer used in the case above.

3. Describe a recent money-making project at your school or in your community. List the factors of production that went into that project, and list the payoff for each resource used. Who makes the decisions regarding whether or not to do the money-making projects? What is the basis (how do they reach this decision) of going ahead with, or deciding not to have, a certain project?

4. An underdeveloped country is unable to meet its citizens' needs for food, clothing, and shelter. Yet in this country is a vast untapped potential for economic prosperity because of its underground copper and uranium fields. How could we, the United States, help this

underdeveloped country to feed its citizens? Choose one of the following options and explain why you think it would be the best way to help the underdeveloped country:

(a) Send them food.

(b) Give them money.

(c) Help them build capital equipment and teach them how to use it.

PART FIVE
ELECTRONIC INFORMATION

17
Information Technology

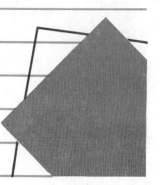

Chapter Objectives

After studying this chapter and completing the activities, you will be able to:

1. Describe the main components of a computerized information system.
2. Explain the procedures used to instruct computers.
3. Identify computer applications used by consumers and workers.
4. List career opportunities in information technology.

COMPONENTS OF A COMPUTER SYSTEM

Each day the computer is changing the way we do business. Electronic banking, shopping by computer, and automated library services did not exist a few years ago. These computer systems allow faster and less expensive processing of information. As computer systems improve, businesses and consumers are able to improve their decision-making skills.

Computers assist with problem solving.

A *computer* is an electronic machine used to process data and solve problems. The combination of several pieces of equipment, as well as the people, needed to do information processing is a computer system. Every computer system consists of four main parts as illustrated in Figure 17-1: input, processing, memory/storage, and output.

Input

Input data start the computer system.

The initial entry of data into a computer system is *input*. This involves a variety of activities including obtaining, coding, and recording. Data to be processed can be names and addresses, test scores, or medical records.

292

FIGURE 17–1
The Main Parts
of a Computer
System

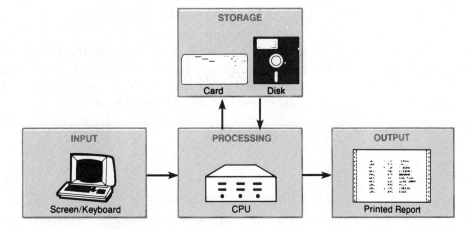

Frequently, input data represent business transactions such as sales, cash payments, or cash receipts.

Data may be entered into a computer system with a variety of devices. A keyboard, similar to the keyboard of a typewriter, is probably the most common. The keyboard is often attached to a screen to make a *video display unit*. Other input devices include punched-card readers, magnetic tape/disk readers, and optical scanners. In all situations, the device must present the input data in a form which the computer can understand and process.

Processing

Processing involves
math and logic
functions.

After entry, data must be converted into useful information. This procedure is the processing phase. The most common computer processes are arithmetic functions—addition, subtraction, multiplication, and division. In addition, computers are capable of making logical decisions such as comparing two numbers, selecting desired items, and creating lists. Each of these procedures is designed to obtain problem-solving information.

The actual processing of data is done by the *central processing unit (CPU)*. The CPU is the main piece of equipment in a computer system. In addition to handling data, the central processing unit also has a "memory." The CPU stores in its memory the instructions and data which will be needed during processing.

Memory/Storage

Data is stored for future
use.

Both raw data (before processing) and information (after processing) must be available for future use. While currently needed material is stored in the computer, other data are filed on magnetic disks and tapes.

This data will be added to the main memory of the computer as needed with the use of an input device.

The storage and availability of data for future decision making is vital to businesses and consumers. A *data base* is a central storage area used by a computer. Examples of data bases are customer accounts of a business or the materials listing of a library. Other data bases are used by many people; these include airline schedule information and summaries of past cases for use by lawyers.

Output

Processing results are output.

The purpose for having a computer system is to have information that can be used. The creation and presentation of information is *output*. Output may be a sales report for a business, report cards for a school, or the monthly bills for a utility company.

The most common forms of output are information displayed on a screen and a printed report. The video display screen, which was first used as an input device, now is an output device. Printers allow the creation of reports, invoices, and checks at a rate of many hundreds per minute.

Types of Computers

The equipment that makes up a computer system is called *hardware*. Hardware includes video display units, tape and card readers, disk drives, printers, and, of course, the main processing unit. Computer systems are frequently classified according to size.

Large businesses use mainframe computers.

Large Business Computers. *Mainframe computers* are the very large ones used by business and government. A mainframe system will usually have connections to many locations—some in the same building and others in different states. Each location, called a *terminal*, has a display screen and keyboard which allow a person to enter or obtain information from the main computer.

Medium-Sized Computers. Smaller versions of a mainframe system are the *minicomputers*. These have an intermediate size and computing power. Minicomputers are used by averaged-sized companies and governmental units.

Microcomputers are used by businesses and in homes.

Personal Computers. *Microcomputers* are small, desk-top systems for business and personal use. The development of the microcomputer has made automated data processing available to small businesses and to individuals in their homes. Even large companies with mainframe computers are saving time and money by using personal computers for day-to-day business operations.

INSTRUCTING THE COMPUTER SYSTEM

A computer is nothing more than wires, electronic circuits, and other parts. While the hardware has tremendous problem-solving potential, nothing will happen without the efforts of people. The computer must be instructed to take certain actions. A *computer program* is a list of detailed instructions for the computer.

Outlining the Instructions

Creating a computer program starts by looking at the detailed steps of the problem. A computer can understand only very simple directions and procedures. As a result, a problem must be broken down into parts. A *flowchart* is a visual presentation of the parts of a process or procedure. Figure 17-2 on page 296 shows the steps for computing net pay. Flowcharts present a problem which the computer can understand.

A flowchart divides a problem into parts.

Talking to the Computer

A *computer language* is the phrases or notations understood by a computer. Figure 17-3 on page 297 lists some of the many computer languages. Each is designed for a specific purpose. BASIC is used with many personal computers, COBOL is used with business computers, and LOGO is used to teach children math and science.

Computer languages allow you to talk to a computer.

Using the Program

Computer programs are commonly called *software*. Software will usually include instructions for using the program. "User-friendly" programs are designed for people with very little computer experience. Software packages for personal computers are available for home budgeting, cooking, foreign language instruction, and video games.

APPLICATIONS OF INFORMATION TECHNOLOGY

The use of computer systems is expanding at a rapid pace. Each day we observe or experience new applications of automated information sys-

FIGURE 17–2
Flowchart for
Computing Net
Pay

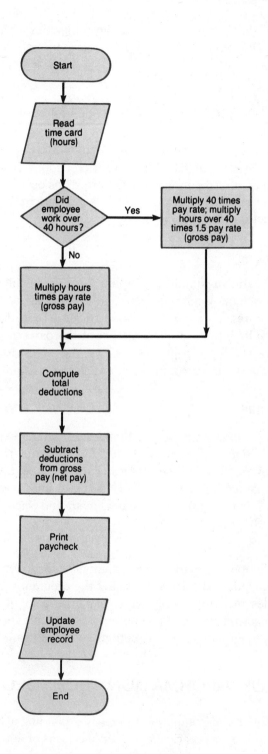

FIGURE 17–3
Types of Com-
puter Languages

APL	LOGO
ASSEMBLER	PASCAL
BASIC	PL/1
COBOL	RPG
FORTRAN	RPG II

tems. These influence our activities in the marketplace, on the job, and in the home.

Banking by Computer

Today, it is possible to conduct your banking activities without ever talking with or seeing another person. As discussed in Chapter 7, electronic funds transfers (EFTs) allow banking through a computerized system consisting of several phases.

Computers handle many banking transactions.

Automated Teller Machines. A computer terminal is a major component of EFTs. An *automated teller machine (ATM)* is a terminal used to make deposits, withdrawals, or loan payments without going to a bank. A debit (or EFT) card is used to activate transactions. In addition, your Touch-Tone telephone allows banking at home.

Direct Deposit. The electronic transfer, by computer, of a paycheck or government check amount is called *direct deposit*. Your employer can communicate your paycheck information directly to your bank by computer. You do not need to take your check to the bank for depositing.

Your pay can be automatically deposited.

Smart Cards. A recent advancement in EFT technology is the smart card. The *smart card* is an EFT access card that can be used to perform banking activities and can store each transaction in the card's memory element. This allows you to maintain a record of the account balance. The smart card can be programmed to reduce the fraudulent and illegal use of bank cards.

Shopping by Computer

Electronic banking is the first step toward a completely automated shopping system. Another development is the use of scanners in supermarkets and other stores. All food items, as well as many other products,

Shoppers are aided by computers.

have been assigned a bar code or *universal product code (UPC)*. Figure 17-4 is an example of the bar code which allows the computer to identify and price items purchased. The UPC system also maintains an up-to-the-minute data base of sales and inventory records for the store.

We are evolving into an *electronic marketplace* in which shopping and other business transactions are handled by automated data processing systems. In some areas of the country, it is now possible to:

1. View product catalogs on a home computer screen or cable television system;
2. Select products desired for purchase; and
3. Pay for the items by electronic banking.

Computers in the Office

Workers use computers.

Automated information systems are also influencing our on-the-job activities. Computers have wide use for processing financial data and correspondence in businesses and other organizations.

Accounting Records. Business computer systems are used most frequently to process financial information. The most common accounting needs of a company are sales/customer, inventory, payroll, and cash receipt and payment information.

FIGURE 17–4
A Bar Code and a List of Items Purchased

```
HOMETOWN FOOD MART

STORE 123   04/20/--


GRO    2.39F CEREAL
GRO     .57F CHILI
MT     5.13F T BONE
NFD     .98C KLEENEX
PRO     .47F BANANA
NFD     .39C DOG FOOD
NFD     .63C GLAD WRAP
GRO     .99D MILK
GRO    2.09D CHEESE
GRO     .89D EGGS


        .11  TAX

      14.64  TOTAL

      20.00  CASH

       5.36  CHANGE


000702   4  4.22PM
```

12345 67890

Word Processing. Increased speed and accuracy when creating letters and reports is another common business computer application. This use, called *word processing*, allows ease of writing, editing, revising, and correcting business communications. In addition, the same letter to be sent to many people needs to be typed only once. The word processing system will repeat the letter and insert each person's name and address.

Computerized letters are faster and more accurate.

Home Information Systems

Personal computers have created an advanced information and entertainment system for the home. Electronic "newspapers" and "magazines" allow instant access to news, weather, sports, and other topics of interest. Sending messages and bills by computer will also become quite common as more people use "electronic mail."

Video games are commonplace in our society. As new information systems evolve, you will be able to compete against people in other geographic locations as well as with members of your household.

CAREERS IN INFORMATION TECHNOLOGY

Computers have created many jobs.

Technological changes mean new and different career opportunities. Computer systems will have a strong influence on future jobs.

Computer-Related Jobs

A variety of careers exist which involve direct use of computers. These work opportunities are in the areas of input/output jobs, computer operations, and programming.

Input/Output. Data-entry clerk and video display unit operator are two of the jobs involved with the input phase of information processing. The creation of business documents is done by a forms designer. A reports analyst evaluates and recommends improved output information.

Computer operators run data processing systems.

Computer Operations. The processing of data is done by a computer operator. Various computer engineers and technicians are involved in the design, creation, and repair of hardware.

Programming. Systems analysts, programmers, and software specialists have the responsibility of developing problem-solving instructions for computers. Workers in this area are needed by business, government, and scientific organizations.

**ILLUSTRATION
17–1**
Computer sys-
tems influence
future jobs.

Information-Related Jobs

Computers will have an
effect on most jobs.

     Most jobs in our economy will be affected by computers. Some areas of business which will be especially affected are:

       Accounting—financial records about company sales and expenses;

       Marketing—data related to consumer buying habits and new product development; and

       Word Processing—development of business memos, letters, and reports.

     Regardless of your career choice, a knowledge of math, business, and computer skills will be valuable to you. As computers influence our daily business activities, a knowledge of information technology will be necessary.

VOCABULARY

Directions: Can you find the definition for each of the following terms used in Chapter 17?

computer   video display unit
input   central processing unit (CPU)

data base	computer language
output	software
hardware	automated teller machine
mainframe computers	(ATM)
terminal	direct deposit
minicomputers	smart card
microcomputers	universal product code (UPC)
computer program	electronic marketplace
flowchart	word processing

1. A list of detailed instructions for a computer.

2. A bar symbol for identifying and pricing food and other purchases.

3. An input/output device consisting of a screen and keyboard.

4. Large computers used by businesses and government agencies.

5. A device used to perform banking activities and store a record of the transactions.

6. The use of computers to create letters and reports.

7. A central storage area for information.

8. The creation and presentation of information.

9. A location away from a large computer which is used to enter or obtain data.

10. The phrases or notations understood by a computer.

11. A computer terminal used to make bank deposits, withdrawals, or loan payments.

12. Computer programs and instructions for their use.

13. Small, desk-top computers for use in businesses or at home.

14. Shopping and other business transactions handled by a computer system.

15. An electronic machine used to process data.

16. The electronic transfer, by computer, of a paycheck or government check amount.

17. A visual presentation of the parts of a process or procedure.

18. The equipment of a computer system including tape readers and printers.

19. The main equipment component which performs the mathematical and logical functions.

20. The initial entry of data into a computer system.

21. Computers with an intermediate size and computing power.

ITEMS FOR DISCUSSION

1. What are the four main parts of a computer system?

2. What is a video display unit? What purpose does it serve?

3. List three examples of input devices.

4. What occurs during the processing phase of data processing?

5. What is the purpose of the "memory" in the central processing unit (CPU)?

6. What is a data base? Give two examples.

7. List three examples of printed output.

8. What are the two most common forms of output?

9. What is hardware?

10. Which type of computer would be best for a small restaurant? Which would be best for the Social Security Administration?

11. Why is a flowchart important when developing a computer program?

12. Why are there different computer languages?

13. How does the UPC system benefit consumers and businesses?

14. What is the electronic marketplace?

15. List some computer jobs related to (a) input/output; (b) computer operations; and (c) programming.

APPLICATIONS

1. List uses of computers in your life which were not present two or three years ago.

2. Prepare a poster or bulletin board display showing a computer system. Obtain or draw pictures of input devices, a processing unit, and storage and output devices.

3. Create a list of data bases which are available to help students, consumers, and businesses.

4. Develop a flowchart for a process or procedure which you do in your daily life.

5. Will computers ever eliminate the need for newspapers, magazines, and textbooks?

CASE PROBLEMS AND ACTIVITIES

1. A local store owner who sells records, tapes, video equipment, and T-shirts cannot decide whether a computer would improve the efficiency of the company's data processing. List the ways in which a computer system could help this business.

2. A company wants to create a data base which would help people who invest in stocks and bonds. What information should such a data base include?

3. Assume that you have a friend who does not believe in electronic banking or shopping by computer. List ways your friend could benefit by these computer systems.

4. Investigate and list the types of computer hardware and software used in your school.

5. Survey local businesses regarding the types of computer systems used in handling business information. Obtain information regarding input devices used, types of storage systems, and output reports.

6. Collect advertisements from newspapers with career opportunities related to computers and information technology. List the jobs in categories such as input/output, computer operations, programming, and other jobs related to information.

7. Investigate the purchase of a personal computer. Compare different brands, sizes, and stores. Also visit various computer stores or use catalogs to determine the software available for computers in your comparison. Make a chart showing the results of your comparison.

8. Interview a person who works with computers. Obtain information regarding job duties, training, and prospects for this career in the future. Prepare a one-page report of your interview.

18
Coping with Technology and Change

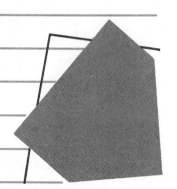

Chapter Objectives:
After studying this chapter and completing the activities, you will be able to:

1. Identify communication strategies for dealing with high-tech, high-touch technologies and change.
2. List characteristics of stress and outline a personal method for stress management.
3. Identify changes in the workplace which accommodate worker needs, and identify personal changes needed to prepare for the future.

TECHNOLOGICAL CHANGE AND COMMUNICATION

There is only one thing for certain: change. Fortunately, we are now living in an era of technological choice rather than with the scarcity of choices in a previous era. This gives us a wide range of opportunities and solutions to our problems. With technology comes complication, sophistication, duplication, and hesitation. We will look at some of these changes.

Telecommunications is the transmission of voice, data, and images.

Telecommunications have been improved greatly through the use of *fiber optics* which transmit sounds in the form of rapid pulses of light through strands of very pure glass, thin as human hair. Already, a half-inch cable containing 30,000 miles of tiny optical fibers runs between New York and Washington. This cable can carry 240,000 simultaneous conversations! Plans are underway to install fiber optic cables undersea between the United States and Europe by 1988 and to Japan by 1990.

The majority of Americans will soon be faced with the vast technological advances made in telecommunications. The standard telephone console may become the only computer terminal most of us will need—text and pictures can be viewed on a video screen attached to the phone while additional data is delivered electronically.

Automatic-transmission devices will allow people to insert into the device a document written in English and have it delivered, in minutes, to a distant point translated into Japanese, Vietnamese, or Arabic. Such advances are very close to becoming a reality in many of our lives. The economic potential of these changes is almost limitless. Says William McGowan, chairman of MCI Communications, "Telecommunications is one business today in which you don't need losers to have winners. There is enough for everybody."

How will you react to the rapid changes that are inevitable?

High-Tech, High-Touch

Major technological advances are occurring almost daily, with the promise of more, better, faster, less expensive, and more efficient models to come. *High-tech* refers to the highly advanced technological processes and machines. Experts predicted in the mid-1970s that the movie theaters would all be closed by 1984—that Americans would choose to rent movies or subscribe to cable services and watch big-screen productions right in their own homes. But it did not happen, and the reason is *high-touch*, which is the human need for personal contact with other living, breathing, communicating human beings. After working all day with machines, computer languages, and advanced technologies, we need human touch. In an era when computers do everything from billing to collection, we cherish more than ever the handmade and the human element. People do not go to the movies just to go to the movies—they go because it is an "event." It is a place where they see and meet others, express emotion, and share feelings in common with others. Grocery shopping is another activity that is considered high-touch. While many Americans may be able to order their groceries through their televisions and telephones, a great number of them will still choose to do the high-touch activities to get away from machines, impersonalization, and technology.

In a high-tech society, people tend to gather where there are other people. The shopping mall is now the third most frequented space in our lives, after home and workplace. People go to crowded areas—malls, movies, concerts, sporting events—in greater numbers than ever before. It is this high-touch that allows us to survive in a high-tech density center such as we see in many of our larger cities. New York is still the largest city, with Los Angeles as No. 2, Chicago as No. 3, and Houston (the nation's fastest growing city) as No. 4 (*Megatrends*).

People need other people.

High-touch activities are popular today.

People move to large metropolitan areas.

Computers used in schools will not take the place of personal teacher-student relationships and influences. A computer cannot teach values, motivation, or human awareness. Computers in the workplace will not replace the need for communication among employees, communication among employees and employers, or good human relations skills.

Communication Among Employees

While upward and downward exchanges of ideas and information tend to be more formal, *horizontal communication* (communication among employees of equal rank) is more informal. Within all groups there are invisible hierarchical ranks and communication barriers. These can be minimized through the use of effective communication abilities and interpersonal relations skills. The most common types of horizontal communications are face-to-face conversations and small group meetings.

Face-to-Face Conversations. Throughout the day, workers stop and speak to each other. They get small clarifications, make statements, and ask questions. Small talk is often a part of the conversation—compliments such as, "You look nice today," or questions such as, "How are you feeling today?" When conversations are personalized, people tend to respond better. Using a person's name helps: "Good morning, Chris, how did the meeting go this morning?" Private conversations that enhance work should be encouraged. Employers can encourage interpersonal communications among employees who should share ideas by providing lunch

Personalized conversation is more effective.

rooms, break times that match, time to meet during work hours, and general open conversation attitudes. A central file of new ideas or work done by employees can be made available to all workers. Then workers can go to the person who had the idea to clarify and explain its use. Employees should feel free to exchange ideas and information because the common goal is the overall benefit of the company.

Small Group Meetings. Small group meetings may be organized (with specific purposes in mind) or they may be spontaneous and informal. Common functions of small group meetings include problem solving, decision making, and information sharing. One of the basic needs (Maslow's Level 3) can be met in group membership. Usually employees who are in small groups are of fairly equal rank. Ideas and suggestions promoted by a group tend to be listened to and implemented more often than when the same information comes from only one person: There is power in numbers. Some companies encourage small group meetings in order to have access to good advice, desired feedback, and varied approaches to problem solving. These companies find that involving employees as a group is a good way to increase employees' commitment to the solution of a problem.

Small groups provide valuable feedback.

Communication Among Employees and Employers

There are two types of communication between employers and employees: upward and downward. ***Downward communication*** is used to keep subordinates (workers) informed, to give them job-related instructions, and to give them feedback about their performance. Downward communication needs to be consistent and fair, with a prescribed method that is easily understood by employees. Some communications will be verbal, some written, and others will occur in private or group meetings. Information and ideas need to be clearly presented so that workers can respond and adjust accordingly.

Downward communication must be understood by employees.

Upward communication is the transmitting of information from employees to their supervisors and employers. Upward communication includes information about job and work-related problems, organizational policies and procedures, and suggestions for improvements of company practices. Upward communication flow should be designed to enhance workers' identification with their superiors. The effectiveness of this type of flow of information and ideas depends on relationships between employers and employees, the quality of the employee's presentation of the message, the extent to which the content of the message is positive or negative, the timeliness of the message, and the extent to which the mes-

Upward communication
should flow freely.

sage is considered useful by the employer. When upward communication is free flowing and encouraged, workers tend to be more productive and efficient because they believe they have a significant role (security) with the company.

Human Relations

Human relations is getting along with others. As technological advances become more complex and sophisticated, our need for genuine and caring human relationships increases. Basically, good human relations are good common sense. To be truly competent in human relations, you need to have a working self-knowledge, an understanding of others (including their needs, desires, and attitudes), and a genuine interest and caring about the needs and feelings of others. Human relations is a fairly new area of study. Until recently, people assumed that human relationships just happened or did not happen—that some people were likable and others were not.

Praise the accomplish-
ments of others.

Techniques for maintaining effective human relations include: setting specific goals, accepting differences, treating others as individuals, empathizing with others, praising the achievements of others, describing problems rather than personalities, accepting responsibility, avoiding dogmatic statements, treating others as equals, trusting others, and controlling your emotions.

1. Set specific goals. Be specific about what you want to achieve, how you want to achieve it, and when you need to have it done. This gives purpose in life and allows concentration on positive aspects of life.
2. Accept differences. No two people are alike; we need to accept others as they are, tolerate differences of opinion, and recognize that other ways of doing things may also be effective. In work situations, we need to learn to disagree without being disagreeable.
3. Treat others as individuals. Take time to discover the individuality in others; learn people's names and call them by their names; take an interest in what others are doing. Your efforts will be appreciated.
4. Empathize with others. *Empathy* is the ability to see others' points of view or understand their feelings. It does not mean you agree with them or what they are feeling but merely that you understand.
5. Praise others. Be consistent in praising the achievements of others.
6. Describe problems. When you have a problem with someone else, you will get the person's cooperation by describing the problem

Describe problems, not personalities.

rather than the person or personality differences. Use passive rather than active voice. For example,

Say: That report was not what was needed by the auditors.

Not: You did not prepare the report properly for the auditors.

7.   Accept responsibility. Take responsibility for your own actions. Everybody makes mistakes; do not avoid taking responsibility for yours. Your willingness to accept responsibility and simply say, "I goofed" will be respected by co-workers and employers.

Avoid dogmatic statements and positions.

8.   Avoid dogmatic statements. A ***dogmatic statement*** asserts an opinion as if it were a fact. If you are dogmatic, you become known as the office "know-it-all." Keep your judgments restricted to possibilities rather than to absolutes.

9.   Treat others as equal. Each person has a valuable role, even though your role may be more valuable than another person's. It is important to treat each person you associate with as though he or she is making worthwhile contributions.

10.   Trust others. Adults, just like children, have a way of living up to, or down to, your expectations. Think the best of others and expect the best. When they know you trust them, most people prove to be trustworthy.

11.   Control your emotions. Withhold your judgments or comments or decisions until the entire matter is resolved and all information is gathered. Reacting emotionally may cloud your decisions, and you may regret later the display of emotions.

TECHNOLOGY AND STRESS

Stress is inevitable in our lives.

Stress is the natural outcome of a society that has high expectations of itself and its individual members. Because we value technology, innovation, and accomplishment, we put pressure on our members who are capable of producing. You may feel this kind of pressure in your personal life, at home, at school, at church, at an activity, or at work.

Stress is the response of the body to any demand made upon it. Because demands are placed on most of us in our daily lives, we will all experience some forms of stress. When we understand what stress is, how it works, and how it can be controlled, we will begin to function effectively in spite of it. Because we cannot eliminate stress, we need to understand it. *Stressors* are the sources or causes of stress. The source can be real or imaginary; if something in your life causes stress, you must deal with it.

Characteristics of Stress

Stress is a chain of
internal events.

To understand the nature of stress, we must study its characteristics. All people experience stress. Stress is all of these things: It is natural; it is a chain of internal events; it can affect your health; it has many causes; it is influenced by personal differences; it affects your activities; and it is manageable.

Stress Is Natural. Because we all make decisions and must face the consequences of our choices, stress is an essential ingredient in our lives. If there were no stress in your choices, you would probably make many wrong decisions because you would not worry about the results. Consequently, you would not gather needed information and take appropriate precautions.

Stress Is a Chain of Internal Events. Our body reacts through its automatic nervous system known as the endocrine system. The brain communicates the need for reactions through chemical reactions. Few people ever "plan" to be stressed over a situation—it just happens through our body's reactions to our thoughts.

We must recognize
stressors in our lives.

Stress Can Affect Health. Many doctors report that various physical ailments and diseases, such as high blood pressure and heart disease, appear to be stress related. Other sicknesses can be caused by or worsened by the presence of stressors in a person's life. Whether the stressors are real or imaginary, the illness or physical reaction of the body can be very real.

Stress Has Many Causes. Stress can be caused by anything. What is insignificant to one person can be a big stressor to another person. What is stressful at one time may be insignificant at another time. Stress can appear at any time, for any reason. Our perception of what is happening can be as significant as what is really happening.

Stress Is Influenced by Personal Differences. Factors such as heredity, physical conditioning (environment), and personal coping abilities and training will influence the effects of stress on our mental and physical abilities.

Stress can affect your
behavior.

Stress Affects Our Activities. Stress can affect your job performance, relationships, personal feelings of self-worth, and even job satisfaction. All aspects of daily life are influenced by the amounts and types of stress we experience, and our ability to manage stress when it does occur.

Stress Is Manageable. There are many forms of coping behavior that you can learn which will reduce the negative effects (physical and mental) of stress.

Stress Management

Once you understand the characteristics of stress, and how each one applies to you, you can begin to manage the effects of stress in your life. *Stress management* involves recognition of stress, understanding its causes and effects, and developing a plan for reducing it, eliminating it, or living with it. Ignoring it will not help. Effectively dealing with stress will lead to stress management skills throughout life.

Recognize the Symptoms. It is important that you be able to step back and realize that you are experiencing stress. Symptoms of stress may include headache, fatigue, restlessness, insomnia (inability to sleep), nervousness, irritability, tension, or guilt feelings.

Symptoms of stress are reactions of your body.

Determine Causes and Effects. When you are feeling one (or possibly more than one) of the reactions just mentioned, try to discover the cause of your distress. The stressors could be at home, at work, or in some activity. The cause of your stress (stressors) may be real or imaginary. Try to pinpoint why you are feeling depressed, angry, restless, or tired. Is it physical or mental? Is it getting better or worse? Is the source pressures you place on yourself, or pressures placed on you by others? Once you have discovered the causes, then you can begin to analyze the effects. How has your behavior changed? How do you feel emotionally? Physically? How are others reacting to you? Report your emotions—discuss them out loud (to yourself or to someone else). Explain what you feel (without placing blame on yourself or anyone else). Be specific, be exact, and be thorough.

Develop a Plan. After recognizing the stress and analyzing its cause and effects, you can begin to devise a course of action for dealing with it. Make a decision to take action, to set the problem aside until a later time (forget about it for now), or to do nothing at all. Some matters cannot be resolved by you because they involve decisions, attitudes, and actions of others. Therefore, sometimes you have to decide to forget about things you cannot control or change. Save your worry and stress for matters that you can control or change.

Make a decision about the stress.

Refusing to deal with your stress (stress management) can be harmful to you. By not dealing with the stress—its origin, cause, and effect—you will have learned nothing from the experience, you will not have resolved the matter, and the next time the same situation occurs, more stress will be added to your already stressed system.

Only you can control your reactions.

You cannot control what others will do or say. But you can control your own reactions, thoughts, feelings, and stress. Start managing stress with small incidents and pressures. As each new situation arises in your life, consider the stressors involved and how you are reacting. Each time you experience a symptom of stress, determine its origin, its cause and effects, and develop a plan to deal with the stress.

CHANGES IN THE WORKPLACE

Because of changes in our personal life-styles and needs, many employers are making changes to meet those needs. Three changes that employers often make to meet various personal needs of their employees and to avoid absenteeism and turnover (employees quitting) are to use flexible schedules, job rotation, and job sharing.

Flexible Schedules

Flextime is advantageous to employers and employees.

Most companies have core times.

Flexible schedules, often called *flextime*, enable employees to select their starting times, usually within a two- to three-hour period. As a result, employees may begin working as early as 6:00 A.M. or as late as 9:00 or 10:00 A.M. Even though starting times are flexible, most employers require employees to work a required number of hours per day. A person arriving at 6:00 A.M. would be finished by 3:00 P.M. (having a one-hour lunch break), while a person arriving at 10:00 A.M. would be finished at 7:00 P.M. Most employers that have flextime also maintain a *core time period*, which is a crucial time during the day when all employees must report to work. This may be between 10:00 and 3:00, when peak business activity occurs for the company.

Flextime decreases absenteeism and tardiness. Production increases because employees are responsible for a full working day regardless of when they arrive on the job. Employees experience greater job satisfaction because flextime helps them fulfill their personal goals. For example, to some people it might be very important to be off at 3:00 P.M.—to pick up children from school. They will have less frustration because public transportation is less congested during travel time. The flextime allows for scheduling of medical and other appointments, and finally, flextime reduces stress caused by pressure of meeting strict work schedules.

Job Rotation

Job rotation is a technique for training employees to be efficient in more than one specialized area. Employees rotate from one area to another. This technique has a fairly high cost to the employer because training is an expensive procedure. Employees are sometimes allowed to perform tasks in each of the areas, while in other instances they simply observe.

Job rotation allows you to explore other jobs.

The use of job rotation allows the company to maximize the opportunities for employee growth and development. Not only does job satisfaction improve, but also productivity increases. Employees benefit from additional training, and job rotation cuts down on boredom and accidents by blue-collar workers performing the same tasks daily. For white-collar workers, it provides the opportunity to learn more about the company and become more valuable, knowledgeable employees.

A major advantage of job rotation for both employer and employee is that information and ideas are voluntarily and freely exchanged among workers so that no one has absolute control over one area. As workers understand how others' work contributes to the overall production, they are better able to get a feel for their personal contributions.

Job Sharing

Job sharing is considered to be an employee motivation strategy. In *job sharing* two people share what was originally a full-time position. Individual salaries and fringe benefits are prorated according to the amount of each employee's contributions. This cuts costs for the employer while tapping into greater expertise and experience.

Job sharing is attractive to certain employees.

Job sharing is especially attractive to people who desire part-time work. Older employees are finding job sharing an attractive alternative to retirement. An increasing number of companies and employees are finding the job-sharing technique helpful in improving employee productivity and efficiency. Advantages include reduced absenteeism and tardiness; flexibility for the employee who needs half days for other activities, recreation or relaxation; less fatigue; and higher productivity levels.

PERSONAL CHANGES

Because the world around us is changing so rapidly, we need to prepare ourselves to meet the challenges ahead. A *self-assessment inventory* lists your strong points and your weak points and gives you an idea of what you need to do to better prepare yourself. As weak points are

The inventory is
designed to identify
weaknesses.
improved, they move to the strong points side of your inventory. By keeping aware of where we stand, what is going on in the world, and what we
need to do to keep up with technological changes, we will not be left
behind in the technological race.

Figure 18-1 is a self-assessment inventory which lists a young person's
assets, liabilities, and plans for action. Can you complete a similar inventory based on your personal qualifications?

ASSETS (STRENGTHS)	LIABILITIES (WEAKNESSES)	PLAN OF ACTION
Education: High school diploma; took business courses	Education: Weak in office skills	Take extra typing classes, build speed and accu- racy
Experience: Cooperative job in office—part-time summer job as clerk; volunteer office work in church	Experience: Need computer application	Look for work expe- rience with com- puters
Aptitudes and Abilities: Good hand/eye coordi- nation; work well with people	Aptitudes and Abilities: Poor speaker; shy around opposite sex	Practice speaking in small groups; lead a class at church; attend more social functions
Appearance: Neat and clean; short, well-groomed hair	Appearance: Wardrobe needs more profes- sional clothes	Start buying clothes appropriate for work

FIGURE 18–1   Self-Assessment Inventory

A comprehensive self-assessment will help you to determine areas that
need work. You might ask another person, such as an employment counselor, to objectively assess your strengths and weaknesses. Another person's point of view can help clarify your self-assessment.

Preparing for the Near Future

Begin preparing now
for the future.
In your personal life, as well as in your work life, you need to make
plans for the future. Because work atmospheres are becoming more
advanced, more high-tech, and less personalized, we need to find ways to
express ourselves and find fulfillment in our personal lives. It is important
to make plans for future years and to have personal life goals to fall back
on and rely upon for expression. In addition to meeting your needs
through work (Maslow's hierarchy), you can find fulfillment and satisfac-

tion in personal pursuits. Leisure activities may include physical fitness programs, crafts and hobbies, and recreation.

Physical Fitness. Good exercise programs begun while you are young will carry over into middle age and beyond. Individual, as well as group activities, should be chosen to keep in shape. You might want to consider skiing, hunting, camping, hiking, jogging, bicycling, dancing, or health club plans. Keeping physically fit will help you work better, feel better about yourself, and keep in shape for the future.

Crafts and Hobbies. Learn to create things, as small and large projects, for yourself and others. This will bring great satisfaction throughout life. You might consider pottery, painting, cabinet making, crocheting or needlepoint, sewing, or making toys, dolls, or gadgets. While your free time may be limited now, at a later time (retirement) you will have more of it, and less energy and desire to learn new skills. A hobby can provide much pleasure in retirement.

Recreation begun today will carry into the future.

Recreation. During vacation times and weekends, plan meaningful outings. Recreation is important to your work attitudes because it enables you to get away—physically and mentally—and readjust your thinking and attitude. Recreation time should be restful and relaxing to avoid returning to work exhausted. Trips, vacations, outings with families, and participation in community activities are examples you might want to consider.

Planning for Retirement

For the first time ever, there are more people over age 65 than there are teenagers in this country. Have you considered what it will be like for you when you become a senior citizen?

Growing older is not a disease; it is a natural process. Many of us fear growing old because old age is not highly valued in our society. All the ads and commercials tell us how to look, act, and feel younger. Models are usually young, slender, and beautiful. Little attention is given by society as a whole to the problems of the aged.

America is a maturing society. The Bureau of the Census projects that by 1990 the number of people between the ages of 30 and 44 will increase by 20 percent. A nearly 60 percent increase in the number of 35- to 44-year-olds in the labor force is expected by the end of this decade (1990).

Now is the time—at the beginning of your work life—to plan for what you will do in your "golden years." Because you can expect to live longer and healthier lives, you must also plan financially for the later years.

Workers should not count on social security benefits being adequate to provide retirement; instead, they should begin at an early age to invest in individual retirement accounts (IRAs), annuities, and other savings and investment programs to provide ample income and security for retirement.

Prepare for a meaningful retirement.

VOCABULARY

Directions: Can you find the definition for each of the following terms used in Chapter 18?

fiber optics
high-tech   stress
high-touch   stressors
horizontal communication   stress management
downward communication   flextime
upward communication   core time period
human relations   job rotation
empathy   job sharing
dogmatic statement   self-assessment inventory

1. The human need for personal contacts with other human beings.

2. A list of your strong and weak points to assist you in future personal plans.

3. Communication among employees of equal rank.

4. Two people share what was originally a full-time position.

5. The transmission of sounds through strands of pure glass.

6. Used to keep subordinates informed, give job instructions, and provide feedback about performance.

7. Getting along with others.

8. Transmitting information from employees to their supervisors and employers.

9. A variation of starting times for employees.

10. A technique for training employees to be efficient in more than one specialized area.

11. The ability to see others' points of view.

12. An opinion stated as though it were fact.

13. The response of the body to any demand made upon it.

14. Recognition of its symptoms, understanding its causes and effects, and developing a plan to live with stress.

15. Sources or causes of stress.

16. A crucial time of the day when all employees must report to work.

17. Highly advanced technological processes and machines.

ITEMS FOR DISCUSSION

1. What is high-tech? What is high-touch?

2. Give two examples of horizontal communication that usually occur in a work setting.

3. What are three purposes of downward communication?

4. List eleven techniques for maintaining effective human relations.

5. Does everybody experience stress?

6. List seven characteristics of stress.

7. List the three phases of stress management.

8. List three changes that employers often make to meet personal needs of employees while helping avoid absenteeism and increasing productivity.

9. What three main categories are listed on a self-assessment inventory?

10. List three major leisure activities that you should consider now so that you will be prepared for the future.

APPLICATIONS

1. List three major technological advances that have affected your life in the last five years.

2. What types of new technology are in your home or school?

3. What events do you participate in that would be considered high-touch?

4. What types of demands cause you stress? What types of demands cause your parents stress?

5. Do you ever have any of the symptoms of stress: headache, fatigue, nervousness, irritability, guilt feelings, restlessness? How often do you feel this way?

6. What have you done in the past to deal with stressful situations you have encountered?

7. If your employer allowed for flexible schedules, what hours would you report to work? Why?

8. If job rotation were available to you, what other jobs would you like to observe and learn more about?

9. In what regular leisure activities do you participate?

CASE PROBLEMS AND ACTIVITIES

1. Read a computer magazine and summarize an article about a new technological advance in telecommunications or computer systems (hardware or software).

2. Explain how high-tech has affected your life and describe the kinds of high-touch activities you enjoy.

3. Interview an office worker in a full-time position. Ask how downward and upward communication are implemented with his or her employer.

4. List some ways that you can work on improving your human relations skills.

5. Write a paragraph about a major stressful situation you have experienced in your life. Describe its symptoms, the cause and effects, and how you dealt with it, or plan to deal with it.

6. Talk to a counselor and ask questions about stress and what advice she or he gives to others about stress in their lives. Take notes and write a one-page report of your findings.

7. Talk to two employees who participate in flextime, job sharing, or job rotation. Ask them to explain why they want it, how they benefit from it, and how their employers benefit from it.

8. Complete a self-assessment inventory, listing your assets, liabilities, and plan of action to make personal changes that will better prepare you to meet the demands of the world of work.

9. Describe what you expect your life to be like when you retire. List activities, hobbies, crafts, and so on, in which you plan to participate.

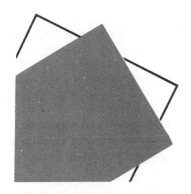

APPENDIX

ANNUAL PERCENTAGE RATE FORMULA

The annual percentage rate (APR) formula is used when there is a down payment, payments to be made on the principal that include interest, and agreements requiring more than one regular payment. Other methods exist, but this formula always proves to be accurate within tenths of a percent. The annual percentage rate is expressed first as a decimal, carried to the fourth decimal place. Then it is changed to a percent by moving the decimal point two places to the right and rounding to the tenths—9.8 percent from .0981. The formula is as follows:

$$R = \frac{2mI}{P(n+1)}$$

Where

    R = the annual percentage rate
    2 = a constant (always used)
    m = the method of payment (m = 12 if monthly payments are made, m = 4 if quarterly payments are made, and m = 1 if annual payments are made.)
    I = the dollar amount of interest
    P = the principal (total amount borrowed—not including the down payment)
    n = the total number of payments
    1 = a constant

An examination of the important parts of this formula is essential in order to make it work properly.

Method of Payment

The method of payment is always 12 when monthly payments are made. Most loans are based on monthly payments. If quarterly payments (four times a year) are made, m = 4. If annual payments (once a year) are made, m = 1 (even if there is only one annual payment).

Down Payment

A down payment is often called a deposit, or amount given as security to ensure that other payments will be made. When a car is purchased, a trade-in is often considered as the down payment because the old car is worth money. The down payment must be subtracted from the purchase price because interest will not be charged on the amount that is paid in the beginning. Most merchants require that the down payment be 10 percent or more of the purchase price. Then the purchaser will have an incentive to keep making the payments and not lose the down payment.

Number of Payments

The actual number of payments to be made under the agreement is entered and 1 is added before any multiplication is done. For instance, if you were to multiply the principal by 36 and then add 1, you would have a much different answer than if you multiplied the principal by 37.

Case Problems

Let us do a case problem to see how this formula works. Assume that a person buys a car for $6,000, making a $400 down payment. The buyer will make 36 equal monthly payments of $170.

ANNUAL PERCENTAGE RATE

$$R = \frac{2mI}{P(n + 1)}$$

$$R = \frac{2(12)I}{P(36 + 1)}$$

$$R = \frac{2(12)520}{5,600(37)}$$

$$R = \frac{24(520)}{207,200}$$

$$R = \frac{12,480}{207,200}$$

$$R = .0602$$

$$R = 6\%$$

I is found by multiplying the total number of monthly payments by the amount of each payment:

$$36 \times \$170 = \$6,120$$

Then subtract the principal from that amount:

$$\$6,120 - \$5,600 = \$520$$

P is found by subtracting the down payment from the purchase price:

$$\$6,000 - \$400 = \$5,600$$

Remember to do what is in the parentheses first (i.e., add 36 and 1 before multiplying).

Use of a calculator will greatly speed these computations.

To make this formula work best, you need to fill in each missing item and then follow through mathematically. Let us work through another example. In this case the purchase price is $1,200, with a down payment of $200 and 12 equal monthly payments of $90.

ANNUAL PERCENTAGE RATE

$$R = \frac{2ml}{P(n + 1)}$$

$$R = \frac{2(12)l}{P(12 + 1)}$$

$$R = \frac{24(80)}{1,000(13)}$$

$$R = \frac{1,920}{13,000}$$

$$R = .1477$$

$$R = 14.8\%$$

P is found by subtracting the down payment from the purchase price:

$$\$1,200 - \$200 = \$1,000$$

I is found by multiplying the total number of payments by the amount of each payment:

$$\$90 \times 12 = \$1,080$$

Then subtract the principal from that amount:

$$\$1,080 - \$1,000 = \$80$$

When using a calculator, carry out your answer to the fourth decimal place. Then round to a tenth of a percent.

PROBLEMS FOR USING THE APR FORMULA

Use a separate sheet of paper on which to work each problem and record the answers.

1. Use the formula, $R = \dfrac{2mI}{P(n + 1)}$, to compute the annual percentage rate (R) for each of the problems below. Show your work.

(a) R = ?
     m = 12 (monthly
         payments)
     I = $240.00
     P = $2,000.00
     n = 24 monthly payments

(c) R = ?
     m = 12 (monthly
         payments)
     I = $292.00
     P = $4,000.00
     n = 18 monthly payments

(b) R = ?
     m = 12 (monthly
         payments)
     I = $16.00
     P = $344.00
     n = 4 monthly payments

(d) R = ?
     m = 2 (semiannual
         payments)
     I = $13.42
     P = $101.00
     n = 2 payments

2. In most cases, installment credit involves a down payment, which reduces the principal amount of the loan. In order to determine the dollar interest cost, you need to multiply the amount of payment by the number of payments being made. This is the amount you will pay back. By subtracting the principal from this figure, you will know the cost of credit (interest). Use the formula, $R = \dfrac{2mI}{P(n + 1)}$, to compute the APR for each of the problems below.

   (a) The car costs $6,000. The down payment (trade-in) is worth $1,000. Payments will be $180 a month for the next 36 months. Compute the annual percentage rate.

R = ?	Remember, principal is the purchase price less the down payment ($6,000 − $1,000).
m = 12	
I = ?	To find the interest, multiply the amount of each payment by the number of payments. Then subtract the principal (36 × $180 − $5,000).
P = ?	
n = 36	

   (b) A refrigerator costs $800. The down payment is 10 percent ($80). Payments are $80 a month for the next 10 months. Compute the annual percentage rate.

   (c) An installment contract provides for a purchase price of $8,000, a down payment of $1,200, and monthly payments of $330 for 24 months. What is the annual percentage rate?

   (d) Purchasing furniture totaling $1,800, you make a $300 cash down payment and agree to pay the rest over 18 months at $100 a month. What is the annual percentage rate?

3. You are buying a television set for $500, putting down $50 cash, and paying the balance at $40 a month for the next 12 months. What is the annual percentage rate?

4. You borrowed $400 for 8 months. You will make 8 equal monthly payments of $55. What is the annual percentage rate?

5. You are buying a house for $80,000, with a down payment of $8,000, and are paying on the balance for 30 years (360 payments) at $750 a month. What is the annual percentage rate?

6. You are purchasing an automobile for $10,200 with a trade-in valued at $2,100. You will pay the balance at $280 a month for 36 months. What is the annual percentage rate?

7. You are borrowing $58 to buy a quality calculator. You will pay your uncle $6 a month for the next 12 months. What is the annual percentage rate?

8. You have agreed to buy a used typewriter for $280, paying $30 down and the balance at $25 a month for 12 months. What is the annual percentage rate?

9. Compute the annual percentage rate.

(a) R = ?
     P = $2,000
     I = $300
     n = 24 monthly
         payments
     m = 12

(d) Purchase price = $8,000
     Down payment = $1,000
     24 monthly payments of
         $325 each

(b) R = ?
     P = $1,000
     I = $100
     n = 12 payments
     m = 12

(e) Purchase price = $1,000
     Down payment = 10 percent
     36 monthly payments of
         $30 each

(c) R = ?
     P = $500
     I = $75
     n = 18 payments
     m = 12

(f) Purchase price = $6,800
     Trade-in = $1,200
     30 monthly payments of
         $240 each

10. You are buying a stereo for $800, less a down payment of $80. You will pay off the balance in 24 equal monthly payments of $40 a month. What is the annual percentage rate?

RULE OF 78

The Rule of 78 is a method of computing the amount of interest the consumer will save by paying off a debt early. The interest refund schedule is based on the number 78, which is the total of the digits for each month of the first year $(12 + 11 + 10 + 9 + 8 + 7 + 6 + 5 + 4 + 3 + 2 + 1 = 78)$. The first month, representing the first monthly payment, has 12 as a factor. Therefore, if you pay off a 12-month loan after you make the first payment, you pay 12/78 of the total interest. The rest of the interest is unearned and, therefore, saved and refunded to you. If you pay the loan off after the third month, you add 12 (first month) + 11 (second month) + 10 (third month) for a total of 33. You will pay 22/78 of the total interest. This calculation is done by dividing 33 by 78 (.4231). The total amount of interest due (example: $30) is multiplied by .4231 to get the amount of interest paid after 3 months ($30 × .4231 = $12.69). The amount of interest paid ($12.69) is then subtracted from the total amount of interest due ($30) to determine how much interest is saved by paying off the loan early ($30 − $12.69 = $17.31). The chart below shows the amounts of interest saved when one-year loans are paid off early.

		RULE OF 78		
Length of Loan	Total Interest	Date of Early Payment	Interest Paid	Interest Saved
1 year	$300.00	After 4th month	(42/78) $161.54	(36/78) $138.46
1 year	$150.00	After 8th month	(68/78) $130.77	(10/78) $19.23
1 year	$100.00	After 1st month	(12/78) $15.38	(66/78) $84.62

When a loan is extended for more than one year, a new base is used. For example, 2 years is $24 + 23 + 22 + \ldots + 3 + 2 + 1 = 300$. Three years begin at 36 and total 666; 4 years begin at 48 and total 1,176. A 3-year loan paid off after 3 months is 105/666 interest paid. To determine the amount of interest paid on a loan of more than one year, you count backwards—the first month of the loan has the highest factor. If it is a 24-month loan, the first month has the factor of 24. When the loan is paid off early, you count backwards: 24, 23, 22, etc. If you pay off a 2-year loan after the first month, you pay 24/300 of the interest and save the remainder, or unearned interest.

Below are examples of the Rule of 78 when computed on loans of longer than 1 year.

		RULE OF 78 (for loans of longer than one year)		
Length of Loan	Total Interest	Date of Early Payment	Interest Paid	Interest Saved
2 years (300)	$240.00	After 2d month	(47/300) $37.61	(253/300) $202.39
3 years (666)	$168.00	After 4th month	(138/666) $34.81	(528/666) $133.19
4 years (1,176)	$818.00	After 11th month	(473/1,176) $329.01	(703/1,176) $488.99

The amount of interest already paid on the 2-year loan is computed by adding together 24 + 23, which is 47. Then 47/300 is the percentage of interest already paid. Multiply 47/300 by $240 to get the dollar amount of interest paid, $37.61. The rest of the interest ($240 − $37.61) is unearned and refunded to you ($202.39).

Not all businesses use the Rule of 78 plan of refunding unearned interest, but each business will outline and explain in the loan agreement the system used. On most revolving accounts, the interest merely stops when the entire balance is paid off. No unearned interest is accumulated because it is computed on the new balance each month. However, a plan for refunding unearned interest is needed on installment accounts because the regular monthly payments include both principal and interest and are calculated to pay off the loan after a set number of months.

PROBLEMS FOR USING THE RULE OF 78

Use a separate sheet of paper to work the following problems using the Rule of 78. Show your computations and underline your answers.

1.

	Length of Loan	Total Interest	Date of Early Payment	Interest Paid	Interest Saved
(a)	1 year	$410	After 3d month	_____	_____
(b)	2 years	$131	After 6th month	_____	_____
(c)	2 years	$68	After 2d month	_____	_____
(d)	1 year	$24	After 9th month	_____	_____
(e)	3 years	$180	After 2d month	_____	_____
(f)	4 years	$2,000	After 8th month	_____	_____
(g)	3 years	$160	After 11th month	_____	_____
(h)	4 years	$811	After 16th month	_____	_____
(i)	2 years	$160	After 14th month	_____	_____

2.

	Length of Loan	Date of Early Payment	Finance Charge	Interest Paid	Interest Saved
(a)	1 year	After 2d month	$30	_____	_____
(b)	1 year	After 11th month	$42	_____	_____
(c)	2 years	After 3d month	$26	_____	_____
(d)	3 years	After 6th month	$211	_____	_____
(e)	3 years	After 18th month	$108	_____	_____
(f)	4 years	After 2d month	$120	_____	_____
(g)	4 years	After 6th month	$120	_____	_____
(h)	4 years	After 28th month	$800	_____	_____
(i)	4 years	After 11th month	$324	_____	_____
(j)	3 years	After 8th month	$216	_____	_____
(k)	3 years	After 22d month	$308	_____	_____
(l)	2 years	After 18th month	$200	_____	_____
(m)	2 years	After 20th month	$380	_____	_____
(n)	1 year	After 6th month	$42	_____	_____

(o) What is the base for a one-year loan? $(12 + 11 + \ldots + 2 + 1 =)$ _____

What is the base for a two-year loan? _____ a three-year loan? _____ four-year? _____

GLOSSARY

Actuarial table. A table of premium rates based on ages and life expectancies.

Actuary. One who calculates insurance and annuity premiums; a specialist on insurance statistics.

Add-on interest. Interest added to the principal; equal payments that include principal and interest are made each month.

Adjusted balance method. Method of computing finance charges in which the monthly payment is subtracted from the balance due before the finance charge is computed.

Adjusted gross income. Income minus allowable exclusions.

Administrative agencies. Groups established by Congress and authorized by the executive branch of government that have the power to enforce administrative laws.

Advanced degrees. Specialized, intensive post-baccalaureate programs.

Agent. A trained professional acting for an insurance company in negotiating, servicing, or writing a policy.

Alimony. Money paid to support a former spouse.

Allowances. Persons who are dependent on your income for support.

American Bankers Association (ABA) number. A number that appears in fraction form in the upper right corner of a check. The top half of the fraction identifies the location and district of the bank from which the check is drawn.

Annual percentage rate. The rate of interest charged on installment contracts.

Aptitude. A natural physical or mental ability that permits you to do certain tasks well.

Arbitration. A process whereby a decision is made by a neutral third party.

Assets. Items of value that a person owns.

Attractive nuisance. A dangerous place, condition, or object that is particularly attractive to children.

Audiovisual aids. Transparencies, slides, and other audiovisual materials.

Audit. The examination of your tax records by the Internal Revenue Service.

Automated teller machine (ATM). A computer terminal used to make deposits, withdrawals, or loan payments without going to a bank.

Average daily balance method. A method of computing finance charges based on the average outstanding balance during a given period.

Balance due. The total amount that remains due on a loan, including both principal and interest.

Basic needs. Ingredients necessary for maintaining physical life.

Bearer. Anyone who presents a coupon bond check to the bank for payment on the date of the coupon.

Beneficiary. A person named on an insurance policy to receive the benefits of the policy.

Benefits. Sums of money to be paid for specific types of losses under the terms of an insurance policy; sick pay, vacation time, and other company-provided supplements to income.

Billing (closing) date. The last date of the month that any purchases or payments made are recorded in your account.

Blank endorsement. The signature of the payee written on the back of the check exactly as it appears on the front of the check.

Bond indenture. A written proof of a secured bond debt.

Borrower. The person who borrows money or uses another form of credit.

Brokers. Members of a stock exchange who do the buying and selling of stocks that are listed with the exchange.

Budgeting. A process wherein expected income is matched to expected outflow.

Business venture. The creation of a business to sell a specific idea, product, or service.

Canceled checks. Checks the bank has processed.

Capital. Property possessed that is worth more than debts owed; a factor of production representing equipment, machines, and other durable but depreciable inputs to the production process.

Carrying charge. *See* Service charge.

Cashier's check. A check written by a bank on its own funds.

Cash management accounts. Money market accounts—services for persons wishing to invest their money at higher rates of return, but with liquidity.

Cash value. The amount of money payable to the policyholder upon discontinuation of a life insurance policy.

Central processing unit (CPU). The main piece of equipment in a computer system which has a memory.

Certificate of deposit. A time certificate—a sum of money deposited for a set length of time.

Certified check. A personal check that the bank guarantees to be good.

Checkbook register. A record of deposits to and withdrawals from a checking account.

Checking account. A banking service wherein money is deposited into an account, and checks are written to withdraw money as needed.

Check safekeeping. The practice of some financial institutions of not returning canceled checks to the customer.

Cherry picker. A customer who buys only loss leaders and super sale items.

Child support. Money paid to a former spouse for support of dependent children.

Claim. A demand for payment for loss under the terms of an insurance policy.

Collateral. Personal property pledged to a lender to secure a loan.

Collectibles. Valuable or rare items, from art pieces to comic books.

Collective bargaining. The process of negotiating the terms of employment for union members.

Collective values. Those things important to society as a whole.

College placement centers. Sources of career counseling available at colleges or technical training institutes.

Collision coverage. Coverage of the insured's own car in the event of an accident.

Commodities. Quantities of goods or interests in tangible assets.

Common stock. A security representing a share in the ownership of a company.

Company advertising. Advertising to promote the image of a store, company, or retail chain.

Competent parties. Persons who are legally able to give sane and intelligent assent.

Compound interest. Interest computed on the sum of the principal plus interest already earned.

Comprehensive insurance. Insurance that covers damage to your car from events other than collision or upset.

Computer. An electronic machine used to process data and solve problems.

Computer language. Phrases or notations understood by a computer.

Computer program. List of detailed instructions for the computer.

Consideration. Something of value that each party to a contract must receive.

Contacts. Relatives, friends, people you have worked for, and others who may be able to provide inside information on job openings.

Contract. A legally enforceable agreement between two or more parties to do or not to do something.

Cooperative work experience program. A program in which students receive high school credits for on-the-job experiences that directly relate to classroom studies in a chosen career area.

Core time period. A crucial time during the day when all employees must report to work.

Corporate note. The written promise of a corporation to repay loans it has accepted from private citizens.

Cosigner. A person with an acceptable credit rating who promises in writing to repay a promissory note if the maker fails to do so.

Counteroffer. A new offer made in response to an original offer.

Coupon bonds. Bonds that have individual coupons attached for each interest payment.

Coverage. Protection provided by the terms of an insurance policy.

Creative listening. A type of listening where all ideas are considered, and the working parts of each are saved.

Credit. What you use when you buy something now and agree to pay for it later, or borrow money and promise to pay it back later.

Credit bureau. A company that operates for profit in the business of accumulating, storing, and distributing credit information.

Credit file. A summary of a person's credit history.

Credit history. The complete record of your credit performance.

Creditor. Any person to whom one owes money or goods.

Credit report. A written report issued by a credit bureau that contains relevant information about a person's credit worthiness.

Critical listening. A type of listening where you discern between fact and fiction.

Currency. Paper money.

Custom. A long-established practice that may be considered an unwritten law.

Data base. Central storage area used by a computer.

Debenture. An unsecured corporate note.

Debit cards. Cards that allow immediate deductions from a checking account to pay for purchases.

Debt collector. A person or company hired by a creditor to collect the balance due on an account.

Decreasing term. A type of insurance policy for which the coverage value decreases each year while the premium remains the same.

Deductible. A specified amount subtracted from covered losses. The insurance company pays only the amount in excess of the amount subtracted.

Deductions. Amounts subtracted from gross pay; expenses the law allows the taxpayer to subtract from gross income.

Deferred payment price. The total amount, including principal and interest, that will be paid under a credit agreement.

Deficit spending. Spending by the government of more money than it collects.

Demand deposit. An account wherein you can demand portions of your deposited funds at will.

Dental insurance. A group insurance plan that covers such expenses as repair of damage to teeth, examinations, fillings, and other specified procedures.

Deposit slip. A form completed each time you deposit money to your checking account.

Direct deposit. The electronic transfer by computer of a paycheck or government check.

Disability income insurance. Insurance that helps to replace the income of a wage earner who cannot work for a prolonged period of time because of an illness or injury.

Discount bond. A bond you buy for less than its cash-in value.

Discount brokerage. A service through which individuals can buy and sell stocks for a reduced fee.

Discount rate. The rate of interest that banks are charged to borrow money from the Federal Reserve System.

Discretionary income. Income left over after the bills are paid.

Disposable income. The money you have to spend as you wish after taxes, social security, and other required and optional deductions have been withheld from your gross pay.

Dissatisfier. Conditions and policies that create dissatisfaction and produce low employee morale and low productivity.

Diversification. The practice of purchasing a variety of investments to protect against large losses and increase the rate of return.

Dogmatic statement. A statement that asserts an opinion as if it were fact.

Down payment. A percentage of the purchase price paid to secure the purchase.

Downward communication. Used by employers to keep employees informed and to give them job-related information and feedback about their performance.

Drafts. Checks.

Drawer. The depositor to a checking account.

Due date. The date on or before which a credit payment is due.

Economics. The study of society's attempts to fill unlimited needs and wants with scarce resources.

Economy. The system or structure of economic life in a country.

Electronic funds transfer. A banking transaction made using an automated teller machine.

Electronic marketplace. Shopping and business transactions handled through automated data processing systems.

Empathy. Ability to see another's point of view.

Employee costs. Expenses paid by employees and not reimbursed by employers.

Endorse. To sign a check across the left end of the back so that the check may be cashed.

Endowment insurance. An expensive type of life insurance policy that functions primarily as a savings contract.

Entrepreneurship. The factor of production that represents management, innovation, and risk-taking.

Equipment. Overhead projectors, screens, and other systems for projecting images and sounds.

Excellent credit rating. A credit rating earned by paying all bills before their due dates.

Exclusion. A part of income that is not, by special exception, taxable; a circumstance or loss that is not covered under the terms of an insurance policy.

Exemption. An allowance a taxpayer claims for each person dependent on the taxpayer's income.

Exempt status. A claim that allows you to have no federal income tax withheld from your paycheck.

Expenses. Money you will need for day-to-day purchases.

Express contract. A contract in which the terms have been agreed upon between the parties.

Extended coverage. An insurance endorsement added to a basic policy so that the insured is covered against loss caused by windstorm, hail, riot, civil commotion, and other specified perils.

Face amount. The death benefit of a life insurance policy.

Factors of production. Land, labor, capital, and entrepreneurship—the components necessary for producing goods and services to meet consumer wants and needs.

Fair credit rating. A rating earned by a customer who usually pays all bills within the grace period, but occasionally takes longer.

Federal Deposit Insurance Corporation (FDIC). A company that insures bank deposits.

Federal reserve bank. A bank for banks and for clearing and processing of checks.

Federal Savings and Loan Insurance Corporation (FSLIC). A company that insures deposits in savings and loans.

Fiber optics. Used to transmit sounds in the form of light through strands of thin, pure glass.

Finance charge (handling charge). The interest or money charged the borrower for the use of credit.

Financial planning. An orderly program for spending, saving, and investing the money you earn.

Financial resources. Sources of income.

Finger dexterity. The ability to use your fingers to move small objects quickly and accurately.

Fire insurance. Insurance that will cover losses from fire damage to your home and possessions.

Fixed expenses. Expenses that remain constant.

Flextime. A variation of starting times for employees.

Floating a check. The practice of writing a check on insufficient funds and hoping to make a deposit to cover the check before it is cashed.

Flowchart. A visual presentation of the parts of a process or procedure.

Formal education. Knowledge gained through attending formal institutions of learning.

Form W-4, Employee's Withholding Allowance Certificate. A form completed for income tax withholding purposes.

Form W-2, Wage and Tax Statement. A form that lists income earned during the year and all amounts withheld by the employer in your behalf.

Free checking. Checking with no service fees involved.

Fringe benefits. Optional or extra benefits provided for union employees.

Full coverage. Liability, collision, comprehensive, and personal injury protection insurances all combined into one policy.

Full disclosure. To reveal to a purchaser in complete

detail every possible charge or cost involved in the granting of credit.

Full-service bank. A bank that offers every possible kind of financial service.

Futures contract. A contract to buy or sell a commodity on a specified date at a specified price.

Gems. Natural precious stones, such as diamonds and rubies.

Goal. An end toward which efforts are directed.

Good credit rating. A rating earned by paying bills on their due dates or within a five-day grace period.

Grace period. The period following the due date of an unpaid premium during which an insurance policy is still in effect.

Gross income. All taxable income received, including wages, tips, salaries, interest, dividends, unemployment compensation, alimony, and so forth.

Gross pay. The total salary, before any deductions are made.

Group health insurance. Insurance that provides coverage for employees or other large groups of people.

Handling charge. *See* Finance charge.

Hardware. The equipment that makes up a computer system.

Health insurance. A plan for sharing the risk of financial loss due to accident or illness.

Hearing. The physiological sensory process of receiving auditory sensations.

Help wanted ads. Brief descriptions of job openings that appear in the classified section of the newspaper.

High-tech. Highly advanced technological processes and machines.

High-touch. The need for human contact.

Homeowners insurance. A policy that combines fire, loss and theft, and liability coverages.

Horizontal communications. Less formal communication among employees of equal rank.

Hospital and surgical insurance. Insurance that pays for all or part of hospital bills, surgeons' fees, and other in-hospital services.

Human relations. Getting along with others.

Identity. Who and what you are.

Illiquid. Not easily converted into cash.

Implied agreement. An agreement that is understood, though not necessarily discussed.

Incentive. A way to encourage employees to do more and better quality work.

Individual health insurance. An expensive policy covering only a single person or a household.

Industry advertising. Advertising to promote a general product group, without regard to where these products are purchased.

Inflation. The increased cost of living.

Initiative. A quality that allows you to do things on your own, without being told to.

Innovations. New ideas, methods, or devices that bring about changes.

Input. Initial entry of data into a computer system.

Insolvent. A term describing a poor credit position, in which one's liabilities are greater than one's assets.

Installment contract. A written agreement to make regular payments on a specific purchase.

Insurable interest. A condition of insurance contracts, wherein the insured must be in a position to sustain a financial loss if the event insured against occurs.

Insurance. A cooperative system of sharing the risk of financial loss.

Insured. The person, partnership, or corporation protected against loss by an insurance policy.

Interest. Money paid by the financial institution to the saver for the use of his or her money; the amount paid for the use of credit; the price paid for using capital.

Interest checking accounts. Accounts on which interest is paid if the depositor maintains a certain minimum balance.

Intermediate goals. Goals you wish to accomplish in the next few months or years.

Internal Revenue Service (IRS). An agency designed to collect taxes and turn them over to the government for the payment of debts, commitments, and benefits.

Investment. The outlay of money in the hope of realizing a profit.

Investment club. A group of people that pools its money, votes on spending decisions, and shares the profits.

Job analysis. A procedure that lists the positive and negative attributes of a given career choice.

Job rotation. A technique for training employees to be efficient in more than one specialized area.

Job sharing. Two people share what was a full-time job, including salaries and benefits.

Joint account. An account opened by two or more persons.

Joint endorsement. The signature, on the back of a check, of both persons named as payees on the front of the check.

Labor. The human factor of production.

Labor unions. Groups of people who work in the same or similar occupations, organized for the benefit of all employees in these occupations.

Land. The factor of production that represents resources that are fixed or nonrenewable.

Layaway. A credit plan whereby merchandise is laid away in your name, and you make regular payments and claim the merchandise when it has been paid for in full.

Letter of reference. A statement, in letter form, written by someone who can be relied upon to give a sincere report on your character, abilities, and experience.

Level term. A type of insurance that is renewable at set intervals, no proof of insurability being required.

Liabilities. Amounts of money that are owed to others.

Liability coverage. A policy that protects the insured against claims for personal injury or damage when the insured is driving his or her car or someone else's car.

Life insurance. Protection against the financial disaster that might otherwise result when a family's primary wage earner dies.

Life-style. The way people choose to live their lives, based on the values they have chosen or rejected.

Limited-payment life. A type of whole life insurance on which premiums are higher because the payment period is limited to a specific number of years.

Liquidity. The quality of being easily converted into cash.

Listening. An active process (skill) that requires mental concentration and effort.

Lobbying. Supporting legislation and political action that is beneficial to a certain profession.

Locked into (a job). The state of feeling trapped in a job because you cannot afford to take the cut in pay that may accompany starting over.

Long-term goals. Activities or plans that will materialize in five to ten years or longer.

Loss. An unexpected reduction or disappearance of an economic value.

Loss leader. An item of merchandise marked down to an unusually low price, sometimes below actual cost.

Mainframe computer. Very large computer systems used by business and government.

Major medical insurance. Insurance that covers both hospitalization and medical services and may be purchased as a separate policy.

Maker. The person who creates and signs a negotiable instrument, agreeing to pay it on a certain date; the person authorized to write checks on an account.

Manual dexterity. The ability to move your hands skillfully.

Marketable. A term describing work of quality such that the employer can use or sell it.

Maturity date. The date on which you must renew a time certificate, cash it in, or purchase a new one.

Median. The statistical middle of a list of figures.

Medicaid. A government health insurance program for indigent persons, regardless of age, who do not qualify for Medicare.

Medical expense insurance. Insurance that pays for doctors' fees for office visits and for routine services other than those connected with hospital care.

Medicare. A medical and hospital insurance program under social security for persons over age 65.

Merit pay. Pay raises for exemplary work.

Microcomputer. Small desk-top systems for business and personal use.

Minicomputer. Smaller versions of mainframe systems of intermediate size and power.

Minimum wage. The legally established lower limit on wages employers may pay.

Minors. Persons under the age of legal majority.

Money market fund. An investment plan for small investors that concentrates on buying short-term government, bank, and corporate notes.

Money orders. Certificates purchased for use when cash or a check cannot be used.

Motivators. Incentives that inspire workers to produce more and better quality goods and services.

Mutual assent. Agreement to all terms of the contract by all parties to the contract.

Mutual fund. An investment wherein someone else is paid to choose and buy various securities for the investor.

National Credit Union Administration (NCUA). An agency that insures deposits in credit unions.

Negotiable. Legally collectible.

Negotiable instrument. A document that contains promises to pay monies and is legally collectible.

Net pay. The amount left after all deductions have been taken out of your gross pay.

Networks. Communication lines established for people to talk to each other and share information.

Net worth. The difference between assets and liabilities.

No-fault insurance. Insurance that provides for the repair or replacement of your car, regardless of who is at fault at the scene of an accident.

Nominal rate. The rate of interest calculated on the principal amount only (does not include compounding).

NOW accounts. Accounts designed to provide the convenience of a checking account with short-term savings gains.

NSF check (not-sufficient-funds check). A check written without sufficient money in an account to cover it.

Odd-number pricing. The practice of putting odd numbers on price tags to make an item appear inexpensive.

Open-ended credit. Credit wherein the lender places a limit on how much a qualifying customer can borrow during a given period.

Optional benefits. Benefits that are not required as part of the total wage package.

Output. Creation and presentation of information—sales reports, report cards, monthly bills.

Overdraft. A check that is written that cannot be covered by the funds in an account.

Over-the-counter exchange. The buying and selling of securities through brokers, but not through a stock exchange.

Overtime. Hours worked in addition to the regular hours.

Paid holidays. Holidays full-time employees who are receiving a salary are entitled to have off, with pay.

Pawnshop. A legal business in which loans are made against the value of specific personal possessions.

Payee. The person to whom a negotiable instrument is made payable.

Peril. An exposure to the risk of loss.

Personal factors. Those influences in a person's or a family's life that determine spending patterns, preferences, and choices.

Personal injury protection (PIP). Automobile insurance that pays for medical, hospital, and funeral costs of the insured and his or her family and passengers, regardless of fault.

Personality. Personal qualities and traits that make one unique.

Personal property floater. Additional property insurance coverage purchased to protect certain specified items of property without regard to location at the time of loss or damage.

Personal resources. Time, money, energy, skills and abilities, and available credit.

Placement services. Organizations that help students find employment, usually without charge.

Point system. A method used in rating consumers' credit worthiness wherein a credit applicant is given points for employment, amount of income, length of residence, type of residence, and other factors.

Poor credit rating. A rating earned by a customer who does not make regular payments, or who misses payments and must be reminded frequently of debts outstanding.

Postdate. To write in a future date on a check.

Precious metals. Tangible, beautiful, desirable substances of great value, such as gold, silver, and platinum.

Preferred stocks. Stocks on which dividends are paid first in the event of company liquidation.

Premium. The sum of money the policyholder agrees to pay to an insurance company periodically for an insurance policy.

Previous balance method. A method of computing finance charges in which the charge is added to the previous balance, then the payment made during the last billing period is subtracted to determine the new balance in the account.

Prime rate. The rate of interest lenders offer their best commercial (business) customers.

Principal. The amount of money deposited by the saver; the total amount that is financed or borrowed and on which interest is computed.

Private counselors. A source of career counseling which costs fom $25 to $75 an hour.

Product advertising. Advertising to convince consumers to buy a specific good or service.

Productivity. A measure of the output of a production unit during a specific period of time.

Professional organizations. Groups that collect dues from members of a profession and provide support services.

Profit. The entrepreneur's reward for taking risk.

Progressive taxes. Taxes that increase in proportion to income.

Promissory note. A written promise to pay a certain sum of money to another person or to the holder of the note on a specified date.

Promotion opportunities. Chances for recognition of your abilities and accomplishments.

Proof. Evidence that backs up or supports information.

Proof of loss. The written verification of the amount of a loss that must be provided by the insured to the insurance company before a claim can be settled.

Property liability insurance. Insurance that protects the property owner against legal claims by persons injured while on the insured's property.

Proportional taxes. Taxes for which the tax rate remains constant, regardless of the amount of income.

Prorate. To divide, as to divide a charge, proportionately over a period of time.

Rate. The interest charge, expressed as a percentage of the principal.

Real estate. Land and anything permanently attached to it.

Reconciliation. The process of matching your checkbook register with your bank statement.

Recorded. Term describing some document or event that has been made a public record.

Recourse. The remedy for situations in which an employee believes that he or she has not received benefits as required by law.

Registered bonds. Bonds for which the corporation keeps a record of the owners.

Regressive taxes. Taxes that decrease in proportion to income increases.

Rent. The price paid for land.

Restrictive endorsement. An endorsement that restricts or limits the use of a check.

Retail stores. Stores that purchase goods from wholesalers and sell directly to customers.

Revenue. Money collected by the government from citizens and companies in the form of taxes.

Revolving account. An account not assessed a finance charge unless the balance is not paid in full by the due date.

Risk. The chance of loss.

Safe-deposit boxes. Boxes in banks rented for safekeeping of valuables.

Salary. The amount of monthly or yearly pay.

Secured loan. A loan that is guaranteed by a pledge of property or other assets to assure the creditor of repayment.

Self-actualization. A level at which workers meet their needs of accomplishment and satisfaction.

Self-assessment inventory. A listing of your strong and weak points and plan of action.

Self-esteem. Feelings of self-worth about ourselves and our accomplishments.

Semiprecious stones. Smaller stones of less commercial value than diamonds, such as garnets, spinels, and opals.

Seniority. The policy that the last ones hired should be the first ones laid off.

Service charge (carrying charge). The amount charged borrowers by merchants or banks for servicing an account or loan.

Service credit. Credit for a service rendered (telephone, doctor).

Setting. Lighting, room layout, speaker's stand, and other physical aspects of speaking.

Share accounts. Savings accounts at a credit union.

Share draft accounts. Credit union checking accounts that have no minimum balance requirements, no service fees, and interest payments based on your lowest monthly balance.

Short-term goal. A goal that is to be achieved in the next few days or weeks.

Simple interest. Interest computed on the principal only. The formula for computing simple interest is $I = P \times R \times T$.

Small loan companies. Finance companies that charge high rates of interest for the use of their money.

Smart card. An EFT access card that can be used to perform banking activities and store each transaction in its memory.

Social Security Act. The first national social insurance program, enacted to provide federal aid for the elderly and for disabled workers.

Social security number. A permanent work identification number.

Software. Computer programs which usually include instructions for using the program.

Solvent. A favorable credit position in which assets are greater than liabilities.

Space. The physical attribute of production that is concerned with dimensional, geographic, and measurable commitments of productive resources.

Special checking account. An account offered to customers who will write only a small number of checks each month.

Special endorsement (endorsement in full). An endorsement that instructs the bank to pay the amount of a check to a third party.

Standard account. A checking account that usually has a set monthly service fee, but no per-check fee.

Standard policy. A contract form that has been adopted by many insurance companies, approved by state insurance departments, or prescribed by law.

Statement. An itemized bill showing charges, credits, and payments posted to an account during a billing period.

Statement of account. A monthly listing of checks received and processed by the bank, plus all other withdrawals and deposits made and service fees charged.

Stock exchange. A place where stocks and bonds of larger companies are bought and sold.

Stock market. A general term that describes the securities market—the place where supply and demand for investment alternatives meet.

Stop payment order. A request that the bank not cash or process a specific check.

Straight life. A type of whole life policy on which premiums are paid throughout life and the face value is paid at death.

Stress. Response of the body to any demand made upon it.

Stress management. Recognizing stress, understanding its causes and effects, and developing a plan for reducing it, eliminating it, or living with it.

Stressors. Sources or causes of stress.

Strike. A process whereby the members of a union refuse to work until an agreement is reached.

Subscribers. Creditors who pay an annual fee to a credit bureau for use of its credit reports.

Sympathetic listening. The type of listening where you listen empathetically, but offer no advice.

Survivorship account. A joint account, so called because any person authorized to sign on the account has the right to the entire amount deposited.

Take-home pay. The net amount of your paycheck.

Target audience. A specific consumer group to which the advertisements for a product are directed.

Taxable income. Adjusted gross income minus deductions, exemptions, etc.

Tax-sheltered annuity. A contract wherein you agree to set aside a certain amount of money each month and defer paying taxes on the earnings until a later date.

Tax evasion. Willful failure to pay taxes.

Tax liability. The amount of taxes due from you, based on your taxable income.

Technology. Advances resulting from improvements in technical processes.

Terminal. Computer location that has a display screen and keyboard.

Term life insurance. A type of life insurance that protects you for a set period of time.

Third World. Undeveloped and underdeveloped nations.

Time. The period the borrower will take to repay a loan; the crucial timing of production so that a product or service is available for consumption when it is desired by the consumer.

True annual percentage rate. The effective rate received when money is compounded and interest is received on interest already earned.

True daily interest. Interest computed on each day of deposit.

Unearned premium. The portion of the original premium that has not been earned by the insurance company and is returned to the policyholder when a policy is canceled.

Unemployment insurance. Insurance that provides benefits to workers who lose their jobs through no fault of their own.

Uninsured motorist coverage. Insurance that protects you as a pedestrian when hit by a car that is uninsured.

Unions. Units or groups of people joined together for a common purpose.

Universal product code (UPC). A bar code which allows the computer to identify and price items purchased.

Unlisted securities. Stocks not listed with an exchange.

Unused credit. The amount of credit above what you owe that you could charge, to a maximum amount.

Upward communication. The transmission of information from employees to their supervisors and employers.

Usury laws. Laws setting maximum interest rates that lenders may charge.

Valid contracts. Contracts that contain mutual assent, consideration, competent parties, a lawful objective, an agreed upon period of time, and a legal format.

Values. The things in life that are important to you.

Variable expenses. Expenses that change according to needs and short-term goals.

Video display unit. A screen or visual monitor on a computer.

Void. To cancel a check.

Voidable contracts. Contracts that contain an element that makes them potentially void.

Void contracts. Contracts that are missing one or more of the essential elements and are, therefore, null and void.

Voluntary compliance. The expectation that all employed citizens will prepare and file income tax returns.

Wage and Hour Act (Fair Labor Standards Act of 1938). A statute providing that persons working in interstate commerce or a related industry could not be paid less than a minimum wage of 25 cents an hour. This act was the basis of current minimum wage policies.

Wages. The total compensation for employment, including gross pay, insurance, sick pay, fringe benefits, and all other types of direct or indirect compensation.

Warranty. An assurance of product quality or of responsibility of the seller.

Whole life insurance. Insurance that pays the face amount to the beneficiaries on the death of the insured.

Word processing. Using the computer to create letters and reports.

Work characteristics. Daily activities at work, such as indoor or outdoor work or working with people or alone.

Workers' compensation. Benefits paid to workers and their families in the event of injury, illness, or death that occurs as a result of the job or working conditions.

Work history. A record of all jobs held and the length of time spent with each employer.

Work permit. A form allowing a minor to work.

Written work rules. Written policies posted in employee work areas for the benefit of all.

Yellow Pages. An alphabetic, subject listing of businesses advertising their services in the telephone directory.

Zero bracket amount. The minimum dollar amount of deductions you need before it is worth it to you to itemize your deductions.

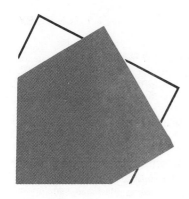

INDEX